Death and memory in early medieval Britain

How were the dead remembered in early medieval Britain? This innovative study demonstrates how perceptions of the past and the dead, and hence social identities, were constructed through mortuary practices and commemoration in the period c. AD 400–1100. Drawing on archaeological evidence from across Britain, including the latest archaeological discoveries, Howard Williams presents a new interpretation of the significance of portable artefacts, the body, structures, monuments and landscapes in early medieval mortuary practices. He argues that materials and spaces were used in ritual performances that served as 'technologies of remembrance', practices that created shared 'social' memories intended to link past, present and future. Through the deployment of material culture, early medieval societies were therefore selectively remembering and forgetting their ancestors and their history. Throwing new light on an important aspect of medieval society, this book is essential reading for all archaeologists and historians with an interest in the early medieval period.

HOWARD WILLIAMS is Lecturer in Archaeology at the University of Exeter. He has published widely on death and memory in past societies and has co-directed archaeological fieldwork at early medieval burial sites in Britain and Sweden.

CAMBRIDGE STUDIES IN ARCHAEOLOGY

Cambridge Studies in Archaeology aims to showcase the very best in contemporary archaeological scholarship. Reflecting the wide diversity and vigour of archaeology as an intellectual discipline, the series covers all regions of the world and embraces all major theoretical and methodological approaches. Designed to be empirically grounded and theoretically aware, and including both single-authored and collaborative volumes, the series is arranged around four highlighted strands:

- *Prehistory*
- *Classical Archaeology*
- *Medieval Archaeology*
- *Historical Archaeology*

For a list of titles in this series please see the end of the book.

HOWARD WILLIAMS

DEATH AND MEMORY IN EARLY MEDIEVAL BRITAIN

CAMBRIDGE
UNIVERSITY PRESS

393.0941
W72d

CAMBRIDGE UNIVERSITY PRESS
Cambridge, New York, Melbourne, Madrid, Cape Town, Singapore, São Paulo

Cambridge University Press
The Edinburgh Building, Cambridge CB2 2RU, UK

Published in the United States of America by Cambridge University Press, New York

www.cambridge.org
Information on this title: www.cambridge.org/9780521840194

© Howard Williams 2006

First published 2006

Printed in the United Kingdom at the University Press, Cambridge

A catalogue record for this publication is available from the British Library

ISBN-13 978-0-521-84019-4 hardback
ISBN-10 0-521-84019-8 hardback

Dedicated to the memory of:
Michael Williamson   24 January 1893–30 July 1965
William John Williams   15 July 1903–5 May 1989
Phyllis Williams   13 August 1911–4 February 2003

CONTENTS

FIGURES

PREFACE

How did early medieval people commemorate the dead? Were mortuary practices not just contexts for personal recollection, but contexts in which perceptions of the dead and the past were created and reproduced? Early medieval graves have been studied for many decades by many researchers, but this particular perspective and line of enquiry has yet to be fully explored and developed. In addressing such an approach, this book is intended as an exploration of new ideas and new perspectives in early medieval archaeology. As such it is intended as a building-block towards future research rather than as a final statement.

My research concerning early medieval archaeology and mortuary archaeology has been influenced and inspired from many directions, and I have many people to thank for inspiration and encouragement. I would like to take this opportunity to thank Mike Parker Pearson, John Moreland and Alex Woolf for introducing me to the study of early medieval and mortuary archaeology during my undergraduate degree at Sheffield. For the development of my ideas during my postgraduate research at the University of Reading, I particularly appreciate the guidance, discussions and debates provided by Richard Bradley and my doctoral supervisor, Heinrich Härke. I also appreciate the innumerable discussions and feedback upon conference presentations, seminars, lectures and publications by many friends and scholars while I was researching and teaching at the University of Reading, Trinity College Carmarthen and Cardiff University. Since being appointed to a position at the University of Exeter in the autumn of 2003, I have enjoyed generous support and guidance from colleagues both in the Department of Archaeology and elsewhere in the University. In addition to those persons already mentioned, I am grateful for beneficial discussions with and support from: Jo Buckberry, Martin Carver, Annia Cherryson, Hella Eckardt, Bonnie Effros, Rebecca Gowland, Catherine Hills, Richard Hingley, Cornelius Holtorf, Andy Jones, Brynmor Morris, Aliki Pantos, Kenneth Penn, Tim Pestell, David Petts, Andrew Reynolds, Julian D. Richards, Martin Rundkvist, Hannah Sackett, Sarah Semple, Chris Smart, Nick Stoodley, Eva Thäte, Victoria Thompson, Sam Turner and Aaron Watson.

Concerning the research and composition of the book, thanks go to the anonymous referees for their constructive and critical comments on earlier drafts. I would like to thank Bonnie Effros, Heinrich Härke, Andrew Reynolds, Sarah Semple and Andy Jones for commenting upon sections of the manuscript. I would also like to thank those who granted permission to reproduce illustrations adapted for use in this volume. The book has benefited greatly from Séan Goddard's illustrations and technical expertise. I am also grateful to Aaron Watson for his innovative artistic impressions. Many thanks for their continued support go to my parents, Phil and Sue Williams, my brother Ralph and his wife Tracey, and my in-laws Keith and Margaret Wilson. Finally, thanks go to my wife, Elizabeth, for her love, patience, encouragement and unswerving enthusiasm for the project. If I have missed anyone from this list of thanks, I defer to the failings of memory . . .

1

Death, memory and material culture

In a Field of old Walsingham, not many moneths past, were digged up between fourty and fifty Vrnes, deposited in a dry sandy soile, not a yeard deep, nor farre from one another: Not all strictly of one figure, but most answering these described: Some containing two pounds of bones, distinguishable in skulls, ribs, jawes, thigh-bones, and teeth, with fresh impressions of their combustion. Besides the extraneous substances, like peeces of small boxes, or combes handsomely wrought, handles of small brasse instruments, brazen nippers and in one some kinde of Opale. (Browne 1658: 21–2)

Had they made as good provision for their names, as they had done for their Reliques, they had not so grosly erred in the art of perpetuation. But to subsist in bones, and be but Pyramidally extant, is a fallacy in duration. Vain ashes, which in the oblivion of names, persons, times, and sexes, have found unto themselves, a fruitlesse continuation, and only arise unto late posterity, as Emblemes of mortall vanities; Antidotes against pride, vain-glory, and madding vices. Pagan vain-glories which thought the world might last for ever had encouragement for ambition and finding not Atropos unto the immortality of their Names, were never dampt with the necessity of oblivion. (Browne 1658: 74)

Introduction

This study begins with two quotations from the 1658 work entitled *Hydrotaphia* by the Norfolk antiquary Sir Thomas Browne. Quoting from Browne's eloquent consideration of mortality and the past inspired by the discovery of some cinerary urns has often been deemed apposite for archaeologists dealing with graves and tombs. For this study, it is so because of the dual significance of Browne's writings for early medieval mortuary archaeology. First, Browne is often attributed with uncovering and describing early medieval graves in Britain for the first time in his account of urns found in the parish of Walsingham in Norfolk. While he wrongly attributed them to the Roman period, Browne was to begin the practice of excavating early medieval graves, describing and illustrating them, and making interpretations as to their date and significance, that has continued to the present day.

Yet there is a second reason Browne's text is significant. Browne was concerned with the significance of the antiquarian discovery of ancient graves for understanding memory. For Browne, graves and ancient monuments were the material manifestations of the futility of remembering. By definition, these newly discovered graves were remains from forgotten times and forgotten people. They had been consigned to oblivion by the passage of time and, as such, had been lost to the memory of their descendants, remaining only as a moral caution against aspirations towards immortality and vanity. The process of antiquarian excavation, as well as the graves that were uncovered at Walsingham, is therefore portrayed by Browne as embodying the misplaced aspirations of ancient people to remember through revering and materialising memories in graves and tombs. In doing so, he is also presumably commenting on the continued post-Reformation emphasis on funerary commemoration in his seventeenth-century England. And yet, Browne is recognising the desire for past people to remember through material culture: from large monuments to modest graves, cinerary urns to portable artefacts.

Thomas Browne and modern archaeologists share both of these aspects in common. In studying the graves, cemeteries, tombs and monuments of the early medieval period (here taken as the period from the fifth century AD following the end of direct Roman rule in Britain, through to the mid-eleventh century when the Norman Conquest of 1066, admittedly somewhat arbitrarily, creates a move into the later Middle Ages), Browne and today's archaeologists share a desire for graves to tell us stories about the past. Yet, like Browne, modern archaeologists are concerned not simply with digging up the graves of the dead: they also aspire to understand the motivations and choices of these past people concerning how they use material culture to commemorate the dead, venerate ancestors, and articulate genealogies and mythologies.

Yet if retaining memories is never easy, so the phenomenon of memory in modern academic research is elusive and difficult to define. Memory is difficult to recognise, since it is a process rather than a fixed entity. Memories are constituted through numerous media: texts, images, stories, songs, rituals and also, importantly for this study, material culture. This is indeed the point where Browne and today's archaeologists might disagree. This is because Browne saw perpetuity in bones and objects to be a 'fallacy', because only in 'names', i.e. in texts and words, was memory thought to reside and be reproduced. However, archaeologists are well-placed to explore the centrality of material culture as both the medium and message of social commemoration in early medieval Britain, operating alongside the spoken and written word. Contrary to the view expressed by Browne, 'names' are not the only way of remembering. Meanwhile, memory need not primarily concern the 'preservation' of memories, fossilising the past in perpetuity and thus achieving immortality. Social memory instead involves the selective remembering and the active forgetting of the past. Social memory is therefore inherently selective, active and performative in nature, and can be mediated by material culture and ritual performances as well as by the written and spoken word.

Throughout human history, the past and its commemoration have been a central concern for individuals and societies attempting to secure and express their perceived rights, aspirations and identities. Memories of the dead and the past in many cultures define the present. The present in turn defines the future. Memory is therefore not only personal, it can be social. To remember is more than to recall events and places: memory operates in a social context and therefore can be regarded, in part at least, as a collective cultural and social phenomenon (Halbwachs 1992). Equally, memory is not a passive phenomenon. To remember is more than to passively recall events and places. Memory in a social sense is a question of active participation and practice: to participate in bodily acts, to perform in rituals (Connerton 1989).

The early medieval period in Britain (c. AD 400–1100) has left us many different sources of evidence for how memories were retained, but also for how they were invented and reinterpreted over time, as a central element of social and religious life. Yet the potential for archaeological evidence to augment this picture, and the centrality of material culture in the production, reproduction and negotiation of social memories, has tended to be underplayed in studies of social memory in the early Middle Ages.

To redress the imbalance, this book aims to explore the ways in which death and burial provided one important context through which social memories and identities were performed and created in this era of social, political, economic and religious transformation. Incorporating the end of the Roman world and the birth of the Middle Ages, the early medieval period was a time of changing commemorative strategies, some coherent and enduring, others innovative and experimental. Some followed traditions that stretched back into the Roman and prehistoric pasts, others were to continue and develop into the later Middle Ages. This diversity and complexity make the study of early medieval death and burial of key importance in the history of death and society, and makes mortuary archaeology pivotal to any understanding of early medieval societies. In addressing this issue, the aim is to develop a richer understanding of early medieval death and burial. Rather than a synthesis of all data, the study is an exploration of selected case studies. On yet another level, the study attempts to show the importance of developing a theorised and imaginative engagement with the early medieval archaeological record.

To introduce the material, ideas and approach of the present volume, this introduction sets the scene in a number of discrete ways. We begin by providing an outline of the history of studying early medieval burial rites, graves, cemeteries and funerary monuments. Next, the chapter introduces current approaches in mortuary archaeology and their potential for providing new insights into death and burial in the early Middle Ages. This appraisal leads us to consider the potential in applying historical, sociological and anthropological perspectives on death, memory and material culture to early medieval archaeology. From these approaches, an archaeological theory is distilled and developed that regards early medieval mortuary practices as technologies of remembrance and mnemonic performances. In the last two sections, this argument is pursued in relation to the archaeological evidence from a single burial site, namely the wealthy, late seventh-century burial from Swallowcliffe Down in Wiltshire. Illustrating many of the themes developed in subsequent chapters, the data demonstrates how mortuary rituals served as memorable events, and how material culture was employed in commemorating the dead and the past. The penultimate part explores the broad patterns and developments in mortuary behaviour from the fifth to the eleventh centuries, charting how social memories were produced and reproduced in early medieval societies before and after the Swallowcliffe burial.

Drawing these elements together, it is argued that links between mortuary practices and social memory span traditional divisions between Celt and Saxon, between pagan and Christian, and between Germanic and Insular and Roman influences in early medieval societies. The link between death and memory therefore offers an alternative perspective in the study of early medieval funerary behaviour. In combination, the introduction hopes to demonstrate that a focus on social memory in the investigation and interpretation of early medieval death and burial helps us to see burials and other mortuary contexts as more than quarries for information about the living in the past. Instead, mortuary practices can be conceptualised as strategies for remembering and forgetting. Before developing this argument, we must review the character of early medieval archaeology and the archaeological interpretation of mortuary practices.

Death and burial in the early medieval period

The early medieval period is known to archaeologists through many sources of evidence, from surviving texts and architecture (e.g. Biddle 1986; Carver 1999) down to pot-sherds and pollen grains (e.g. Fyfe & Rippon 2004). Archaeological sites take many forms and include the dwelling-places of early medieval people, from farmsteads and villages, high-status 'manors', fortifications, 'wics' (early markets and trading-places) to towns, minsters, monasteries and (by the end of the period) parish churches. Portable artefacts are derived from many of these sites, from houses, huts, rubbish pits, ditches and wells, and also from deliberate deposits, such as hoards. Few early medieval remains survive as above-ground features, although there is a range of fragmentary elements, such as linear earthworks, stone sculptures and crypts preserved in later church architecture (for introductions to early medieval archaeology, see: Hinton 1990; Reynolds 1999; papers in Wilson 1976). Moreover, much of the character and form of the later medieval landscape itself was formed in this period. The patterns of settlements, fields, routes, boundaries and territories of later centuries can often be shown to owe their roots to the period between the end of Roman Britain and the Norman Conquest that saw dramatic changes to land-use, tenure and economy (e.g. Fyfe & Rippon 2004; Hooke 1999; Rippon 2000). Furthermore, the landscape of early medieval Britain inherited and incorporated elements of the past, including the ruins and monuments of earlier times, such as the ruins of Roman buildings to the burial mounds, ceremonial monuments and hillforts of prehistory. Many of these sites attracted early medieval interest and activity for both ritual and more prosaic reasons (Eaton 2000; Williams 1997).

Among this rich body of archaeological data are burials, cemeteries and mortuary monuments. Indeed, graves have loomed large in the development of early medieval archaeology because they often provide secure contexts for dating and studying early medieval communities through the evidence their inhabitants left behind – their own bodies, the artefacts placed with them, the structures used to contain them and the monuments raised over them. From such contexts, the history of the early medieval period has often been written and rewritten (recent reviews include Carver 1999; Hadley 2001; Lucy 2000; Lucy & Reynolds 2002). A number of pervasive themes have dominated the interpretation of graves by archaeologists and historians. These have tended to focus on six inter-related themes: (1) the collapse of Roman control and culture; (2) barbarian invasions, including Anglo-Saxons in the fifth century and Scandinavians in the ninth; (3) conversion to Christianity; (4) the formation and development of early medieval kingdoms; (5) the Viking presence and influence; and (to a lesser extent) (6) the Norman Conquest. The burial evidence is often thought to chart this narrative history of the 'origins' of medieval society through socio-political fragmentation, ethnogenesis, religious change, socio-political evolution, colonisation from Scandinavia and the Norman take-over.

As we shall see, although archaeologists have had very different approaches to the study of graves, one thing they agree on is that graves are the intentional outcome of mortuary rituals. In the material remains left to us we can glimpse many aspects of early medieval life and attitudes to death, as well as how these ideas and practices changed over time and between localities and regions. Outside the western world, funerary rituals and subsequent 'ancestral rites' can be highly visible, theatrical and multi-sensuous series of actions and performances in which material culture can have prominent and profound roles (Metcalf & Huntingdon 1991).

If seen in this way, early medieval graves are not simply an indirect way of finding out about the living in past societies. Graves first and foremost provide direct insight into the responses, attitudes and practices surrounding death. As such, the portrayal of the dead can be devised as intentional statements or 'discourses', relating to world-views, ideologies and concepts of personhood, rather than a reflection of living society (see Barrett 1994). Moreover, these statements, often both social and sacred in character, are made to promote ways of thinking and being related to contemporary society, but they are also intended to evoke links with the past and aspirations for the future. They are therefore intended to be memorable in themselves, and mediate the production and reproduction of social memory: how groups envision their pasts and futures, and hence their identities.

If this argument is accepted, then how can we develop archaeological theories for the study of early medieval mortuary practices that help us to approach and explore the relationships between death and memory? Before developing a perspective, it is necessary to review past and current approaches towards early medieval mortuary data.

Early medieval mortuary archaeology – new approaches
Ancient graves, including those of early medieval date, have been uncovered since the Middle Ages itself. Early discoveries were often attributed to the Romans (Browne 1658; Smith 1856). They were first recognised as pertaining to the early Middle Ages by the late eighteenth-century barrow-digger James Douglas (Douglas 1793).

Following his precedent, from the Victorian period early medieval graves discovered during barrow-digging or during agricultural or industrial activities were increasingly reported amidst the pages of the publications of the burgeoning antiquarian and archaeological societies (e.g. Smith 1848; 1856; Wylie 1852). For instance, at Chessell Down on the Isle of Wight the local antiquarian George Hillier excavated part of an early medieval cemetery and illustrated the richest grave (Arnold 1982a; Smith 1868; fig. 1.1). Since these discoveries there has been a tendency to use the burial evidence to compensate for the fragmented and problematic historical and linguistic evidence for the 'barbarians' who succeeded Rome, their racial and religious affiliations, and the progress of their conquest and settlement of Britain. Consequently, burials have been used to write the history of peoples, kingdoms and their conversion to Christianity. Developing upon these Victorian precedents, early and mid-twentieth-century approaches took the form of 'culture-history': charting the history of tribes and ideas, and their origins, movements and evolution through burial rites and the artefacts contained within graves (Childe 1945; Trigger 1989; see Leeds 1913; 1936; 1945; Myres 1969; 1977).

Alongside these interpretations, the data-set of early medieval burials has continued to grow over the last century, and the range of methods and techniques employed in their study has burgeoned (Dickinson 1980). This applies both to research excavations intended to explore them, as well as 'rescue' excavations aimed at recovering them before their destruction by development. Therefore, while the historical evidence for the period has remained static, and can even be regarded as diminishing, since sources once deemed reliable have been increasingly regarded as fanciful myth, the archaeological evidence has dramatically increased (fig. 1.2). This rise of new evidence has enabled new perspectives to be developed in how we interpret early medieval graves. While the primary focus of popular interest in these graves remains the stories they are thought to tell us about the origins of 'peoples' such as the 'Saxons' or the 'Picts', over the last thirty years archaeologists have adopted alternative perspectives from traditional culture-history, witnessing the influence of new theoretical paradigms employed throughout archaeology.

With the 'New Archaeology' or 'processual' archaeology that became popular both in America and England by the 1970s, the focus changed from using graves to chart the history of peoples and the spread of ideas towards the use of mortuary data to reconstruct social structures and their evolution. In this context, burial evidence was seen as a means of identifying changing social and economic complexity (Binford 1971; Chapman & Randsborg 1980). Early on, difficulties were identified in focusing purely on social stratification and the many problems with its identification (e.g. Brown 1980), and the integration of vertical differentiation in mortuary behaviour with horizontal variation was deemed essential, including age, gender and kinship (e.g. Shennan 1975).

The 'social' and 'economic' approach applied to burial data by the 'New Archaeology' came under sustained criticism during the 1980s by various 'post-processual' critiques that focused on the problems with such social analyses. These included the lack of consideration of symbolism, power and ideology in past mortuary

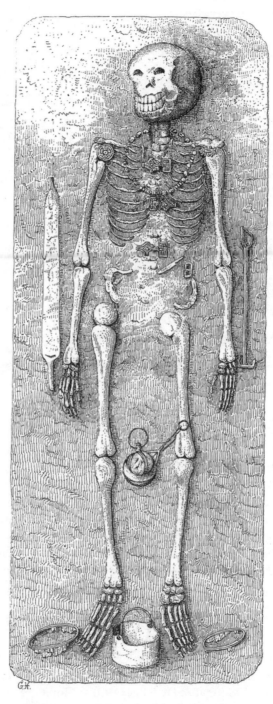

Figure 1.1 Drawing of grave 45 from Chessell Down, Isle of Wight, containing an adult skeleton, furnished with female-gendered artefacts and dating to the late sixth century AD. The grave was uncovered by the Victorian antiquary George Hillier (after Smith 1868).

Figure 1.2   Three seventh-century inhumation graves pictured during excavations directed by Mark Stedman and Nick Stoodley at Shavard's Farm, Meonstoke, Hampshire in 1998 (photo by the author).

contexts. Burials were not a direct reflection of living society or a means of charting directly the 'history' of peoples. The meaningful and 'active' role of burials and the material culture they contain was emphasised, and a more 'contextual' approach was advocated. Rather than a direct window onto social structure, burials have been seen as comparable to written sources in the sense that, although they contain messages, they require an awareness of source criticism to understand them, as well as a self-critical awareness of one's own biases as a reader. With careful consideration, symbolic statements, and the ideologies of which they formed a part, can be inferred from burial contexts (Hodder 1980; Parker Pearson 1982; 1999c; Shanks & Tilley 1982). While initially developed as a critique of the New Archaeology's social approach to burial data and the cross-cultural use of ethnographic analogy, many studies were developed that incorporated post-processual elements within a primarily 'social' study of mortuary evidence (e.g. Carr 1995; Morris 1992).

For early medieval archaeology, processual and post-processual archaeologies have only been slowly and partially adopted (see Austin 1990; Bradley 1987; Carver 1999; Driscoll 1984; 1988; Hedeager 1992a; Moreland 1997; 2001; Pader 1982). Yet early medieval mortuary archaeology has often played a central role in both the processual and post-processual debates about how to read evidence from graves. As a classic 'case study' in which methods and theories can be developed and tested, early medieval burials were deployed in processual and 'social' studies of mortuary archaeology (e.g. Alcock 1981; Arnold 1980; Härke 1997d; Hedeager 1992a; Ravn 2003; Shephard 1979). They have equally involved critiques of the traditional explanation for the introduction of furnished burial rites as evidence of migration (Halsall 1992; James 1980; 1988; Lucy 2002). Similarly, 'post-processual' critiques of the social approach have focused on the active roles of mourners in burial ritual (i.e. the grave may say more about the mourners than the deceased) as well as the symbolic and historical context of mortuary expressions (Cannon 1989; Lucy 1998; Pader 1980; 1982; Samson 1987). Interpretations of mortuary symbolism have been developed through the study of early medieval burial data, although in terms of methodology they have tended to share much in common with processual approaches (e.g. Härke 1990; 1997a and b; Richards 1987). These perspectives have also inspired studies that focus upon graves as materialised ideology (e.g. Carver 1995; 2000; 2001; 2002) and self-dubbed 'contextual' studies that combined social and symbolic perspectives (e.g. Lucy 1998; 2002). Alongside these approaches, the older themes of using graves as quarries for cultural and religious history can still be identified (e.g. O'Brien 1999; Taylor 2001; Welch 1992; Wilson 1992).

Yet a key criticism of early medieval mortuary archaeology over the last decade has been that a number of further theoretical approaches have yet to be explored in relation to the data. These approaches – explored more fully in prehistoric contexts – have sought to escape from the polemic of either a purely 'social' or an overtly 'symbolic' approach, focussed neither solely on the material itself nor the meanings behind burial rites. Instead, a theme linking them is a concern with the active and performative role of mortuary practices – both structuring and structured by past social structures and associated cosmologies in which the living actors engage and interact with the dead (e.g. Barrett 1994; Parker Pearson 1993). Mortuary practices are considered simultaneously a religious, a social, an economic and a political realm, rather than parcelled into one single category. The rituals can affect and direct past societies' and individuals' views of themselves and the world around them, their links to the past, aspirations for the future and links with the supernatural. There is no single theme in these approaches; instead there is a constellation of related issues and debates which we need to explore in turn to appreciate their significance for developing new perspectives on early medieval graves and cemeteries.

The first issue of debate concerns the meaningful, active, ritualised and symbolic nature of mortuary practices. The symbolic role of material culture from funerary contexts has often been addressed, and it is generally accepted that mortuary practices are a symbolic medium, compared by some to language (e.g. Richards 1992), texts (Pader 1980; 1982) and even to poetry and theatre (Carver 2000). This has led to two perspectives. First, symbolism is often seen as purely social in focus, i.e. symbolism is seen as subservient to the role of mortuary practices in communicating the social identity of the deceased, and, in turn, mortuary variability is perceived as indicating social structure (e.g. Richards 1987; Härke 1997d). Alternatively, there has been the tendency to restrict discussions of the symbolic to those artefacts and practices that defy a 'prosaic' or 'practical' explanation, such as amulets and the decoration upon objects, rather than broader patterns in burial data (e.g. Meaney

1981; Wilson 1992). Yet symbolism has many forms, and complex chains of signification can embody mortuary events and their material culture. Symbolic, iconic and metaphorical messages can all be made through monuments, artefacts and the body in death linked to the social identity of the deceased but also to cosmology, mythology and ideology. For example, the issue of pervading metaphors in mortuary contexts is one explored by Chris Tilley (1999) and addressed in relation to early medieval monuments by Anders Andrén (1993). Andrén considers how Gotlandic picture stones of the first millennium AD can be understood as metaphors of otherworld journeys as well as socio-political statements through the scenes depicted upon them, and through their shape and monumental scale. In other words, mortuary practices can be concerned as much with cosmology as with the representation of society, as Oestigaard (2000) has discussed for first-millennium AD cremation rituals and Price (2002) for Viking-period artefacts and graves. Similarly, drawing upon historical and archaeological information, Bonnie Effros has demonstrated the complex early medieval social and metaphorical significances of food and drink in mortuary contexts (Effros 2002a), as well as the numerous symbolic associations of clothing when used to adorn the early medieval dead (Effros 1996; 2002b: 13–39). While it may not always be possible to reconstruct cosmologies any more than it is possible to reconstruct social structure from mortuary variability (*pace* Gräslund 1994; see Jennbert 2000), the possibility that metaphors and symbols relating to cosmology may have been as important as signalling social identity in mortuary practices is now widely considered (Williams 2001b).

A theme closely connected to 'the meaning of things' concerns the social agency of mortuary practices and the artefacts, structures, bodies, monuments and spaces they incorporate. 'The dead do not bury themselves' is a constant point of emphasis in recent studies: burial rites are the contrivances and media for the survivors, and it is their role in mortuary performances that, it is suggested, should be emphasised. A focus on the agency of participants in mortuary ritual leads us to appreciate how mortuary traditions develop and retain their consistency, but also to how they evolve and transform over time through collective and individual decision-making and negotiation. This is a theme explored in a series of prehistoric studies of burial data (see Barrett 1994; Chapman 2000; Gillespie 2001). However, it is also an issue to consider the agency of non-human agents in mortuary contexts, since, in many societies, death and the dead are regarded as continuing to have a presence and agency, as well as being transformed through the agency of supernatural powers, after the cessation of vital signs (Williams 2004b). Indeed it could be argued that identities in mortuary practices (of both the dead and the living) are mediated by the 'agency' of objects, rather than any symbolic meanings they hold or evoke. The agency inherent in non-human materials and beings that are present in early medieval funerals has similarly received limited attention. By this it is meant that the material presence of bodies, objects and indeed monuments, architecture and spaces influences the ways in which mourners interact with each other, with the dead and with the supernatural. For instance, a key guiding idea behind the sacrifice of animals in many societies is the expectation that their spirits might serve as guides for the deceased to the next world; an animal in this light is not just a symbol of material wealth, but a non-human agent essential to the proper transformation of the dead in social, cosmological and ontological terms (Eliade 1954; Williams 2001b; 2005b).

This takes us to the issue of personhood in past mortuary practices (e.g. Fowler 2004). Archaeologists deal with the study of bodies in past mortuary practices, and these are often taken as the disposal of personalities that retain their individuality upon death. However, both anthropological and historical research has challenged the imposition of such rigid definitions of the social person in life and death outside western modernity. The relationship with animals, objects and monuments can involve the exchange of qualities and attributes between people and their environment in life, and the same can apply to mortuary contexts. This is supported by the anthropology and sociology of death (Bloch & Parry 1982; Davies 1997; Hertz 1960; Metcalf & Huntingdon 1991) that emphasise the dissolution, transformation and (sometimes) the negation of individuality in death rituals in the process of societal and cosmic regeneration and the creation of ancestors. The argument has usually been developed in relation to the complex, multi-stage mortuary rituals of later prehistory, in which bodies are transformed, fragmented, curated and circulated *through* monuments and among the living (e.g. Fowler 2001; 2002; 2003). Yet this argument may apply to mortuary rituals that bring substances, materials and monuments into association with each other within graves and cemeteries. Even when the cadaver is interred singly and whole, its posture, position and the objects and structures connected to it can evoke more than the individual identity of the interred person (Brück 2004; Fowler 2004: 131–54). In most cultures, identities can be *distributed* between biological individuals and through material culture, monuments and places, and therefore have 'dividual' and even 'fractal' qualities (see Fowler 2004 for discussion). For example, Jos Bazelmans (2000; 2002) has developed these ideas in discussing the ideologies of artefact exchange behind early medieval literary sources such as *Beowulf* and explored their implications for understanding the roles of the exchange and deposition of artefacts in commemorating dividual personhood and the roles of early medieval graves in constituting early Christian attitudes towards the body and the cosmos.

Linked to these issues is the question of whether mortuary practices ever represent the beliefs, ideologies and practices of *one* group, since, as public events, funerals and other mortuary rites involve the interaction, competition and conflict of many different social groups defined in numerous ways in relation to age, gender, status, family, household, religion and ethnicity, or a combination of these simultaneously. Mortuary practices have been considered as 'ritual discourses', but they are often as much about conflict as they are contexts for 'social integration' (Barrett 1994; see Williams 1999a). In some instances, it is possible to consider mortuary practices as operating as symbolic and social violence as much as contexts of mourning and group-definition. For example, when considering the evidence from the early Middle Ages, Julian D. Richards has emphasised the assertion of Scandinavian pagan identity involved in the Viking appropriation of existing Christian cult sites at Repton. This included the reuse of a Mercian royal mausoleum and the overt display of cremation and mound-burial at Ingleby. Together, these were alternative ways of asserting a distinctive socio-political and religious identity in the face of a larger indigenous population. As such, they constituted the commemoration of shared origins but may have been communicated as a statement of conflict and contestation towards other groups (Richards 2001; 2002; 2003; 2004). Mortuary practices and the social memories they evoke can concern both group inclusion and exclusion.

Related to this is the issue of the emotional aspects of mortuary practices, a theme that has yet to be addressed fully in early medieval archaeology. A number of scholars have recently emphasised the need to consider the somatic experiences of mortuary practices by mourners (e.g. Meskell 1996) and in particular the role of emotion in influencing their context, character and form (Tarlow 1999; 2002). Expressions of emotion might be seen as personal grief and therefore a matter of psychology. Alternatively, emotional expressions in funerals might be seen as mere social convention. Either way, emotional responses to death might be perceived by archaeologists as a topic we cannot address. On the contrary, if we consider the multi-sensuous elements of mortuary practices and their role in connecting the living with the dead, then an understanding of the social context of bereavement becomes an important element for understanding death and material culture in the past. For instance, we might wish to consider in terms of bereavement the choices of artefacts added to graves, as well as the stylised portrayal of the dead within the grave and upon monuments, as being intended to evoke specific emotional responses. Equally, early medieval archaeologists have underplayed the centrality of both fear and abjection in early medieval mortuary ritual, themes that are common motivators for ritual practices in other societies and periods (Nilsson Stutz 2003).

Connecting the themes of meaning, agency, personhood, discourse and emotion is the role of mortuary practices in the production and reproduction of social memory. Because this element serves as a lynchpin for many of the other themes in recent mortuary theory, this is the central theme adopted for this book. Studies of mortuary practices focusing on social memory have become centre-stage over the last decade in archaeology but also in a range of other disciplines, including history, sociology and anthropology. In archaeology, discussions have focused on the different forms of commemoration, the complex relationships between monuments and social memory through their architectural spaces and places (e.g. Barrett 1994; Edmonds 1999; Thomas 1996; 1999; 2000; 2002), and the landscape and monumental contexts of commemoration (e.g. Bradley 1998b; Thomas 1999; Tilley 1994; 1996b), as well as the 'biographies' of commemorative monuments as they are built, used and reused in different contexts over time (Holtorf 1996; 1997; 1998).

While studies of memory have tended to focus upon monuments in past societies, there have also been discussions on the relationship between monumentality and other forms of social commemoration, such as the disposal of portable artefacts in graves and hoards (Bradley 2002; Rowlands 1993). The interplay of mortuary practices and monuments has been discussed in most detail in connection with the 'collective' mortuary monuments of the early Neolithic (Barrett 1994; Fowler 2001; 2002; 2003; Thomas 2000) as well as the 'genealogies' constructed through the repeated augmentation with graves and structural alterations of early Bronze Age burial mounds (Barrett 1990; 1994; Kuijt 2001; Last 1998; Mizoguchi 1993). Similarly, discussions of place and cemetery organisation in terms of social memory have been aired in relation to New World archaeological data-sets (Chesson 2001; Joyce 2001; 2003). Discussions have also entertained the mnemonic qualities of artefacts and the role of the grave as a focus for artefact display in relation to the body (Brück 2004; Jones 2001a and b; 2002; 2003; 2004). The complex roles of portable artefacts in social remembrance are, however, only beginning to be addressed in archaeological research (Lillios 1999). Hamilakis (1998), Meskell (1996) and Tarlow (1999; 2002) have, from different perspectives, tackled the issues of corporeality and embodiment in strategies of remembrance: how bodies, living and dead, interact to create memories. Meanwhile, Parker Pearson (1993) and Meskell (2003) have highlighted the importance of going beyond the cemetery to compare and contrast the roles of settlements and burials in commemorating the dead and ancestors.

Few of these approaches have been explicitly applied to early medieval burial archaeology, although they have gained solid grounding in other areas of historical archaeology. Their potential for the study of historical mortuary archaeology and combining evidence from documents, images and material culture is illustrated by the recent discussions of Roman monumentality by Valerie Hope, in which she discusses the role of gravestones as a focus for written, visual and ritual forms of remembrance (Hope 1997; 2003). Equally, Meskell's (2003) study of mortuary practices in New Kingdom Egypt combines textual and archaeological evidence to explore the different memory practices involving both houses and tombs. These themes have been addressed in later medieval and post-medieval archaeology, from the study of gravestones and church monuments (Finch 2000; Tarlow 1999; 2002) to the commemoration of conflict (Lahiri 2003; Saunders 2003; Tarlow 1997).

If we intend to develop these theories in relation to early medieval mortuary archaeology, we can build upon the insights of scholars investigating other periods and places, together with the reappraisal of the many valuable studies and the wealth of data available for early medieval burials and cemeteries. In doing so, we can begin to provide exciting new interpretations of the ways memories and identities were constructed in mortuary contexts. These studies challenge contemporary approaches in early medieval mortuary practices as a reflection of social structure or materialised ideologies. Instead they focus on the complex interactions of the living and the dead during mortuary practices and on how the social person was transformed and selectively remembered. Yet recent popular descriptions of early medieval mortuary archaeology, while paying lip-service to archaeological theory, retain a core of empirical description that, it might be argued, does not do justice to the potential of early medieval mortuary evidence to provide insights into ways of remembering and forgetting in the early medieval period.

Therefore, the challenge for the next decade of early medieval mortuary archaeology is to move beyond rigid alternatives of cultural, social and ideological readings of the burial data towards considering the themes of metaphor, agency, personhood, emotion and memory.

Perspectives on death, memory and material culture

Let us now consider further the key theme of 'social memory': the ways in which mortuary practices serve to commemorate the past, and sometimes also to evoke aspirations of the future. Yet in order to pursue this approach, we need to look beyond early medieval archaeology and archaeological theories from other periods. This is because other disciplines can offer us a range of insights into the relationships between death, memory and material culture that enable us to appreciate early medieval data in new ways.

Historical perspectives

Historical sources for the period from c. AD 450 to c. AD 1100 are varied, including histories, chronicles, genealogies, saints' lives, laws and wills as well as Gospels. When not explicitly biblical in their focus, they have specific concerns, notably the actions of the elite, including kings, noblemen, saints, bishops, abbots and abbesses. Moreover, their focus often appears to be concerned with life, not death and mortality. However, many of these sources, in different ways, combine a common interest in the representation and dissemination of selected past events, and, in other ways, in death, the dead and their commemoration. Therefore, while accounts of funerals in early medieval Britain are few and brief, many of these texts are explicitly intended as mnemonic documents, aiding memory and promoting particular interpretations of the past. For example, this argument can be developed for the Venerable Bede's (somewhat selective) recording of the lives of the seventh-century abbots, abbesses and bishops of Northumbrian monasteries and ecclesiastical centres, including descriptions of their deaths and tombs (e.g. Webb 1965; see Karkov 1999).

Increasingly, historical documents are considered less as a source of reliable factual information about what happened in the early Middle Ages, tending more to be regarded as documents written within specific socio-political and religious contexts, often with an overtly commemorative and propagandist agenda (e.g. Sims-Williams 1983). Yet, rather than being abstracted from the world around them, written sources often bear testimony to the complex interaction of oral traditions and their recording in texts. In this way, social memories were created, transformed and reproduced through the medium of the spoken and written word (Innes 1998; Fentress & Wickham 1992: 144–5). For example, the production of a saint's life, including the choice of miracles recorded and the manner and sequence of their recording, would simultaneously involve the reuse of tropes and parables from earlier lives and from the miracles of Christ to create the memory of the saint's cult and community. Equally mnemonic are secular documents such as genealogies, intended for recitation in public performances and serving to enhance the appearance of longevity and prestige, as well as the divine and mythical ancestry of early medieval kings and their families, households and kingdoms (Dumville 1985). Even early medieval charters – which, if taken at face value, are little more than descriptive accounts of the transaction of land – are commemorative of the relationship between kings as givers and lords and religious houses as receivers of land. They are also a means of marking onto the landscape the boundaries of such gifts.

Against this background, the study of social memory in early medieval Europe has been a developing focus of research over recent decades, closely connected to considering the complex and situational construction of early medieval elite identities, including gender and ethnicity (e.g. Geary 1991), and inspired by sociological theories of memory (see below; Connerton 1989; Fentress & Wickham 1992). The social processes of both remembering and forgetting can be seen to be important in constructing identity at many levels, from the individual and the family, through to religious communities, ethnic groups, kingdoms and broader conceptions of pre-Christian and Christian society and cosmology. Memory involved many different types of social actor, including the clergy, monastic communities, royalty and aristocracy, and was no less important for the social memories of communities and families lower down the social spectrum, although inevitably the written sources that focus on the highest echelons of early medieval societies have very little to say directly about them in this period (Fentress & Wickham 1992).

The theme of social memory has been explored through many different types of text and context in the early Middle Ages beyond simply chronicles and genealogies. For example, scholars have discussed the legal and social importance of wills as a means of social commemoration (Crick 2000). Others have explored the role of oral traditions and ritual in monastic remembrance (e.g. Cubbitt 1998; 2000; Innes 1998). While theorising about social memory in explicit ways, historians have tended to overlook the roles of material culture in the production and transmission of memories, and how this in turn could serve in the construction of social identities in early medieval Europe. There are exceptions to this bald statement. For example, Patrick Geary (1994a and b; 1999) has emphasised the role of the dead in the commemoration of the past, in particular by making associations with the Roman and Germanic past through links with pagan gods, heroes, emperors and kings. Geary does engage directly with the role of landscape in mortuary commemoration and also with the importance of swords as heirlooms in connecting real or imagined ancestors to the present.

Another important study has been conducted by Elizabeth van Houts (1999), who has addressed the role of material culture in early medieval remembering and forgetting. Van Houts explores the role of the cadaver, artefacts and even embroidery in the transmission of elite mythologies and monastic and family histories; the same argument could be applied to a wide range of secular and sacred treasure passed down the generations and exchanged between individuals and groups (see chapter 3). Objects are regarded as 'pegs' for, and serve to negotiate, social memory (van Houts 1999: 99–100). Matthew Innes (2001) has built on these insights to discuss the importance of material culture as a medium for communicating family and monastic memories across the generations through their display and exchange. What is lacking from this research is a clear attempt to draw upon the rich range of literary and historical evidence for mortuary practices and, more broadly, to see how death and the dying were perceived and to consider how these ideas and practices would have mediated social remembrance.

Central to this appreciation of texts and social memory is the consideration of early medieval manuscripts as a form of material culture. They were expensive, composite objects in themselves, the text produced in a specific style, elaborately illustrated, bound and decorated, and forming the focal point of public rituals, whether they were the performance of Mass in church, the declaration of oaths at a meeting-place or the declaration of charter bounds in the landscape (Moreland 2001).

Complementing this rise in early medieval studies of memory are new perspectives on early medieval death. Victoria Thompson's (2004) innovative and interdisciplinary study of dying, death and burial in later Anglo-Saxon England breaks new ground by exploring the rich symbolism and complex associations linking mortuary material culture to the textual evidence. Although not the primary focus of the study, her analysis of sculpture and burial rites suggests not only symbolic meanings of the rites, but also their commemorative functions (Thompson 2002; 2003a; 2004). Similarly integrating archaeological with historical data is Dawn Hadley's recent synthesis of early medieval death, burial and commemoration linking texts, tombs and graves in studying mortuary commemoration (Hadley 2001). Thompson and Hadley do not, however, integrate fully the theme of social memory in the study of the early medieval mortuary evidence. Consequently it is necessary to pursue further some of the sociological concepts behind early medieval studies of social memory.

Sociological perspectives

The types of memory that need to be envisaged in the study of early medieval mortuary practices have not only personal recollections and biographies, or simply myths and sacred histories, but also the social performance and experience of 'shared' or 'collective' memories. Building on the work of Maurice Halbwachs (1992), sociologists have developed approaches to how social memories are constituted and reproduced. While memory certainly could incorporate personal reminiscences and personal interactions with events, places and persons, it was mediated through social contexts of engagement and experience. Following Paul Connerton (1989), we can identify two overlapping types of social memory. First, there are those that focus on rituals and commemoration but that can also be concerned with monuments, images and texts; these might be referred to as 'inscribing practices' of remembrance. In contrast to them, we can identify 'incorporating practices' of remembrance that focus primarily on the body, its movements and dispositions. Material culture of all forms, from portable objects to monuments, from the corpse to art, can be implicated in both these forms of commemoration.

Recent work in sociology has explicitly investigated the role of mortuary practices and bereavement in remembering and forgetting the past and, in some instances, has considered art, material culture and the body as vehicles for memory. Elizabeth Hallam and Jenny Hockey (2001) explore a diverse range of contexts and artefacts, from tombs to photographs, arguing that material culture holds an 'agency' that affects the evocation, suppression and distribution of social memories for those using it in mortuary and commemorative contexts. For example, Hallam and Hockey emphasise how tombs and graves serve to portray death and the dead in specific ways that can challenge decomposition and time. Moreover, they chart how the grave and the tomb are but some of the contexts for commemoration in recent and contemporary British deathways, and more private and personal contexts have tended to come into fashion.

A further instance of the value of analogies from modern society comes from the research of Douglas Davies (1997) exploring the diversity of ways in which cremation in modern Britain encapsulates many religious traditions and forms of commemoration and is mediated by the architecture of the crematorium and portable objects. Similarly, Marcia Pointon (2002) has articulated a sophisticated discussion of how the role of hair and social memory in Victorian society provides a series of lessons for archaeologists concerning the way in which quite modest objects intimately connecting the living and the dead can serve in remembrance. These insights are focused upon western modernity, yet they provide an insight into the complexity and variety of interactions of material culture and memory in mortuary contexts. In many ways, however, it is only a false distinction between western and non-western societies that prevents these studies from being of value in considering the mnemonic roles of mortuary practices in the early medieval period.

Anthropology and ethnography

Anthropological approaches, and ethnographic analogies, have long inspired archaeological studies of past mortuary behaviour, and they provide us with legitimate and valuable insights into the possible commemorative roles of mortuary practices in early medieval Britain (see David & Kramer 2001; Parker Pearson 1999c).

In terms of general anthropological theory, social theories of dying, death and the dead have been dominated by the influential work of Robert Hertz (1960) and Arnold van Gennep (1960). In particular, Hertz's essay – both sociological and anthropological in character – emphasised that, in contrast to Western medical perceptions of death as a biological event, in non-Western contexts death is almost always a ritualised transition. Drawing upon accounts of funerals recorded from south-east Asia, Hertz's study addressed how fear of death and the dead varied according to the status of the deceased and focused upon the process of transforming body, soul and mourners through the ritual process from live individual to dead ancestor. Similarly, van Gennep conceptualised death as a *rite de passage* comparable to other lifecycle rites in which the dead person moves through rites of separation, a liminal period and finally rites of incorporation into a new identity. Both scholars regard 'death' as a journey and a process rather than a cessation of life-signs. Each has implications for the connection between death and social memory. For instance, they help to indicate the potential for considering the *process* of the funeral as a means of selectively remembering and forgetting, rather than as simply the end-points when the body is incorporated into a tomb, monuments are raised and ancestral rites are conducted. While the role of material culture and technologies in these rites was discussed only in passing by Hertz and van Gennep and in most subsequent discussions of death as a ritual process, this body of literature provides a basis upon which archaeologists can consider the choices of treatment of the dead in mnemonic terms.

More recently, studies have developed an appreciation of the role of material culture in the ritual process of death in non-Western societies. Indeed, Maurice Bloch has argued that material culture operates in a parallel and distinctive cognitive medium for social communication, discourse and commemoration alongside the spoken and written word. It may often be able to communicate messages that words may find difficult (e.g. Bloch 1998). For mortuary practices, rather than a formulaic 'system' transforming the person into ancestor, material culture can be considered as part of a ritual performance of selectively remembering and forgetting, serving to reconfigure 'memories' of the dead from dangerous 'ghost' to that of an 'ancestor'. This fruitful way of reformulating Hertz's model of death as a transition by Metcalf and Huntingdon (1991) can be augmented by regarding the transition as a mnemonic one. This theme has been pursued by Piers Vitebsky for the Sora of India (Vitebsky 1993). Among the Sora, the funerary sequence involves the negotiation of memory between the living and the dead, in which shamanic trances serve as a means by which the dead person communicating with the living is 'forgotten' as a person and is embedded in the surrounding landscape. A parallel development in social anthropology's approaches to death is to consider the relationship between emotion, the treatment of the body in death and social memory, as discussed by Loren Danforth and Nadia Sedematakis for rural Greece (Danforth & Tsiaras 1982; Seremetakis 1991). These rites involve secondary burial rites (i.e. where the dead are exhumed after a designated period for reburial) in which expressions of mourning through laments mediate between the living and the dead. Similarly, ethnographies highlight the two-way interaction between the corpse and the living, showing how the cadaver is more than a passive substance at the centre of the funeral: it can 'act upon society' through the funeral rites, influencing mourners and their understandings of death and the past, and serving as a focal point for social tensions and conflict (Connor 1995).

Melanesian ethnographies have explored in detail the relationship between concepts of the social person, the commemoration of the dead and the complex social exchanges that are integral to the redistribution of identities and resources during and after funerals. In many Melanesian societies, exchange is the medium for commemoration, while the consumption of food and drink during funerals can be a further means of exchange central to the process of both remembering the dead as ancestors and also forgetting and redistributing the identities of the dead person among the living. Examples include Richard Eves' discussion of feasting and Deborah Battaglia's study of exchange, portable artefacts and the body (Eves 1996; Battaglia 1990; 1992; see also Foster 1990). In contrast, Susanne Küchler's work on the *malanggan* of New Ireland provides an example of another use of material culture in commemoration. Rather than exchange, it is brief display and subsequent destruction of sculptures known as *malanggan* in the final phases of complex mortuary ceremonies that forms the centre-piece of mortuary 'forgetting' (Küchler 1988; 1999; 2002).

Therefore, Melanesian ethnographies focus on the commemorative roles of portable artefacts and feasting activities and other forms of 'ephemeral' monuments that serve in the construction of memory through display and destruction. In contrast, ethnographies from Madagascar illustrate the roles of permanent monuments in the commemoration of ancestors in non-Western societies. Studies of the Merina and Zafinimiry of Madagascar by Maurice Bloch serve to illustrate the interplay of cadavers, the mortuary process and monuments in commemoration (Bloch 1971; 1995). The wrapping and management of bodies is an important medium for commemoration, both before and during primary burial and subsequently when they are disinterred and carried for secondary burial in communal tombs. In this process, the cadaver of a known and commemorated family member is reconfigured and translated in order to augment the collective order of the ancestors who are materialised in the tomb (Bloch 1971; Kus 1992; Kus & Raharijaona 2001; Raharijaona & Kus 2001). Once placed in the tomb, the collective remains of ancestors serve as an expression of identity for the disparate kin group, serving to create a focus for fertility and continuity that challenges the disruption and discontinuity caused by death (Bloch 1971; Bloch & Parry 1982).

These sources of evidence are reasonably familiar in archaeological discussions of death and burial, and there has been a long history of exploiting ethnographies, as well as anthropological, sociological and historical theories, for insights into past mortuary behaviour revealed in the European archaeological record (e.g. Ucko 1969). Their application is not without its problems and challenges, however, for these societies are likely to be very different from those we shall encounter in early medieval Britain (see also Parker Pearson & Ramilisonina 1998). Yet their strengths lie in showing the multiple and interweaving strategies of commemoration possible before, during and after funerals in non-Western societies in which portable artefacts, bodies and monuments, as well as the landscape itself, are implicated in remembering and forgetting. These can be strengthened through ethno-archaeological research and through the study of recent and modern mortuary behaviour by archaeologists themselves (e.g. Downes 1999; Høilund Nielsen 1997a; Parker Pearson 1999b; Parker Pearson et al. 1999). They also serve to challenge us not to write the early medieval past as if memory then was identical to the individualistic commemorative responses that are all too familiar to us in modern Western society; instead, they show us alternative ways of remembering and forgetting.

For our study of early medieval death and material culture, it is the combination of historical and sociological, as well as anthropological and ethnographic, perspectives that allows us to build a strong foundation for a new explicit theory for early medieval mortuary archaeology centring on death as a context for commemoration. Social memories can be mediated by writing and oral histories, but material culture in a diverse range of forms can also mediate in remembering and forgetting. Memories also involve many different forms of material culture, from artefacts and the body to monuments and the landscape. They can be as much concerned with forgetting as with remembering; and they can be concerned not only with projections of the past but also aspirations for the future. Memories connect the living and the dead but mediate with the sacred, too. If these general points are accepted, there still remains the lack of a precise archaeological theory to link the broader theories we have discussed to the data that we have available.

Technologies of remembrance – mortuary practices as techniques

While it has been argued that an understanding of social memory is central to understanding mortuary practices past and present, the definition and scope of the term 'social memory' is extremely broad. Almost anything and everything in the archaeological record has the potential to be invested with social memories, and since death was a frequent occurrence in past communities, we can anticipate that many objects had some connection with the dead, even if they were not necessarily placed in graves.

What we cannot do as archaeologists is get inside the minds of past people and consider what they consciously thought about the dead and the past. What we can do, though, is consider the ways in which ritual practices could mediate the past and create memories afresh: the performance of social memory. Material culture simultaneously provides a context, a medium and a message by which these memories could be produced and reproduced within individual funerary sequences and between funerals.

A useful way forward is therefore to focus not on 'what' was remembered precisely – something we cannot hope to gain direct access to – but 'how' commemoration took place and 'why' it took the form that it did. This involves an emphasis on the link between memory and ritual practice, rather than the overarching cosmologies and ideologies that undoubtedly influenced the way that commemoration took place during early medieval funerals. In this regard, a useful concept is one developed by Andy Jones in relation to Neolithic and early Bronze Age mortuary practices, namely regarding funerals as 'technologies of remembrance' (Jones 2003). In Jones' formulation, this serves to emphasise how mortuary practices are sequences of acts and practices ('techniques') that together create chains of actions that connect to transform the social person and reconstitute them in a new form in death. The intended outcome may not always be reached; it might be the subject of negotiation between different groups; and a range of practical, economic, socio-political and religious factors might influence how the technology of the funeral proceeded. Yet it helps to understand that funerals in the past were not repeated and formulaic procedures reflecting the identity of the dead directly, but that they were ritualised performances. Conversely, mortuary practices in this light were not unstructured and impromptu, but the result of informed decisions and choices by mourners who actively remembered past funerals and sought to reproduce and reformulate remembered templates in appropriate but also innovative ways.

In order to illustrate this approach, we can amend Hertz's (1960) theory of death as a transition following the lead of Metcalf & Huntingdon (1991). Mortuary practices negotiate the changing relationship and status of the mourners, the physical body (i.e. the cadaver) and its metaphysical elements (i.e. the soul). The mortuary process can be regarded as a set of practices and technologies concerned with the transformation

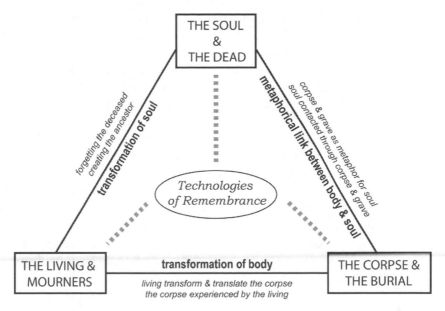

Figure 1.3   A reconfiguration of Metcalf and Huntingdon's interpretation of Hertz's theory of death as transition involving the relationship of mourners, the body and the soul. In this interpretation, technologies of remembrance that involve the deployment of material culture have been attributed a central role in the ritual process. Through the two-way interaction between these three 'agents' (the mourners, the body and the soul), social memories are transformed and reconstituted (diagram by the author).

of the relationship between these three 'agents'. The mourners transform the corpse, and in so doing, the body affects the living through its presence and changing form, influencing the way the funeral is remembered and how the dead are regarded. Linked to this process, the mourners selectively forget elements of the deceased's identity and create a new 'ancestral' identity for the deceased through the ritual process. Central to the process of transforming body and soul is the metaphorical connection envisaged linking them together in many cultures (Hertz 1960; Metcalf & Huntingdon 1991). The soul is manifest within the body and communicates to the living through it, while the body can be regarded as materialising the changing status of the soul through the funerary ritual (fig. 1.3).

From this perspective, memories of the dead were performed and composed through the funeral. However, we must not consider the ritual process of death a 'closed system' unrelated to other times in social life. Memorable events and sequences of acts of funerals not only transformed body and soul, they also structured how subsequent funerals were to proceed by setting up a precedent that could either be followed or challenged in subsequent funerary rituals. Memory is therefore both practice and a structuring principle of mortuary practices. The mnemonic technologies of funerals provide the glue that binds rituals and participants together, but also the innovation that drives traditions forward in new ways. The advantage of perceiving past funerals as 'technologies of remembrance' is that it helps us to get closer to the actions of past people and to how these practices were directly implicated in remembering and forgetting. The emphasis of such an approach is not upon seeing mortuary practices as direct windows onto more abstract sets of belief, identities and affiliations. It is instead an approach that may help us to understand instances of considerable uniformity and conservatism in the burial record, with the repetition of similar funerals culminating in the same landscape locations. Yet it equally allows archaeologists to imagine how innovation and the adoption of new 'technologies of remembrance' can equally serve in creating distinctive identities and relations with the past.

Admittedly, there remain problems with this 'mnemonic' approach. First of all, memory is a diffuse term that needs precise definition. This study has broadly conceptualised 'social memory' as a term, but this requires explicit clarification as a term in relation to both theory and data. Moreover, as with discussions of 'ideology' and early medieval burial, there remains a temptation and tendency to focus on 'elite' burial rites. Furthermore, there is a tendency to consider memory in purely 'social' terms without addressing the religious and sacred context in which commemoration might take place (both pagan and Christian) in early medieval Britain. One particular area of criticism concerns the debate over the interpretation of 'ancestors' in archaeological research. In a fervent attack upon the ubiquitous and uncritical application of the concept throughout recent studies of memory and monumentality in British prehistory, James Whitley (2002) has strongly cautioned against an over-reliance on and conflation of all mortuary rituals and rituals surrounding monuments to the cult of ancestors. This argument is pertinent for the study of early medieval societies. While the commemoration of the dead and the veneration of ancestors are likely to have been a prominent part of social remembrance in early medieval mortuary rituals, ancestors were clearly only one element of the remembered and invented past, alongside genealogies, heroes embodied in legends, origin myths and (following conversion to Christianity) biblical history.

These are but some of the problems, and in subsequent chapters I hope to explain the ways in which it appears that memories (and what types of memory) were being performed in early medieval mortuary practices. Yet, as a starting-point, this approach allows us to consider both uniformity and variability in early medieval mortuary data in new ways. The remainder of this introduction will pursue this idea through burial data, by first charting the broad trajectories of commemoration in early medieval Britain between the fifth and eleventh centuries AD, and secondly by exploring a single burial context to discuss how a mnemonic approach might help us to explain the material evidence we encounter.

Remembering and forgetting in early medieval mortuary practices

It is often tempting to assume that mortuary practices are among the most traditional and conservative aspects of any society, and with this view in mind, it would be expected that, for much of the past, we should find practices and traditions in disposing of the dead that are slow to change. While in terms of the perception of early medieval people this may often have been so, yet the long-term processes revealed by the archaeological record show that mortuary practices underwent dramatic changes in the period, mirroring the dynamism of societies as they adjusted and reconfigured

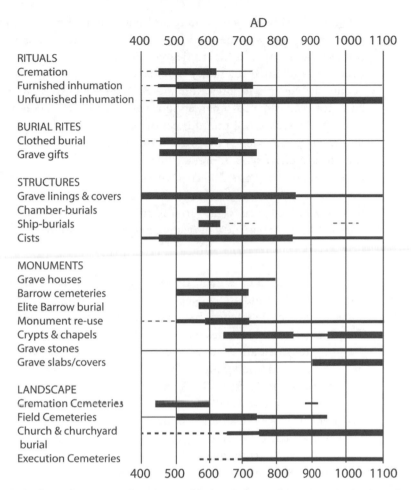

Figure 1.4 A schematic representation of some of the key elements of mortuary practices in early medieval Britain and their changing frequency over time (diagram by the author).

themselves (Carver 1999). Therefore, while crude and broad distinctions between 'Celtic' or 'British' areas and 'Saxon' ones can be suggested, and between 'pagan' and 'Christian', the early medieval period as a whole can be regarded as one of considerable variability, with rapidly changing and fluctuating 'technologies of remembrance' evident in the way the dead are disposed of and monumentalised. Even in a book, it will not be possible to explore this variability in full, and only select examples will be discussed to identify certain issues, showing how both selective remembering and forgetting were mediated by material culture and ritual performances (fig. 1.4).

The Roman Iron Age background
The starting-point for our discussion has to be the emerging uniformity of mortuary practices in the late Roman world. The mortuary practices of later Roman Britain show an increasing uniformity and regularity over time, with the appearance of 'managed' extra-mural urban cemeteries suggesting that either a Christian and/or

secular civic elite was controlling and maintaining burial grounds (Philpott 1991). Yet diversity can also be identified, with cremation persisting alongside inhumation, and a variety of different degrees of uniformity between and within cemeteries (Watts 1991). Such regularity may have been counter to the structural social and economic tensions in later Romano-British society that culminated in the decline and rapid collapse of Roman administrative and socio-economic systems in Britain in the early decades of the fifth century AD (Esmonde Cleary 1989). In any case, the overall pattern tends towards inhumation, and with minimal grave goods by the later fourth century, comprehensible (at least broadly) within the Christian world of late Antiquity (Petts 2004). Dynamic changes occur in the fifth century, when new forms of mortuary behaviour can be observed. The 'sub-Roman' period can therefore be categorised in burial terms as a period of divergences and innovation rather than the usual view of decline and fragmentation.

Divergences

The fifth and sixth centuries AD in Britain are regarded in many different ways by current historical and archaeological scholarship, with different researchers opting to suggest different degrees of change and continuity. Few would dispute, however, that the fifth and sixth centuries were periods of marked social, political, economic and religious transformation. To what extent this change was caused by Germanic immigration alone, and how much it was the result of indigenous change brought about by both economic and political change, remains a focus of dispute (see Hills 2003).

Regardless of how the fifth century is perceived in other spheres, in terms of mortuary practices we see a period of departures and innovation in a number of senses. First, we see the establishment of new 'Germanic' or 'Anglo-Saxon' cemeteries in southern and eastern England. The rites exhibit notable similarities with those found in southern Scandinavia and northern Germany, especially in the cremation rites. These 'Germanic' burial rites were internally complex and diverse between localities and regions. Even the same cemeteries show considerable variability in the mode of interment selected (inhumation or cremation) and variability in grave goods in terms of type and quantity, as well as diversity in the orientation, posture and spatial location of graves (see Arnold 1997; Hills 2003; Lucy 2000; Welch 1992). There is also a clear propensity towards cremation in eastern England and inhumation in southern England, although the two rites overlap in differing proportions between regions (Lucy 2000: 142–3; Williams 2002a).

These 'Germanic' burial rites are found over eastern and southern England, but they are only consistently discovered in select regions and are absent from others. This suggests that the societies of the time were characterised by complex socio-political and ethnic fragmentation with many local patterns. Consequently, the furnished burial rites visible may be only part of the overall picture of mortuary variability in late fifth- and sixth-century Britain.

Charting a linear evolution of burial rites over time for early medieval graves is a difficult enterprise. We can see a shift to new sites for cemeteries in the late sixth and early seventh centuries, new 'final-phase' cemeteries being established with a reduced provision of grave goods. These furnished burials have been interpreted by some as the residue of pagan superstition, by others as an overtly Christian adaptation of furnished burial tradition (see Boddington 1990; Geake 1997). Simultaneously in the seventh and early eighth centuries there are other categories of cemetery focusing upon churchyards with west–east orientations and no grave goods (Geake 1992; Lucy & Reynolds 2002). There are also for the first time clear indications of a separate elite burial rite consisting of mound-burials with a range of innovative grave goods prior to, but perhaps overlapping with, the elite adoption of church-burial (Webster 1992). Therefore, if the 'migration period' of the fifth and sixth centuries was a time of great mortuary variability, the seventh and early eighth centuries cannot be said to show any greater uniformity despite the gradual decline in placing grave goods with the dead.

The possible burial rites that might have taken place in these 'gaps' between areas of Germanic burial rite are found over areas of lowland Britain outside Roman control. This is the burial rite of west–east-orientated burials in ordered rows that David Petts (1998; 2000; 2002a) has referred to as the 'Central Rite'. Many of these sites seem to be newly established, but in association with Roman structures and buildings. These burials are generally findless, although modest grave goods do occur. A variation on this theme is found further west. In the south-west and Wales we also discover west–east burials, but with less evidence of orderly rows. There is also evidence for rectangular and square grave structures and long-cists. In combination these features constitute elements of what Petts refers to as the 'Western Rite'. Moving into northern Britain, we have well-ordered west–east-orientated graves forming 'long-cist' cemeteries in a discrete region of northern England, southern and eastern Scotland. Long-cist cemeteries are also found in Ireland (O'Brien 2003). Finally, in central and northern Scotland we have the 'Pictish' square barrow cemeteries, although increasingly there is evidence of overlap between these rites and the long-cist cemeteries to the south (Alcock 1992). Where radiocarbon dates are available, these cemeteries can be dated from the fourth and fifth centuries through to the eighth and ninth centuries AD. Therefore there is not only chronological, but also considerable regional variation in western and northern Britain, a variety that cannot easily be conflated into a simple distinction between 'Celt' and 'Saxon'.

Convergences
Throughout the seventh, eighth and ninth centuries it appears that unfurnished field cemeteries continued in the 'Celtic West' as well as in 'Anglo-Saxon England', some attracting churches at a later date. Where cemeteries are attracted around minster churches and monasteries we find evidence of multiple burial grounds serving the religious community and the lay population of the environs (e.g. Daniels 1999; Hall & Whyman 1996; see Hadley 2000; 2002). Yet it was only by the tenth and eleventh centuries that most parish churches were firmly established with their accompanying churchyards (see Gittos 2002; Hadley 2000; 2002). Consequently, the decline in the provision of grave goods does not seem to have led to any less spatial complexity in the burial rites found across Britain, and in fact the opposite could be argued, with

an enhanced diversity and complexity evident in terms of both location and burial rite. The ninth century (the traditional advent of the 'Viking period') brought shifts and changes associated with the decline of monasteries, but it was not fundamentally a period of massive change in the same way as the fifth and seventh centuries (see Thompson 2004). From the ninth century, funerary sculpture developed and varied considerably in quantity and context. Yet despite the apparent uniformity of unfurnished west–east orientated graves that provide the ubiquitous norm from the eighth to the eleventh century, variability can still be identified in burial rites (Bailey 1980; 1991). A variety of grave structures and furnishings developed within the supposed 'uniformity' and 'equality' of west–east orientation and extended supine posture (Buckberry forthcoming; Hadley 2000; 2002). Nor was the Norman Conquest the clear watershed in terms of mortuary practices that it is often portrayed to be in other spheres. While grave slabs developed and proliferated, there were continuities in mortuary practices and mortuary topography across the mid-eleventh century divide between Anglo-Saxon and Norman England (Daniell 1997; 2002; Finch 2000).

Dying in the eleventh century no doubt involved a very different set of ritual practices from those in the fifth century, just as dying in Orkney would have involved different burial rites from those in Kent, but a set of core themes can be isolated and developed from this book's discussion. The shift from the deployment of furnished burial rites to a focus upon permanent stone tombs is only one element of this change, but it was one that should not be overemphasised to the exclusion of others. The evolution of churchyard burial should also not be seen as a simple evolutionary narrative. Nor can we necessarily chart a simple linear evolution in the history of attitudes and practices surrounding death. Diversity is still the key, and the emergence of church burial can perhaps be regarded as simply a development of existing strategies of remembering and forgetting, rather than an immediate and radical instigation caused by conversion to Christianity.

Explaining mortuary variability through social memory
Explaining this variability is a difficult challenge for archaeologists, and the theoretical paradigm we employ will very much govern which elements of the mortuary practices we value for study and which we suppress. The variations in the treatment of the dead are broadly related to the social identity of the deceased and the mourners, but the precise manner in which the dead were remembered is clearly connected directly to a series of strategies for evoking the dead in particular ways, and linking them to broader cosmological, mythical and social views of the past, present and future. Communities were very much treating death as a performance, using death as a changing 'stage' upon which to express their identities and connections with the dead, the ancestors, the sacred and the past in general. Simultaneously, attempts were being made to construct aspirations for the future, both for the dead in the hope of achieving a final destination in an afterlife and for the living in affirming their land, possessions and resources.

Defining this variability in terms of social memory and the contrasting strategies recognised as 'technologies of remembrance' provides a broad, crude but helpful

Figure 1.5 View of the downland ridge in south-west Wiltshire known as Swallowcliffe Down, looking north. In the early medieval period, the burial mound, reused for a wealthy bed-burial, would have been sky-lined (photo by the author).

framework that cuts across the usual ethnic and religious divisions usually imposed upon the evidence. It is from this perspective that the rest of the book will develop.

Memories through mortuary practices: Swallowcliffe Down, Wiltshire
This broad review provides an initial illustration of how a focus on social memory allows us to engage with traditional questions of cultural, social and religious change identified through mortuary practices with an appreciation of the role of burial rites as both a form of *habitus* and a materialisation of ideology. We have seen that the configuration of mortuary practices as 'technologies of remembrance' helps to express the interaction of ideology and practice and the transformative social and mnemonic quality of mortuary practices; they are ritual performances that not only reflect and express society and ideology, but also actively transform and reproduce identities and social memories. To introduce the way in which we can explore the role of early medieval mortuary practices as 'technologies of remembrance' through a detailed and contextual study of archaeological evidence, this section introduces the main themes of the book crystallised into a single grave.

In August 1966, archaeologists excavated the wealthiest and most complex female grave ever uncovered in the history of British archaeology. The excavations were conducted by Faith Vatcher on behalf of the Ministry of Public Buildings and Works on Swallowcliffe Down, on the boundary between the parishes of Swallowcliffe and Ansty in south-west Wiltshire.

The burial was located in a chamber inserted into the centre of an early Bronze Age burial mound on the apex of the Down (figs. 1.5 and 1.6). Grave-robbers and antiquarians had got there first: much of the top and middle of the grave had been disturbed, and some of its contents may have been removed, although the character

Figure 1.6   View looking north-west from the site of the Swallowcliffe mound, now imperceptible due to erosion, plough-damage and excavation (photo by the author).

of the grave can be assessed with some certainty from George Speake's assessment and publication of the excavation archive (Speake 1989). For the burial rites of early medieval Britain, the grave cannot in any sense be regarded as 'typical' in terms of the quality of preservation, wealth, structure or isolated location. Indeed, while the Swallowcliffe grave forms part of a group of 'final-phase', richly furnished burials of adult females, it is in many ways unique. Yet for the purposes of this volume, the Swallowcliffe grave provides a useful introduction that encapsulates many of the potentials and challenges with using archaeological data to interpret social strategies of remembering and forgetting. The argument is that the artefacts, body, grave, monument and location all combined in the construction and commemoration of the social person in death (fig. 1.7).

Artefacts
The grave goods from Swallowcliffe Down represent a range of objects and materials placed in and around the cadaver in five discrete assemblages (fig. 1.8). The artefacts date the grave to the later seventh-century AD, a time when burial with grave goods was increasingly rare. At the west end of the grave were two vessels, an iron pan or skillet and a large yew-wood iron-bound bucket (assemblage A), while at the foot end of the grave was a bronze-mounted bucket placed on a ledge on the side of the grave (assemblage C). Beside the right forearm are two glass palm cups (assemblage E). By the left leg was a maple-wood casket containing a range of items, including a bronze sprinkler, a silver spoon, four silver brooches, a strap mount, one amber and two glass beads, an iron spindle, two knives with horn handles and a comb of bone or antler (assemblage B). By the right leg was a satchel of wood and leather decorated with an openwork disc mount of copper alloy with gold and silver repoussé foils (assemblage D). Some of these items were connected with feasting (the buckets, pan and cups),

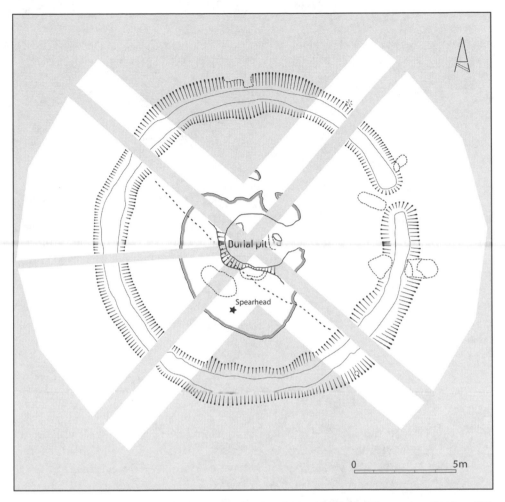

Figure 1.7 Plan of the 1966 excavations of the reused, early Bronze Age burial mound on Swallowcliffe Down. The seventh-century bed-burial was uncovered centrally placed within, and deliberately reusing and remodelling, the earlier monument (redrawn by Séan Goddard after Speake 1989).

some with Christian ritual practices (the sprinkler), and others were elements of burial costume, although not actually worn by the deceased (the brooches), while the comb was concerned with the presentation of the body in life and perhaps also in death. Items of burial costume including pin-suites and beads were not found, but such remains may have been disturbed by the antiquarian exploration of the grave.

The meanings and associations of these objects may have been complex, varied and layered. Some would have been on display for mourners to see and therefore made an overt statement of identity, while others were concealed from view, hidden away within containers. The artefacts could have had different associations with individuals and groups, some being personal possessions of the deceased, some being items belonging to the deceased's family and others still being gifts brought from far and wide by families and individuals who owed allegiance or shared friendship

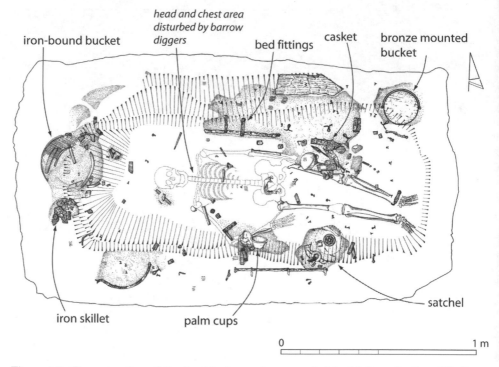

Figure 1.8 Reconstruction of the furnished seventh-century bed-burial from Swallowcliffe Down (adapted by Séan Goddard after Speake 1989; reproduced with the kind permission of English Heritage).

with the deceased and her family. Some may have had a clear iconographic message, as with the openwork disc with its Christian-cross and chi-rho symbolism (Speake 1989: 80), while others may have communicated wealth and hospitality, status, age and gender. The biographies of the objects may also have been important: some were probably contemporary with the deceased, whereas others may have had longer histories of use – biographies that perhaps stretched over generations – and some may have been heirlooms. While each object may have made a statement, the composition as a whole may have been more important than the sum of its parts, serving as a tableau for all at the funeral to see and remember. Other objects had more specific, sensuous associations. As with Melanesian ethnographies showing the importance of feasting in mortuary practices, many of the artefacts in the Swallowcliffe Down grave are associated with eating and drinking, and therefore evoke the positive associations and social bonds created during their use. The 'story' created by the grave goods is therefore complex, involving symbols, metaphors and memories to create a powerful and memorable spectacle for those attending the funeral.

The body

The body was poorly preserved and had been disturbed by the antiquarian intervention. When examined, the remains were shown to be those of an adult female aged between 18 and 25 years at death and around 5 ft 3 in. in height. The circumstances of her death are unknown, although even at this young age her bones show some signs of pathology. The body had been laid in an extended posture for all to see, orientated west–east in Christian fashion, and again we can consider its mnemonic associations: the posture serving to display the body to onlookers, the orientation serving to evoke links with a Christian past, present and future. Orientation was not a clear indicaton of religious belief, since a west–east orientation was common for pre-Christian as well as conversion-period and churchyard burials. The final assemblage of 'grave goods' is actually better described as an element of the grave's structure connected to the disposition of the body. It consists of the ironwork of the bed, consisting of single and double cleats, stays, side rails, eyelets and nails. The placing of the body upon a bed may have communicated status and comfort, but perhaps also the metaphor of death as akin to sleep.

We must remember that at least two dead bodies were involved. The grave-digging must have involved the discovery of Bronze Age skeletal material and its removal. By analogy with other Bronze Age burials, the cutting of the grave into the centre of a Bronze Age barrow would probably have revealed many different burials, some primary, some added at later dates in the site's use. The Swallowcliffe burial mound is likely to have originally covered at least one crouched inhumation burial and received a series of secondary inhumation and cremation graves, and indeed the excavations revealed traces of cremated material in the grave fill of the Saxon burial suggesting earlier disturbed graves.

At a time when minster churches were being newly established, early medieval communities were yet to become accustomed to the regular disturbance of older graves caused by the pressures upon the use and reuse of the churchyard for burial (Williams 1998). Yet it is equally difficult to imagine that such remains would not have been recognised, and choices had to be made about how to respond to these remains: either to ignore them or to treat them with respect.

The grave

The grave was no ordinary early medieval inhumation burial space: it was a chamber measuring just under 3m by 1.5m. There are indications that there may have been wooden corner-posts supporting wooden walls, and there is even the suggestion that clay was brought from the valley to line and seal the grave (Speake 1989: 14), which was perhaps originally painted or covered with textiles, with a range of soft-furnishing padding the bottom of the grave and covering the bed.

The artefacts, body and grave would have interacted to create a complex sequence of practices and performances in the funeral. We can imagine the digging of the grave, perhaps the lining of the grave with timber shorings, and perhaps a temporary shelter over the grave in the hours or days until the body was ready for burial. We then have the lowering of a bed into the grave, followed by the clothed body together with a set of discrete deposits. Each would have required persons approaching the grave and passing them down to those in the grave itself with the body. Finally, after the funeral had approached completion, the grave would have been back-filled and the mound raised.

The burial mound

The grave was found at the centre of a burial mound with a circular ditch almost 13m in diameter and a causeway on the eastern side. Yet this was not a new monument raised once the grave had been back-filled in a single event. Instead, it was a pre-existing monument thousands of years old when it attracted the secondary Anglo-Saxon burial in the later seventh century, and it seems to have had at least two phases of construction. The primary monument was a bell barrow made of chalk lumps covered with turves and flints around which was a large berm (a flat, raised area between the mound and the ditch) before the ditch. In a second stage, this mound was extended, doubling its size and extending the mound to the very edge of the ditch. The exact dating of these phases is unknown, but both phases are likely to date to the early Bronze Age, at least 2,500 years before the seventh-century burial mound. Over such a distance of time, the likelihood of a preserved 'memory' of the original function of the burial mound is unlikely to have survived. Instead, the choice to 'reuse' the site is likely to have been a deliberate appropriation of an unknown past, imbuing the monument with new meanings that served to create connections to an invented ancestral past, and perhaps also to stake claims for the future.

The reuse consisted of a centrally placed secondary burial of seventh-century date inserted into the prehistoric monument and dispersing the original primary interment (Speake 1989: 6). This was not a case of expedient reuse. The digging of a large and sizeable chamber may have been made easy through the use of an earthen mound rather than attempting to cut through the chalk bed-rock, but for a standing monument the creation of such a large and deep grave must have been an act of considerable effort in itself. This reuse also required the opening of the centre of the monument and the destruction of the original primary grave, and the complete remodelling of the monument once back-filling was complete. A prominent post may have also been erected to commemorate the site of the grave. Therefore, rather than a passive veneration of an earlier structure, the Swallowcliffe Anglo-Saxon burial involved the wholesale reconfiguration of the monument. The monument reuse at Swallowcliffe was an enduring element of the funeral that contributed to the creation of a new monument out of the old (see Williams 1997).

The landscape

Given the restriction of excavations to the mound itself, the possibility that other early medieval graves were not situated around the monument cannot be ruled out. The discovery of an early medieval spearhead on the southern side of the burial mound could represent traces of other graves or other instances of ritual deposition at the monument. Nearby and visible from the burial mound on Swallowcliffe Down, at Winkelbury Hill on the northern edge of Cranborne Chase, a similar grave was found. Reusing a Bronze Age burial mound was a central interment (also a bed burial) that seems to have been one among a series of early medieval burials focusing upon the prehistoric barrow cemetery.

On the same ridge at Swallowcliffe, a Saxon burial, thought to be a primary interment within a burial mound, was found only 250m away over the parish boundary,

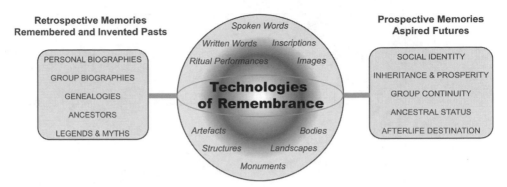

Figure 1.9   Schematic representation of the retrospective and prospective elements of social memory mediated by technologies of remembrance (drawn by the author).

suggesting the possibility of a diffused set of burial foci on the ridge top. Yet the central positioning of the burial within the earlier monument, its west–east orientation and its wealth suggest that this was the remains of a member of the Christianised West Saxon aristocracy. The grave was situated on a ridge with all-round views, its creators possibly selecting a prehistoric monument that was also well-placed to be visible from long-distance routeways noted by a later charter reference to a *herepath* (army road) traversing the ridge upon which the mound was situated. It is also possible that the burial was located upon a contemporary territorial boundary: either the mound was integral to the boundary's creation or the monument affirmed its significance (Reynolds 2002; Williams 1999b). The grave can be dated on chronological grounds to the late seventh century, forming part of a discrete group of barrow-burials in this period of conversion and kingdom consolidation (see Geake 1997; 2002; Ozanne 1962–3).

Conclusion: Swallowcliffe in context

The material evidence at Swallowcliffe gives us only a partial view of the burial occasion: a range of different social groups would have been involved in the funeral as participants in particular obligations and rituals, and simply as observers. Moreover, the material culture, structures and monument are incompletely preserved. Many other materials and substances may have been deployed, exchanged and disposed of in ways that leave no material trace in the grave itself. Perhaps most important to remember is the fact that the burial itself was probably only one stage (and not necessarily the final one) in a long sequence of ritual acts. From the settlement itself where the person may have died, through a series of spaces and places, the body was transformed and translated until it finally reached the hilltop where the cadaver was interred. Yet the themes connecting these technologies of remembrance are their public nature and a concept of death as transition. Connected to the use of material culture may have been other 'technologies of remembrance' that leave little archaeological trace: songs, dances, feasts and other ceremonial events that punctuated the transformation of the dead person into their new social, ontological and cosmological identity. Images, the spoken word and the written word may also have

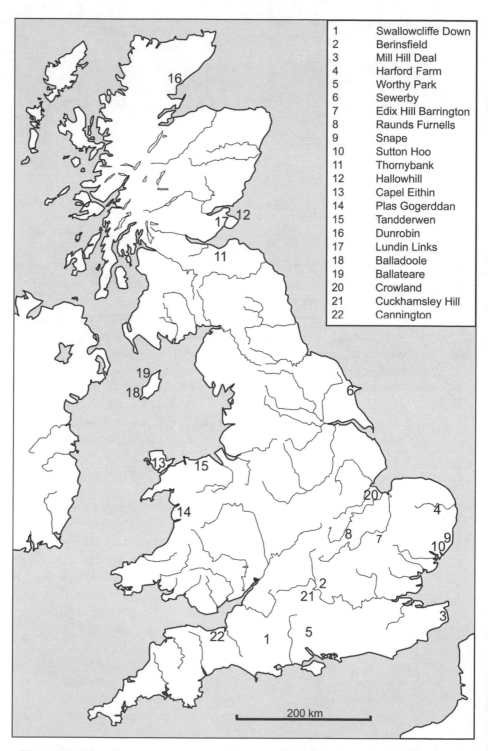

1	Swallowcliffe Down
2	Berinsfield
3	Mill Hill Deal
4	Harford Farm
5	Worthy Park
6	Sewerby
7	Edix Hill Barrington
8	Raunds Furnells
9	Snape
10	Sutton Hoo
11	Thornybank
12	Hallowhill
13	Capel Eithin
14	Plas Gogerddan
15	Tandderwen
16	Dunrobin
17	Lundin Links
18	Balladoole
19	Ballateare
20	Crowland
21	Cuckhamsley Hill
22	Cannington

200 km

Figure 1.10 Map of the sites used as case studies in the book, numbered in order of discussion.

guided the commemoration of the dead person interred on Swallowcliffe Down, connecting imagined and remembered pasts with aspired futures for the dead person and the living community (fig 1.9).

Despite the limitations of the data for a complete picture of how memories were composed and reproduced, we can draw together the themes of artefacts, body, structures, monument and landscape as means of exploring and theorising the mnemonic significance of mortuary practices in early medieval Britain. Together they allow us to consider the different types of mnemonic at work in the one burial. The evocation of pasts and futures for those attending the funeral and those encountering the burial mound in the early medieval landscape was performed through the mortuary rituals, culminating in the creation of the grave and monument. Placing the furnished, high-status burial rites conducted at Swallowcliffe in context is the aim of this book.

The book begins by focusing upon portable artefacts from within and beyond early medieval graves (chapter 2) and the role of the dead body itself in social remembrance (chapter 3). We then focus upon the role of graves as contexts of commemoration in which artefacts, materials and bodies are displayed and concealed (chapter 4). In combination, these chapters hope to explore the interactions of objects, bodies and contexts in creating and transforming 'memorable' scenes at death. The book then moves on to a consideration of monumentality and memory, in which we look at the interaction of monuments as a part of the ritual process and as foci for remembrance (chapter 5). Finally, we consider the significance of cemeteries and graves as places of memory in the evolving early medieval landscape (chapter 6).

Many archaeological sites will be mentioned on this thematic journey through the use of material culture to commemorate the early medieval dead, but the focus will centre upon twenty-two sites from across Britain (fig. 1.10).

2

Objects of memory

Introduction – rethinking early medieval mortuary artefacts
The study of portable artefacts, particularly those discovered from graves, has traditionally been one of the mainstays of early medieval archaeology. As explored in the introduction, while a consideration of 'commemoration' might tempt us to focus this study upon burial mounds and gravestones, this book will begin by considering the role of portable artefacts and materials in the remembering and forgetting of the dead.

The choice of early medieval communities to clothe the dead and place artefacts on and around the cadaver is the very reason that these graves have become such a visible and diagnostic feature of the archaeological record and an invaluable resource for understanding the early medieval period. The high visibility of furnished graves is not without its problems for archaeologists, since graves with objects have tended to dominate archaeological studies at the expense of the many regions and periods within the early Middle Ages where grave goods were sparse or absent – because they do not survive, because they were placed with the dead but were recirculated among mourners or deposited elsewhere, or because they were never a part of mortuary ceremonies (see Lucy & Reynolds 2002). Yet for those communities practising furnished burial rites, placing selected artefacts and materials with the dead could serve as an important means of configuring and transforming social memories of the dead and the past, and, in turn, social identities.

In this chapter we shall explore how archaeologists have begun to address the portable artefacts found in graves and other contexts from a mnemonic perspective. Rather than regarding grave goods as functioning to display a static social role that was 'held' by the deceased, we can see portable artefacts as an important medium for the complex, sequential and selective process of remembering and forgetting the social person throughout the funeral and culminating in the burial. It will be shown that furnished burials created an 'image' of the dead through the selective deployment of artefacts that influenced the production and reproduction of social memory.

Moreover, it is argued that the contrast between furnished and unfurnished burial is not one between early medieval societies that commemorate through portable artefacts and those that do not. Instead, it is argued that the selectivity of grave goods placed in furnished graves suggests that those artefacts involved in the funeral but circulated and exchanged among the living also had a mnemonic significance. The decline of grave goods in seventh-century England is more than a change in the context of commemoration towards permanent memorials (*pace* Effros 2003) but an extension of the mnemonic significance of artefacts through their biographies and away from the display of deposition.

Early medieval furnished burials – previous studies

Since the nineteenth century, studies of early medieval burial have, often myopically, focused upon the study of these artefacts in and of themselves with only occasional consideration of the mortuary contexts from which they derived. In the antiquarian and culture-historic traditions, artefacts were (and to some extent continue to be) used as an important means of dating graves, as well as of assessing the racial and cultural identities, along with the religious beliefs, of their occupants (e.g. Leeds 1913; 1936; 1945). More recently, as archaeologists adopted an explicitly social perspective in mortuary archaeology inspired by the New Archaeology (Binford 1971; Chapman & Randsborg 1980), but perhaps also by German approaches and methods (Samson 1987; Härke 2000b), the variability of grave goods was regarded as an index of social position and wealth (e.g. Alcock 1981; Arnold 1980; Dommasnes 1982; Jørgensen 1987; Shephard 1979; Solberg 1985; see also Härke 1992; 1997d). Subsequent studies appreciated the crude nature of focusing purely on 'vertical' social differentiation and have attempted to look at regional and local variations (Fisher 1988; 1995; Lucy 1998; 2002; Pader 1982; Richards 1987), as well as 'horizontal' social differentiation, including how gender, age and kinship might have influenced the provision of grave goods (Crawford 1993; 2000; Fisher 1988; 1995; Gowland 2001; Härke 1990; 1997d; 1998; Stoodley 1999a and b; 2000; Tyrell 2000). National surveys have revealed important patterns in the deployment of grave goods (Härke 1990; 1992; Stoodley 1999a; 1999b; 2000). Meanwhile, in some instances large-scale cemetery excavations have provided data adequate enough to recognise clear patterns in artefact-provision within individual cemeteries, the scale of analysis most relevant to the ritual practices of past communities (e.g. Ravn 1999; 2003). Moreover, further studies have explored the variability in the provision of specific artefact-types in more detail, as with studies of weapons and belt-fittings (Dickinson & Härke 1992; Härke 1989a; 1990; 1992; Marzinzik 2003). This research has been greatly facilitated by cross-referencing the provision of artefacts in graves with osteological evidence for age, sex, biological distance and pathologies. Such methodologies have usually been applied to inhumation burials, but increasingly it has also been applied to early medieval cremation burials as well (McKinley 1994; Richards 1987; Ravn 1999; 2003; Williams 2003).

While early social approaches attempted to infer social organisation directly from the burial evidence, within much of the subsequent research there is an acute awareness that caution is necessary in naively 'reading' the identity of the dead directly from their treatment in death (Härke 1990; 1997c; Samson 1987). There are seven main issues in this regard.

1. *Survival.* We must be cautious over the differential survival of artefact types, given that leather, textile and other perishable remains rarely survive, and bearing in

mind the question whether the number and type of the metal, ceramic and glass objects reflect the original grave assemblage in terms of quality and quantity (Lucy 1998). For example, the textiles that swathed the corpse may have been more significant than the metal dress fasteners that archaeologists assume were the important objects for symbolising identities (see Effros 2002b; 2003).

2. *Selection*. Early medieval graves do not represent individuals who expired and fell into the grave with the objects they happened to have with them when they died! Artefacts were selected from the possessions of the deceased and their kin, as well as gifts from ritual participants and those attending the funeral. Because archaeologists tend to have only the grave preserved for their investigation, many other stages that constitute the 'transition' of death or *rites de passage* of funerals being no longer visible (see Bartel 1982; Hertz 1960; Metcalf & Huntingdon 1991; van Gennep 1960), it is easy to forget the innumerable objects that might have come into contact with the corpse and had special roles in the funeral but that did not enter the grave. For instance, the employment and association of objects with the dead might have taken place during the washing, dressing, translation, transformation and interment of the cadaver, and there might also have been objects associated with the distribution of property among kin and mourners, and with the feasting and other practices that might have accompanied the funeral. These artefacts need not necessarily have ended up in the burial deposit, even though they might have had important and prominent functions in the mortuary process.

3. *Regional and chronological change*. Geographical and temporal changes in mortuary practices will affect the quantity and quality of artefacts placed in the grave, so that caution must be taken in comparing cemetery with cemetery and region with region, as well as with cemeteries of different date-spans (e.g. Arnold 1980). For instance, we should be acutely aware that the provision of artefacts in different regions might have had different significances within similar social structures, or that different social structures might have involved the comparable provision of artefacts in graves. Similarly, over time the frequency and nature of artefacts and their disposal might have changed (see Cannon 1989). Reading social structure directly from these changes may overlook changes in fashion, cycles of competitive consumption and even the deliberate suppression of mortuary expenditure (Morris 1992).

4. *Symbolism*. As discussed in the introduction, artefacts in graves may be present because of their meanings, and these may relate to the social identity of the deceased, but they might also relate to broader cosmological themes (see also Parker Pearson 1982; 1999c; Shanks & Tilley 1982). Since furnished burial is neither exclusively 'pagan' nor 'Christian' in early medieval contexts, this theme is applicable both to pre-Christian cosmologies (e.g. Andrén 1993; Price 2002, but see also Williams 2001b, Gräslund 1994) and Christian world-views (Effros 1996; 2002b and 2003; Thompson 2002; 2003a and b; 2004).

5. *Context*. The social and symbolic messages of artefacts may depend as much on context as the function, form and decoration of the object itself. For example,

subtle differences in the location of artefacts in relation to the body might have held important social and symbolic messages (Lucy 1998; Pader 1982), and these may have been 'read' by different audiences at different levels. Moreover, the significance of a given object might have changed depending upon the age, gender and status of the deceased as constructed by mourners, the combinations of other objects it occurs with, and its location in the grave in relation to the posture and orientation of the body (see Sofaer Derevenski 2000; Stoodley 2000). Consequently, using the simple quantification of grave goods to infer social identity may miss many of the statements made in early medieval graves.

6. *Agency of mourners.* A related issue concerns the agency of mourners in how they portray the dead. Archaeologists have repeatedly emphasised that the 'dead do not bury themselves', and the treatment of the dead body in the grave might say more (or as much) about the identities and socio-political claims of the living than it does about the 'roles' of the dead themselves (see Lucy 1998; Parker Pearson 1999c; Samson 1987). It is possible, and perhaps even likely, that the roles and identities of the living person are not reflected wholly or accurately in the manner of their mortuary portrayal. The social identity of the dead might be invented, enhanced, suppressed or even inverted from those held in life (Halsall 1998; 2003; Pader 1982; Parker Pearson 1982; 1999c). For instance, the artefacts interred with the dead are as likely to be 'gifts' from mourners as they are possessions of the deceased, and this should not be restricted to the distinction between costume and grave offerings (*pace* Crawford 2004; King 2004).

7. *Ideology.* Mortuary practices are the results of the intentional actions of mourners and are theatrical, ritual displays. They were therefore ideological statements (Carver 1986; 1995; 2000; 2001; 2002; Halsall 1998; 2003; Theuws & Alkemade 2000). From such a perspective we can imagine portable artefacts as having an overt role in legitimising and reproducing, but also transforming, identities and social structures, and as being fundamentally enmeshed in power relations that involve competition and conflict, domination and resistance. Mortuary practices can therefore embody myths of origin (Härke 1997a, b and c).

In combination, these issues caution archaeologists against reading social structure directly from early medieval mortuary variability without taking into account the many practical, methodological and theoretical problems that a social reading of burial data entails. An emphasis upon mortuary variability and the provision of grave goods may still have much to tell us, but it is not a direct reflection of social organisation, or even simply its stylised portrayal in an ideological context, that mortuary practices provide. One way forward might be to consider not only the symbolic and ideological context of grave goods provision, but also the mnemonic roles of portable artefacts.

Memory and early medieval grave goods
With these ongoing issues and debates in sharp focus, we must reappraise the way we think about early medieval grave goods. In particular, the possibility that artefacts

were not only intended to symbolise identities, but also to evoke social memories has received limited consideration by early medieval archaeologists (Hallam et al. 2001: 129–54). A number of studies have already begun to consider the mnemonics of early medieval artefacts, focusing upon their form, iconography and decorations to suggest their role in displaying and communicating status, and also origin myths. For example, Heinrich Härke (1997c) has discussed the Germanic origin myths that may have been asserted and reproduced through the deployment of weapons in graves. Meanwhile, the significance of Styles I and II animal art as symbols of Germanic political allegiance and mythical origins has been raised by numerous writers, both for the Scandinavian and Continental material, and for Anglo-Saxon finds (Dickinson 1991; 1993; 2002b; Hedeager 1992b; 1998; 1999; 2000; Høilund-Nielsen 1997b; 1998). If the form and decoration of objects communicated and constituted a range of memories and associations with idealised pasts, then their burial with the dead could have served to emphasise their symbolic meaning and connections with ancestors. The deployment of these objects would simultaneously enhance certain ways of remembering, but equally they would serve to suppress and 'forget' others, making their use a strategy of distinction and exclusivity as well as inclusiveness and group membership. In the context of the shifting political allegiances that typify the early medieval period, this interpretation is appealing because of its focus upon the 'active' role of style in creating new pasts for elites and their followers. Moreover, this approach finds close parity with historical research showing the use of myths (biblical and heroic) by early medieval elites to portray themselves as legitimate successors to the past (e.g. Pohl 1997).

These studies have made important contributions, yet there remains the need to address the manifold ways in which grave goods might have influenced other forms of social remembrance within the mortuary process itself, both through their presence and through their associations with other artefacts and the corpse. For example, while mythical memories may have been evoked by some artefacts, such as those with elaborate decoration, others may have evoked the past through their circulation and curation and consequently their association with a series of famed social actors, as discussed in relation to the gift-exchanges recorded in the Anglo-Saxon poem *Beowulf* (Bazelmans 2000). This is a theme explored by Heinrich Härke concerning the circulation of weapons in early and middle Anglo-Saxon society (Härke 2000a).

Other artefacts still would have been valued not only for their antiquity but also for the distance they had travelled from far-away places with exotic and prestigious associations, as well as for the manner of their conveyance – as such the exotic objects deriving originally from the Byzantine, Frankish and British spheres, or those objects inspired by Scandinavian exemplar found within the mound 1 ship-burial at Sutton Hoo (Carver 1998a; 2005; Williams 2001a). Some objects may have developed mnemonic significance because of the lack of a known and remembered history, as has been suggested for Roman objects from early medieval graves likely to have been discovered rather than curated (Eckardt & Williams 2003). Meanwhile, the potential role of heirlooms as exhibitors of memory is a well-known theme from early medieval written sources as well as from occasional archaeological finds, as in the case of 'named' and inscribed swords (e.g. Ellis Davidson 1962; see also Lillios 1999). Even the incorporation of old materials (i.e. 'spolia') into a new object, such as the Alfred Jewel, could have been an important way of creating links to the past (e.g. Kornbluth 1989; Wilson 1964; Webster & Backhouse 1991). Conversely, the production of new objects with an exclusive mortuary function may have served to distance the deceased from the past and instead emphasise a new identity, as in the case of gold-foil crosses placed or sewn onto early Christian funerary attire (in parts of the Continent) or placed on the corpse (e.g. in the recently discovered early seventh-century chamber-grave from Prittlewell in Essex) (MOLAS 2004; see also Effros 2002b).

While artefacts could be memorable for their 'special' qualities derived from their biographies and mythologies, their significance for commemoration could come from more mundane and prosaic sources. There might also be objects with mnemonic roles cultivated from their use in daily life, as parts of the household or through their use in daily, regular or seasonal social and economic practices, such as spindle-whorls and knives (e.g. Härke 1989b; see Hoskins 1998), or their intimate use in connection with the body, as with combs or tweezers (Williams 2003; 2004a; see chapter 3). An apotropaic role might also be important, as for prized amulets used to protect the person and their identity from spiritual and physical harm (Eckardt & Williams 2003; Meaney 1981; White 1988). In these senses, commemoration derives from their functional qualities (both practical and symbolic) and their close involvement with the *habitus* of early medieval technologies of the body and daily activities.

The mnemonic role of objects need not be restricted to the evocation of different temporalities of the past (i.e. mythical, genealogical, biographical and so on), but apply also to conjuring aspired or prospective memories of the future. For instance, objects may evoke a social identity never achieved in life but attributed to the deceased in death (see Hope 1997; 2003; Thompson 2003a; 2004). Examples include the provision of some infants and children with weapons that they could not have wielded in their lifetime (see below; Härke 1992).

We also need to consider the wide range of attributes that made portable objects important as foci for remembrance. Traditional studies have focused on the form and decoration of early medieval artefacts, but these are only some of the features that may have informed their use in mortuary commemoration. For instance, the colour and brilliance might be aspects that were as important as form and decoration (Gage et al. 1999; Jones 2002; 2004; Hosler 1995; Saunders 1999; 2002). It may have also been important whether they appeared new and shiny or worn by time and use. In addition to these qualities, the treatment of artefacts might influence their meaning: whether they are produced, exchanged, consumed, fragmented or destroyed (or a combination of these) during the mortuary context (e.g. Jones 2003; Williams 2003). It is only by considering the diversity, complexity and biographies of the many objects often referred to collectively as 'grave goods' that archaeologists can begin to engage with their significance for early medieval societies.

These broad principles help us to consider the commemorative roles of artefacts in mortuary practices, but it is important to remember that what are often called 'grave goods' may relate to many divergent types of artefact with different associations with the cadaver, including clothing, artefacts placed on or around the body, and elements of the structure of the grave itself (see Barrett 1994). In this light, artefacts can have many different mnemonic associations, and each object may relate to the deceased's and mourners' identities in contrasting ways. Yet, in combination, artefacts helped to compose a final and striking 'tableau' of the dead within the grave or upon the pyre (e.g. Carver 2000; Geake 2003; Halsall 2003). This image of the deceased was composed to create a memorable 'scene' that simultaneously emphasised certain aspects of the deceased while 'forgetting' others (see chapter 4).

If we allow for the possibility of artefacts having a role in creating social memories, then we can imagine that they were not simply adjuncts to commemorative practices performed primarily through the medium of the written or spoken word, or by the raising of permanent memorials over graves. Instead, artefacts deployed during the funeral and selectively placed with the dead may have been an important medium for commemoration, serving as a mnemonic interface between the corpse and the mourners. This involved the enhancing of some memories and the suppression of others: a process of both remembering and forgetting.

Early medieval grave goods – a mnemonic approach

If we take this mnemonic approach, how does it help us understand the changing uses of portable artefacts in early medieval mortuary practices? The use of portable objects in graves was not a unique development of the early medieval period, for many prehistoric and Roman-period communities across north-west Europe employed a diverse range of artefacts in graves. Yet the distinctive assemblages of material culture found in graves dating to the later fifth and sixth centuries AD in southern and eastern England have tended to be regarded as representing the introduction of a new mortuary tradition. Archaeologists have regarded these new furnished burial rites of early medieval Britain as 'pagan' and 'Germanic': part of a broader pattern of furnished cremation and inhumation rites that have their origin in Scandinavia and 'free Germany' beyond the edge of the Roman Empire (Hedeager 1992a; Hills 2003; Todd 1992). The spread of furnished burial in the fifth and sixth centuries is usually seen as reflecting Germanic migration, although different scholars have interpreted the process of invasion and settlement in contrasting ways. In addition, more recent studies have moved away from seeing migration in isolation towards the consideration of other possibilities, including elite take-over rather than mass migration, and an ideological change involving the imitation of Germanic groups and social practices (e.g. Higham 1992; Hills 2003). The issue is further complicated by the fact that, despite a decline in grave-good provision in late Roman cemeteries, and the accepted major changes in society that took place from the fourth to the sixth centuries, the furnishing of graves was an integral element of late Romano-British mortuary practices (Gowland in prep.; Philpott 1991). Considering furnished burial as a form of commemoration related to the evolving social and political context of competition and conflict in the period may be a fruitful way of integrating these different viewpoints. Seeing mortuary practices as a context for creating new relationships with the dead, ancestors and the past makes these debates somewhat redundant. While not denying either the likelihood of a series of migration events over the fourth to sixth centuries or native continuity in many areas, we can say that furnished burial came into its own in this context of social and political transformation.

The first new furnished burial rite of the fifth century AD is urned cremation burial. Cremation involved the provision of objects on the funeral pyre, after which the ashes were collected and placed in a cinerary urn. The pots, often decorated, contained the cremated remains and a range both of pyre goods (artefacts placed on the pyre and present in the grave in a fragmented, distorted and often incomplete state, including glass beads, ivory bag rings, combs and spindle-whorls) and grave goods added largely unburned to the burial (such as further bone and antler combs, and iron and bronze toilet implements, including tweezers, shears, razors and earscoops) (Richards 1987; 1995; Williams 2004b). The artefacts placed in these graves seem to have had a particular association with the management of the body, and the presentation and cutting of hair and nails in particular (see chapter 3). The fragments that survive in the urn are therefore a selection of a far greater number of objects placed with the dead on the pyre. This is attested at the cremation cemetery of Spong Hill (Hills 1977; 1980; Hills & Penn 1981; Hills, Penn & Rickett 1987; 1994) not only by the discovery of fragments of dress accessories (brooches and beads), but also by fragments of glass vessels and burnt pot-sherds that must have been placed or smashed on the pyre prior to, or during, the cremation (Evison in Hills et al. 1994).

Accompanying these cremation rites, sometimes at the same cemeteries, but also in many newly established sites, are furnished inhumation graves – unburned corpses accompanied by a range of grave goods, including weaponry, vessels and items of costume, such as belt buckles, dress fasteners and necklaces. There were probably greater similarities in the mortuary processes of both rites than their remains suggest, for the furnishing of inhumation graves must in many ways have resembled the decking-out of the funeral pyres of those destined to be burned (McKinley 1994). These two forms of mortuary practice have different distributions, cremation predominating in east Yorkshire, the east Midlands and East Anglia, and inhumation found over all of southern and eastern England. Mixed-rite cemeteries, in which both rites are found to a similar degree, are a southern English phenomenon. Meanwhile, three areas – south-west Wessex, east Kent and Northumbria – have produced limited evidence of cremation as a common burial rite. In all other regions, cremation and inhumation are found alongside each other in varying proportions. This variation in the mixture of rites may not be entirely random or directly connected to the Continental origins of immigrant groups. It may be that the choice of rite was a deliberate and active choice to symbolise socio-political affiliations with particular ideas, practices and groups while simultaneously creating a visible distinction from others (Williams 2002a; see also Lucy 2002).

As interesting as these new furnished burials are, there are equally those areas of eastern and southern England where few furnished burials are found. Some of these areas are likely to have had a sparse population in the period, while others, such as Hertfordshire, Essex and West Sussex, were populous in the Roman period, and here other explanations must be sought. One is that these remained British areas and continued variations of Roman burial rites into the fifth and sixth centuries, and perhaps in places even later (e.g. Dark 1994; 2000). A further, less explored, possibility is that furnished inhumation and cremation are only two of the more visible types of burial rite in the period and that others existed that leave little archaeological trace. In areas where these other rites were more commonplace, burial sites may be harder for archaeologists to find. Possible alternative rites include unfurnished inhumation and unaccompanied cremation, or the excarnation (ritual exposure and dismemberment) of the dead. Whatever the precise explanation, it is likely that we have visible to us only some of the complex variability in the provision of grave goods in early medieval burials of the fifth and sixth centuries AD.

Moving into the seventh century, we encounter the phenomenon of 'final-phase' burials. There remains considerable debate over when sixth-century burial rites disappear and when new cemeteries are established. Helen Geake (2002) has suggested an early seventh-century hiatus, in which there is a proliferation of largely invisible burial rites, with only the wealthy barrow-burials at sites like Sutton Hoo and Snape attesting to continued burial traditions. Others perceive a more seamless transfer of burial rite and burial location, although both may not have happened at precisely the same moment for the entire population and in each region (Boddington 1990). Through the seventh and into the early eighth centuries AD in southern and eastern England we see the decline of weapon-burial, more modest and Byzantine/ Frankish-inspired high-status female mortuary costumes in selected graves, and an overall reduction in the frequency and quality of grave goods placed with the dead.

The decline of grave goods in the seventh and eighth centuries has also been attributed to a range of explanations. A simplistic view is that grave goods represent pagan beliefs and their subsequent decline reflects the replacement of localised pagan cults of the dead with a new Christian orthodox doctrine of death sustained and supported by the involvement of the clergy in mortuary practices (Taylor 2001). There is no question that mortuary practices were Christian in and around early Christian centres. These would be the graves of the inmates of the religious communities themselves, as well as the secular elite and their retainers who were most closely associated with them. However, numerous objections have been raised to the view of the decline in cremation, the decline in furnished burial and the increased popularity of west–east orientation as evidence of a new belief system imposed on the population. The lack of direct historical evidence for an active clerical influence on burial before the tenth and eleventh centuries is one argument (e.g. Bullough 1983; Effros 2002a; Gittos 2002; Hadley 2001), but it is also clear that field cemeteries continued long after the conversion to Christianity (Hadley 2001; 2002; Zadora-Rio 2003). More complex socio-political and economic explanations have been sought in changing patterns of inheritance and the circulation of moveable wealth, and in the possibility that taxation by an increasing church and secular administration of kingdoms encouraged the decline in grave goods (Boddington 1990; Geake 1992; 1997; 1999a and b; Hadley 2001; 2002; Shephard 1979). It is also possible that, while not *control-ling* burial rites (see Geake 2003), Christianity brought with it from the Merovingian kingdoms, Ireland and western Britain a commemorative emphasis upon topography and monumentality at the expense of portable artefacts (Effros 1997). Whatever the case, it is the argument of this chapter that although their role changes, portable artefacts continued to be enmeshed in evolving technologies of remembrance.

Alongside these final-phase cemeteries, others of contemporary date had already adopted a findless and Christian burial tradition almost bereft of any deliberately placed artefacts (Geake 1992; 1997). This suggests that rather than a coherent and linear trend from furnished to unfurnished inhumation burial, together with the cessation of cremation rites and the preference for west–east orientation, we are looking at alternative strategies of commemoration in contemporary operation. For some communities, burial with grave goods was encouraged and developed in certain contexts, but for others artefacts were circulated and disposed of in other contexts.

Grave goods did not die out as completely as it might first appear. A range of artefacts has been recovered from cemeteries of the seventh to eleventh centuries, including knives, whetstones, buckles, coins, beads and combs (Hadley 2001: 95–7). Evidence of a range of grave structures, including chests, coffins, biers and charcoal layers, has been recovered. Meanwhile, shroud pins, brooches and knives are among the items that continue to be found with some graves (Daniell 1997). Moreover, the late seventh-century tomb of St Cuthbert uncovered in Durham Cathedral strongly illustrates that the placing of artefacts with the dead could serve as a votive practice compliant with Christian practice and belief, rather than contrary to it (Campbell 1982; Coatsworth 1989; see also Crawford 2004). There is also the possibility, as Hines (1997b), Härke (2000a) and Stocker & Everson (2003) have argued, that weapons were ritually deposited elsewhere, as in watery contexts (see chapter 6), a practice found in cult sites from Scandinavia (Jørgensen 2003) and possibly associated with funerary ritual both before and after conversion to Christianity.

Outside southern and eastern England, other artefact-poor burial traditions were practised, often seemingly developing from later Roman west–east-orientated Christian-style burial rites. These graves are again characterised by a lack of grave goods, and yet at these sites there are, sometimes, instances of artefacts from graves. At the sub-Roman cemetery of Cannington in Somerset, for example (see chapter 6), we have a range of modest artefacts found in a minority of graves, including knives, coins, beads and pins (Rahtz, Hirst & Wright 2000: 87). Also, there is interesting attention to grave structure, including the placing of quartz pebbles in some graves, as at Capel Maelog in Powys (Britnell 1990) and Capel Eithin on Anglesey (White & Smith 1999).

Meanwhile, the ninth century sees a brief interlude, when furnished burial rites return associated with the raiding and invasions of the Danes and Norsemen. Most famously in the Northern and Western Isles of Scotland, in Ireland and on Man, we see a new phase of furnished burial within existing Christian cemeteries. Yet similar graves have been found across England, evident in the unusual cremation barrow-cemetery at Ingleby in Derbyshire (Richards et al. 1995; Richards 2004). Other furnished burials include those from churchyards or prominently located burial mounds found from the Isle of Man and Cumbria to the Western Isles, Orkney and the northern Scottish mainland (Bersu & Wilson 1966; Freke 2002; Graham-Campbell & Batey 1998; Richards 1991).

These general trends in the provision of furnished burials can be related to traditional narratives of migration, conversion and kingdom formation, but they may also be related to patterns of socio-political structures, tensions, crises and transformations. By considering furnished burials as a commemorative strategy to create a memorable image of the dead, we can pursue the significance of the rite further. Let us now move on to look at a selection of the grave goods found in furnished burials, and how they may have served in remembering and forgetting the dead.

Brooching the subject

Dress fasteners were an important part of costume and identity in the early medieval world, and brooches are a common element of furnished burial rites across north-west Europe and Scandinavia. While the traditional approach to brooches is to create typologies and chronologies and identify their Continental origins (Welch 1992; Hines 1997b; see Effros 2004 for a review of Continental approaches), more recent studies have complemented such insights with assessments of their function as a part of early medieval costume and their contextual associations in mortuary contexts, as well as the symbolic and iconographic meanings of brooch form and decoration (e.g. Dickinson 1991; 1993; 2002b; Owen-Crocker 2004). In early Anglo-Saxon graves, brooches are found predominantly with adult females and some child graves, although they could in rare instances occur as an element of male-gendered costume (Stoodley 1999a). There is considerable local and regional variation in the provision and use of brooches as an element of dress (e.g. Fisher 1988; 1995; Hines 2002; Lucy 1998; 2002) but as a general rule brooches tend to be used in fastening female costume, being often found in pairs at the shoulder or chest (Owen-Crocker 2004). It is by no means certain that the dead were dressed in their own brooches, nor is it clear whether mortuary costume was a direct reflection of the costume worn by the living person. Yet it is clear that brooches show signs of use and wear and were therefore used as an element of the costume of the living (Hines 1997b; Stoodley 1999a). As such they were an extremely visible element of the mortuary display both during the preparation of the corpse for burial and within the grave itself (fig. 2.1). Between brooches we often find strings of beads, some only ten or twenty in number but in rare cases numbering well over 100 beads, that worked in combination to create a mortuary display.

Berinsfield, Oxfordshire

The brooches from the early Anglo-Saxon cemetery excavated at Wally Corner, Berinsfield (near Dorchester in Oxfordshire) provide us with a case study through which we can explore in more detail the relationship between brooches, beads and the mortuary construction of social memory and identity. The cemetery lies on

Figure 2.1 An artistic interpretation of the rituals involved in preparing and dressing an adult female cadaver for burial within the context of a settlement of the sixth century AD. The image serves to emphasise the likely public nature of the entire early medieval mortuary process from dying and death to disposal. It also illustrates the prominent role of dress accessories and other portable artefacts in the funeral (artwork by Aaron Watson).

the second gravel terrace and forms part of a concentration of early Anglo-Saxon cemeteries and settlements clustering along the Thames and its tributaries, close to the location of the Romano-British small town of Dorchester where, by the early seventh century, the first West Saxon episcopal see was established (Boyle et al. 1995: 4, 137–43). The cemetery consisted of 114 inhumed skeletons and 4 cremation burials uncovered during a salvage excavation by the Oxford Archaeological Unit ahead of gravel extraction. The cemetery was in use from the mid-fifth to the later sixth century AD (Boyle et al. 1995: 124–7). The discoveries are thought to represent between half and two-thirds of the cemetery, and by the time of its abandonment it is possible that the cemetery had received up to c. 300 burials (Boyle et al. 1995: 112). Many graves were disturbed by the removal of the topsoil, and others may have been completely destroyed. This is particularly likely for cremation burials, for when they are found, they tend to be interred in very shallow positions (Boyle et al. 1995: 8). Despite the limitations of the evidence, the Berinsfield cemetery is one of the few early Anglo-Saxon cemeteries recorded and fully published from the Upper Thames valley (Blair 1994; Hawkes 1986; see also Boyle et al. 1998; Scull 1992).

The Berinsfield graves have featured prominently in recent studies of burial and identity in the period because of the relatively good skeletal, contextual and spatial information they provide (e.g. Stoodley 1999a: 133–4). Focusing on this cemetery does not allow the statistical surety of regional and national surveys, however. Moreover, a reappraisal of the bone evidence by Rebecca Gowland is likely to require the qualification of some of the relationships between osteological age, sex and the provision of artefacts with the dead (Gowland 2002; in prep). Nonetheless, this summary study provides a perspective on how the body, artefacts and cemetery space interacted in commemorating the dead.

No single brooch-type was used as a badge of identity or group affiliation at Berinsfield. As well as brooch-types common in 'West Saxon' areas with saucer and disc brooches predominating (see Dickinson 1979; 1991; 1993), there are also 'South Saxon' button brooches (Avent & Evison 1982), 'Kentish' square-headed brooches and 'Anglian' small-long brooches (Hines 1984; Leeds 1945). At Berinsfield, as with other cemeteries, we find the occasional reuse of Roman brooches (White 1988). This variability is common for early Anglo-Saxon cemeteries and need not reflect the ethnic affiliations or origins of individuals wearing these objects, but the complex exchange patterns and interactions between neighbouring localities and regions (see Hines 2002; Malim & Hines 1998). It is almost unknown for the female graves from a single cemetery to display the same brooch-type in such a way as to tempt one to consider them as symbols of mutual affiliation (see also Brugmann & Parfitt 1997; Hirst 1985). Yet, equally, the central importance of brooches in the mortuary display of female-gendered identity suggests that they were not bereft of significance in symbolising the identities of the deceased and mourners before the closing of the grave. How then did brooches serve the construction of social memory at Berinsfield?

Despite the variation, the brooches were located in the Berinsfield graves in such a way as to suggest that permutations around a common formula were employed

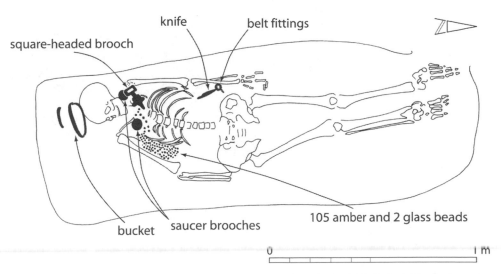

knife   belt fittings

square-headed brooch

bucket   saucer brooches   105 amber and 2 glass beads

0   1 m

Figure 2.2   Plan of the adult female burial from grave 102 from Berinsfield, Oxfordshire (redrawn by Séan Goddard after Boyle et al. 1995).

in dressing the dead (figs. 2.2 and 2.3). In 22 of the 24 Berinsfield brooch-burials, pairs of brooches were found. In all cases but one, pairs of brooches are found at the collar, suggesting their use in dressing the corpse in a peplos-style garment with two fastened straps, one over each shoulder (Owen-Crocker 2004; fig. 2.4). Of the paired brooches, most (19/22) were of the same type, while more rarely (3/22) they were of different types. The combination of a saucer and square-headed brooch in burial 107/1 in grave 107, in which the square-headed brooch was already broken when buried, might indicate a second-best or *ad hoc* use of the brooch (Hines in Boyle et al. 1995: 85). In the other cases, the pairings also involved rare brooches: a Roman and small-long brooch combination in grave 83, and a disc and equal-arm combination in grave 8. The two instances of three brooches both involve pairs of saucer brooches at the shoulders and a third, great square-headed brooch that may have had different functions, as a cloak-fastener in one instance (grave 107, fig. 2.2) and as a pouch-fastener in the other (grave 77). In some cases the pairs of brooches were accompanied by pins, as in grave 91 (Boyle et al. 1995: 50).

In further instances this formula seems to have been rejected. In the case of grave 83, the posture of the burial was tightly flexed, and the brooches do not appear to have been placed in the grave as clothing, since one was found near the left hand, the other by the pelvis. A variation occurs in grave 73, where the pair of saucer brooches was not located at the collar (Boyle et al. 1995: 47). One saucer brooch and pin were placed at the shoulders, and the second small saucer brooch was found on the left side of the chest.

Of the two instances of single brooches, one was a saucer brooch from a heavily disturbed grave (grave 22) that probably formed one of a pair (the other half now lost), while the other was a rare *stützarmfibul* found with an infant (grave 64). The latter find was an extremely old and worn brooch, perhaps not used by the deceased

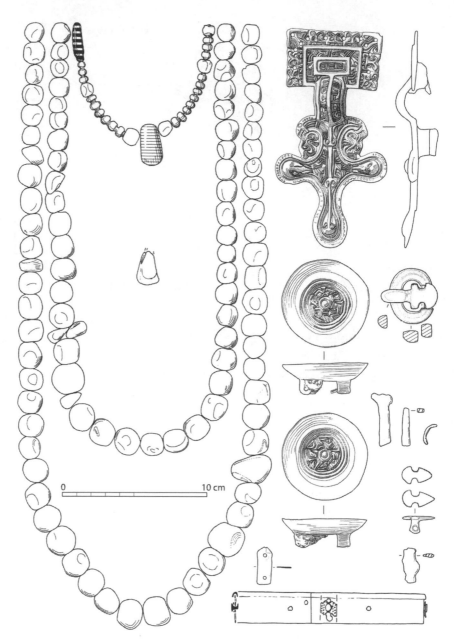

Figure 2.3   The artefacts from grave 102 from Berinsfield, Oxfordshire (adapted by Séan Goddard after Boyle et al. 1995; reproduced with the kind permission of the Oxford Archaeological Unit).

but placed on the body by mourners as a commemorative act. This review indicates that brooches were used following a set formula, but different types of brooch were employed in contrasting ways, and some individuals were denied the burial rite involving brooches afforded to others.

Brooches were clearly an integral material aspect of gendered identity for the early Anglo-Saxon community interred at Berinsfield, with just over half of the adult

Age at death	Disc	Saucer	Applied saucer	Button	Stützarm-fibul	Small-long	Square-headed	Brooch combos
0–1								
1–7					1			
7–15	2		1			1		
15–20		1		1			2	
20–30	1	2				2	1	1
30–40	1	2	1					
40+	1	1						
adult			1					1

Figure 2.4   The brooch types buried with graves from Berinsfield correlated against osteological age at death.

females buried with brooches (17/31). On occasion, there are cases of adult males with female dress assemblages, and one of the female-gendered graves from Berinsfield was tentatively sexed as male on osteological grounds (grave 104; see Stoodley 1999a: 33, 189; Gowland pers. comm.). This grave seems typical for adult females in terms of grave goods and posture but was distinguished by the provision of an uncommon (but not rare) brooch-type. However, the grave is also marked out by the placing of charred logs down both sides of the grave (Boyle et al. 1995: 52). This is a rite found in other early Anglo-Saxon cemeteries (e.g. Cook & Dacre 1985) and may reflect a means of purifying the grave (see chapter 4). In combination this suggests that the burial was marked out as different in the choice of burial rite to complement the unusual provision of artefacts for the biological identity of the deceased.

Brooches were less common with children, even if half are presumed to be female (only 6/34 children aged under 15 had brooches). This supports a more general pattern in the increasing provision of brooches not only as a symbol of gender, but also of age, in early Anglo-Saxon mortuary practices (Stoodley 1999a and b; 2000). No brooch-types seem to be restricted to any particular age-group, but there do appear to be broad differences in the age of individuals given each brooch-type. The wealthiest brooch-type in terms of size and craftsmanship is the square-headed brooch, restricted to burial with sub-adults, and young adults. Meanwhile, saucer brooches seem restricted to adults, while disc and applied saucer brooches were also found with sub-adults. The old Continental brooch was clearly an heirloom, and it is notable that it was interred singly with an infant, a pattern identified in other cemeteries of associating old objects with young deaths (Crawford 2000).

Were these brooches actually visible in the grave? It seems that they were visible at many stages of the funeral, but they may not have been so prominent as they appear in the excavation reports, where they are associated with the few other artefacts that have survived over one and a half millennia in the soil together with human bones. With the clothing present, and perhaps wrapped, they may have been more subtle aspects of the mortuary costume. These were objects that may have held their greatest significance at earlier stages of the funeral, during the washing and dressing of the corpse and its display prior to burial. They may have been visible on the corpse as it was laid 'in state', carried to the burial site and lowered into the grave (fig. 2.1). However, there are instances where textile preservation suggests that, in some cases, the Berinsfield brooches were overlaid by outer layers of clothing, either cloaks or blankets placed over the corpse. Moreover, in some cases a head-veil may have been laid over the head and shoulders. Certainly in two instances (graves 5 and 91) there is evidence of a head-dress or cloak placed over the corpse and secured by a ring and pin. Therefore the association of the brooches and the body was intended as an element of display, but one that was restricted to those who paid close attention in proximity to, and had roles to play in the dressing of, the corpse, its procession and interment.

Next, we must explore how the 'image production' of adult-gendered dress is played out through the spatial organisation of the cemetery (fig. 2.5). The Berinsfield cemetery consisted of a series of separate burial plots radiating from a common focus upon a Romano-British ditch running roughly north–south through the site (Boyle et al. 1995; see Stoodley 1999a: 133–4). There are three discrete plots and a more dispersed spread of graves westwards from the ditch. Each area has localised clusters, lines and rows of graves within the broader distribution. Although it is not possible in many cases to demonstrate a deliberate and intentional spatial association this is feasible, given their similar orientations. It must also be borne in mind that the graves are likely to have been marked with mounds and posts (Hogarth 1973). The location of earlier graves may have provided mnemonic prompts for subsequent burials. The brooch-burials are found in all burial plots, but they are particularly uncommon in the eastern plot, where most of the graves are either of children or adult males.

There are instances of brooch-burials interred adjacent to each other, notably graves 104 and 91 and graves 42 and 49. However, while the first pairing look almost identical in terms of grave-size and orientation, burial posture, and the provision of pairs of small-long brooches and beads, as well as the fact that both individuals were of a similar age at death (20–5 years), there are also subtle differences in the grave assemblages. Grave 104 does not have a copper-alloy pin, while grave 91 does. Also, grave 104 had over twice the number of beads, and from their location they do not appear to have been suspended from the neck but placed in the grave by mourners. Grave 104 also had three iron rings to the left of the waist and charred logs placed along the grave sides, together with a fragment of a stamp-decorated vessel, all elements not found in the burial rite for grave 91. Given the apparent care and attention to make similarities between the two burial rites, these differences are worth noting and may have been intentional. Against this evidence it should be remembered that grave 104 is an instance of an osteological male buried with a female-gendered grave assemblage (see above).

A similar interplay may be witnessed in the adjacent graves 42 and 49, both of adult females aged over 45 years at death. The former was interred with two saucer brooches, sixteen amber beads, an iron buckle loop and an iron knife. On a slightly different orientation, grave 49 had an identical posture but was interred with two disc brooches. Regardless of how we read the interplay between these two burials, their similarities are unusual at Berinsfield. In all other instances, adjacent graves appear to select different combinations and types of brooch and bead from their neighbours. Whether this was due to expedience or conscious choice to differentiate new interments from existing graves, it is evident that each burial was a distinctive

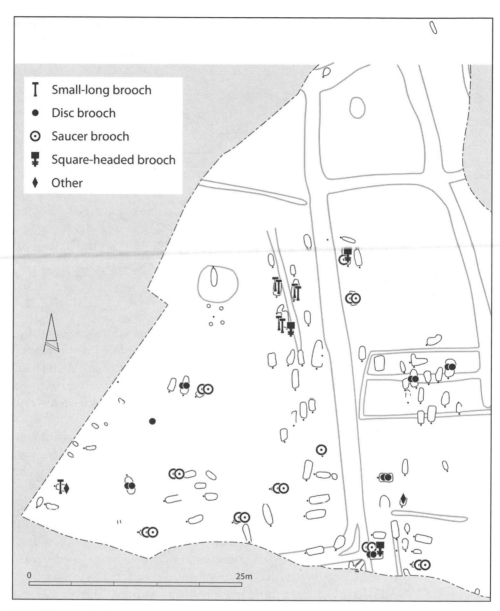

Figure 2.5 The distribution of brooch types from the Berinsfield cemetery excavations (redrawn by Séan Goddard after Boyle et al. 1995).

performance that evoked similarities with other funerary rituals but that also marked differences in terms of orientation, posture and grave assemblages.

Consequently, while brooch-burial may have intercut status groups as an expression of gendered identity and perhaps also household and group affiliation (see Stoodley 1999a), it is clear that each individual performance was attempting to distinguish new burials from existing, remembered, neighbouring graves. Whether

Grave	Unusual posture	Spatial distinction	Unusual orientation	Complete lack of grave goods
4				x
25	x	x	x	x
106	x	x		x
108		x		x
109	x	x	x	x
134		x	x	
152				x

Figure 2.6 Table of brooch-less adult female burials from Berinsfield.

motivated by competition or not, it is possible that this was at least partly concerned with the subtle manipulation of a commonly expressed mortuary 'image' created in the grave as the culmination of the funeral.

When image failed – adult female burials without brooches
Having reviewed the uses of brooches as an integral element of display within the grave, we must ask why some adult females were buried without brooches. Of the fourteen adult females without brooches, seven cases can be explained by post-burial disturbance and truncation, and brooches may very well have been originally present. There are only seven cases where the lack of brooches appears to reflect the choices of the early Anglo-Saxon mourners (fig. 2.6).

In all seven unambiguous adult female burials at Berinsfield without brooches, the absence of brooches correlates with unusual aspects of burial practice. Graves 4 and 152 appear to be standard extended supine burials, but without any grave goods. However, the five other adult females are distinguished by their posture, orientation and spatial location (fig. 2.7). Grave 108 was a young female aged between 20 and 25 without grave goods found in an extended supine position on the edge of the cemetery. Grave 106 was a female of well over 45 years of age, buried on the edge of the eastern male burial group and a row of graves in the northern group. The body was, unusually, positioned on its left side, with legs flexed and left arm bent, with hand near shoulder, and no grave goods were found. Grave 109 was also a female of over 45 years of age and, although buried in an extended position, was inserted into an extremely narrow grave so that the arms were tightly folded over the body. It is also noteworthy that this grave was situated adjacent to brooched females, but on the very edge of the cemetery; again, no grave goods were found, and the burial had a different orientation from that of the nearby graves. Grave 25 was an adult of indeterminate age buried in a bent or curved position in the Romano-British ditch running through the cemetery, and the grave seems to be situated between the south-east and western burial areas. Grave 134, an extended supine female of over 45 years of age, was again distinguished by its peripheral position to the west of the northern group within a Bronze Age pond barrow. The grave was also distinguished by its unusual orientation: rather than the prevailing south–north of the adjacent northern group graves, or the west–east of the more southerly burials, burial 134 was orientated north–south. The burial was the only one of the group of seven to receive any grave goods, which consisted of six beads (two amber, four glass), a bronze pin and an iron knife.

Although each burial is different, many show clear distinctions from the normative burial rite of extended supine posture with grave goods and following an orientation shared with the rest of the burial plot. They also tend to be positioned on the peripheries of burial plots (fig. 2.7); this author does not accept that these burials are necessarily later than furnished graves because of their peripheral position (*pace* Boyle et al. 1995: 133). They have burial postures that would make the display of costume difficult (either crouched, flexed or constricted), and in all but one case they do not simply have fewer grave goods, they have none at all. Moreover, when we look at the age profile, we see a propensity towards older individuals, while those with brooches show a tendency towards the younger end of the age-range. The sample is too small to argue with certainty, but it appears that the burial rite distinguished those not afforded a role in image production. This may have been because of their social status and identity in life, but it could equally concern the interaction of the deceased's identity with that of the mourners or the circumstances of death. The active role of mourners in deciding who was buried how is illustrated by the case of grave 83 mentioned above (p. 49). There, the adult female was interred in a flexed position with brooches, but the brooches were not apparently worn on the body but placed over the cadaver, perhaps as part of clothing added by the mourners. In this instance we may be seeing a person destined for an image-less burial subject to a change of status and afforded a supine burial with artefacts by mourners at the grave side.

It is difficult to disentangle which factor was more important. Were these adult females denied the ideal posture because of the absence of appropriate brooches for mnemonic display? Or was the absence of brooches a reflection of their distinctive posture? Either way, it is clear, as other authors have noted (e.g. Haughton & Powlesland 1999; Hirst 1985), that there is a close connection between posture and burials denied pairs of brooches on their mortuary costume in sixth-century graves. Both elements may relate to the inability to grant certain adult females the same mnemonic display as was the aspired norm for many adult female graves – or, indeed, the actual wish to deny them it.

Memories at the cutting edge

Having discussed the provision of brooches in predominantly adult female graves of the later fifth and sixth centuries, let us now discuss a set of artefacts with male associations: weapons. In late fifth and sixth centuries, weapons, knives and belt buckles were the most consistent material markers of male identity in mortuary practices (Härke 1989a; 1990; Marzinzik 2003). The weapon burial rite continues

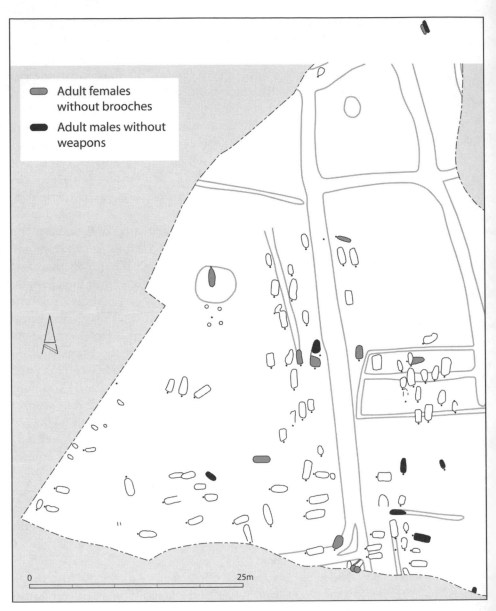

Figure 2.7   The distribution of adult burials without clearly gendered grave goods in the Berinsfield cemetery (redrawn by Séan Goddard after Boyle et al. 1995).

at some sites through the seventh century, increasingly employed as a sign of status (Härke 1992). Spears and shields are the most frequently uncovered weapons (Dickinson & Härke 1992; Swanton 1973). Less common are finds of spathae (double-sided swords; Ellis Davidson 1962), while other infrequent items include seaxes (short swords), franciscas (axes) and (very rarely) arrowheads (Härke 1990: 25–6; 1992). Helmets and mail corselets are the least common weapon-types, found in

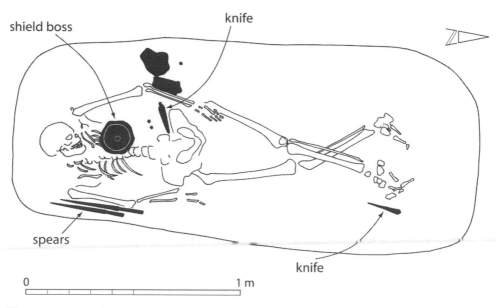

Figure 2.8 The adult male weapon-burial from grave 28 from the Berinsfield cemetery (redrawn by Séan Goddard after Boyle et al. 1995).

only a few of the very richest graves (Härke 1990: 26). Weapons are among the most frequent and distinctive sets of grave goods placed in burials of the fifth to seventh centuries in southern and eastern England, a pattern that is reflected more widely throughout early medieval northern Europe and Scandinavia (figs 2.8 and 2.9).

Weapons have been subject to a wide range of archaeological studies. In addition to discussions and reports of weapons from particular graves and cemeteries, they have been discussed as evidence for the racial and religious affinities of those interred (e.g. Wylie 1857; Leeds 1913) and the occupation of the deceased as a 'warrior'. Meanwhile, studies have addressed weapon typology and chronology (e.g. Dickinson & Härke 1992: 4–30), construction techniques (e.g. Dickinson & Härke 1992: 31–54; Ellis Davidson 1962) and their use in combat (e.g. Dickinson & Härke 1992: 55–61; see Härke 1990: 22–4 for a literature review of approaches). The broader social context of weapon-use has also been discussed. In addition to their use in combat, weapons could have a variety of roles in socio-political and ritual display (Dickinson & Härke 1992: 61–2). In the burial context, weapons could be a means of displaying the identities of the dead and hence allow us to read the social organisation of the burial community (e.g. Arnold 1980) or to identify changing uses of weapon deposition as an act of conspicuous consumption at the funeral (Arnold 1980; Theuws & Alkemade 2000). The most detailed and influential study of the symbolism of weapon-burial to date has been the work of Heinrich Härke. By looking at the variability in the provision of weapons in early Anglo-Saxon graves, Härke compiled a range of evidence to argue that although weapons are often found buried with male adults who *could* have used them during life, they were not principally symbols of 'warrior' status. Instead, Härke interpreted the presence of weapons (and the

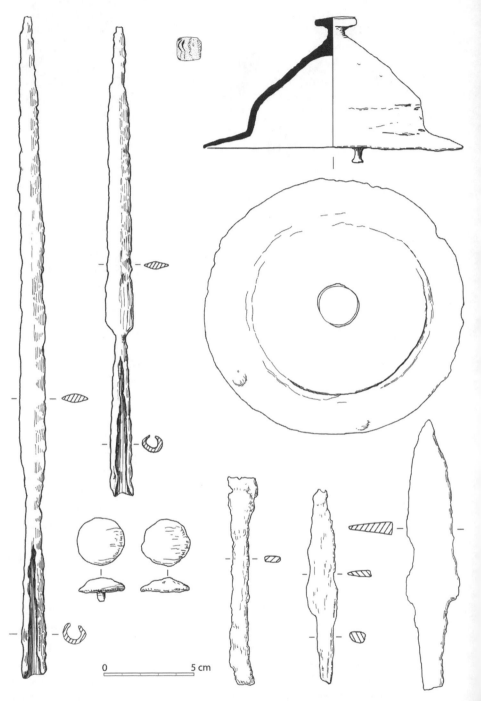

Figure 2.9   The artefacts from grave 28 from Berinsfield, Oxfordshire (adapted by Séan Goddard after Boyle et al. 1995; reproduced with the kind permission of the Oxford Archaeological Unit).

choice of weapon combinations) as forming a multi-layered and polysemous symbolic act relating to the social identity of the deceased (Dickinson & Härke 1992; Härke 1989a and b; 1990; 1992). In turn, the frequency and character of weapon provision can be seen to vary within and between cemeteries, whereas changes over time were seen to reflect regional and chronological changes in social structure and Anglo-Saxon ethnogenesis (Härke 1989a; 1990: 26; 1992: 159–64; see also Stoodley 1999a; 2000). While there has been a reluctance by some to accept Härke's arguments concerning the ethnic symbolism of weapon burial (e.g. Lucy 2000; Tyrell 2000), his study suggests that the burial of weapons constituted a Germanic ethnic origin myth, symbolising perceived and/or real cultural origins through the burial ritual (Härke 1997c). In this sense, weapons not only symbolised social identities, but also connected past and present through their use in the funeral.

These archaeological theories and studies have augmented historical and literary studies of the social and ritual roles of weaponry (Härke 2000a). Weapons were produced, circulated, displayed, fragmented and taken out of circulation in social and ritual practices that served not only to construct and reproduce power relations but also to formulate and communicate distinctive concepts of the ideal social person (Bazelmans 2000; Theuws & Alkemade 2000). In this light, the weapon burial rite did not simply construct real or imagined links to a Germanic past and mythic ancestors. It also employed weapons that may themselves have had long cultural biographies of use and reuse as complex composite artefacts that connected known individuals and groups to each other through cycles of exchange (Theuws & Alkemade 2000). In this light it is important to make the distinction with female burial costumes that, composed by mourners, were closely connected with the preparation of the body. By contrast, weapons were arranged around the body and could often be placed outside coffins (where present), and therefore they need to be regarded more as 'gifts' added during the composition of the grave.

What has not been thoroughly addressed to date, however, is how weapons, as such a prominent, if changing, part of funerary rituals in the fifth, sixth and seventh centuries in early medieval Europe, served in social remembrance. Certainly the weapons themselves may have been symbols of mythical origins, but memories were also promoted by the composition of the burial deposit. The display of weapons formed part of a tableau composed using the dead body and artefacts. This symbolic text was intended to be read by mourners and onlookers as part of a ritual performance and display (see Halsall 1998; 2003).

Weapon burials and identity
We can identify broad national patterns in the provision of weapons in graves, as well as regional and local patterns in how different social groups employed the rite (Härke 1992; Lucy 2002; Stoodley 1999a). Sam Lucy has even suggested that different cemeteries in the same regions and indeed different burial groups show contrasting uses of what at first appears to be a very similar rite (e.g. Lucy 1998; 2002). Without attempting to suggest that the site selected reveals all the patterns in

Death and Memory in Early Medieval Britain

Age at Death	No weapons	Spear	Shield	Spear & shield	Two spears & shield
0–1					
1–7		1			
7–15		2			
15–20	1		1		
20–30		1	3	2	
30–40	5	2		5	
40+	3	2		1	1
adult			3		

Figure 2.10 Table of weapon-burial combinations correlated against osteological age from Berinsfield.

weapon provision, we shall again focus upon the cemetery of Berinsfield (Oxfordshire).

At Berinsfield, a slightly higher than average number of adult males for the region were interred with weapons, but the combinations were typical (fig. 2.10). With no swords recovered, most graves contained a spear (eight instances), a shield (seven instances) and a shield and spear (eight instances). There is also one grave with a shield, two spears and two knives. Given that knives might also have been fighting weapons in some instances, single weapons need not represent non-functioning weapon-sets. Spears were placed on either side of the body and shields tended to be placed over the chest or stomach (Härke in Boyle et al. 1995: 68–9). Osteological sex and weapon provision are closely correlated, with no cases at Berinsfield of skeletons sexed as female interred with weapons. It is also clear that age correlated with the combinations of weapons placed with the dead. First, those adult males without weapons tended to be mature or old individuals, with only one young male interred without weaponry. To put it another way, older individuals were less likely to receive weapons upon death, while all younger adults received weapons (Härke in Boyle et al. 1995: 69). Also, weapon burials tended to be wealthier in other artefacts than those of adult males without weapons. Single spears had the greatest range, being found with children and juveniles as well as adults from 20 to over 40 years of age, the smaller spearheads being found in child and juvenile graves (Härke in Boyle et al. 1995: 69). By contrast, a number of bodies were interred with shields alone, and these tended to be younger adults: no child or juvenile burials had shields. By contrast yet again, the combination of spear and shield was found in mature adults aged 30–40, whereas the only individual with two spearheads and a shield was over 40 years of age. Therefore, different weapon combinations were selected to communicate subtle differences in social identities. Although the interpretation of non-metric traits remains open to debate (see Mays 1998; Tyrell 2000), Härke did observe that individuals with weapons had different traits from those without, hinting at possible family relationships between those interred with weapons and more distant relationships with those not selected for weapon burial. Whether read as ethnic differences, as Härke suggests, or as indicators of familial divisions, the evidence does suggest that groups with different social/biological relationships had a different treatment in death.

Image production in weapon-burials

So far we have discussed the combinations of weapons, following on from the work of Härke and using Berinsfield as an example. However, the way in which we create these patterns assumes a degree of objective overview that would not have been possible in the early medieval period. In other words, for those attending early medieval funerals, earlier funerals and the way weapons were placed may have been remembered, and broad expectations and patterns would have been recognised in what, how and where weapons should be interred. Yet, since many months may have separated each interment, and years may have separated the deaths of two individuals whose age, gender and status required comparable burial procedures, we should not expect hard-and-fast rules over interment, but merely trends. This is because we must recall that such variations may be reproduced through the vagaries of personal memory, oral tradition and the consensus reached over what occurred in earlier funerals. Consequently, burials that to the archaeologist appear very different may to the past population have been little more than the continuation of a rigid, orthodox tradition. Equally, those elements that are the same need not be those valued in the past.

When considering weapons, we must be aware that, for each successive burial, the community and those controlling the burial ritual (elders, shamans or cunning women: Dickinson 1993; Price 2002), as well as those looking on (relatives, allies, friends, subordinate groups, hired mourners etc.), may have had a clear set of expectations formed by social memory concerning how the dead should be disposed of. When composing the grave, attempts may have been made simultaneously to evoke recollections of past funerals and to ensure that artefacts were placed with the dead in an appropriate fashion. Other efforts may also have been made to distinguish the current funeral from earlier events as the dead or mourners assert their agency to alter, manipulate and transform the sets of rules and expected procedures from which they were building their burial rituals.

For any particular cemetery, the patterns we identify are therefore trends that accrue throughout the lifetime of the cemetery, a process that in some instances may stretch over a century. How were these patterns reproduced? As John Barrett astutely observed (Barrett 1994), each successive burial involved a set of choices about how to portray the dead, whether to follow earlier burials (as far as they were remembered) and evoke similarities with the past, or to emphasise differences, distinctions or deliberate juxtapositions of differing disposal images of the dead. Both choices involve acts of remembering and rely on the sets of images constructed through the use of portable artefacts. In most cases, a mixture of the two (both similarities to and differences from the past) will be sought, both to evoke elements of earlier funerals in the treatment of the dead, and to distinguish the burial: in other words, a compromise between dogged orthodoxy and innovation.

Memory reproduction

At Berinsfield, we can see how these ideas might begin to play out. The distribution of weapon-burials at Berinsfield is much more clustered than their female equivalents (fig. 2.11), with three or possibly four groups evident: an eastern sector, a south-east group and a western group that in turn might be split into an eastern core and a western scatter. When the different weapon combinations are plotted, it is evident that they are interspersed. We can focus on two sets of graves in the eastern half of the western group that seem to be related in terms of location and orientation: the three burials 28, 52 and 53, and the four burials 20, 24, 29 and 30. Taking the first group, it is evident that different locations were chosen for each, burial 28 with two spears on the right side of the head and a shield over the chest, burial 52 with a spear on the left side of the head and shield over the pelvis, and burial 53 with the spear on the right side with the shield over the pelvis.

The same distinctions can be seen in the clear row of burials 20, 24, 29 and 30. Moving from north to south, burial 20 was disturbed but the spearhead was on the left side of the head, burial 30 was disturbed and the original position of the spearhead is unknown. Burial 29 had a shield placed over the stomach area, as did burial 24, but in addition a spearhead was situated on the left side of the head.

Indeed, these subtle distinctions are repeated with almost every closely positioned pair of weapon burials in the cemetery. This 'pattern' can be recognised at other cemeteries, with even clearer patterns in the deposition of groups of weapon-burials, for example, at Mill Hill, Deal (Parfitt & Brugmann 1997). At this site, the late fifth- and sixth-century graves congregated around an early Bronze Age burial mound (fig. 2.12). Many graves were clustered against the mound, perhaps seeking a close connection to whatever ancestral or supernatural associations the monument evoked, and perhaps to connect the newly dead to imagined pasts and myths of origin (Williams 1997; 1998). Yet a group of weapon-burials was located, evenly spaced, on the eastern side of the monument, leading the excavators to speculate that small mounds had originally been placed over each grave (Parfitt & Brugmann 1997: 13). The weapon-burials are, because of their proximity and orientation, clearly related, and yet the position of the interred objects and the posture of the body varied considerably with each interment. Given the unknown number of years that may have passed between each burial, it is not possible to prove that there was a conscious desire to reference earlier burials while creating subtle differences or to commemorate earlier graves through the presence of weapons. However, it is suggested here that the intention was to do both: to evoke the past through re-enacting the earlier burial rite, and also to make a distinctive image that played off against, but did not replicate, the earlier interment. If this argument is accepted, then it challenges attempts to limit social mortuary archaeology to the reading-off of broad patterns. Instead, it asks us to look at how each individual burial was a ritual performance serving not only to create a memorable image of the deceased, but also to respond to and evoke earlier interments through burial rite and location. This image production and image reproduction combined to sustain the mortuary tradition and create links between the living, the recently dead, and possible concepts of ancestry and ancestors through the use of grave goods in the funeral.

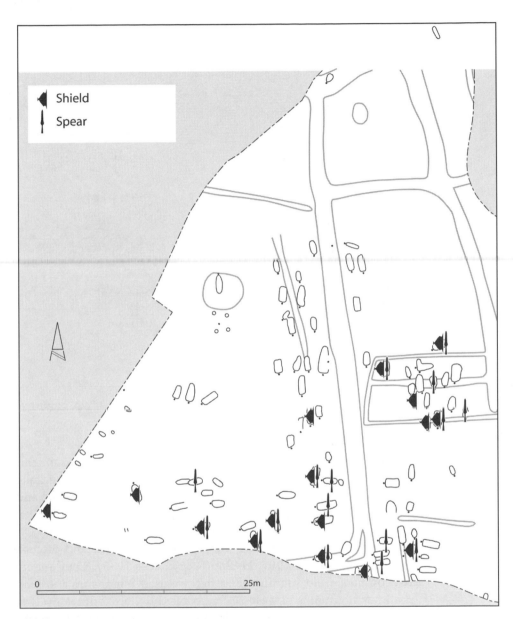

Figure 2.11   The distribution of weapon-burials in the Berinsfield cemetery (redrawn by Séan Goddard after Boyle et al. 1995).

Metaphors, biographies and gift-giving

As already discussed, the practice of furnishing the dead was, however, neither ubiquitous nor static in early medieval Britain. First, not every grave, and in some cemeteries only a minority of late fifth- and sixth-century Anglo-Saxon burials, was furnished. As we have seen, in other areas the rite is absent. Also, the rise and subsequent
decline of the furnished burial rite illustrates that, over time, the deployment of dress
accessories, artefacts and grave furnishings was increasingly avoided as a means of

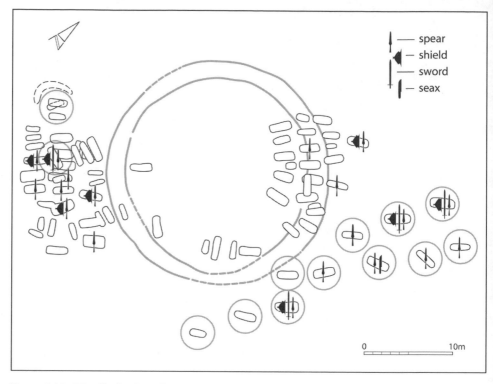

Figure 2.12 The distribution of weapon-burials from the Mill Hill, Deal cemetery (redrawn by Séan Goddard after Parfitt & Brugmann 1997).

promoting memory. Why was this the case? When social commemoration is discussed, it is often assumed that grave goods were only a fleeting experiment during a period of ethnic and political change, as well as social upheaval and competition. Exploring the changing provision of grave goods in the final-phase cemeteries of the seventh century suggests an alternative explanation.

Final-phase cemeteries have long been characterised and discussed (e.g. Boddington 1990; Geake 1997; Hyslop 1963; Leeds 1936). They are often situated in new locations from late fifth- and sixth-century burial sites and tend to consist of small burial grounds of west–east orientated burials with relatively sparse furnishings. Classic type-sites include Winnall II near Winchester in Hampshire (Meaney & Hawkes 1970) and Chamberlain's Barn, Dunstable, in Bedfordshire (Hyslop 1963), although final-phase graves are sometimes found overlying early Anglo-Saxon cemeteries, as at Finglesham in Kent (Hawkes 1982), Lechlade in Gloucestershire (Boyle et al. 1998) and Edix Hill, Barrington, in Cambridgeshire (Malim & Hines 1998). While many graves contain few objects, some burials are still furnished with elaborate and sophisticated material culture assemblages, including items of personal adornment, bag and box collections, and vessels. Indeed, alongside these cemeteries, the late seventh century is also defined by a series of isolated barrow-burials, some of which, particularly female graves, were especially wealthy (Geake 1997; 2002;

Shephard 1979). In the introduction, we reviewed the evidence from the female burial placed on a bed and surrounded by rich furnishings within an earlier Bronze Age burial mound on Swallowcliffe Down (chapter 1). This burial encapsulates the fact that this furnished tradition appears to straddle the conversion, with many graves containing implicit and explicit allusions both to pre-Christian and Christian ritual practices (Speake 1989).

Harford Farm

A full review of seventh- and early eighth-century burial sites is beyond the scope of this discussion. This study will instead focus upon a recently published cemetery of the final-phase type from Harford Farm, near Caistor St Edmund, Norfolk (Penn 2000). The excavations were conducted ahead of road construction, revealing forty-seven burials in forty-six west–east orientated graves in two burial plots focusing upon two of a series of prehistoric burial mounds (fig. 2.13). The site was located on a locally prominent gravel spur between the valleys of the rivers Yare and Tas. The graves in area A were thirty-one in number, were west–east orientated and were arranged in rows on the southern side of a prehistoric mound. To the south (area C/D) was a second group of fifteen graves, also west–east in orientation and scattered on the west and east sides of a prehistoric monument. This practice of monument reuse was a common feature of seventh-century burial sites (see chapters 1, 5 and 6).

The two groups of graves at Harford Farm appear broadly contemporary, although those in area A frequently showed traces of wooden coffins, whereas the more scattered and less ordered arrangement of graves to the south indicated other types of furnishing interpreted as pillows and beds of textile, leather or some other organic material. Because of the sands and gravels into which the graves were cut, few human remains were preserved. The bodies were revealed only through stains in the soil indicating that all identified cases were of adults, positioned supine and extended in most instances (Penn 2000: 74). Despite the fragmentary evidence, the surviving grave goods paint a picture of the very end of the furnished burial tradition, with only some of the burials receiving elaborate assemblages of grave goods. Yet the proportion of graves with artefacts is very high at Harford Farm when compared with other final-phase cemeteries. Only thirteen out of forty-seven had no grave goods at all. Meanwhile, a further eighteen had knives or knives and buckles, leaving sixteen graves with a range of more elaborate grave goods. Of these, eleven were regarded as 'modestly equipped' with knives, buckles and sometimes chatelaines, including one instance of 'weapon-burial': grave 25 interred with a seax. Since many of the graves produced evidence of coffins and other organic linings to graves, it is possible to question the assumption that the decline in metallic objects was accompanied by a comparable decline in other grave furnishings. Therefore, when we discuss 'findless' burials and a decline in furnished burials, we may only be seeing the decline in the deployment of metal dress fittings and metal artefacts: the provision of grave structures, clothing and other textiles may have continued. Indeed, this is demonstrable

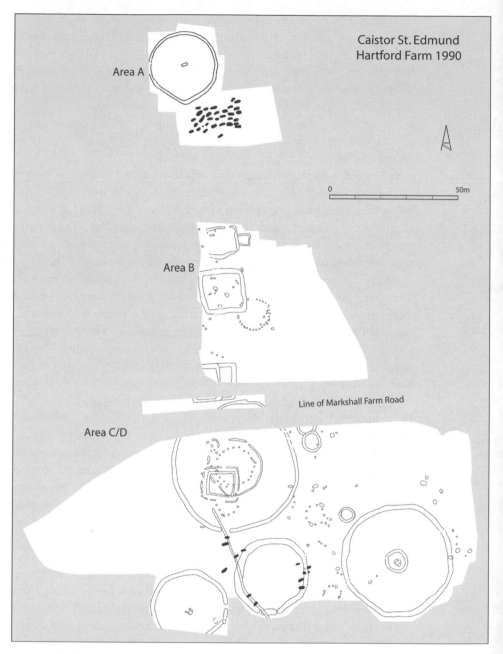

Figure 2.13   Plan of the excavations at Harford Farm, Caistor St Edmund, Norfolk showing two groups of seventh – early eighth-century burials focusing upon a Bronze Age barrow cemetery (redrawn by Séan Goddard after Penn 2000).

through the archaeological evidence for middle and later Anglo-Saxon burial rites in which a wide range of grave furnishings is employed (see chapter 3).

This leaves five graves – 11, 18, 22, 28 and 33 – that were clearly distinguished from the rest of the graves, since the number and quality of the artefacts retrieved during excavation were far in excess of those from the other burials (figs. 2.14–2.18). Interestingly, these burials are not set apart in terms of location, nor are their graves any larger than the others; in addition, more poorly furnished burials from the cemetery produced more evidence of organic grave furnishings revealed by soil-stains. Therefore it appears that these individuals were afforded a comparable burial rite to their lesser-furnished companions, but the choice was made to include a range of portable artefacts on and around the body.

All of the five rich burials from Harford Farm are female-gendered assemblages, although the osteological sex of these individuals could not be ascertained due to the poor bone-preservation. Moreover, the artefacts were not always located where one might expect if they were elements of the deceased's mortuary costume. This suggests that many of these artefacts had other roles in the composition of the burial assemblage, rather than simply being elements of mortuary costume. It is argued that these grave assemblages can be understood only partly as 'clothing' used in the production and reproduction of an 'image', as occurred in sixth-century fur-nished burials. Certainly, this is still likely to be part of the story, but the location, character and form of the objects suggest that many were mnemonic objects placed with the dead because of their biographies and metaphorical associations rather than because they were associated exclusively or even primarily with the identity of the deceased. Moreover, each burial assemblage was unique, suggesting little in the way of a repeated mnemonic image reproduction at Harford Farm, as was the case at Berinsfield. Their deposition in a grave is argued to have been less about the personal identity of the deceased and more a powerful strategy of social commem-oration for the mourners demonstrating perhaps family, household or community remembrance. A brief description of the graves provides the basis for developing this interpretation.

Grave 11

With traces of a coffin-stain surviving over the burial, the body in this grave sur-vived in a semi-flexed position orientated west–east and visible only as a soil-stain (fig. 2.14). The cadaver was interred with a costume consisting of elaborate precious metal accessories. They comprised a gold, silver and garnet composite disc brooch and three silver-wire rings, that from their position, seem to have been suspended from the neck of the corpse. Also suspended from the neck or placed on the chest were a further eight to ten silver-wire knot rings associated with a silver toilet set of three items – a perforated spoon and two picks (figs. 2.16 and 2.17).

Upon the disc brooch, a product of the early seventh century (c. 610–50), was a runic inscription running from the back-plate onto the pin-mounting. The Old English inscription is interpreted as 'luda:giboetæsigilæ', translated as 'Luda repaired this brooch.' Associated with this runic inscription are a series of zoomorphic

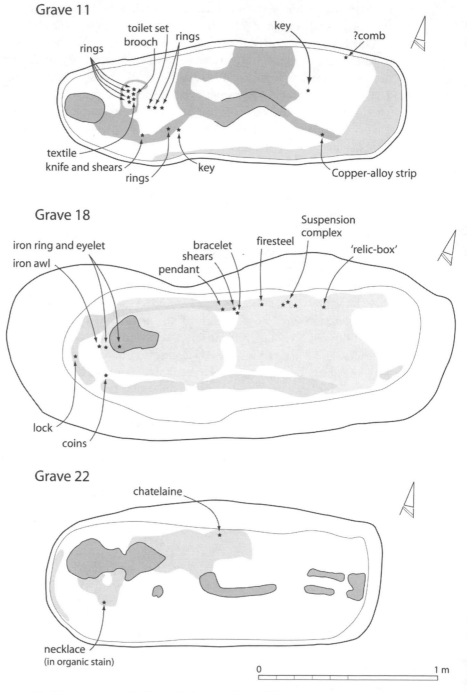

Figure 2.14 Plans of graves 11, 18 and 22 from the Harford Farm cemetery (redrawn by Séan Goddard after Penn 2000).

Grave 28

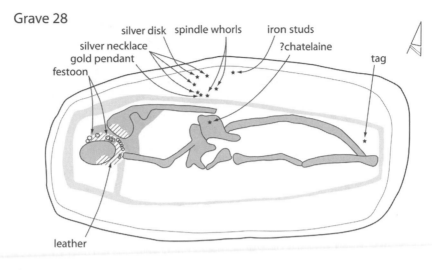

leather

Grave 33

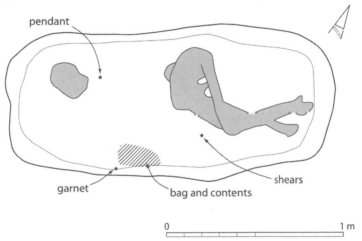

Figure 2.15 Plans of graves 28 and 33 from the Harford Farm cemetery (redrawn by Séan Goddard after Penn 2000).

inscriptions, presumably also added by the craftsperson during repair. The seemingly mundane inscription is notable as one of the earliest known of this variety, most being eighth and ninth century (Hines in Penn 2000: 80; Penn 2000: 45–9; see below). The object is an early seventh-century brooch of Kentish manufacture and therefore may have been at least fifty years old when interred towards the end of the seventh century in this Norfolk grave.

Between the right arm and the chest were placed a knife and shears, while at the belt were three iron suspension rings and a key. Another key and a comb were placed beside the feet and copper-alloy fragments hint at further objects towards the foot end of the grave (Penn 2000: 14).

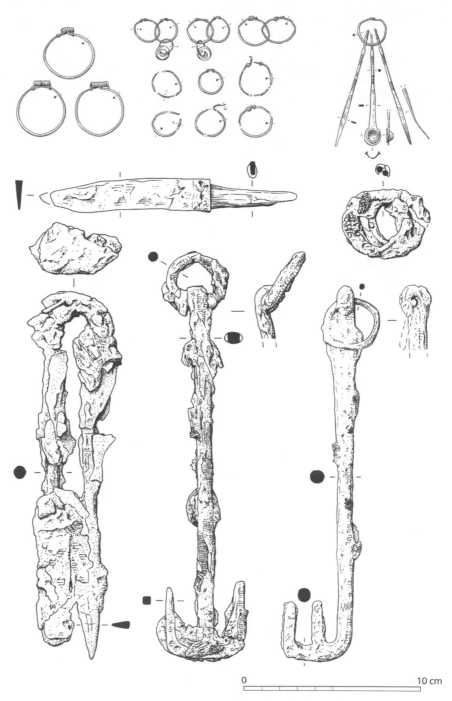

Figure 2.16 Artefacts from grave 11 from the Harford Farm cemetery (adapted by Séan Goddard after Penn 2000; reproduced with the kind permission of Norfolk Landscape Archaeology).

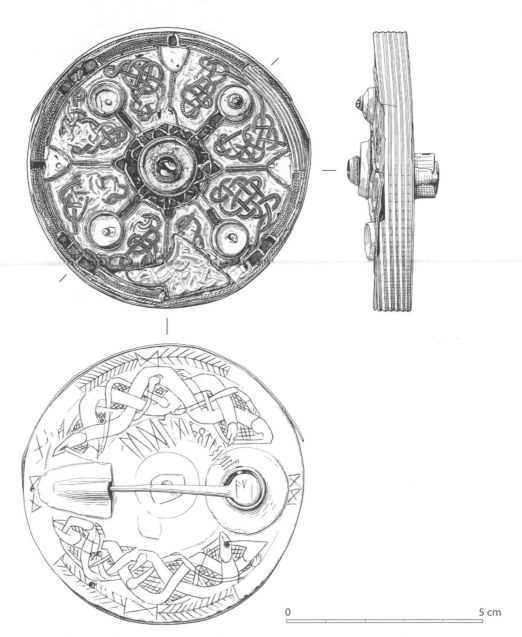

Figure 2.17 The disc brooch with animal-decoration and a runic inscription added at a later date on the back from grave 11 from the Harford Farm cemetery (adapted by Séan Goddard after Penn 2000; reproduced with the kind permission of Norfolk Landscape Archaeology).

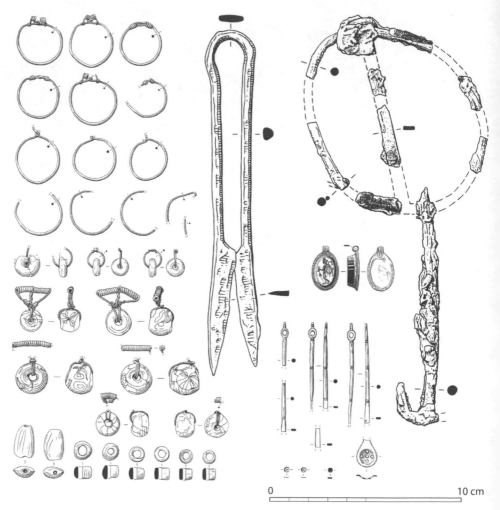

Figure 2.18 Artefacts from grave 11 from the Harford Farm cemetery (adapted by Séan Goddard after Penn 2000; reproduced with the kind permission of Norfolk Landscape Archaeology).

Grave 18

This was another encoffined burial, with an iron barrel-lock and key fragment found at the far western end of the grave, suggesting a wooden box containing an iron awl had been placed adjacent to the head (Penn 2000: 65; see fig. 2.14). Also found in the grave were a gold and garnet pendant, shears, a copper-alloy bracelet used as a suspension ring, an iron purse-mount and a collection of suspended objects of unknown function (possibly an inkpot and pen-case). Of special note is a suspended bronze cylinder of a type often described as a 'relic box'. It contained a silver pin-suite and linking chain (Penn 2000: 66–7).

None of these items was situated on the body as elements of costume. Instead they were located alongside the northern edge of the grave in the area of the left side of the waist and left thigh, all seemingly beside or upon the coffin. The final item is one of only two pin-sets characteristic of final-phase Byzantine-style jewellery from the cemetery, and its position shows that it was not placed on the body as an element of costume but concealed with the relic box. It appears that two sceattas (silver coins) were added to the grave, possibly placed on the coffin to the right and above the head. These diagnostic items date the grave to the very early years of the eighth century (Penn 2000: 75).

Grave 22

This burial contained surviving stains suggesting an extended supine posture was encoffined with two groups of artefacts (see fig. 2.14). The first group consisted of the remains of a necklace or festoon at the neck, comprising silver-wire knot-rings, silver bullae and glass beads. The other concentration of objects was on the left side of the waist (i.e. as with grave 18, along the northern side of the grave either in or on top of the coffin). These artefacts are interpreted as a chatelaine (an ornamental chain, usually found by the waist of female burials), consisting of a copper-alloy ring linked to wire rings, as well as beads, a buckle, a knife, a tool (possibly a pair of tweezers) and two keys (Penn 2000: 27–9).

Grave 28

Also thought to have held a coffin, this grave contained a further division between objects located by the neck and two groups of objects by the waist (fig. 2.15). A festoon of fifteen silver wire rings and a single silver bucket shaped pendant were found at the neck. However, other items of jewellery were found in a cluster situated outside the coffin, but within the grave, on the northern side adjacent to the waist and left forearm of the skeleton. These included eleven bullae of a silver necklace, as well as an open-work gold pendant. Also placed outside the left forearm were two spindle-whorls, two silver decorated discs, five iron rivets that may indicate the presence of a comb, and a knife. Finally, placed upon the left hip was a chatelaine consisting of an iron ring, shears, a steel, a key and a series of other undiagnosed iron objects. Evidence of dress for burial is evident from a copper-alloy shoelace tag found by the left foot (Penn 2000: 25–7).

Grave 33

The fifth and last wealthy female-gendered burial from Harford Farm seems to have been interred without a coffin and the only one of the five to be found in the southern, most dispersed, burial group (see fig. 2.15). The body seems to have been positioned in a semi-flexed posture. By the neck was a Roman intaglio mounted in a frame of twisted and beaded gold wire showing signs of wear. On the right side of the body were found two gold discs with garnets that may have adorned the outside of an adjacent leather or textile bag. The contents of the bag consisted of a necklace made of silver-wire knot-rings with seventeen beads of either glass or amethyst. Also in the bag was a silver toilet set of three implements (one of which was a perforated spoon) like those suspended from the neck of grave 11, and the remains of a chatelaine consisting of an iron ring and key. Finally, by the right leg was a pair of shears (fig. 2.18).

Assessment

Elements of these graves evoke the sixth-century mortuary practices from Berinsfield described earlier. Despite Berinsfield being 'pagan', to use traditional terminology, and Harford Farm being an 'early Christian' cemetery, it is difficult to avoid the close similarities that these mortuary practices exhibit. The dead are clothed and furnished in their graves, and while artefacts are restricted to fewer graves at Harford Farm, the *structure* of the burial rite seems comparable. It may be possible to argue that the composition of artefacts and the body was intended for display within the grave in a manner suggested for sixth-century graves. Graves 11, 22 and 28 had necklaces in place by the neck, suggesting they were worn as part of the mortuary costume. In addition, grave 11 had the disc brooch associated with its necklace. A silver toilet set was positioned just below, hinting that they may have also been suspended from the neck. Finally, grave 33 has a gold intaglio pendant suspended or placed by the neck. The location of chatelaines (bag groups) near the waist in graves 11, 22 and 28 is also consistent with their being part of the mortuary costume dress, or at the very least, with their having been placed there to give the impression of being so, as part of the mortuary display. These items show signs of curation, hinting that they were treasured not only for their form, decoration and 'value', but also because of their antiquity and provenance as received gifts or acquired treasures.

However, this is only part of the picture. There are indications that many of the items were placed upon and around the corpse, rather than used to dress the dead. The knife and shears in grave 11 were over the right arm, a position that does not correspond to the usual waist-side location of these items. The same applies to the key and comb by the feet of this burial. Moreover, while the items on the northern (left-hand) side of grave 18 could have been suspended from the waist, they are strung out, suggesting a deliberate placing within the coffin unattached to the corpse. They included a gold and garnet pendant that would have been a prominent element of the costume had it been placed on the corpse itself. It is notable that the 'relic box' contained and concealed the silver pin suite, rather than this item being on display and positioned on the corpse. In grave 28 most of the items, including a silver necklace, were clustered on the left side of the waist but do not seem to have been worn. Among this group was a gold open-work pendant, a striking object indeed if it had been placed suspended from the neck of the dead person. Instead, these items appear to have formed part of a bag or other organic container added to the grave by mourners and separated from the chatelaine that overlay the left pelvic bone. Finally, in grave 33, the bag collection was separate from the body, on its right side, and within it was the silver necklace and silver toilet set, as well as the remains of a chatelaine group. Once more, these were items that could easily have been displayed upon the body itself but were instead selected for interment adjacent to it.

The same observation applies to other prestigious objects placed in the Harford Farm graves. The one certain weapon-burial from the cemetery (grave 25) had a seax enclosed in a leather sheath placed on the northern side of the grave, possibly over the left side of the corpse's torso. As well as this position suggesting the blade was laid on the corpse, it was placed upside down, the blade facing the head of the corpse – the opposite of what one would have expected had it been an element of 'dress' (Penn 2000: 25). Furthermore, many of the basic elements of burial 'costume' at Harford Farm are not present in these five wealthy graves. Only two of the five have knives, and none of the five have belt buckles. It is therefore difficult to see these graves as augmenting a common repertoire; rather they were also making a distinctive statement by showing elements of being dressed for death (such as the shoe-lace tag from grave 28), but with many of the items placed around the cadaver.

Harford Farm in context

The marked lack of elaborate grave goods in the majority of graves means that the assemblages placed within these five wealthy female gendered graves could be seen as evidence of the high status of the deceased and/or the mourners. Yet the selection of objects for interment may signify more than the straightforward classification of artefacts as 'personal possessions and jewellery' linked to 'mundane' associations suggests (Penn 2000: 98). Certainly, the Harford Farm graves form part of the phenomenon of wealthy female graves that are found across England in the later seventh and early eighth centuries (Geake 1997).

Similar patterns can be found elsewhere in adult female 'final-phase' burials. For instance, grave 93 from the Boss Hall cemetery at Ipswich in Suffolk produced a composite brooch with evidence of repair and of some antiquity when buried, while the gold pendants and silver toilet set from the grave are interpreted as being placed in a pouch at the neck and therefore potentially not a visible part of the burial costume (Webster in Webster & Backhouse 1991: 51–3). Meanwhile, grave 14 at Lechlade in Gloucestershire contained a female aged between 14 and 16 years. A silver pin-suite and a necklace of silver-wire rings, silver pendants on silver-wire rings, and a bead necklace together with a mounted beaver-tooth pendant were all found at the neck, forming a part of the mortuary costume. However, the other items, including iron shears, a cowrie shell, fragments of a glass vessel, glass beads and a relic box, were hidden from view within a wooden box left of the lower legs of the interment (Boyle et al. 1998: 58–9, 156).

A further instance can be recognised in the wealthy bed-burial placed into a prehistoric mound at Swallowcliffe Down discussed in chapter 1. Although found to have been previously disturbed when excavated, with the consequence that items of jewellery may have been removed by antiquarian barrow-diggers prior to excavation, none of the five deposits related to the body itself, but were placed around the cadaver as gifts from the living. The first point about this burial is that the items were not only concerned with display, but also with concealment. Personal items were concealed away within boxes before or during burial, making the process one of enclosure, rather than a tableau of burial display within the grave itself. Second, in addition to the themes recognised at Harford Farm, we can identify a particular emphasis upon vessels for food and liquid in this grave. Despite the undoubtedly wealthy character of the grave, most of the wealth is dedicated not to overt display, but to specific practices and functions within the burial ritual and within life. Drinking rituals may have been part of aristocratic hall-centred social life in the later seventh-century, and drinking may have been a means of commemoration. But drinking could have served as a form of exchange and incorporation by which the living and the dead could be connected to memory transmission. In other words, drinking vessels at Swallowcliffe and other high-status early medieval burials are less about the personal identity of the deceased so much as the mnemonic interaction of the living and the dead expressed as a form of gift exchange and incorporation. The messages are metaphorical and sociological rather than propagandistic and mythological. These were items not necessarily connected to the identity of the individual, but to communal, social and ritual practices. The burial ritual at Swallowcliffe was therefore not only related to the gendered identity of the deceased, but also to wider themes of commemoration through the display and concealment of objects belonging to a range of groups, brought as possessions and gifts to celebrate the remembrance of the dead.

The wealth of these graves was clearly part of the burial ritual in which objects were placed in the grave to articulate the identity of the deceased and their status, gender and socio-political affiliations, as well as the identities of the living. However, while some objects were displayed upon the body, others were concealed around the edges of the grave, within bags and boxes, some seemingly placed separate from the body itself. In the case of the two coins from grave 18, it appears that objects were sometimes added after the coffin had been closed. This evidence combines to suggest that, rather than being elements of mortuary costume, these were items placed on the corpse by mourners separate from the body, and often concealed from view during the final display in the grave.

It is difficult to explain these rites as either 'pagan' or 'Christian'. Instead, they make more sense as socio-political statements of display (Bazelmans 2000; Effros 2003; Halsall 1998; 2003; Janes 2000; Marzinzik 2000). Helen Geake (1997) has argued that rich female dress assemblages demonstrated aristocratic status and also ideological affinities with the Roman and Byzantine world, a form of 'renaissance' linked to the closely connected dual processes of Anglo-Saxon kingdom formation and religious conversion. Sonja Marzinzik's study of late seventh-century belt buckles has recently stressed the 'Frankish' rather than 'Roman' or 'Byzantine' affinities of these burial rites, adapted and adopted for the English context (Marzinzik 2003). However, this does not explain the rite and its mortuary significance.

A number of writers have recently challenged the ubiquity of the term 'grave goods', suggesting that this phrase lumps together many different types of artefact located on the cadaver, around the cadaver and outside the coffin and/or grave structure (see also chapter 4). King (2004) has recently addressed the fact that 'gifts' (offerings not placed with the body but added to the grave) from early Anglo-Saxon graves may have had an important role in the reproduction of social relations. As items added to the grave by mourners, the rich artefacts from Harford Farm would fall into this category. However, King does not address the mnemonic roles of placing these artefacts with the dead.

Sally Crawford (2004) comes closer to the mark when she emphasises that these wealthy female burials may best be described as 'votive' offerings within a Christian context, rather than grave goods in a traditional, pagan sense. Yet this contrast is equally predicated upon the false distinction of 'possessions' and 'gifts', the former regarded as costume, the latter as objects added to the grave by mourners. These cannot be neatly separated chronologically or according to pagan or Christian belief. Despite these limitations, her principal argument resonates closely with those presented here. These were items not necessarily connected with costume per se, but items enclosed with the dead to mediate relationships between living individuals and communities and the memory of the dead person. But we must still ask why these objects, and why for these particular graves?

Discussion

The objects used in wealthy final phase female burials served to mark status. They were also those objects closely connected to the body: items of costume such as pendants and necklaces, objects that may have symbolised involvement in or supervision of agricultural tasks, such as shears, or objects that were concerned with the presentation of the body, such as toilet sets. Rather than 'mundane' objects, these were items with biographies closely connected to the regimes of bodily management and display during life, as well as social practices within the household and farmstead. No single metaphor or theme runs through these items, but collectively they provide a constellation of aristocratic and female-gendered associations. In particular, the careful use of brilliant and precious objects of silver, gold and gems is notable, even when these objects were hidden from view within containers.

Other objects clearly had much longer biographies. The 'keep-sakes' of bag collections, which included functioning brooches (as in grave 18 at Harford Farm), may suggest the curation of objects important and valued in relation to dead persons. The choice not to wear such an item may have been governed by its mnemonic associations with a previous owner. In fact, these objects are better explained as gifts or heirlooms rather than objects appropriate for the display of the deceased's personal identity. Possibly older still than these keep-sakes was the composite disc brooch from grave 11, perhaps over fifty years old when buried. It is also an object rarely found outside Kent, where these brooches were produced. It was repaired at some stage in its use, evidenced by the runic script and decoration added to the back. It may have only recently come into the possession of the Norfolk community among which it was buried, but it seems equally likely to have been a valued object for the household, associated with the history and identity of the social group, and not simply a personal trinket. The decision to place such an item with the dead must have been a statement not simply about the personal identity of the deceased but also about the wider kin group and household, and their social memories. This argument is sustained when we realise that such investments of wealth in graves may have accompanied only certain funerals, perhaps at times of crisis, stress or competition between groups, when such statements were necessary to affirm links to the past (see Stoodley 1999a). Consequently, those buried with artefacts may not necessarily have been of any higher status than the unfurnished or poorly furnished graves around them: it may have been the timing of the mortuary rite that governed the choice of displaying or concealing these items with the corpse.

Conclusion: rethinking grave goods

In this chapter we have challenged the traditional conception of grave goods as symbolising a static identity held by the deceased upon death and have attempted to overcome the usual perception of grave goods as 'reflecting' social identity directly. Instead, we have suggested that grave goods had a range of mnemonic roles. Focusing upon brooches and weapons, we have seen how memories were created for the dead through the creation of an image in the grave (image production) and also the referencing of earlier interments to emphasise both similarities and differences (image reproduction). Moving into the seventh century, we recognised that image production became complemented by an increasing value placed on the biographies of specific objects. Rather than relationships with specific individuals, these objects could have been more, not less, significant in commemoration through their circulation in society and only occasional deposition with the cadavers of select individuals. The 'final-phase' burial is often regarded as the end of 'pagan' burial rites and the 'superstitious' beginnings of new Christian funerary mores. Yet this discussion suggests that, while this may in part be the case, what was changing was the relationship between death, memory and material culture.

3

Remembering through the body

Introduction – the early medieval body in death

Hair, skin and flesh are almost never preserved from early medieval graves; in the vast majority of cases, bones are all that survive. Over large areas of the British Isles soil conditions are such that even bone can be in very poor condition or completely obliterated. For example, in the previous chapter we saw that at Harford Farm in Norfolk soil-stains alone indicated the position of the body in the graves dating to the seventh and early eighth centuries AD (see also Bethell & Carver 1987). Excavation methods and techniques are also a factor influencing the degree and quality of the recovered skeletal material (Mays 1998: 13–32). When corporeal remains are identified and recovered, what can they tell us as archaeologists?

When it has been excavated, a great deal can be said about the early medieval body in death: whether it was interred intact, in what position it was placed (extended, flexed or crouched), whether it was supine (facing up), on its left or right side, or prone (facing down). We can discern the body's orientation and whether it was placed alone or together with other bodies. As we saw in the last chapter, regarding Berinsfield, such variations show us differences in the way the deceased was treated and commemorated by those participating in the funeral. Yet the analysis of the bones themselves can tell us a great deal about the life of the dead person.

Osteologists have made an increasing and important contribution to early medieval mortuary archaeology. Just forty years ago, detailed osteological reports were only occasionally and partially employed in the study of early medieval cemeteries, but today human remains are studied as an integral part of excavating mortuary sites. Using human remains, osteologists can inform us about the age at death of the skeleton from developmental and degenerative changes to the teeth, skull and postcranial skeleton (Chamberlain 1994; Mays 1998: 42–73), while in many cases the attribution of sex has been attempted on the basis of the morphology and robusticity of the pelvis, skull and long bones (Mays 1998: 33–42). From this data archaeologists have attempted to reconstruct the demography of past populations, although this remains a difficult enterprise, given a range of theoretical, methodological and practical difficulties (e.g. Boddington 1987b). Yet, as we saw in chapter 2, age and sex data (and to a lesser extent stature and pathological evidence) have been compared with aspects of mortuary practice to suggest the differential social treatment of different biological categories (e.g. Crawford 2000; Lucy 1997; Stoodley 1999a and b; 2000). There remain ongoing debates over the accuracy of ageing and sexing methods and the subsequent social inferences built upon them (Gowland in prep.), but the comparison of 'biological' with 'cultural' data has long been recognised as providing many new perspectives on early medieval burial rites, as well as challenging old assumptions made without resort to bone data (e.g. Buikstra 1981).

Qualitative and quantitative methods have also been employed to investigate questions of kinship and biological distance. The methodologies and theories that formed the basis of attempts to reconstruct the racial affiliations of ancient skeletons have long been discredited because of their racist motivations and abuses in the past. Therefore limited detailed craniometric (metric trait) research into early medieval skeletal samples appears to have been conducted by modern researchers (Mays 1998: 74–101). However, similarities in a range of dental and skeletal non-metric traits have been used to suggest biological relations between individuals. There have been attempts to correlate these 'non-metric' or 'epigenetic' traits (Mays 1998: 102–21) with aspects of mortuary practice in order to recognise burial procedures connected to particular families (Härke 1990), although there remain debates over the reliability of the results and the assumptions that lie behind them (e.g. Tyrell 2000; see also chapter 2 here).

The study of health and disease in early medieval populations has also been a burgeoning area of research (e.g. Bush & Zvelebil 1991). As well as congenital, metabolic and neoplastic conditions, bones can reveal specific types of infection, most famously conditions such as tuberculosis, leprosy and even syphilis, where archaeological excavations are increasingly providing details of the epidemiology of these conditions. There is also a range of non-specific infections and degenerative dental and skeletal changes that, while not restricted to a single condition, have been used by osteologists to infer the level of health and environmental stress upon past populations (Mays 1998: 122–61; Roberts & Manchester 1995). In turn, attempts have been made to correlate these conditions with aspects of mortuary practice in order to identify the relationship between health in life and treatment in death, although once more a raft of theoretical and methodological problems, including some inherent ambiguities in the nature of osteological data, have cast doubt on these attempts (see Wood et al. 1992). Skeletal remains reveal a range of trauma evidence upon early medieval skeletons, evidence that can sometimes suggest overall stress and occupational hazards faced by early medieval people leading to accidents and even such medical procedures as trephination/trepanation (e.g. Parker 1989). In other instances we can identify evidence of interpersonal violence, and, in some, osteologists have inferred evidence of execution (e.g. Pitts et al. 2002; Wenham 1989) and ritual practices associated with death, such as post-mortem decapitation (Harman et al. 1981; Mays 1998: 163–81).

Particularly over the last decade, a range of new scientific techniques has been applied to ancient human remains. For instance, attempts to ascribe sex, biological distance, palaeo-diet and population movements have been addressed through attempts to retrieve ancient DNA from human remains (Mays 1998: 197–206). The extraction of ancient DNA remains a considerable problem for archaeological research, given the poor bone-condition retrieved from many early medieval cemeteries and problems of contamination. To date, only some results have been published for this period (Arrhenius 2002).

More successful have been studies of bone chemistry, particularly carbon, oxygen, nitrogen, lead and strontium isotopes. The ratios of these isotopes can sometimes reveal evidence of diet, and, on other occasions, evidence that certain individuals grew up and lived in areas with contrasting environments from that in which they were buried. Hence, ancient migrations of individuals and groups can potentially be recognised (e.g. Montgomery et al. 2000). This has allowed archaeologists to begin to reassess and revisit traditional questions of migration, and this has once more brought to the fore the question of whether mortuary practices reflect the cultural origins of past groups. Recent studies have identified expected local origins for some burials (Pitts et al. 2002) but also evidence of immigrant groups in early medieval cemetery populations. For example, in a study of the late Roman (fourth-century) Lankhills cemetery, where a group of furnished burials have in the past been regarded as immigrants with distinctive Pannonian material culture, isotopic evidence has indeed indicated a central European origin for some of the male graves (Stoodley, in prep); meanwhile, for the West Heslerton cemetery (fifth to seventh centuries AD), isotopic analysis has suggested a mixture of immigrants and local people interred (Budd et al. 2004; Montgomery et al. 2005). In a further example, a Viking woman from Adwick-le-Street in Yorkshire with distinctive oval brooches produced an isotope signature consistent with a childhood spent in Norway, confirming that correlations of mortuary dress and places of origin can seemingly bear out a traditional culture-historic interpretation (Speed & Walton Rogers 2004). However, the potential for integrating isotopic analysis into the systematic social analysis of mortuary variability has yet to be undertaken for the early medieval period and will require the study of larger samples of graves with well-preserved human remains (see Bentley et al. 2003).

All these are ways in which archaeology and the archaeological sciences have regarded human remains from early medieval cemeteries as a valued source of information about the structure and condition of past individuals and the societies they composed. Yet there are increasing uses of osteological evidence that tie much closer into the study of mortuary practices by examining the ritual technology of early medieval inhumation and cremation rites, including the transformation of human remains and their position, posture and orientation.

The study of the ritual technology of inhumation, how the sequential treatment and disposal of the body in the grave served in affecting the role of the funeral as a context for experiencing death and commemorating the dead, has considerable potential (see Garland & Janaway 1989). Evidence of disturbance has been used to infer the duration of the funeral and the movement of bodies prior to interment in later medieval contexts (Boddington 1996; Brothwell 1987). Moreover, variations in bone preservation, as well as the posture of the body and the location of the bones, may be used to infer the presence of shrouds, coffins and other grave structures (e.g. Reynolds 1976). There is considerable potential for the application of even more detailed analyses of burial position and posture in early medieval graves in order to identify the influence of practical and ritual actions concerned in the construction of the grave and the burial of the dead. Such an approach has been pursued to good effect in examining the variety of positions and postures from inhumation graves of the southern Scandinavian Mesolithic (Nilsson Stutz 2003). These studies not only challenge the division between practical and ritual action in grave composition, but also foreground the centrality of the cadaver in past mortuary ceremonies. For example, at the cemetery of West Heslerton, a diverse range of burial postures was recognised. The majority of the bodies were crouched or flexed (Haughton & Powlesland 1999: 90), with a significant minority of not only extended burials but also twelve instances of prone burial. Within this diversity, and where bone preservation allows, a myriad different postures and positions can be identified; this variety could be related to practical attempts to fit the body, together with the desired artefacts, into the pit available, but, as argued in the previous chapter, it could relate to contrasting strategies of commemoration.

The study of cremation provides another case study where detailed osteological analysis has enhanced an understanding of mortuary practices. Assessments of the age, sex, non-metric traits and pathologies are possible, if hampered by the fragmentation, shrinkage, distortion and discolouration caused by the intense heat applied to the bone. Yet detailed analyses of cremated remains can reveal whether the body was cremated while still fleshed or after decomposition, elements of pyre technology such as whether the pyre was tended, and the posture and location of the body on the pyre, as well as evidence for pyre material, pyre-tending, duration and temperature. Osteological study can also reveal aspects of the post-cremation treatment of the ashes, including how the remains were collected, whether fragmentation took place, and their association with artefacts, containers and other cremation deposits (Mays 1998: 207–24; McKinley 1994: 82–105).

We can extend these discussions to account for material culture in close connection to the body: the discovery of flowers and other aromatic substances as well as plaster, charcoal and ashes used to suppress the experience of decomposition. Moreover, there are hints from the written sources that crude forms of embalming may have been performed to assist in the 'miracles' witnessed when exhuming the remains of saints (Chamberlain 1994; Chamberlain & Parker Pearson 2001; Gransden 1994). Osteological discussions can be extended to the study of animal sacrifice and the provision of animal bones in graves. Without detailed osteological analyses, animal bones can often be missed or misinterpreted. The frequency of animal sacrifice, for example, was an important part of early Anglo-Saxon cremation practices, with whole horses, cattle and dogs, and joints of mutton and pork frequently added to pyres alongside a less frequent range of wild animal species (Bond 1996; McKinley 1994: 121–35). Despite the many theoretical, methodological and taphonomic challenges faced by archaeologists when analysing osteological data, this discussion allows us to recognise the value of human remains not only for reconstructing the lives of past people, but also for understanding how they were treated in death. To develop such an approach requires the combination of osteological and cultural data, and also a more developed archaeological theory of the body in death.

The social body in death

Early medieval human remains are more than hoards of data to be quarried with scientific techniques. For people conducting the funeral, the cadaver was a decomposing and potentially physically and spiritually harmful set of substances. Equally, the body may have been the point of convergence for bereavement and veneration, but could also have been a source of fear and aversion. As archaeologists approaching early medieval dead bodies, we must go beyond osteological techniques to consider the social quality of the body in death.

We only have to move forward to the later Middle Ages to appreciate the rich meanings surrounding depictions of the cadaver and human bones as reminders of mortality, a metaphor for death itself and a symbol of aspired resurrection (e.g. Binski 1996). Moreover, the later medieval and early modern periods preserve a rich folklore associated with the fear of the dead: not only ghostly apparitions but corporeal revenants. Such stories show the powerful impact that a bad death or the possessed dead can have if not properly and fully transformed by mortuary practices (see Barber 1988; Caciola 1996; Daniell 1997). Archaeologists have, for other periods and regions, extensively theorised the transformation of the body in death as a key social, cosmological and ontological expression of the changing status of the living and the dead (Fowler 2001; Shanks & Tilley 1982; Thomas 1999; 2000). For early medieval societies, we can develop such perspectives with reference to the evidence for Christian religious conceptions of the body provided by written sources. Although largely dating from the very end of our period, literary discussions of the body as a container for, and antithesis of, the soul present us with a graphic example of how the dead body is central to eschatological thought. A particular theme evident in the written sources is the early Christian desire to associate the dead body with symbols of humility and penitence (Effros 2002b; Thompson 2002; 2003b; 2004). Yet in the context of the cult of saints, the dead body is a focus of desire and aspirations of miraculous healing (Brown 1981; see also Karkov 2003). As throughout the later Middle Ages, there were likely to have been other understandings of the body in death unsanctioned by the Church, and this is certainly the case for pre-Christian (by definition) and for early Christian societies, where pastoral care by the clergy would have been extremely limited. Yet this insight into Christian eschatology provides one valuable avenue into the potentially diverse and complex symbolic and mnemonic significances of early medieval cadavers. It also reminds us that early medieval people were not savvy to modern scientific and medical concepts of the body as a biological entity, and that they perceived death as a process and a journey, not an event. We must remember that the definition of 'death' and when it begins was still a matter of medical controversy throughout the eighteenth and nineteenth centuries, when fears of 'live burial' were at their height and doubts were widespread about the ability of the medical profession to diagnose death (Bondeson 2001). During the transition of death, including both the process of dying and the subsequent treatment of the corpse (see Hertz 1960), the cadaver may have been a focus of both fear and veneration, a vehicle through which the identity of the social person was transformed and reconstituted, and also a medium for the commemoration of the deceased (Hallam et al. 1999; Nilsson Stutz 2003: 81–95).

Some useful discussions have set the stage for such an approach by considering early medieval bodies as social entities. For instance, Tyrell has addressed the problems of imposing racial characteristics upon early medieval bodies (Tyrell 2000). Moreover, the impact of both social and biological life-histories upon how individuals were treated in death has been considered by Gowland in her study of late Roman and early Anglo-Saxon burials (Gowland 2004; in prep; see also Robb 2002). Meanwhile, Victoria Thompson (2002; 2003a; 2004) has built upon her discussion of Anglo-Saxon literature (see above) to consider the implications for understanding a range of archaeological evidence, including mortuary monuments and structures, as responses towards, and treatments to manage, the body in death. Yet Thompson does not extend her ideas about the meanings of the body to consider the cadaver as both person and material culture. It remains therefore somewhat surprising that archaeologists have almost ignored the corpse as a symbol and as a social and mnemonic force in early medieval mortuary practices.

The cadaver as mnemonic

Mortuary practices raise particular issues concerning the body as a focus of identity and memory. On an ontological level, mortuary practices involve a close engagement with and realisation of one's own mortality, and on a psychological level, they involve (especially for close kith and kin) an emotional crisis over the loss of a person. The move from a living person to a dead person is rarely a simple and straightforward affair; there was no static 'boundary' between life and death (Thompson 2002). Rather than a concealed and hidden process managed by doctors and hospitals, death in the early Middle Ages would have been a commonplace, visible and somatic experience in which the cadaver becomes a focus of bereavement.

Therefore, while the appropriate treatment, transformation and disposal of the corpse are, from a Western perspective, treated primarily as a hygiene and environmental issue, in non-Western societies they are often an integral element of mourning, commemorating and celebrating the deceased's life and aspirations for their future existence in an afterlife. The treatment and transformation of the corpse constitute a process through which the relationships between the corpse, the soul and the mourners are all reconfigured. Disposing of the corpse is a means of disposing of the soul and is consequently about both remembering and forgetting in order to render the identity of the deceased into a new physical and metaphysical form. A usual configuration of the dangerous and potentially harmful memories of corpses is the concept of death pollution, in which the corpse is believed not only to be physically repulsive, but contagious in a spiritual sense (Hallam et al. 1999: 124–41). The aim of treating the body is often to disperse, manage and transform these out-of-place experiences and memories and create a new identity. By the end of the funeral, the corpse is usually provided with a new stable form, residence and identity that, rather than fear and revulsion, can provide a focus of veneration and commemoration in a durable state (e.g. Bloch & Parry 1982; Danforth & Tsiaras 1982; Metcalf & Huntingdon 1991).

During this process, the corporeal remains can evoke emotions and memories (Tarlow 1999; 2002), not simply because the remains look like the living person, but also because the dead body is rarely inert. Following rigor mortis, in which the body stiffens visibly, we have the process of decomposition beginning, in which colour and aroma signal the changing. Bodies are known to emit noises and movements as well as smells, and these biochemical changes are often misinterpreted as continuing signs of life, or attempts by either the deceased or possessing demons to contact the living (Barber 1988; Williams 2004b). In this sense, bodies are foci for mnemonic agency, and the tense interaction with bodies can influence the nature of commemoration.

These are questions that might be thought to be beyond the realm of archaeological research, but they can be identified through the way in which the corpse is treated in death. Technological procedures used to change the state of the corpse are often intended to obscure and conceal decomposition, such as clothing the corpse, wrapping it in a shroud and encasing it within a coffin. However, even these methods create their own distinctive experiences of the body.

With these ideas, it is tempting to reduce the variation of early medieval funerals to a cross-cultural formula through which the corpse is transformed from flesh to bone, from living person to venerated ancestor (Bloch & Parry 1982; Metcalf & Huntingdon 1991). However, as numerous commentators remind us, mortuary practices are as much about the living as the dead, and we need to consider not only the experiences of the cadaver on the living, but the bodily practices of the living, involving the use of space, material culture and interactions with the corpse. By this is meant the roles of somatic experience in death rituals: ways of moving, and indulging in or restraining from such bodily practices as singing, dancing, drinking, feasting, fighting or sacrifice (Hamilakis 1998). All of these practices and many more besides might overlap with, and pertain to, acceptable modes of expressing bereavement. These can be considered 'techniques of the body', or incorporating practices, ways of bodily disposition and action that will often remain invisible to the archaeologist, but they can be revealed indirectly in some startling ways from the data preserved in graves (see Connerton 1989).

Therefore, while we have already seen how the body might be treated, adorned and displayed during early medieval mortuary practices as a symbolic or mnemonic text, we need to extend this approach to the body itself. The corpse can be regarded as a range of substances that have a mnemonic agency of their own, influencing the way the dead are perceived and selectively remembered and forgotten through the funerary process. The living body also needs to be considered as a medium through which memories are performed and experienced in dialogue with, and in confrontation with, the cadaver.

The body in transformation – early medieval corporeal technologies
The archaeology of early medieval Britain offers us many different corporeal technologies. The first thing to be aware of is the possibility that a considerable proportion

of the burial population is invisible to the archaeologist. The familiarity of archaeologists with the discovery of buried human remains and associated objects should
not fool us into believing that all of the dead, or all parts of the dead, reached the
ground in a final burial deposit. In other words, we should not assume that the division between furnished inhumation and furnished cremation burials was necessarily
the only, or the most important, distinction between the burial of the dead. We must
bear in mind that a range of disposal methods would not necessarily leave behind a
clear and coherent archaeological signature, including water-burial and excarnation.

Next, when considering the mortuary practices of early Anglo-Saxon furnished
inhumation graves such as those already discussed at Berinsfield and Harford Farm,
we can suggest a sequence of engagements between the bodies of the living and the
dead mediated by material culture. We have already considered the importance of
inhumation rites in preparing and displaying the dead. The washing and dressing of
the body and the corpse's posturing for the funeral are likely to have been important
elements of the pre-burial rituals. Similarly, the orientation of the grave and its
location in relation to earlier bodies may have been important. Equally relevant is
the lack of evidence that early Anglo-Saxon inhumation graves were deliberately
reopened or disturbed after initial burial, suggesting a desire to avoid the experience
of the body once interred, a strong fear of the dead and careful control over cemeteries
by their surviving kin (Härke 1997d). When multiple burials do occur, they tend to
be contemporary or within a very short space of time (Stoodley 2002). Exceptions do
occur, and require further consideration, such as grave 80 from Edix Hill, Barrington,
tentatively interpreted as an Anglo-Saxon charnel pit (Malim & Hines 1998: 76).
Similarly, grave 7 from Wigber Low in Derbyshire contained two disarticulated adult
male skeletons. The grave was provisionally dated to the post-Roman period and
was inserted into a prehistoric cairn as part of a small secondary burial group (Collis
1983: 22, 30–2). However, there is evidence from the pattern of disturbance in the
bones of some graves and the presence of insect pupae mineralised on the metalwork
from them that burial may not always have occurred immediately upon death (see
chapter 4). For the early Anglo-Saxon cemetery at Empingham it was argued that a
wooden burial cover protected the body for some period after burial (Reynolds 1976;
Timby 1996; see also Butterworth & Lobb 1992: 26). This evidence can be read in
different ways, but two options are that burials were displayed for some period prior
to burial and/or graves were sometimes given only temporary covers for a period
after burial, perhaps to facilitate the addition of further artefacts.

Early Anglo-Saxon cremation rites can broadly be reconstructed on the basis of
osteological analyses from the cemeteries at Spong Hill and Sancton (McKinley
1994; Timby 1993). They reveal that the rite involved a more complex and developed relationship between corporeal transformation and ritual technology. Cremation rituals provide a complex sequence of interactions with the corporeality of the
dead. From the washing and preparation of the body, through its placement upon
the pyre together with sacrificed animals and artefacts, cremation focused primarily
on the public transformation of the dead body. This would have been followed by the
visible destruction of the body's integrity and surfaces and its transformation into

heat, flame, smoke, steam, ash and bone. Unlike in the modern crematorium, this process would have been a public experience witnessed by mourners, participants and onlookers. The corporeal interaction of the living and the dead did not end there; it would have continued once the pyre had cooled and the ashes were searched for the remains of the dead. The selection of artefacts and bone from the ashes and their placement in an urn would have involved an intimate engagement between the bodies of the dead and the living. Finally, after a procession to the burial site, the interment of the ashes in the cinerary urn would have been the final connection between the living and the dead. In this light, we can challenge a view of cremation as a rapid and singular event of destruction concerned solely with theatrical display, and instead see it as a process in which the living and the dead were connected through a staged and sequential corporeal interaction (Williams 2004b). We rarely have preserved the actual sites of cremation (although see Carnegie & Filmer-Sankey 1993). Yet from the artefacts that are absent from cremations but common in inhumation graves of similar date, it is possible to suggest that many items, including knives and weapons, were placed on the pyre but afterwards selected from among the ashes for recirculation among the living (Williams 2005a). It is also clear from the archaeological evidence for cremation from sites like Spong Hill that not all of the ashes ended up in the cinerary urn. While it is possible that the 'efficiency' of retrieval may explain this variability, and that consequently the remaining ashes were simply left on the pyre site, it is equally possible that cremated bone was circulated among the mourners (McKinley 1994). At the least it is very possible that cinerary urns were stored above ground for long periods of time before the decision was taken to inter them in the cemetery either singly or as a group of cinerary urns.

With the decline of cremation in the seventh century, inhumation rites prevail, in which the body seems to have been taken out of the world of the living with less and less elaboration. However, the high-status seventh-century barrow-burials do indicate that the body could be a focus of elaboration and display alongside artefacts in a period when cremation was on the decline (Carver 2005). The discovery of cremation burials at the St Mary's Stadium site in Southampton suggests that, in the complex social and ethnic mix of the proto-urban wics, cremation could remain a viable disposal strategy through the seventh century (Birkbeck 2005: 11–81).

The adoption of Christian burial rites might be regarded as ushering in an era of unity and coherence in beliefs and practices surrounding the treatment of the dead body. The separation of body and soul was an integral element of Christian thinking but did not mean that the treatment of and care for the body in death was any less important in mortuary ritual. However, the archaeological evidence suggests considerable diversity. At one level, corpses become less important in mortuary display with the decline both of furnished inhumation and cremation rites. Connected to this decline in mortuary display came a focus on objects and structures that served to conceal and contain the sensory experience of the cadaver, such as coffins, cists and charcoal burial (Thompson 2004). However, in some instances the conversion to Christianity presided over a sustained corporeal engagement. The desire for burial *ad sanctos* within churches and churchyards, and in the most holy places therein, became an increasingly overriding consideration for choosing where to inter the dead (Effros 1997; 2002b). Together with the restrictions on the space for burial through the use of boundaries around churchyards, particularly in urban environments, and with church-building in stone requiring deep foundations, the accidental discovery of human remains became a commonplace element of new mortuary rituals (see Cherryson, in prep.). Indeed, this was a theme common to medieval burial rites from the middle Saxon period right up until the emergence of cemetery burial and cremation as alternatives to churchyard burial in the nineteenth century.

Christian-period mortuary practices often developed a more complex relationship with the body in death than simply a concern for its spatial positioning and management. The bodies of the 'very special dead' retained a role as repositories of the *potentia* of saints and conduits to the sacred (Brown 1981). In this context, the saint's cadaver – whether whole or in part, whether miraculously preserved or surviving only as bone – as well as associated 'secondary' relics and architectural spaces containing them became powerful vehicles for social remembrance (Geary 1986).

The 'secondary' burial rites found in the *Life of St Cuthbert*, for example, suggest that the exhumation and translation of the saint's corporeal remains were a public and planned occasion. The rituals served to enhance and legitimise both the sociopolitical and sacred expectations of the living, and to enhance and legitimise not only the saintly identity of the deceased and his place as a 'founding father' of a monastic community but also the royal and aristocratic dynasties from the region associated with that community (Colgrave 1940).

Yet middle and later Saxon archaeology shows that the exhumation, translation and management of human remains after death were not the exclusive preserve of the cult of saints. It was a strategy that may have been more widespread than we are willing to suspect, armed as we are with the incorrect assumption that 'Christians' do not actively or deliberately disturb the dead once interred. Whether interpreted as a pagan war memorial or as a Christian ossuary, the western mausoleum excavated at the early medieval monastery at Repton provides one such instance. The evidence indicates that a chapel or mausoleum of the Mercian royalty was reused in the later ninth century for the interment of 264 disarticulated skeletons (almost all adults, with a high proportion (82 per cent) of males). It has been suggested by the excavators that this unusual event was associated with the wintering of the Viking army at the site in 873–4 and may represent the use of the mausoleum as a collective grave for those who died on the campaign (Biddle & Kjølbye-Biddle 1992; 2001). Meanwhile, at the cemetery of Addingham, North Yorkshire, we have evidence that with the abandonment and relocation of the church, the old churchyard was partially emptied of its dead, perhaps for burial around the new church (Adams 1996: 163–5).

In northern and western Britain, mortuary technologies may have been just as complex and variable. However, large regions produce few burials at all, and many of those found do not preserve good bone-evidence, making conclusions about the treatment and transformation of bodies difficult to reach. However, while

inhumation is the preferred method of burial over much of western and north-
ern Britain, there are hints that cremation was employed, particularly in northern
Scotland, such as among the burials excavated at Hermisgarth on Sandy, Orkney
(Downes with Morris 1997; see also Ashmore 2003).

   Complex corporeal engagements in early medieval Britain are suggested by the
results from the excavation of a square cairn at Cille Pheadair on South Uist in the
Outer Hebrides. Beneath the square-kerbed cairn, found in a beach location, was
a long-cist containing the extended supine body of an adult female aged about 40
years. The grave was dated to the seventh or eighth century AD, orientated with the
woman's head to the south by south-east (Mulville et al. 2003: 25). The soil conditions provided excellent bone preservation, allowing details of the post-mortem
manipulation of the cadaver to be identified. The skeleton had received interference
when in a state of advanced decomposition, possibly when the temporarily covered
grave was revisited months after the original burial event. The original supine position of the skeleton was altered. Her back was wedged from the right side with a
second kerb stone, tilting the corpse onto the left side. The ribcage was splayed,
as her sternum had been removed, perhaps as some form of curated amulet in its
own right and/or to provide some form of access to the interior organs of the chest.
Finally, the right hand was moved from beside the jaw to the area of the groin, an
event that took place when the hand was in an advanced state of decay, evidenced
by the fact that some fingers were left in their original position near the neck. The
excavators propose that the body had been left exposed or given a temporary cover
and revisited months after death, when her posture was amended. Only after this
was the decision made to raise a square cairn over the grave (Mulville et al. 2003:
27). Interpreting the significance of this evidence is problematic. Is this an exceptional and 'deviant' burial rite? Or are similar cases rare across the British Isles in
the early Middle Ages because we cannot identify such evidence for post-mortem
disturbance without the excellent bone preservation and careful excavation methods
available at Cille Pheadair? At the very least it hints that seemingly straightforward
early medieval inhumation rites could have been drawn-out affairs involving multiple
stages of engagement with the decomposing cadaver, sometimes following months
of temporary interment.

   In starkest contrast to the curation of human remains because of their sacred
associations in the case of the cult of saints and perhaps other venerated, high-status
individuals and groups, we have the use of human remains to create memorable
scenes of a very different kind in early medieval execution cemeteries. A full study
of execution graves has been undertaken by Andrew Reynolds (see also Reynolds
1997; 1999; 2002; also Carver 2005: 315–59; Semple 1998; 2004b; Pitts et al.
2002), but it is possible to consider here the mnemonic implications of formalised
execution sites as places of infamy – the commemoration of 'bad deaths' (Williams
2001a). For example, during the excavations in 1987–8 by the Norfolk Archaeological Unit focusing upon a large prehistoric round barrow 29m in diameter at South
Acre, Norfolk, evidence was found of its reuse in the Saxon period by over 100
secondary burials (Wymer 1996). None of the bodies appear to show any signs of

'ceremonial placing' within the grave (Wymer 1996: 67); many graves were shallow; some contained multiple burials; and none contained any grave goods. Further, the complete lack of infants and young juveniles was unusual, even when the preferential destruction of immature individuals is taken into consideration (McKinley in Wymer 1996: 82). The preponderance of younger adults is also distinctive. Eight individuals showed signs of having been decapitated, an interpretation substantiated by associated cut marks in three instances, and by body position in the remaining five cases (McKinley in Wymer 1996: 86). Seven individuals were located in prone positions, and in some cases their posture appears to indicate that they lay where they had fallen within the grave. In further cases the hand positions suggest the individuals had been bound (McKinley in Wymer 1996: 86–7). Rather than the remains of a single massacre, this site appears to represent a *cwealmstow* – an execution place – of the middle and later Saxon period (Wymer 1996: 89; Reynolds 1997; 2002).

The reuse of a prehistoric barrow may have deeper supernatural significance (Reynolds 1997; Semple 1998), but the location would certainly have been a prominent marker in the surrounding landscape: a place where selected felons were killed in a ritualised and public display. In doing so, the aim was to materialise the authority of those enacting the execution and also to make the event *memorable* – promoting the fame of the executor and the infamy of the executed over time (see also M. Williams 2003; Whyte 2003). Placed in prominent locations, often on boundaries and routes, the named and infamous dead were suspended physically and conceptually between heaven and earth. The slow disintegration of their corpses through being pecked by birds may have augmented the execution itself to create a visual and olfactory statement. Killing and execution therefore created a mnemonic spectacle in early medieval societies. As such, it stood in antithesis not only to 'proper' burial but also to the veneration of the bodies of saints as the ultimate means of commemorating those who fail to achieve salvation through churchyard burial, and who are thus excluded from society in this world and the next (Reynolds 1997).

In combination, these examples serve to illustrate the rich potential of carefully exploring the treatment and management of the corpse as a way of gaining insights into the use of the body as a focus of commemoration during and after early medieval funerals. From the burial of the cadaver or the transformation of the body by cremation to the exhumation, translation and veneration of cadavers, the early medieval burial record contains a diverse set of technologies and practices aimed at transforming the body in death and employing the corpse in commemorative strategies. Let us now pursue three archaeological case studies of how the body provided a medium for social commemoration in mortuary practices. We will begin by addressing the transformation of cadavers by fire, the contrasting postures afforded to corpses, and lastly the positioning of the dead in churchyards.

Transforming cadavers

As argued above, cremation was a technology of remembrance in which the body was the key ingredient: acted upon by fire, but resistant to complete destruction. Transforming the body involved transmuting the cadaver from hair, skin, flesh and bone into heat, light, steam, smoke, ash and cremated bone. The impact of the animated fire upon the body would have been a multi-sensuous experience: a memorable event in which all the senses would have been affected (fig. 3.1). Moreover, while cremation can be seen as speeding up the decomposition process, it was still a ritual sequence rather than an event. The preparation of the pyre, the cremation itself, and the subsequent exploration of the ashes and their selection and interment might have been a prolonged sequence of ritualised stages of commemoration that extended over days, weeks or potentially years (Williams 2004b). One element central to early Anglo-Saxon cremation rites seems to be the metaphorical and mnemonic significance of hair and artefacts associated with its management.

Portrayals of the body in early medieval art are relatively rare compared with the Roman world or the later Middle Ages. When they do occur, both in pre-Christian and Christian contexts, depictions of the human form emphasise the centrality of head- and facial hair in visual appearance. This is certainly true of the gold bracteates – Germanic transformations of Roman imperial coinage – in which the length of head-hair is a common and exaggerated attribution (e.g. Axboe 1981; Gaimster 1992; 1998; Hedeager 1999). A comparable representation of flowing locks is often portrayed on Scandinavian gold-foil figurines ('guldgubber') dated to the seventh century (Watt 1999). Similarly, head- and facial hair have a prominent role in many types of Migration Period (early Anglo-Saxon) art from Britain, including the portrayal of human heads upon button brooches and square-headed brooches (Avent & Evison 1982; Hines 1984; 1997b; Owen-Crocker 2004).

Cross-culturally, we can suggest that objects used to maintain hair during daily rituals, and employed in burial rituals to articulate the transformation of the body, had a special role in symbolising and constituting aspects of selfhood, including age, gender, kinship, status and ethnicity (see Williams 2003). Hair and nails often have specific associations in the mortuary rituals of many societies: they are elements of the body that are liminal, being both a part of the body but at its edges and separable without pain. Once separated, they can be well preserved and can continue to be invested with memories connected to the person long after death, becoming enduring 'artefacts' of the body (Pointon 2002). It is moreover possible that hair and nails, because of their connection with the cadaver, may provide a metaphorical 'surface' between the living and the deceased, and hence a potent medium for commemorating the dead person specifically and the ancestral past more generally. They are therefore both integral to the presentation of the body and could operate as a way of symbolising identity, but they are easily and readily transformed to articulate a change in identity through the ritual process of death. Both for mourners and the cadaver, the management of hair and nails can be regarded as a means of articulating the transformation of body and soul during mortuary practices.

With these ideas in mind, we can appreciate those artefacts added to cinerary urns during post-cremation rituals in eastern England in the fifth and sixth centuries AD. Many items found in cinerary urns were pyre goods deliberately selected from the pyre along with the cremated human and animal bone. Moreover, new objects were deliberately associated with the dead in the early Anglo-Saxon post-cremation rite.

Figure 3.1   An artistic interpretation of an early Anglo-Saxon cremation ritual. The image emphasises the sensuous engagement of mourners with the corporeal dissolution and fragmentation of the dead (artwork by Aaron Watson).

The most frequent unburned items found in cremation graves are the cinerary containers themselves. It remains unclear whether these richly and (sometimes) bizarrely decorated vessels were made especially for the funeral or selected for their qualities from among pots used in the domestic setting, but it does appear that they differ from the normal range of domestic assemblages found in early Anglo-Saxon settlements (Richards 1992). Moreover, as Richards (1987) has argued, the identity of the deceased seems to have had a bearing on the form and decoration of the pot selected to contain the remains of the dead (see also Williams 2005b). Leaving aside the details of this variation, we need to ask what these objects were doing in the post-cremation rite after the spectacle of the burning pyre was long passed. The early Anglo-Saxon cremation rite placed great emphasis upon the urn as a container for a sizeable proportion of the human and animal bone from the pyre. In this sense, urns provided a new corporeal and material 'body' for the deceased, and the decorated surface of the urn articulated a new surface or 'skin' for the ancestor.

A range of other items was placed within cinerary urns. The most common artefacts had associations with hair, including 'toilet implements' consisting of bronze or iron tweezers, razors and blades, shears and earscoops, some of them full-sized functional objects, others miniatures possibly serving as amulets among the living or specially made for the funerary ritual. Hardly any of these items show signs of heat-damage, which, for the copper-alloy objects at least, strongly suggests that they had not been placed with the corpse on the pyre. For the iron toilet implements we cannot tell, but it is likely that many of these items were also added to the cinerary urns in the post-cremation rites (Williams 2004a). Other frequently found objects in cinerary urns are bone and antler combs. Some of these had been placed on the pyre and show traces of burning, but many also seem to have been added after the event, and some appear deliberately to have been snapped and placed in the urns in a fragmented state (Williams 2003). For these items, a related but slightly different association is represented, suggesting that the retention of part of the comb was an important way of connecting the living with the dead.

This evidence can be seen in the context of cremation as a corporeal technology. Not only would the effects of fire and heat create a visually tangible and sequential dissolution of the corpse, the bones remaining would provide their own distinctive colours, shapes and textures that mourners would recognise through the handling and burial of the ashes (Williams 2004b).

Given that cremation served to rapidly transform the body to ashes and mask decomposition, the placing with the ashes of objects connected with the management of hair seems paradoxical. Toilet implements were probably used to pluck, shave and cut head- and facial hair as part of regimens of body management, and combs were probably used to remove lice and prepare head- and beard-hair, and may have formed parts of daily washing rituals. These artefacts may have also been used in lifecycle rituals to alter the appearance of initiates to emphasise their transition from one state to another. In mortuary practices themselves, combs and toilet implements might have been used to prepare the corpse for cremation, as well as used by mourners to alter their appearance to symbolise their state of mourning. These were items connected with purification and the management of death pollution. Similarly, these items might have marked the end of the liminal period in rites of incorporation as they were used to alter the hair of mourners once more. For example, if the period of mourning required the cessation of shaving and washing for mourners, then the use of these items may have marked their return to normal regimes of body management. Conversely, if mourning involved particular ways of shaving or presenting hair, then their cessation of use might have been the significant moment when mourners returned to the world of the living from their liminal state. Either way, the disposal of these objects with the dead might have been connected to the identities of the mourners. Indeed, these items perhaps served their function by soaking up the death pollution and so could not be kept by the mourners.

However, given the fact that the soul, corpse and mourners in many societies are believed to undergo parallel and recursive transformations during mortuary practices (see Hertz 1960; also chapter 1 above), it is possible that the significance of toilet implements and combs also lay with the changing corporeality of the deceased. Just as the cremation destroyed the surface of the body, so the incorporation of the dead into a new ancestral identity might have been most appropriately articulated by the creation of a new corporeal form or 'body' in death (Serematakis 1991). In particular, new skin and hair might have been thought to re-grow for the dead after cremation as the skin dessicates and recedes. The placing of the ashes within a pot provided a body, and perhaps the combs and toilet implements provided the metaphorical 'skin' for the body in the grave and the soul in the afterlife. In this sense, the addition of such objects was more than a means of marking the end of the period of mourning: it was a form of prospective mnemonic embodiment, metaphorically constituting the dead in a new form.

In this light, there may have been a logic to the placing of combs and toilet implements in urns. These items were connected to the transformation of identities of both the living and the dead through the funerary process, in which corporeality was the focus of identity rather than the form, decoration, function or symbolism of the objects themselves.

We can see these ideas in action in the large cremation cemeteries of eastern England, such as Newark in Nottinghamshire (Kinsley 1989), Sancton in East Yorkshire (Timby 1993) and Spong Hill in Norfolk (Hills 1977; 1980; Hills & Penn 1981; Hills et al. 1987; 1994), as well as the mixed-rite cemeteries of southern England, such as Abingdon Saxton Road in Oxfordshire (Leeds & Harden 1936) and Appledown in Sussex (Down & Welch 1990). Each cemetery appears to manifest the theme in different ways, suggesting that rather than a uniform conception of the body in death, the relationship of hair, transformation by fire and reconstitution following cremation took on varied significances over time, between communities and perhaps also between age-, gender- and status-groups.

One version of this theme occurred at a mixed-rite cemetery in Hampshire. At Worthy Park, Kingsworthy, excavations in 1961 and 1962 revealed ninety-four inhumation graves and forty-six urned cremation burials (Hawkes & Grainger 2003: 1–11, 113–32). Artefacts were not particularly frequent among the cremation

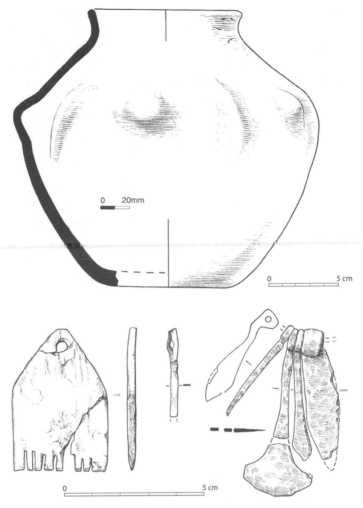

Figure 3.2 The cinerary urn, miniature comb and miniature iron implements from grave C. 23, from Worthy Park, Kingsworthy, Hampshire (adapted by Séan Goddard after Hawkes & Grainger 2003; reproduced with the kind permission of the Oxford Committee for Archaeology).

burials, but those that were placed in cinerary urns were almost exclusively combs and toilet implements. In urns 2, 3, 5, 11 and 23, there were bone or antler combs, while two combs were placed in 31. Moreover, placed in urns 2, 11, 23 and 31 were iron toilet sets (fig. 3.2). Yet the mnemonic significance of these items did not end there, for while two of the combs (urns 5 and 11) were composite combs like those found occasionally in inhumation graves and settlements, the rest (urns 2, 3, 23 and the two from 31) were single-piece miniature combs, in two cases pierced for suspension. It is likely that these were not intended as functioning items, but miniatures made for the funeral. A distinctive pattern is also found in the toilet implements. Unlike inhumation graves, where the majority of toilet implements are made from copper alloy, without exception those from the Worthy Park cremations were iron, and all appear to have been deliberately made as miniatures. In urn 2, ten miniature toilet implements were suspended from an iron ring, while from urn 23 four miniature items were recovered (Hawkes & Grainger 2003: 124, 130). The vast majority of urns did not produce these artefacts, but it is possible that those receiving the miniature objects were the graves of ritual specialists, or that they embodied a principle that was widely recognised but that only on some occasions entailed the objects actually being disposed of rather than simply recycled.

The selection of small and miniature objects for inclusion in cinerary urns as a means of reconstituting the dead has parallels in other uses of 'amuletic' objects in ritual practices found across northern Europe in the late Iron Age and Viking periods, and can sometimes be connected to non-Christian ritual specialists (e.g. Callmer 1994; Price 2002: 203–4). For example, Gunnar Anderson (2005) has discussed the symbolism that may have lain behind the provision of iron rings upon which were suspended miniature hammers and other tools within cremation burial rituals of central Sweden in the Viking period. Moving beyond a generic 'pagan' significance linked to the cult of Thor, he suggests that the combination of ring and hammer may have been linked to themes of reproduction, fertility and protection. Such themes may have had specific mythological associations, but they may also have made sense in terms of the ritual process of cremation: the post-cremation rites were the moment when the regeneration of the dead was required. Moving back to the miniature combs and implements at Worthy Park, we might envisage a comparable theme, albeit manifest in a different form and in a different society. The miniature quality of these items may have actually distilled their regenerative qualities, just as the fragmentation and shrinking of the bones of the dead by the cremation pyre did not seemingly weaken, but rather enhance, the bones' mnemonic significance.

This argument suggests that a deliberate and intentional selectivity took place in the items and objects placed with the dead in the post-cremation rites. The objects interred were not merely the vestiges of an earlier impressive spectacle randomly shovelled into pots for rapid and secretive burial. Nor were they items that would have easily proved useful in impressive and elaborate social displays and in symbolising social identities to a wide audience. It is instead argued that the symbolism and efficacy of these objects were concerned with transformation, rather than solely with signifying aspects of social identity. The concern was for artefacts to have an agency as indexes or 'secondary agents' simultaneously of the mourners and the cadaver (see Gell 1998). Toilet implements and combs were deployed to reconstitute social memories and create ancestors from ashes.

Corporeal fear and respect

Exploring the responses to and treatment of individual burials is often frowned upon by archaeologists, given their usual emphasis upon statistically supportable patterns when studying mortuary practice. However, having explored general trends in the interaction of mortuary technologies, artefact provision and the transforming corporeality of the dead in cremation rites, we can move on to examine specific responses to the biography of the human body and how the life-history of the deceased affected the

Sewerby, Grave 49

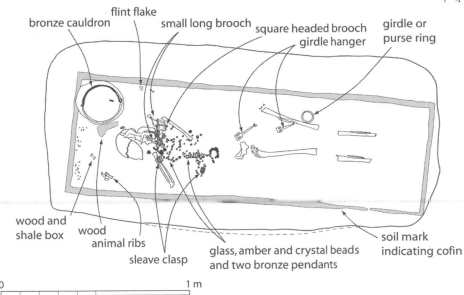

Figure 3.3   Adult female grave 49 from Sewerby, East Yorkshire, positioned in an extended and supine position. The burial was situated below grave 41 (redrawn by Séan Goddard after Hirst 1985).

treatment of the corpse in mortuary practices (see Hallam et al. 1999). This is because while archaeologists have recently highlighted the cultural and social biographies that both artefacts and even monuments might undergo, the biography of the body as well as the deceased's social identity may influence and contribute to strategies of remembrance. It is the biography of the body itself that is likely to influence the manner of its disposal in mortuary practices (Robb 2002; Gowland 2004). By 'biography' we can mean the circumstances of death and the social identity of the deceased upon death, in addition to the history of this person and whether his or her body conformed to the ways in which funerals were employed to commemorate the dead.

To explore these ideas, I shall focus on graves that are deliberately distinguished from the contemporary mortuary 'norms' in death as a means of responding to and emphasising a distinctive social memory. To do this, I wish to explore on the most famous 'deviant' burial from early medieval contexts: a sixth-century grave from Sewerby (East Yorkshire) where two bodies are superimposed in the same grave. We shall contrast this with a discussion of a seventh-century burial from Edix Hill, Barrington, in Cambridgeshire, where a dead individual was attributed a high-status burial in spite of a distinctive 'osteo-biography'.

Sewerby graves 41 and 49
The partial excavation of a sixth-century inhumation cemetery at Sewerby in East Yorkshire produced just over fifty burials, many of which were furnished. Grave 49

Grave 41

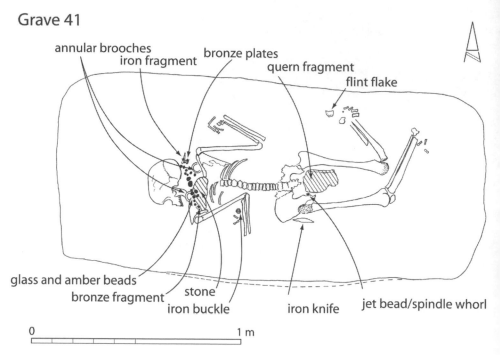

Figure 3.4 Adult female grave 41 from Sewerby, East Yorkshire, placed in a prone posture in the grave over grave 49 (redrawn by Séan Goddard after Hirst 1985).

(fig. 3.3) was the wealthiest female grave from the cemetery, with the longest string of amber beads, three bronze brooches, two girdle hangers, wrist clasps and over 200 beads. A bronze cauldron was also found near the head. The body had a sizeable grave with a coffin, one of only four from the cemetery (Hirst 1985: 32). In every sense, this was a 'good death', though not because the person lived particularly long, dying between 17 and 25 years of age – indeed, the provision of wealth in the grave could reflect the out-pouring of bereavement by a kin-group and community at the loss of a young female who was denied a full and complete life and who may have failed to produce heirs for her household (Hirst 1985: 34).

After grave 49 was partially filled in, or soon after back-filling when the grave cut was still clear, a second female burial (grave 41) was inserted at a shallow depth, exactly reusing the existing grave fill. In terms of the age of death, grave 41 had reached full adulthood, dying between 35 and 45 years of age (Hirst 1985: 34; fig. 3.4). However, the position and associations of the grave suggest the burying community received the death as a 'bad' one. The skeleton was placed prone, with the face inclined to the left, with arms bent at the elbows. The bones from the right hand survived in a clenched position. The right and left legs were both bent back on themselves, the lower right leg rising into the subsoil. It is also notable that in grave 41 the head was at the east end, the orientation of the grave being the reverse of grave 49 and the cemetery as a whole. The body had been clothed upon burial, with a pair of annular brooches on the chest, and with fifteen beads of amber and glass around the neck, together with bronze pendants and a jet bead or spindle-whorl. A buckle was found next to the left arm and a knife by the left hip. A further distinction can be identified in the stones found over the corpse: the first was a flint between the shoulder-blades, the second a fragment of beehive quern placed over the lower back. There were no signs of any 'grave goods' such as the bronze vessel, animal bones and box of wood and shale accompanying grave 49. After the burial was partially filled in, a wooden vessel was placed over or adjacent to the skull.

After this burial, a spread of chalk lumps was brought, probably from the nearby beach, and placed over the surface of the grave, forming a mound. It is also possible that traces of post-holes recovered indicate the presence of an above-ground structure raised on the chalk platform (Hirst 1985: 38–9). The chalk covered not only the double grave of 41/49, but also a juvenile in the adjacent and parallel grave 42. All three burials were associated with female-gendered grave goods, although it is possible that the association of the chalk spread with this grave was fortuitous.

The excavator, Susan Hirst, interpreted grave 41 as a 'live' burial thrown into the grave and weighed down with stones and by throwing soil onto the body. Hirst considered numerous possibilities to explain this practice but focused upon the possibility that the 'live' burial was the punishment of a criminal or perhaps the ritualised murder of a witch (Hirst 1985: 39). The interpretation of such instances as executions has been suggested on other occasions (e.g. Hawkes & Wells 1975) but has been challenged on both practical and theoretical grounds that we cannot easily determine the precise cause of death, and burial posture can often have multiple interpretations (Reynolds 1988). The possibility of human sacrifice or punishment cannot be easily ruled out, the posture reflecting a violent end or perhaps a statement of deliberate disrespect for the deceased.

Other less gruesome explanations remain available, however. A body suffering from rigor mortis when discovered might have been buried in this posture for the practical reason that the limbs could not be moved. Similarly, it has been noted that the posture resembles closely cases of 'cadavaric spasm' (Knüsel et al. 1996): when death occurs in stressful circumstances, such as house fires, the body sinews tighten and cannot be moved. Whichever explanation is sought, there seems a connection between the unusual posture and a 'bad death', whether caused by violence inflicted as punishment or sacrifice, or by untimely and dramatic circumstances.

Without being able to narrow down precisely the circumstances of death, we can instead seek for other factors that might explain the nature of the burial. It is clear that the communal cemetery was still deemed an appropriate place for burial, unlike in later cemeteries, and indeed, the addition of the burial above an earlier grave suggests a deliberate association. Indeed, the graves can be considered in terms of a series of contrasts in posture, furnishings and orientation (fig. 3.5).

Despite these contrasts, there are also some similarities. The prone burial posture does not interfere with the expression of female identity through material culture, as both graves were provided with a costume upon death (Stoodley 1999a: 103). Both had comparable *klapperschmuck* – bronze triangular plates used as pendants as part of the necklace. Also, the location of vessels to the right-hand side of the skull appears comparable in both graves, even if the vessel in grave 49 was bronze and that in grave 41 was largely of wood.

49	41
Head to west	Head to east
Supine	Prone
Extended	Arms & legs bent
Encoffined	No coffin
Square-headed brooch–cloak?	No cloak
Animal food offering	No food offering
Coffin	No coffin
No stones	Stones over body

Figure 3.5 A table comparing and contrasting the mortuary rituals and artefacts associated with graves 41 and 49 from Sewerby, East Yorkshire.

These factors lead us closer to an interpretation of the burials in relation to each other. If the body in the second burial had died under untimely or inauspicious circumstances, then it appears the burial rite selected was intended to pay reference to the earlier grave, both in terms of location and in terms of conscious comparisons and contrasts. One possibility is a concern over death pollution: a fear that the corpse might harm the living. The posture and location may have been intended to disperse the pollution of death by association with an existing 'ancestor'. Indeed, the stones over, and the posture of, the body may have been an attempt to prevent the cadaver from literally rising out of its grave. Whether death was caused by violence or other circumstances, the cadaver was regarded as a 'bad death' and treated so as to 'manage' death pollution and associate the body with an existing 'good death'. Such practices illuminate the association of the body with a supernatural agency that manifests itself in different ways throughout European prehistory and proto-history (Taylor 2002).

Edix Hill, Barrington grave 18
The excellent preservation of the skeletal remains from Edix Hill, Barrington, in Cambridgeshire, provides many insights into the health of early medieval communities living in the Cambridge region in the late fifth and sixth centuries AD, with a number of graves also dating to the seventh century AD (Malim & Hines 1998).

Of the 148 skeletons examined, two instances (one definite, one ambiguous) of lepromatous leprosy were identified from the very diagnostic bony changes that the disease brought about to the skull and the extremities of the limbs. Leprosy is an ancient disease and seems to have reached Britain by the late Roman period. By the later Middle Ages, the theological and social perception of the disease led to the popularity across Europe of the charitable acts by kings, nobles and bishops of establishing hospitals for lepers (leprosaria). Lepers were regarded as the walking dead, who went through a form of burial ritual upon entering leper hospitals, where they remained segregated from the rest of the population. Archaeological evidence illustrates that hospitals were afforded their own cemeteries, and that therefore

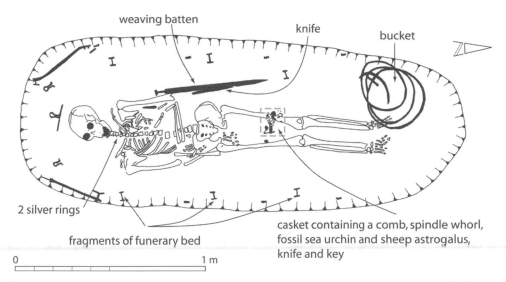

Figure 3.6 Adult female grave 18 from Edix Hill, Barrington, Cambridgeshire (redrawn by Séan Goddard after Malim & Hines 1998).

sufferers of the disease were often separated in death as well as life (P. Richards 1977; Lee & Magilton 1989; Magilton & Lee 1989; Manchester 1987; Roberts & Manchester 1995: 142–50). In contrast, skeletons with the diagnostic bony changes caused by leprosy have been found in a range of late Roman and early medieval skeletons from communal cemeteries, suggesting a different social and religious response to the disease (Manchester 1987).

The one unambiguous instance of leprosy at Edix Hill was a seventh-century wealthily furnished burial, grave 18, in which a supine, extended skeleton of a female aged between 17 and 25 was uncovered (fig. 3.6). The bony changes indicate that the individual concerned would have had substantial changes to her face, including nodules and profuse discharge from the nose, as well as tooth loss. The osteologist Corinne Duhig notes that 'the fact that she had been given a bed-burial casts an interesting light on the attitude of the Anglo-Saxons to disfigurement and obvious disease' (Duhig in Malim & Hines 1998: 177). What is most striking is the wealth of her grave: her condition did not relegate her to a 'deviant' burial of someone whose remains were denied clothing and furnishing or an appropriate burial posture. Not only was she placed upon a bed – a rare and possibly high-status rite in this period – but she was associated with a range of high-status seventh-century artefacts, including a weaving batten, as well as a box containing a comb and key, and a bucket by her feet. Therefore, while we cannot reconstruct the precise cause of her death (and it need not necessarily have been directly from her leprous condition or associated infections), we can suggest that her death would have involved intimate handling of her remains, including the washing and dressing of her leprous cadaver and the provision of objects in close association with her.

We cannot get inside the minds of the early medieval mourners to find out their emotional responses to her death. However, we can observe that her treatment stands in stark contrast to the fear engendered by the disease in the later Middle Ages as well as throughout the world today. It is possible to suggest that she died at an age when she would have been the greatest loss to her community, and as such she was afforded an extremely rich burial, perhaps signifying an aspired status never fully achieved in life (see Hope 1997). In chapter 2 we have already suggested that artefacts placed in wealthy female burials had wider social and communal significance in commemoration than functioning to symbolise the personal identity of the deceased. Moreover, given the long course of lepromatous leprosy as a disease, the woman's demise might have been anticipated and perceived as inevitable, providing the time for preparations for the funeral and a recognition of the fate that awaited her. The 'good death' afforded to her suggests that the social status of her kin and the gifts provided by mourners for the composition of her grave surpassed the disfiguring ailment of her teenage years. There is enough evidence to hint that the biography of her dying and death could have contributed to the manner of her commemoration, providing her with one of the wealthiest graves from the cemetery. Either her relatives were powerful and wealthy enough to provide ritual specialists to 'compose' her grave while they kept at a 'safe' distance from the death, or their attitudes to the disease were in marked contrast to later responses. Of further note is the fact that over the grave two more skeletons were found: a child and an adult. Over these was a further grave cut, in which an unsexed adult of over 45 years was interred, with an iron knife. This suggests that the reuse of the grave site could have been motivated by the wish for the association with the 'good death' represented by the bed-burial, as may have happened at Sewerby (see above).

The Sewerby and Edix Hill graves represent contrasts in the relationship between social memory and the cadaver in death. The 'bad death' of burial 41 at Sewerby is symbolised by unusual posture and artefacts despite the appropriate clothing of the deceased. A close association with the primary occupant of the grave is suggested by the grave goods, and the possibility is entertained that the location of the burial may have been intended to diffuse the death pollution of her bad death through association with the good death of an earlier burial, perhaps from the same community.

In contrast, the extreme deformity of the adult female from grave 18 at Edix Hill was denied or masked by the elaborate and high-status treatment of her grave. In both cases, the cadaver was not ignored, rather the osteo-biography of the deceased set in motion a complex series of commemorative choices responding to the identity of the deceased and the circumstances of death. These may be rare and perhaps extreme cases, but they portray a broader contrast concerning the ways in which furnished burial served to manipulate memories through the actions of the living on the dead body and to manage the impact of the dead body on the living.

The cadaver postured, positioned, protected and disturbed

We have seen how social and cosmological conceptions of the body in life and death may have been closely connected to the interaction of mortuary technology, bodily transformation and artefact provision in the cremation and inhumation rites of the fifth to seventh centuries AD. By way of comparison, I wish to move the discussion forward to the supposedly 'familiar' and 'Christian' conception of the body in death to identify how these ideas played out in practice in the treatment of the dead in late Saxon churchyards. Here we move beyond the body and its transformation through mortuary technologies to consider also the way the body is orientated, postured and situated in relation to previous graves, monuments and the church.

The discussion of the diversity of middle and later Saxon graves has been aided by a series of research studies in recent years, including those by Chris Daniell (1997), Dawn Hadley (2000; 2002), Andrew Reynolds (2002) and Victoria Thompson (2002; 2003a and b; 2004), with ongoing work by Annia Cherryson (in prep.) and Jo Buckberry (in prep.) providing a broader consideration of mortuary practices and mortuary variability. For example, excavations beneath York Minster revealed that the potential complexity of grave structures and features associated with a late Saxon cemetery could rival and surpass those of any early Anglo-Saxon furnished burial site. As well as the use of stone and wooden coffins, two biers were identified. In other cases, domestic storage chests were reused as coffins, and in one instance a boat served as a container for the cadaver. Some graves had pillow stones and ear-muff arrangements, others were fully lined with tile and stone, creating cists, and some were filled with charcoal. Furthermore, graves were marked by stone sculpture in the form of markers and slabs (Phillips & Heywood 1995), burial rites laden both with religious symbolism and elements of socio-political display, in which the enclosure, containment and protection of the body seem to have been the primary focus.

To provide a detailed case study in which we can approach this complexity and diversity in terms of social memory, this discussion intends to focus upon the site of Raunds Furnells in the Nene valley, one of central importance. Excavations of a church built adjacent to a late Saxon manorial complex in the late ninth or early tenth century provide an ideal case study for discussing the treatment of the body in a Christian context, facilitated by a detailed and interpretative excavation report by Andy Boddington (1996). The sequence of the archaeological evidence from Raunds Furnells begins with the development of a small, single-celled church built without a graveyard (fig. 3.7). With the addition of a chancel, a graveyard was established by digging a boundary roughly 40m by 30m sometime in the mid-tenth century. In total, 363 individuals were excavated, which excavators estimate may represent a community of around 40 individuals at any one time.

The church had a relatively short life-history of a little over 200 years, with a new church built in the late eleventh or early twelfth century, by which time burial had all but ceased. This church was in turn converted into a manorial building in the late twelfth or early thirteenth century. Consequently, excavations provide a rare glimpse of the state of a rural churchyard prior to the Norman Conquest and before the successive use and reuse of the same space for a further millennium had fragmented and obscured the late Saxon phases. In his study of the cemetery, Boddington allows an unparalleled insight into the beginnings, development and end of a Christian Saxon church and churchyard, in which patterns in the spatial distribution, orientation and structure of graves, as well as evidence for grave covers and markers, could be linked to the treatment of the evidence for skeletal age and

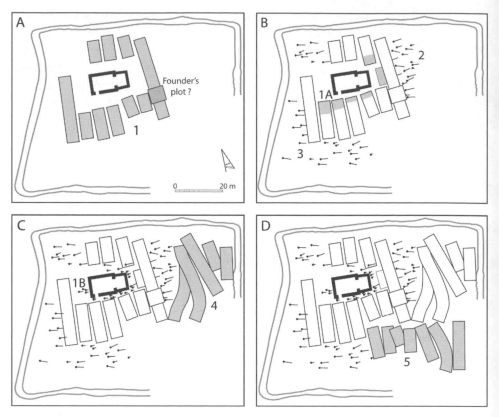

Figure 3.7   Andy Boddington's reconstruction of the developmental sequence for the late Saxon church-yard at Raunds Furnells, Northamptonshire (redrawn by Séan Goddard after Boddington 1996).

sex and of the evidence for the disturbance and reburial of bodies. All these elements combine to provide us with an insight into the strategies of deploying the cadaver in social remembrance in tenth- and early eleventh-century England.

The body positioned

The evolution of the churchyard involved new burials being added to existing planned rows, up to twenty-three rows being identified in total, with some breakdown in planning evident at the ends of rows and on the edges of the churchyard (Boddington 1996: 53; see fig. 3.7). These rows originally focused upon but respected the church by 2–3m (zone 1). Subsequent overspill to the west and the east did not follow a row arrangement (zones 2 and 3). Meanwhile, burials gradually encroached upon the walls of the church without respect for the row arrangement (zones 1a and 1b). However, counteracting an evolutionary progression from initial order to subsequent disorder, new rows were laid out to the east and south-east of the original focus on the church (zones 4 and 5). Throughout, therefore, we see a tension between ordered burial and the desire to be placed *ad sanctos*, between identifying a place for the body in the churchyard and the desire for close association with sacred foci within it (see also Effros 1997).

As the cemetery developed, there appears to have been an increasing propensity for spatial clustering in terms of the osteological sex and age of the deceased. Boddington noticed that sexed male burials tended to be concentrated to the south of the church in the earliest phase of burial (zone 1). By way of contrast, a greater number of sexed female skeletons were found in the areas without rows to the east and west of the first ordered burial area (zones 2 and 3). Infants are placed almost exclusively under the eaves of the church (zone 1b; see Crawford 1993) and are rare in the outer zones of burial (zones 4 and 5), which Boddington interprets as a spatial division according to age in the later phases of the churchyard's use.

Within this broad structure, there is also evidence for burial plots in which we see specific references to earlier graves. The first response is one of avoidance, seemingly identified by the 'respect' shown to the location of grave 5283. The grave sat in the centre of a 1.5m (E–W) by 1.6m (N–S) area free of burials apart from two infant graves. It appears that this may be a 'founder's grave' (Boddington 1996: 11, 51–2, 67), with a stone sculpted grave cover (see fig. 3.12) and possibly marked by a stone cross. The addition of infant graves to this area mirrors the attraction of similar burials to the eaves of the church in the later phases of the churchyard's use, suggesting that this grave may have been equally perceived as a 'founder's grave'. A further focus of commemoration is a single-infant burial, unique for its location within the chancel of the first church, although it was not clear whether it was a primary or later insertion (Boddington 1996: 21). Notably, the grave cuts across the threshold between the first church and the chancel, and it is tempting to see this as a grave afforded a special status and commemorative significance for the Christian community (Boddington 1996: 24).

Further foci of commemoration other than the church and the 'founder's grave' occur with a series of four graves (three adults and one adolescent) placed in a line orientated upon a large post-hole, possibly the base of a wooden cross (Boddington 1996: 50). In another group, a 'burial plot' of five graves cut each other successively, each burial being placed to the north of the previous one. All are associated with a linear slot connecting two post-holes, an arrangement reminiscent of that expected for the original placing of tenth-century 'hogback stones' between two crosses (Bailey 1980; Boddington 1996: 50; see Lang 1984; fig. 3.8). The structure appears to have created a focus for a succession of burials, referencing the position of each other, but increasingly placed closer to this monument. Further instances of referencing earlier interments relate to children interred over or in the graves of adults at the same time or soon after the first burial (Boddington 1996: 52–3). There are further instances of burials disturbing earlier ones, but Boddington (1996: 53) regards this as fortuitous. However, in the light of the other cases mentioned, it is possible that the location of graves made overt reference to earlier burials. In the light of these spatial patterns, it is possible to consider the position of the body as a carefully remembered and respected phenomenon, with careful choices made about where subsequent burials were added to earlier graves.

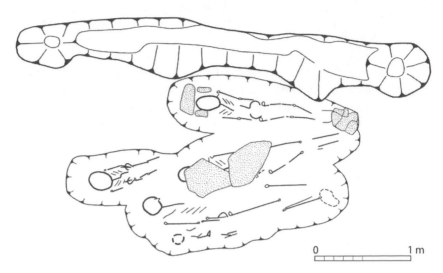

Figure 3.8 Possible burial groups associated with a timber structure within the churchyard at Raunds Furnells, Northamptonshire (redrawn by Séan Goddard after Boddington 1996).

The body postured

Over the years there have been many theories to explain patterns in the alignment of early medieval graves, from religious belief through to orientation on the rising sun. The repeated orientation of bodies west–east at Raunds Furnells is expected, given the Christian context, but the alignment of graves was not true west–east: instead, it followed closely upon the orientation of the first church (fig. 3.9). Burials were also laid out in clear rows, referencing earlier interments (see above). In addition, orientations varied from this set alignment around the edges of the site, where adjacent churchyard boundaries were more influential. Not only was the church used as a focus of commemoration respected by the graves, the alignment of the building was carefully respected (Boddington 1990; 1996: 31–2).

Orientation was therefore more than 'tradition' or mere unthinking repetition of a set 'rule'; the practice clearly had religious significance, but in connection to the local mortuary and commemorative topography, rather than to a ludicrous degree of celestial or astronomical accuracy (Hawkes 1977; Wells & Green 1973; but see Longley 2002). It is tempting instead to regard orientation as simply a reflection of the organisation and authority of church authorities in 'controlling' burial. However, as Boddington (1996) emphasises for the site as a whole, we need to consider the late Saxon funeral as a point of intercession between many groups that we collectively call 'mourners', including the family, the clergy and the wider community. The careful referencing of the church and churchyard boundaries by each burial cannot be simply explained in terms of Christian doctrine. Instead, it is important to consider two related mnemonic results of the same repeated orientation. First, orientation in medieval Christian culture was often connected to prospective memory: the aspiration of salvation on the day of judgement, and hence the need to face east. Second, orientation created a mnemonic structure, connecting each new burial to

Figure 3.9 The overall plan of the churchyard at Raunds Furnells, Northamptonshire (redrawn by Séan Goddard after Boddington 1996).

those that went before and creating a social history of commemorative mortuary events through repeated ritual action. Orientation is therefore argued to have been of central importance, but not in terms of precise compass-alignment connected to the 'control' of the clergy and an obsessive compliance to religious doctrine. For the Raunds Furnells community, the significance would have been through the dual mnemonic practices that the orientation evoked, creating connections to past burial events and aspired future salvation.

All of these elements help to explain the careful positioning and management of the body itself during mortuary practices. The Raunds Furnells skeletons show a marked consistency in the provision of body posture. All graves were supine, with arms at the sides and the legs straight. Head position varied, facing the foot of the grave or to one or other side. Despite some subtle variations, such as cases of crossed hands and feet, the overall impression is of a remarkable consistency due to the careful management of the burial by the clergy and/or mourners. There were, however, two clear distinctions in the posture and preservation of the skeletons. The first was a noticeable difference between many skeletons in a 'parallel' posture, with arms close to the body and feet together, seen as indicative of burial within a shroud and/or coffin, and those in an 'unparalleled' posture, with legs or arms splayed, suggesting burial clothed but without a coffin. Both types of burial were found throughout the churchyard, but with more 'parallel' burials found in the central, earlier zone of burial around the church. Associated with these earlier 'parallel'-postured graves are others with evidence of bone-tumble, particularly among the vertebrae, apparent in one-third of these graves. Bone-tumble is particularly common among the lumbar vertebrae and is generally restricted within the area of the trunk, referred to in the report as 'internal tumble' (Boddington 1996: 36–7, 47–8). A variant of this, referred to as 'external tumble', occurred in a distinct group of burials in which bones had moved away from the trunk to overlie the skeletal frame or to rest between the legs. All of the ten adult remains with this evidence were males, and their graves clustered around the southern side of the church, the same area where graves with stone coffins suggest a high-status zone of burial close to the church. This pattern may simply indicate decomposition within the coffin before it collapsed, but Boddington (1996: 48) regarded this as unlikely, arguing instead that it suggests the movement of skeletal elements prior to burial when the body was in a semi-putrefied state. This might be indicative of cadavers that had been transported considerable distance for burial or had been stored in an above-ground mortuary prior to burial, or perhaps a mixture of both (Boddington 1996: 48). This evidence suggests the importance for the community of a repeated burial posture, but it also suggests prolonged mortuary ceremonies for select individuals.

The body protected

Late Saxon burials are characterised by a series of structures that have received a variety of interpretations. At Raunds Furnells, Boddington identifies the prevailing theme of the graves as one of protection (Boddington 1996: 48). No charcoal burials were recovered from Raunds Furnells, but burnt pieces of wood occurred alongside the burial or against the grave cut in four graves (Boddington 1996: 37), conforming to a wider picture of burning as a means of purifying and protecting graves (see also Heighway & Bryant 1999: 202–5). Soft furnishings within graves included clothing, feathers and layers, although some graves hinted at the presence of organic pillows (Boddington 1996: 37). Coffins were probably present, given the evidence for bone-tumble, posture and context, while in other graves wooden covers were supported by stone and clay linings (Heighway & Bryant 1999: 208–16).

In around half the graves (both with and without traces of coffins), stones were found that had been used to protect the body, the head in particular (fig. 3.10). A variety of stone arrangements was recovered from cists found to contain child graves, stone linings (see above), stone and clay linings, 'ear muffs' on either side of the head to protect it and ensure it faced down the line of the body, and stones covering or surrounding the head. These structures were found in all age and sex groups, but head pillows were twice as likely to be found with males than females (Boddington 1996: 41).

A concern with the osteo-biography of the individual is evident in the case of skeleton 5074: the left proximal tibia of the adult male shows signs that it was swollen, suggesting that the knee was crippled and could not be laid straight when the body

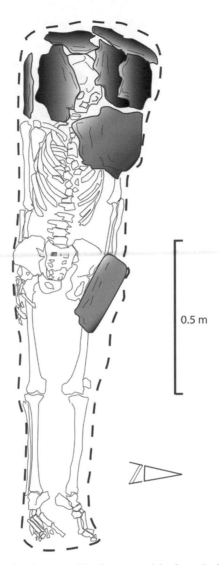

0.5 m

Figure 3.10 A grave with the head protected by limestone slabs from the Raunds Furnells churchyard (redrawn by the author after Boddington 1996).

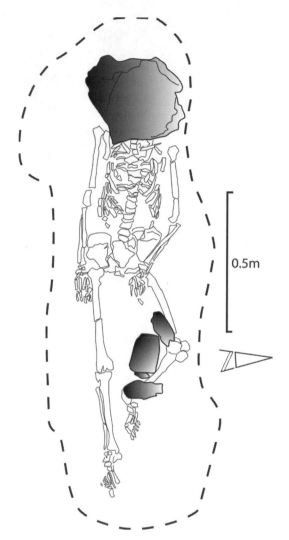

Figure 3.11   A grave from Raunds Furnells with the head covered by a layer of clay and a limestone slab, and three stones used to protect the left knee (redrawn by the author after Boddington 1996).

was buried. Therefore, in addition to the head being protected with a large stone resting on clay so as to prevent the skull from being crushed, three stones were placed to protect the sensitive knee (Boddington 1996: 42; fig. 3.11). It may also indicate that the body in death was regarded as more than unwanted substance. This instance is revealing of the emphasis placed upon the protection of the body in later Saxon burial rites. It suggests that death was not instantaneous in the minds of the mourners, and that for them the cadaver still held elements of the deceased's personhood bound into its flesh and bones (see Karkov 2003; Thompson 2003b). Moreover, the care evident in the placing of stones around the head and ailing limbs may allude to the prospective memory of salvation: the aspired healing of wounds and resurrection of the body on the day of judgement. The process of grave construction may therefore have materialised cosmological and eschatological beliefs through the response to bodily disease and suffering.

The highest-quality grave structures at Raunds Furnells were stone coffins, at least five of which were recovered, although only one remained *in situ*. Again the emphasis upon protection can be identified in stone coffin 1117, where a head-shaped recess was carved that served simultaneously to frame the skull and perhaps also to keep the head facing upwards. Both elements may be linked to the desire for the perceived social and religious status and virtue of the deceased in life to be manifest in the posturing of the body in death (fig. 3.12). Finally, we have evidence for grave covers and grave markers. Two sculpted limestone grave covers were found, possibly reflecting high-status graves, although the possibility that further wooden counterparts may have existed cannot be ruled out. The elaborate crosses and interlace decoration would have spoken to the audience of the funeral and those visiting the cemetery (if indeed it remained visible) of status, but it would also have served to frame and contain the body, providing an apotropaic shield against forces of physical and spiritual decay (see Thompson 2004; fig. 3.13). Grave markers consisted of head- and foot-stones, as well as stone crosses, and we can imagine these had wooden counterparts that have not survived. For example, in a particularly well-preserved area north of the chancel, we have the best-preserved evidence for a wooden cross-footing and a large post grave marker, as well as stone head- and foot-markers for two child graves (Boddington 1996: 45–7). The significance of protecting and marking the body seems therefore to have been twofold: fixing the dead in place as 'ancestors' within the cemetery space, and promoting the aspiration of salvation for the dead through protecting their mortal remains.

The body disturbed

The final element of commemoration through the body at Raunds Furnells is a not infrequent aspect of Christian practice: the reuse of graves and the occasional translation of human remains. This occurs in a number of instances at Raunds Furnells, where we have examples of the disturbance of earlier graves. Given the evidence for grave markers and grave covers, and the likelihood that burials were overlaid by visible mounds, all creating a general pattern of respect for earlier graves, examples of grave reuse and translation require a specific interpretation.

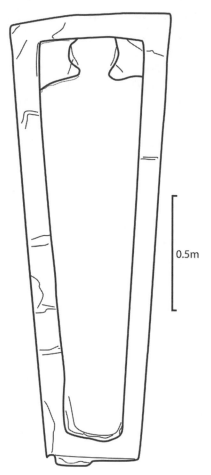

0.5m

Figure 3.12 The stone coffin with head recess from Raunds Furnells, Northamptonshire (redrawn by the author after Boddington 1996).

The disturbance of graves for reuse could be seen as an expedient practice contradicting the respect and protection afforded to the dead. Yet there are instances where this is far from the case. The disturbance focused on the area around the first church, suggesting that a desire for burial *ad sanctos* encouraged repeated burial in the most favourable conditions. However, there is evidence for the reuse of graves involving reverential treatment of earlier remains. For example, there are cases of bones being laid at the foot of the new occupant, as in the reburial of an adult male at the feet of female skeleton 5128 in precise arrangements (Boddington 1996: 30; fig. 3.14). When it is considered that these bones would have to have been handled and arranged, and would have been a prominent and visible element of the burial ritual, it is difficult to reduce their reburial to expedient and practical responses to earlier human remains, whether they were disturbed intentionally or not. In particular, old bones, when repositioned in the grave, would have been for the mourners the

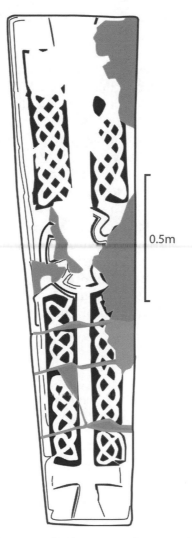

0.5m

Figure 3.13 The cross-adorned, stone, sculpted grave-cover from Raunds Furnells, Northamptonshire. Grey shading = area of disturbance and most damage (redrawn by the author after Boddington 1996).

last and most visible remains of the dead before the closing of the grave (Boddington 1996: 50).

The cessation of the first church's use and the building of a second church seem to have been associated with some new rituals. The second church's foundations appear to have disturbed only thirteen burials. Three further skeletons were dumped into two pits to the north of the north wall of the second church, possibly from stone coffins broken up to be used in the making of the second church. Similarly, the position of the disarticulated bones in grave 5239 suggests that they were reburied within a sack (Boddington 1996: 29; fig. 3.15). What is notable is that these two pits were extremely large for their contents, being 2m across, which hints at some special respect shown to these remains (see also Heighway & Bryant 1999: 205–6). Another reburial, which seems to have been collected in an organic container, was found in the northern part of the graveyard. Meanwhile, a more political motive might explain the replacement of the original occupant of stone coffin 5282, located immediately south of the church, by at least one subsequent skeleton. It is tempting to see the replacement of this high-status burial, prominently positioned outside the church entrance, encased in a stone coffin and provided with an elaborate grave cover, as not just a practical reuse, but a deliberate replacement by a new 'founder'.

Discussion

Recent discussions of later Saxon burial rites have focused upon understanding the increasing control of burial by the Church (Gittos 2002; Hadley 2000; 2002) and the origins of churchyard burial, as well as using written and visual evidence to provide an historical and ideological context for understanding the practice of burial. However, the approach taken here, albeit focusing upon only one site, is to emphasise the importance of ritual performance and display in the burial procedures. It is argued here, by looking at the evidence from Raunds Furnells, that we can see a tension between ordered control and protection of the body in death, and the desire for burial *ad sanctos*, interacting in creating both retrospective memories linked to earlier graves and prospective memories of salvation. The focus was not upon funerary monumentality as such, but upon the spatiality and corporeality of the dead.

Conclusion: cadavers in motion

This chapter has explored three themes concerning the cadaver's transformation and treatment in death that, in different times and places, may have contributed towards the commemoration of the dead. More than any other aspect, death in the past and present focuses attention onto the dead body, its transformation and translation. We need to rethink our views of the body in early medieval death as more than a source of osteological data and a backdrop to the provision of objects, graves and tombs. Instead, we should be encouraged to consider the corpse as a mnemonic agent in early medieval mortuary practices: a focus of memory and a medium for the transformation and constitution of personhood through mortuary

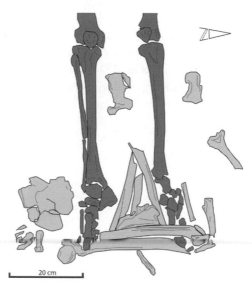

Figure 3.14 Evidence for the careful reburial and arrangement of human remains associated with the insertion of new burials at Raunds Furnells. The shading serves to differentiate the bones belonging to each skeleton (redrawn by the author after Boddington 1996).

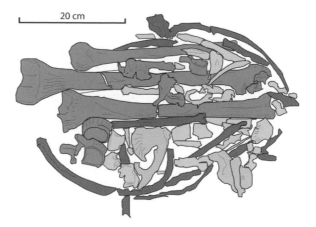

Figure 3.15 Evidence for the exhumation and reburial of a late Saxon skeleton within a bag from Raunds Furnells, Northamptonshire. The excavator, Andy Boddington, speculates that this may have been the original occupant of the stone coffin featured in fig. 3.12. The shading serves to highlight the different anatomical parts of the same skeleton found in the bag (redrawn by the author after Boddington 1996).

practices. The dead body can be seen as a composite of substances, layers and essences that are managed, transformed and fragmented during mortuary practices in the composition of memory. In each case we can see how the mourners acted upon the body as a vehicle of commemoration and how, simultaneously, the body acted back upon society, exhibiting a memorable scene to those participating in and looking on during the funerary process.

Graves as mnemonic compositions

Introduction – remembering through the grave

Whereas in previous chapters the mnemonics of the contents of graves – artefacts and cadvavers – have been discussed, this chapter aims to develop a consideration of the different roles of the burial context itself in the production and reproduction of social memories. Through a consideration of three case studies – the sequence of grave composition at Snape (Suffolk), the intact burials and chambers found beneath mounds 1 and 17 at Sutton Hoo (Suffolk), and the cist graves from Thornybank (Lothian) and Hallowhill (Fife) – we can consider the grave as a mnemonic composition in its own right.

What is a grave?

In mortuary archaeology, graves are often taken for granted as something familiar and therefore not requiring theoretical consideration (see Kaliff 2005). Graves are sometimes seen in terms of their size and elaboration as a further index of the labour and wealth invested in early medieval burial practice (e.g. Stoodley 1999a). Yet by regarding the grave itself as an unproblematic and universal phenomenon, as simply a cut feature and an empty space in which the ritual deposition of body and objects takes place, archaeologists are avoiding the very context that they are intending to theorise and interpret. Graves may be regarded as containing and restraining ritual activity, but as a feature they tend to be regarded as a purely functional space.

Yet graves and the deposits interred within them cannot be separated. They interact with each other and can take on many different meanings and roles in the ritual process in different societies. For instance, a grave is by no means a necessary requirement as the end-point of a funeral: bodies can be disposed of by a variety of other means, including exposure and water-burial. Consequently, grave-digging and the form of graves are not environmentally determined, other than in cold climates where below-ground burial is impossible owing to the frozen soil. Moreover, when grave-digging does takes place, the size and shape of the graves are not predetermined and can vary considerably, as ethnographic studies show us (David & Kramer 2001: 390–7). Graves can also serve as places of religious worship, acting as the points of intercession with ancestors and the supernatural (Kaliff 2005). In some societies, graves are not even the end-point of single funerals, since graves can be reopened, receiving successive burials (e.g. Shanks & Tilley 1982). Furthermore, graves can be only temporary containers of the dead: in many societies, bones and artefacts can be retrieved from them for a variety of motives, from tomb-robbing to ancestral rites (e.g. Hertz 1960).

It is also useful to regard grave-digging as a ritual activity in its own right, performed as a precursor to and facilitating rituals, whether conducted by ritual specialists, as an obligation to the deceased and his or her kin, or perhaps even by kin-group members themselves. Also, the act of digging is a repeated practice, one of many that can create mnemonic connections to earlier funerals and that can itself be a 'performance' involving different actors and bodily actions. Therefore, when considering early medieval 'graves', it is necessary to consider them as mediators of ritual and memory, rather than simply as functional dug features.

Graves as texts

The idea of the early medieval furnished burial as a tableau created for the display of the deceased's identity as envisaged by the mourners has become a common theme in recent research (see chapter 2). Emphasising the *context* of the grave as the appropriate scale at which to examine the interaction of bodies and objects, studies have examined the use of the grave as an environment for creating 'images'. For example, Guy Halsall (2003) has explored the significance of furnished burials as symbolic communication by regarding the burial as akin to a text containing many meanings formed by the arrangement of objects and the body and intended to be 'read' by mourners. In so doing, Halsall emphasises the role of mourners in making an active choice concerning how the dead might be interred from a range of possible alternative positions, postures and artefacts. In this sense, burial rituals, including the choice of clothing for the body and of grave goods, structure, orientation and position, are always a dynamic and innovative ritual display. This is as true of instances where mortuary rites appear novel and distinctive as of when they appear imbued with an aura of conservatism (see also Halsall 2000). When considering these assemblages we must be aware of the precise location of objects and structures, as well as the sequence of actions involved in the funeral, all of which might affect the meanings and statements made by the grave as a whole (Halsall 2003: 62–3).

A key theme in this discussion is not only the meanings of individual objects and their relationships in the grave but also the question of how the entire assemblage within the context of the rural cemetery provided a context in turn for competitive discourses between families (Halsall 2003: 66). Halsall is nonetheless aware that the textual analogy has its limitations for understanding furnished graves. Unlike a fixed text, funerary rituals are public performances that are unique and cannot form the basis for another performance, while a text can be read aloud many times. Burial rituals are therefore more prone to innovation, adaptation and improvisation than rituals governed strictly by the written word. Equally, funerals can involve texts, words and acts, and in this sense are 'multi-media' performances, in contrast to linear, 'mono-media' texts (Halsall 2003: 66–7). Furthermore, Halsall sees the textual metaphor as too optimistic, as much of the 'text' by which the burial is related has been lost and cannot be translated into the present. Yet he admits that in studying mortuary variability we can identify the 'grammar of display': the rules that influence how material culture and burial rites are performed repeatedly to their intended audiences (Halsall 2003: 67).

Halsall sees this working through the creation of memorable 'scenes' in the grave that are then reproduced through their remembrance between funerals (Halsall 2003: 68). However, he argues that the brevity of these displays is equally central to their nature and efficacy. Rather than investing in permanent, above-ground commemorative monuments, Halsall (2003: 69) sees the creation of memorable scenes *within* the grave as significant. In so doing, he very clearly sets a theoretical agenda for interpreting the mnemonic significance of furnished graves.

Martin Carver (2000) has applied similar ideas to his consideration of the two largely complete burial assemblages from Sutton Hoo: mound 1, excavated in 1939 by Basil Brown, and mound 17, excavated in 1993 at the end of Martin Carver's campaign of excavations on the site. Carver's perspective on these rich assemblages is to address both the meanings and socio-political context behind these bold 'statements' (Carver 2000: 36). Carver suggests that the rich assemblages of artefacts operated in a manner analogous to Anglo-Saxon poetry. Both were comparable to theatrical performances aimed at informed but sizeable audiences. Both involved material and symbolic props – in the case of the grave, the body and the artefacts associated with it. Moreover, both grave and poems can be 'read' at different levels of symbolic meaning and in different ways by contrasting sections of the audience:

> A grave is not simply a text, but a text with attitude, a text inflated with emotion. It is not the reality behind *Beowulf*, because a burial is itself not reality and is not meant to be; like poetry it is a palimpsest of allusions, constructed in a certain time and place. But the allusions themselves are so numerous and their interweft so complex, that the time and the place are the last things we can easily ascertain. It is the allusions themselves which must first be studied. In brief, burials have a language.
> (Carver 2000: 37).

These layers of meaning and manifold allusions are seen by Carver as making clear statements about the dead person, the mourners and the wider social group that both belonged to, although he admits that the grave may have been viewed in different, even contradictory, ways. Graves can draw upon allusions from many regions and many periods of time conflated into one ritual display.

While concurring with Carver's approach, we can take his poetry analogy further by suggesting that both poetry and graves can act not only as statements in the present, but also as mnemonic performances aimed at constructing the present in relation to the past and the future. In this sense, his poetic analogy was not so much about making a statement concerning the dead person or mourners, but about the connections of both to mythical pasts and to aspirations of future status and power.

Graves, like poems, have the ability to shift between and sometimes conflate past, present and future, rendering temporal distinctions ambiguous and transformed.

Remembering and forgetting

In order to develop such a view, we must build upon the ideas of Halsall and Carver to explore how the 'texts' created in graves operated in remembrance by emphasising how graves are *not* like texts or poems. First, while the textual and poetical analogies help us understand the meaning of objects, graves are not simply concerned with composition: they are also concerned with transformation. Whereas poems can vary between performances and texts can be read in different ways, graves are not concerned with a static set of ideas, symbols and materials, but with their reconfiguration, manipulation and rendering in a different form. Rather than being a single composition, graves sometimes involve a sequence of different 'scenes' in a logical progression of change, from death-bed and funerary procession to burial and monument-raising. In this sense, graves concern 'scene-making', as Halsall argues, but can also involve the creation of a sequence of connected scenes that often form elements of what might be referred to as the unfolding mnemonic 'narrative'. In other words, the final composition of the grave, as seen by archaeologists, may not have been as important as the process of making it. The sequence of performances leading from scene to scene created memories and identities rather than a static tableau.

Second, as Halsall notes, funerary rituals concern performances composed of acts, materials and practices, not simply sets of ideas and abstract symbols. Graves undoubtedly contain symbolism, but an intellectual engagement with meaning is only one element of their significance. Instead, we might think of the 'impact' or (to use the anthropological phrase) 'agency' of the grave in relation to the audience. The piles of treasure on display, the intimate act of fastening a brooch by the cadaver's neck, the lowering of the coffin, the throwing-in of the first soil over the assemblage: these are practices with potential mnemonic significance, as much as the objects themselves and their contextual relationships. They are also acts that create the sequence of commemoration, although in and of themselves they may have no symbolic meaning at all. Their significance comes from their role in ritual performance, serving to mediate between the living and the dead.

Third, graves are not only about scene-making, but also about concealment – a theme already touched on in chapters 2 and 3 (see also Halsall 2003). Despite recognising that the strength of furnished burial rites in creating memorable events relies on the brevity of the experience, Halsall sees this as also an inherent weakness as a mnemonic strategy, confined to periods 'where status and power could be won and lost within a lifetime' (Halsall 2003: 69). While the insecurities and therefore the immediacy of power and status in early Merovingian society may explain the choice of furnished graves over permanent monuments, as Halsall argues, it is important to realise that these need not be opposing, but complementary means of commemoration. However, by failing to develop his explanation of the role of remembrance through scene-making, Halsall continues to regard the transient nature of furnished burials as a weakness, to some extent considering them a temporary phenomenon in the social 'evolution' of more enduring mechanisms of commemoration, rather than a strength in creating memories in a different and distinctive way from erecting permanent monuments (see also Effros 2003). In other words, graves are not only about experience, they are about managing and altering experience: some enhanced, others suppressed. Consequently, materials, substances and artefacts placed with the dead can be as much concerned with the management of sensory experience of the body and grave goods as with display. This is an idea developed by Susanne Küchler (2002) in relation to the *malanggan* sculpture of New Ireland – mortuary monuments constructed for display for brief periods of time prior to their abandonment or destruction. The 'scene-making' qualities of furnished burials may have operated in a similar way, memories being enhanced, rather than weakened, through their unique form and brevity of experience.

Fourth, what is invisible can be as significant as what is tangible. Focusing on the material over the immaterial is an inevitable consequence of archaeologists working within a social context. The rejection of simplistic associations between mortuary practice and religious belief aside, the possibility that graves are ontological and cosmological spaces as well as social ones should lead us to consider the grave context as potentially imbued with physical and spiritual qualities by early medieval people. The display of grave goods and the body involved the identity of the deceased and survivors but perhaps may have been created to manage the transformation of the ghost into an ancestor, as well as manage the assistance or hindrance of other spiritual beings (deities, spirits and demons, for instance). Without entertaining these elements, we risk the danger of rendering graves as equivalent to the ostentatious display of modern consumer goods and imposing a modern materialist perspective upon early medieval communities.

Having developed this idea, let us now explore some familiar archaeological furnished grave assemblages to see how they operated in constructing remembrance.

Graves and grave structures in early medieval mortuary practices
Traces of early medieval grave structures are more common and diverse than is usually supposed. As well as the traces of wooden coffins and grave structures which can sometimes survive as stains in the soil, in rare cases the actual wood can be preserved in anaerobic conditions. However, there remain doubts over the precise interpretation of many of these features. For instance, even the features identified as 'coffins' in the modern sense of a transportable container for the body may often have been simply wooden grave structures that facilitated the display of the body within the grave for some time before the final back-filling.

A range of other features in and around the grave can be uncovered. The preservation of organic linings and coverings as soil-stains in some cemeteries hints that a range of wood, textile, leather and plant materials could have been employed in early medieval graves more commonly than they are actually found (see below). This is sometimes supported by tentative evidence from the position of bones, where bodies have decomposed in a cavity created by a covering before earth filled the grave (Reynolds 1976). Further grave structures include ledges, post-holes that supported canopies and grave markers, and stones placed around the edge of the grave or over the body, as well as the occasional placing of burnt logs within the grave (Cook & Dacre 1985; Hogarth 1973).

For the cremation rite, furnishings on or around the pyre itself can only be surmised by analogy with the contents of inhumation graves. However, it can be said that there is no reason to assume that early Anglo-Saxon cremation pyres were any less elaborate than their inhumation counterparts. As well as the stack of wood that forms the basis of the pyre, we can expect layers of textile as well as kindling to have covered the corpse, and perhaps even a catafalque overlying the pyre. Structures are also found with the cremation burials themselves, and about these we have direct evidence. Cremation graves are usually shallow and modest in size, and grave cuts often cannot be identified in the soil conditions. However, in some cemeteries there are traces of stone or tile cists provided for the urns, as well as slabs and tiles acting as covers over the urns, as at Caistor-by-Norwich (Myres & Green 1973). Meanwhile, at Spong Hill in Norfolk there are instances of stone cairns placed over groups of urns, perhaps to protect them and to mark their location (Hills 1977; Hills & Penn 1981; Hills et al. 1987; 1994).

We have already reviewed many of the diverse grave structures found in middle and later Anglo-Saxon burial rites. These include ships (chapter 3 and this chapter), bed-burials (see chapter 1 and this chapter), coffins with or without iron nails and those sometimes made from reused ship timbers (e.g. Rodwell & Rodwell 1983: 310–12), and domestic chests (Hall & Whyman 1996). These were all objects that had clear 'biographies', perhaps valued objects (or parts of such), and their reuse in graves may have had mnemonic significance. The diversity of stone grave structures was seen at Raunds Furnells (chapter 3): stone pillows, 'ear muffs', cists, sarcophagi and grave slabs (see Boddington 1996; Hadley 2001; Thompson 2004). A range of features is also found within graves, such as the charcoal graves, with layers of charcoal below, surrounding or over the grave, found principally at urban, ecclesiastical and minster churchyards. Alternative explanations for this practice have been reviewed by Daniell (1997). Elements towards a convincing explanation for the practice include the importance of charcoal in soaking up the juices and odours of decomposition or in distinguishing the status of the deceased directly, but also in managing the dissolution of the body through the lengthy funeral services that high-status individuals might expect. A spiritual interpretation of the rite – that charcoal was part of a broader pattern of social status represented through an ideology of humility and penitence – seems a likely context for the rite (see also Thompson 2002; 2003a and b; 2004). Another instance of grave structures is provided by the 'wands' found in late Saxon burials, as at Barton-upon-Humber, that may be regarded as pilgrims' staffs and hence also symbols of penitence and humility (Rodwell & Rodwell 1983). Recent work by Jo Buckberry (in prep.) has shown that many of these grave structures varied in their frequency according to the age, gender and social status of the deceased. In other words, grave structures and layers operated in a comparable (if not identical) way to early Anglo-Saxon grave goods, dismissing the assumption that 'Christian' burials are less concerned with the expression of social differentiation.

There is no reason that this constitutes the full range of potential grave structures. Perishable forms of grave container could equally have included complex structures made of different materials, such as wood, leather, textile and plant remains rich in symbolism and central to the commemoration of the dead. Bonnie Effros (2003) has recently emphasised the importance of clothing, coverings and containers in the symbolism of Merovingian graves. Rarely do they survive, although the coffin of St Cuthbert (Coatsworth 1989) shows the potential for coffins from Britain to contain a range of religious scenes comparable to their stone counterparts.

One way of explaining the shift from furnished to unfurnished burial might be to follow a recent suggestion by Helen Geake (2002) and contrast the ritual tableau constructed by early Anglo-Saxon furnished burials with the enclosing and protecting of corpses emphasised both by later Anglo-Saxon graves and their western and northern British counterparts. The work of Victoria Thompson (2002; 2004) has clearly pointed the way towards an understanding of later Anglo-Saxon grave structures and grave slabs by addressing their role at the interface of secular and religious elite culture and the symbolism of humility and salvation. Yet the diversity of grave structures employed in the careful and sequential commemoration of the body through mortuary practices has yet to receive the attention it deserves.

In western and northern Britain, we find some of these grave structures, but others too, partly because of the availability of stone but also because of different mnemonic strategies. In terms of grave coverings, a notable example is the use of quartz to cover and mark 'special graves', such as those at Cannington in Somerset (Rahtz et al. 2000; see chapter 6), Capel Eithin on Anglesey (White & Smith 1999; see chapter 5) and Capel Maelog, Powys (Britnell 1990). In areas with widespread available stone, we find the use of cists, particularly in parts of Wales, northern England, Scotland and Ireland (Alcock 1992; James 1992; O'Brien 2003). When and where cists are not employed, we find evidence of other burial containers. For example, from the monastic site of Whithorn in Dumfries and Galloway excavations produced evidence of long-cists, dug-out log-coffins and plank-coffins. The rest of this chapter will focus on a number of case studies to illustrate the role of grave structures in social remembrance.

Layers of memory – Snape

At many early Anglo-Saxon cemeteries the focus has been upon the study of metal grave goods. Despite the acidic soils destroying both artefacts and bone in many of the cemeteries of eastern England, some cemeteries have yielded good organic preservation, and the mineralised remains of organic material and textiles have been found adhering to metal artefacts.

The cemetery of Snape in Suffolk is central to such discussions, where excavations between 1985 and 1992 produced evidence for a wide variety of burial traditions. In terms of the quality of bone and artefact preservation, post-cemetery disturbance and partial excavation, the Snape excavations offer less evidence than many other recently excavated early medieval cemeteries. However, the excavations were invaluable in revealing the extent and character of a 'mixed-rite' late fifth- to sixth-century communal cemetery that preceded the construction of the rich ship barrow-burial towards the end of the sixth century (Davidson 1863; Filmer-Sankey & Pestell 2001). Consequently the Snape excavations have provided both comparisons and contrasts with the barrow cemetery of Sutton Hoo, now also known to have been discrete from, but close to, a sixth-century communal cemetery (Carver 2005; Filmer-Sankey & Pestell 2001). Moreover, the cemetery is well known for the diversity of mortuary practices uncovered, including cremation burials, inhumation graves, annular and penannular ring-ditches, grave markers, boat-burial and evidence of horse-sacrifice. The excavations also produced a rare example of a cremation pyre, as well as burnt stone features that may reflect evidence of ritual feasting during mortuary rituals (Filmer-Sankey & Pestell 2001).

For the purposes of this book, the excavations have a further value, for despite the poor preservation of human bone and the disturbance of many of the graves, this cemetery, more perhaps than any other, provides us with insights into the sequence of ritual practices involved in grave construction. There are two main reasons for this: first, because of the high quality of the excavation techniques employed under research conditions (see also Haughton & Powlesland 1999). Most early medieval graves are recorded with a single plan. However, the careful excavation of the Snape graves by spits involved recording multiple plans and sections. This made it possible to see the sequence of actions involved in the burial ritual in the stratigraphy of the burial deposit. Second, the sandy, acidic soil conditions left stains where the human remains had been deposited, as well as where many artefacts had been mineralised and destroyed (Filmer-Sankey & Pestell 2001: 16). This evidence showed that a range of organic objects of horn, leather, animal hair, wood (Cameron & Fell in Filmer-Sankey & Pestell 2001: 204) and textiles (Crowfoot in Filmer-Sankey & Pestell 2001: 207–14) had once been placed around the corpse, as well as metal objects (fig. 4.1). From their sampling and analysis, together with their shape and location, it was possible to infer a variety of grave goods and structures.

The theme running through much of the variation is not the production of a single 'scene' in the grave, but the sequential production, followed by the concealment and consignment, of successive 'scenes' during grave composition and back-filling.

Furnishing the dead
Let us now review the evidence that shows the complex ritual sequences at Snape. First, we have evidence for the duration of the proceedings. Insect remains have been used to suggest that the bodies of the dead in early Anglo-Saxon England were not interred immediately, but were left within structures or in the grave where they could be accessed. At Snape, as with other cemeteries, mineralised fly pupae attest to this, although the precise length and manner of exposure remain unclear. For example, in grave 32, the buckle and knife of the male grave assemblage were

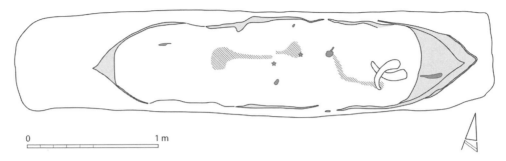

Figure 4.1 Plan of boat-grave 4 from Snape, Suffolk, illustrating the poor bone preservation but the unusual survival of organic grave goods as soil-stains. Artefacts that could be discerned include a pair of drinking-horns, and the grave structure consisted of a dug-out boat used to contain the body (redrawn by Séan Goddard after Filmer-Sankey & Pestell 2001).

covered with 250 fly puparia and a beetle (Filmer-Sankey & Pestell 2001: 75, 77–9). This indirectly supports the argument that the grave-side and grave-focused rituals were only one stage towards the end of the funerary obsequies (see also chapter 3).

Further aspects of the duration and character of mortuary practices were recognised for grave 17. Within this grave, two cinerary urns were placed on a shelf of natural bedrock above the head of a west–east-orientated furnished adult male-gendered inhumation, seemingly as integral elements of the inhumation burial rite (Filmer-Sankey & Pestell 2001: 53–5). Although we cannot rule out the possibility that the occupants of these urns had died in the days or weeks when the inhumation was being prepared, it is likely that these cinerary urns had been curated for some time before being interred in the grave as an element of the inhumation rites. Indeed, cases such as this beg the unanswerable question of how long cinerary urns containing the ashes of the dead circulated among the living before finally being buried.

In most cases, the grave cuts at Snape were considerably larger than was necessary to contain a body, suggesting the explicit intention of creating a sizeable container in the earth to receive the inhumed body and a range of materials and artefacts. In grave 9, there was a shelf at the bottom end of the grave which could have been made to allow a mourner to stand in the grave to position the body (Filmer-Sankey & Pestell 2001: 36–8). Moreover, in two instances, structures were clearly present. Grave 47 was surrounded by a four-posted structure, one post in each corner of the grave; this may represent only part of a much more complex grave-lining, if these were only the load-bearing posts (Pestell in Filmer-Sankey & Pestell 2001: 238; fig. 4.2). Meanwhile, grave 2 revealed traces of a complex internal structure, with clay deposits that may have acted as post-pads supporting a superstructure over the grave at the eastern end. Other traces of above-ground structures were present, including ring-ditches (see chapter 5), suggesting that above-ground post-funeral commemoration was enhanced by these structures. At the very least this evidence

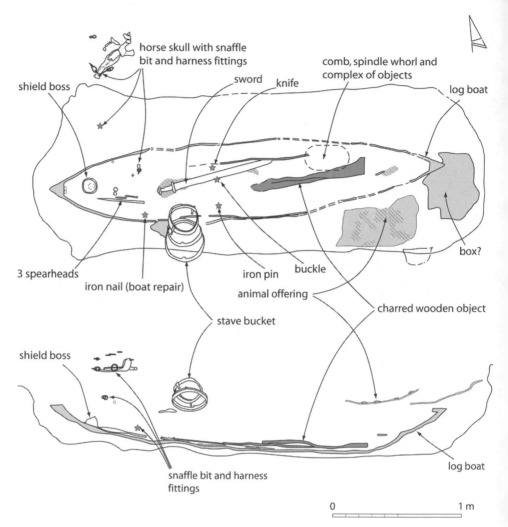

shield boss

horse skull with snaffle
bit and harness fittings

sword   knife

comb, spindle whorl and
complex of objects

log boat

3 spearheads

iron nail (boat repair)

iron pin   buckle

animal offering

stave bucket

charred wooden object

box?

shield boss

snaffle bit and harness
fittings

log boat

0   1 m

Figure 4.2 Plan and section of boat-grave 47 from Snape, Suffolk, illustrating the range of grave goods placed with the dead, including spears, a sword and a shield. The presence of a buckle suggests the body was clothed for death. Afterwards the body was placed in the boat, and a bucket, bags and boxes (possibly associated with food offerings of meat), as well as a burned log, were added to the grave. Finally, a horse's head and bridle were situated beside the grave (redrawn by Séan Goddard after Filmer-Sankey & Pestell 2001).

might explain the lack of intercutting between graves in most fifth- to seventh-century cemeteries (Pestell in Filmer-Sankey & Pestell 2001: 239). Yet it is clear that these structures built around the grave must have influenced the nature of the funerary process itself, allowing the grave to remain secure and open for an extended period of time (if required) and perhaps protected by a canopy from the elements. Simultaneously, it allowed the grave to operate as a small, restricted arena for ritual activity.

Preparing and assembling the grave

This argument is supported by other aspects of the graves at Snape. Prior to the placing of the body, a deposit of ash was buried at the base of grave 39, perhaps connected to rituals of preparing the grave. In some cases the structure of the grave was also used to facilitate the posture of the body: in at least three burials, pillows of iron-panned sand were identified beneath the heads of the cadavers (in graves 7, 14 and 37). Although graves were often large enough to contain the body and objects, the practicalities of selecting and positioning objects meant that, in three instances, hollows were later cut into the sides of the graves to fit objects that were too large for the grave cut. This suggests a desire to include artefacts in a prescribed location around the body, and for the objects and the body to operate together within the grave to create the appropriate display (Pestell in Filmer-Sankey & Pestell 2001: 239).

Containers

Identifying the evidence for burial containers at Snape was hampered by the nature of the soil conditions, but twenty-eight out of the forty graves investigated had some form of container or structure. Rather than these being an exception, it is possible to suggest that Snape hints at the range of possible burial containers that cannot be identified in other cemeteries excavated in rescue conditions or within soil matrices that do not facilitate organic survival (see Harford Farm in chapter 2). From the Snape evidence, the excavators challenge the assumption that early medieval burials revealing traces of organic linings necessarily indicate coffins, suggesting instead that a range of different burial containers was utilised. At Snape, there were three instances (two certain) of boats being used as containers for the body. The discovery of heartwood in grave 3 supports the view that a log-boat fragment was added to the grave (Gale in Filmer-Sankey & Pestell 2001: 226). There were a further seven possible coffins that would have been held together with wooden pegs, and at least one instance of a bier, possibly made of wicker hurdle. In addition, there are at least ten cases of textile, bark or animal hide layers beneath the body, either objects designed especially or perhaps reused cloaks or blankets.

Artefacts and the body

Next we have the body and its accompanying objects, and once again we encounter multiple layers of material. The individual objects were also contained or covered. It has long been realised that many of the 'bag collections' were, by definition, hidden from view within containers. At Snape, it is also clear that other artefacts were wrapped in textiles. Moreover, textile remains suggest that some of the corpses at least were covered by veils, suggested from tabby weaves in grave 68. Similarly, a fragment of mineralised hemp tabby curling round a brooch in grave 19 suggests that a head-veil covered the corpse (Crowfoot in Filmer-Sankey & Pestell 2001: 211). This evidence emphasises the roles of clothing as elements of display, but also as a means of wrapping and masking the corpse.

The female costume at Snape follows a broader 'Anglian' pattern, with an undergarment of long sleeves, their cuffs decorated with tablet-woven bands and fastened with wrist clasps, worn with an overgown of either tubular or peplos pattern. This would have been fastened on the shoulders with a pair of brooches and a necklace of beads. At the waist was a belt with a buckle. Sometimes a third brooch was worn, possibly attaching a cloak, but in the Snape instances, the third brooch was occasionally used to hold up the central part of the dress (Crowfoot in Filmer-Sankey & Pestell 2001: 211). Male costume is more difficult to reconstruct, but at Snape, as at many other cemeteries, it is clear that weapons may have been wrapped separately for burial (Crowfoot in Filmer-Sankey & Pestell 2001: 212; but see Harrington, in prep.). Similarly, the lyre in grave 32 was buried in a bag (Crowfoot in Filmer-Sankey & Pestell 2001: 212). Elizabeth Crowfoot speculates that some of the Snape textiles may have had biographies of their own, having been brought long distances or curated for significant periods of time comparable to the life-histories of individuals and households. Certainly it is easy to overlook the wealth and social significance invested in textiles in early medieval societies in favour of the more visible metal artefacts. Therefore, rather than being subsidiary to the metal objects found in graves, textiles were perhaps a medium for expressing wealth, status and the identity of the deceased, as well as serving to contain, consign and conceal artefacts within the burial context.

Stains in graves appear to indicate the presence of organic artefacts and materials. In some instances these are related to metal finds, as in grave 20, where the soil stain of a spear shaft was recovered (Filmer-Sankey & Pestell 2001: 61–3). In other cases they reveal wholly organic objects. In grave 32, the remains of a wooden bowl, possibly made of walnut, were identified (Filmer-Sankey & Pestell 2001: 75, 77–9), while in grave 4, a pair of drinking-horns made of cattle horn was arranged symmetrically at the feet of the corpse, evidence of a ritual that would have been lost in the soil conditions of most early Anglo-Saxon cemeteries (Filmer-Sankey & Pestell 2001: 25–9). Other organic grave goods recovered include wooden vessels and associated stains, suggesting joints of meat were buried with the dead. A plum stone from grave 32 hints at the range of other food offerings that may have accompanied the burials at Snape but that have failed to survive in the soil conditions.

Layers
Other stains cannot be explained in this way but may instead be regarded as structures and layers of material placed in the grave as part of the rituals surrounding burial. In four cases, the organic layer (sometimes folded to make double layers) was seen to extend up the sides of the grave cut, suggesting that the entire grave was lined to receive the body, and was perhaps attached to wooden structures to maintain rigidity (Pestell in Filmer-Sankey & Pestell 2001: 241). Such linings may have been thick layers of textile, perhaps made especially for the funeral, or perhaps they were taken from the walls of houses. They may have been adorned with designs and, if edged, may have had tablet-woven borders, making them impressive surfaces ready to receive the body. For instance, in grave 16 tablet weaves were identified, suggesting

that large blankets lining the grave and clothing the body may have been adorned with woven horsehair patterns (Crowfoot in Filmer-Sankey & Pestell 2001: 211). These textiles clearly had a role in creating the burial context, but they may also have been used to wrap the body prior to interment and then been used as a lining, revealing the body to viewers for the final time prior to the back-filling of the graves. For each of these layers, it is important to remember that every element may have been more common than even the good preservation at Snape reveals. The Rippenköper (a twill weave with reversed ribs) from grave 37 from Snape suggests that we are dealing with garments similar to those found in Alemannic graves (Crowfoot in Filmer-Sankey & Pestell 2001: 208–9). Meanwhile, concerning the tablet-woven borders of cloths, these may have been treasured and reused (Crowfoot in Filmer-Sankey & Pestell 2001: 211). A related issue concerns the appearance of these textiles. Many have been dyed with bright colours used only for restricted garments, perhaps associated with high-status clothing (Walton Rogers in Filmer-Sankey & Pestell 2001: 212).

Concealing and consigning the dead

So far we have evidence for elaborate grave structures employed to construct an 'image of death' comparable to our discussions of the use of brooches, beads and weapons in chapter 2. However, the Snape evidence illustrates that this was only part of the significance of the mortuary sequence, for with the composition of the grave there is subsequent evidence for the importance of layering and concealing the dead prior to the final back-filling of the graves. In two graves, 36 and 37, textile layers were found overlying the body. The evidence was clearer for grave 37, where two different heavy-wool weaves, one of which was decorated with stripes, could be identified (Crowfoot in Filmer-Sankey & Pestell 2001: 208).

Further evidence for ritual actions during the closing of graves derives from four-teen textile samples from six graves of a purple organic material seemingly added to the graves. One interpretation is that this may derive from grasses, bracken or flower stems strewn over the body. Stems and leaves were found to overlie the corpse in grave 47, while bracken and vegetation were identified in graves 3 and 32, and possibly in grave 8.

Other ritual acts involve the deposition of charcoal logs in the grave fill for many burials. This consisted of charred wood, mostly oak and gorse, but also willow/poplar, hazel and blackthorn/cherry. The charcoal consists of roundwood, suggesting the use of branches incorporated into the grave fill (Gale in Filmer-Sankey & Pestell 2001: 226). Evidence of some kinds of charred wood, from small flecks to large burnt timbers, was identified in thirty-three out of forty graves (Filmer-Sankey & Pestell 2001: 243). Tim Pestell notes that many were carefully positioned as covering layers of the body, as for instance in grave 9 (fig. 4.3). There seems to be a particular emphasis upon the placing of charred timbers over the head of the cadaver, as in graves 8 and 39. In grave 9, it appears from the section of the grave that the burnt oak timbers formed a pile rising in height towards the head (western) end of the grave. At the foot (eastern) end of the grave was a shelf upon which no burnt timbers were found. It is possible that a mourner or mourners could have used this as a

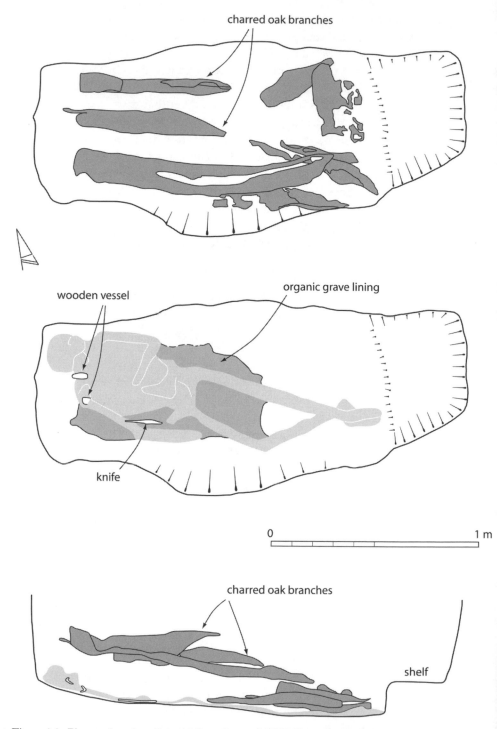

Figure 4.3 Plans and section of grave 9 from Snape, Suffolk, illustrating the organic grave lining beneath the soil-stain of the corpse and the charred oak logs added over the grave. Also note the ledge at the bottom of the grave itself (redrawn by Séan Goddard after Filmer-Sankey & Pestell 2001).

step upon which to stand to place the timbers over the corpse during the burial rites (Filmer-Sankey & Pestell 2001: 36–8).

Trampled sand noticed at the base of graves 9 and 40 suggests ritual activities within the pit prior to final back-filling. Snape also produced evidence for the organisation of the back-filling of graves, with at least two or three people involved, identified from different areas of back-fill soil composed of contrasting colours, and in one case (grave 45) distinctive tip-lines were recognised. For example, the patchy mix of back-filling in graves 2, 6 and 16 suggests the involvement of at least two people, while for the boat in grave 4 there is evidence of at least three people being involved in the back-filling. Moreover, spoil was used to create structures within the grave: in grave 47, a tripartite division of fill extended into the boat-stain, with grey topsoil fill at the centre and yellow-brown redeposited natural on either side, while sand was used to pack the boat in place. Meanwhile, in grave 32, the topsoil back-fill was used as the base for the organic layer's edges to be laid on.

Objects were also included in the grave fill. These included a large quartzite saddle quern inserted into grave 20, a large quartzite stone in grave 47 and the prow of a ship in grave 10 (fig. 4.4). Moreover, pottery scatters were identified in at least eight graves, suggesting the deliberate breakage of pottery over graves either during or towards the end of the back-filling of graves. Burnt flints were also recovered from the fills of several graves, which, while difficult to prove as deliberate inclusions, could reflect further evidence of burial ritual (Filmer-Sankey & Pestell 2001: 244). For example, in grave 27, twenty-four pieces of charcoal – and beneath them, sixty-two burnt flint chippings – were recovered from the grave fill. In grave 2, meanwhile, the fragments of a brooch were found in the back-fill (Filmer-Sankey & Pestell 2001: 21). Finally, there is even the suggestion that the deposition of human remains could be associated with the back-filling of graves, since cremated bone was recovered from many grave fills. While some may have been accidental inclusions of disturbed earlier cremation burials, in grave 11 a mass of bone and a few burnt objects were sealed in the fill across the whole area of the grave, suggesting a deliberate scattering of cremated bone in a manner analogous to the position of burnt timbers and artefacts (Filmer-Sankey & Pestell 2001: 43–4, 246). As mentioned above, regarding grave 17, two cinerary urns were placed on a shelf of natural bedrock at the head end of the grave (Filmer-Sankey & Pestell 2001: 53–5; fig. 4.5). Once the cremation process had been completed and the ashes collected up (see chapter 3), there would have been no reason for a rapid interment of the ashes in a ceramic container. It is quite possible that cinerary urns were displayed above ground, in houses, and transported over considerable distances before final disposal. In this scenario, it is possible that cremation urns were buried only once a possible inhumation funeral was conducted. In grave 19, these rituals were taken one stage further with the addition of an unburnt human body, apparently 'thrown in' prone over the first interment. Identified most famously at Sewerby, East Yorkshire (Hirst 1985; see chapter 3), these 'deviant' burials, sometimes interpreted as evidence of human sacrifice, appear to be additional rituals augmenting the placing of materials, layers and artefacts over the original interment (Filmer-Sankey & Pestell 2001: 58–60). As the excavators note, the size

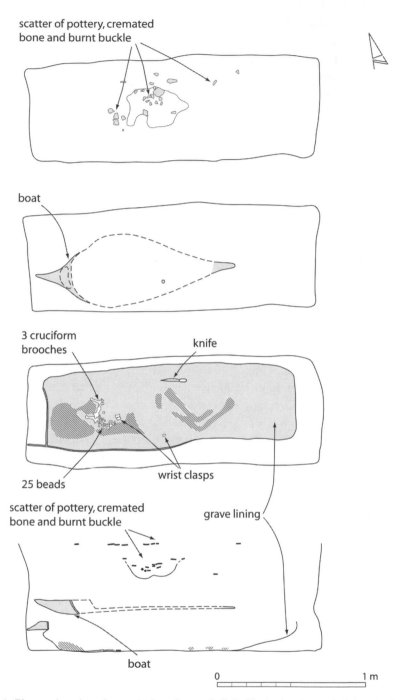

Figure 4.4 Plans and section of grave 10 from Snape, Suffolk, illustrating the grave lining, the furnishing of the corpse, the subsequent addition during back-filling of a part of a boat, and a scatter of cremated bone and artefacts (redrawn by Séan Goddard after Filmer-Sankey & Pestell 2001).

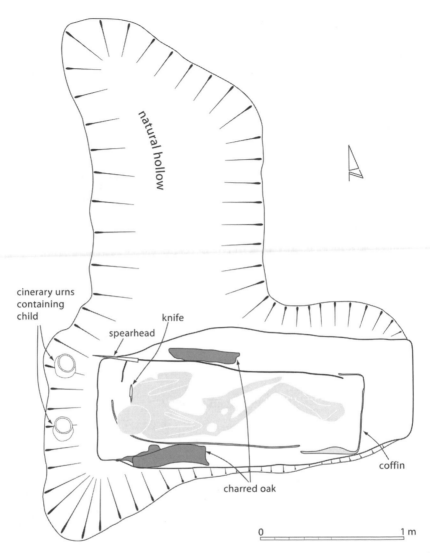

cinerary urns
containing
child

natural hollow

knife

spearhead

coffin

charred oak

0   1 m

Figure 4.5 Plan of grave 17 from Snape, Suffolk, inserted into a natural hollow and accompanied by charred logs and two cinerary urns placed on a ledge above the head of the interment (redrawn by Séan Goddard after Filmer-Sankey & Pestell 2001).

of the grave seems to 'anticipate' the inclusion of two burials, suggesting that the intention to add a second body was an integral element of the burial ritual rather than an 'after-thought'.

Snape grave 47

We can pursue many of these elements through the discussion of one of the wealthier sixth-century graves excavated at Snape: grave 47 (Filmer-Sankey & Pestell 2001: 102–11; see fig. 4.2 above). As discussed above, bulges in the corners of the grave suggest a four-post-hole structure was originally erected over it. Following the construction of the grave, charred wood was placed at the bottom. Next, an oaken boat was laid in the grave, showing evidence of charring on a small patch at the western end of the grave, possible only on the interior. An iron nail found near the boat may be the remains of a patch, suggesting a vessel with a history of use. A shield was next laid over the gun-whale. Alongside a range of other grave goods placed with the body, a pillow was deposited at the foot of the grave, identified by the presence of mineralised feathers. An iron sword sheathed within a scabbard of wood and leather lined with animal hair was interred within the boat. Before the back-filling of the grave, a decapitated horse's head, still wearing its harness, was placed beside the boat. The bridle was draped down into the main burial deposit. A stave bucket of yew planks was rammed snugly into the grave edge. Once the grave was partially back-filled, textile fragments covered by an alkanet colorant were located in two patches laid over the eastern bow of the boat. This suggests that the boat was interred and slightly back-filled before being covered or lined with textiles and having further grave goods laid within and upon it. A bundle of three spears wrapped in textiles may have been added to the grave at this stage. Subsequently, three large burnt flints and two flint flakes may have been deliberately added to the grave fill. The precise sequence of these ritual acts cannot be accurately and exactly reconstructed, but it is clear that these events involved both display and concealment in a staged sequence.

Discussion

This discussion has far from exhausted the evidence from Snape for burial ritual. Inevitably, despite the wealth of evidence produced by soil conditions and careful excavation for the structured deposition of artefacts, bodies and grave structures, we cannot identify exactly when, for how long and in what way the grave assemblages were involved in display. Yet the evidence suggests that at each stage of the funeral, different artefacts and layers were present, revealed and then enclosed and hidden from view. Rather than a single 'image of death', Snape reveals that graves were a sequential arrangement of both display and concealment. We can see the grave lined with textile and other organic remains. The body was clothed, and, in some instances, linings placed over the body. This begs the question of how, if at all, the corpse was actually displayed in the manner suggested, and to what extent organic layers of textile and animal hide were used to furnish, wrap and conceal the corpse from view. Drawing this evidence together allows us to challenge the 'ritual tableau' view of early medieval furnished burial rites as only one upon many stages in a sequential process of display and concealment. Indeed, it may be possible that these ideas are influenced by the contemporary 'Americanising' of the British funeral industry, where embalming techniques have facilitated the increasing popularity of open-casket funerals (Metcalf & Huntingdon 1991: 200–4; Mitford 1963). We can take this idea one stage further. Instead of focusing upon the 'impression' and visual impact of corpse, artefacts and structures on a passive observer, we need to consider early medieval graves as being actively composed. This can be considered akin to the process of archaeologists excavating a grave, but in reverse: a process of revelation and concealment.

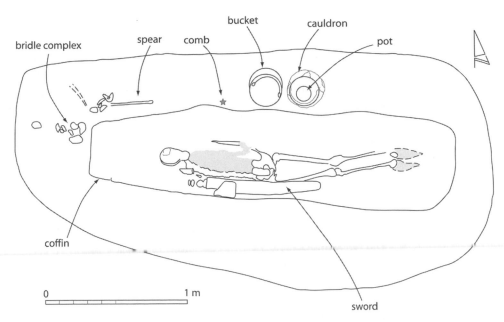

Figure 4.6 Plan of the wealthy adult male weapon-burial from beneath mound 17 at Sutton Hoo. Other objects not illustrated were a tub found over the bridle at the western end of the grave and a shield placed underneath the coffin (redrawn by Séan Goddard after Carver 2005).

Brilliant graves at Sutton Hoo

The grave was a restricted context for display, but with the princely burials of the later sixth and early seventh centuries we see the grave turn into a ritual theatre, with the use of chambers and ships serving as contexts (or settings) for the display of objects and the dead. This section will look at two rich burials of this kind, identifying the ways in which multi-sensual experience of the grave and the sequence of ritual actions may have served to create a memorable scene of a kind and scale that the graves at Snape could not have achieved. Indeed, it could be argued that, more than the quality and quantity of the objects interred, it was the acts of composition that set these high-status burials apart from their predecessors and made them unique performances. Building upon the results of the interpretations of Martin Carver (1998a; 2000; 2005; see above), we shall consider the only two intact burial deposits found beneath large mounds at Sutton Hoo: mounds 17 and 1. We shall discuss mound 17 first.

Sutton Hoo mound 17
Mound 17 covered two separate graves, each with a body. The northern grave contained a horse, the southern grave a man (fig. 4.6). The sequence suggested by Carver (2005: 115–37) for the assemblage of the human burial can be crudely summarised and adapted for our discussion here as follows:

1 The grave pit was excavated for the human burial (Carver 2005: 127–8).
2 The grave was lined with moss and grass (Carver 2005: 128).

3 Two spears were laid flat on the bottom of the grave (Carver 2005: 125, 128).

4 A shield was placed over the spears (Carver 2005: 125, 128–9).

5 Three deposits were located along the north-east edge of the grave: (i) an iron-bound bucket, (ii) a cauldron containing a ceramic pot, and (iii) a bronze bowl containing lamb chops positioned in a haversack (Carver 2005: 129).

6 A harness, bridle, body harness and saddle were placed at the western end of the grave (Carver 2005: 131–2).

7 A wooden tub was laid over the harness at the western end of the grave (Carver 2005: 132).

8 The wooden dug-out coffin was lowered into position, containing the extended supine body of a young adult male accompanied by a sword, knife, buckles and a purse (Carver 2005: 134–5).

9 An antler comb was either thrown into the grave or slipped off the coffin lid (Carver 2005: 132).

10 The stallion was sacrificed and interred in an adjacent pit (Carver 2005: 135).

11 Both human and horse graves were back-filled.

12 A single mound was raised over both the human and animal grave consisting of stacked turfs (Carver 2005: 137).

The sequence of overlapping objects could be explained by the confines of the grave, yet it is evident that the sequence suggests different roles for the grave goods at different stages of the burial rite. The spears and shield, which as we saw in the previous chapter were usually closely associated with the body and identity, were separated from the cadaver in this grave, being placed beneath the coffin. The subsequent placing of vessels and horse gear represent a discrete set of offerings again, seemingly preparing the grave to receive the coffin. These items may have been gifts from retainers, possibly connected to the sacrifice of the horse in the adjacent pit prior to, and building up to, the lowering of the coffin itself into the grave. The coffin would in turn have obscured and concealed these items, especially if it had been covered with layers of textiles. In turn, the coffin enclosed the clothed body and the sword – the weapon that would serve to symbolise elite status and identity more readily than spears and shields (Härke 1990). The coffin's contents would presumably have been composed and displayed the deceased above ground at an earlier stage in the rituals, but it remains unclear whether the final act of concealment took place above ground or in the grave itself. Finally, a comb was thrown into the grave, an act that is seen by Carver as a more personal remembrance by a mourner (Carver 1998a: 112), but it is noteworthy that this use of combs in final commemorative acts mirrors the fifth- and sixth-century deposition of broken comb fragments in early Anglo-Saxon cremation urns (Williams 2003). Consequently, the comb may have been regarded by tradition as an appropriate symbol of the closing of the mourning process, perhaps an object used to manage the hair of the living and the dead, and polluted by association with death.

One explanation of this ritual sequence would be to see a tension existing between the desire to follow convention in interring the dead in a sizeable, but still confined, grave, and doing so while making apparent a degree of wealth that in hindsight required greater space for its adequate display. After all, despite the best intentions, funerals in all societies can be chaotic affairs in which decision-making rarely lies with one person and inappropriate decisions (whether for practical, aesthetic, emotional or social reasons) can often be made. However, in the light of the discussion of Snape above, the sequence in mound 17 appears deliberate. While the objects added to the grave had to be inserted in some sort of order, it is difficult to regard the sequence as purely random, being instead part of a carefully orchestrated funerary sequence (see Carver 2000). For instance, while the area around the coffin may have been packed with organic grave goods that have left no trace, this does not explain why the weapons were interred beneath the coffin rather than along the sides of the grave for all to see. If this observation is accepted, then a hypothetical narrative of different meanings may have been evoked by the sequence of depositions:

1 Retainers' gifts of weapons and feasting gear evoking the military, social and cer-emonial life of the aristocrat.
2 Horse gear evoking hunting and military campaigns in which horses would have been an exclusively aristocratic element.
3 The cadaver presented in an idealised state, dressed for death.
4 Horse sacrifice and comb deposition serving to mark the end of the mourning process.
5 Back-filling the grave and mound-raising serving to seal and fix 'memories' in place.

Sutton Hoo mound 1
In many ways, the composition of the grave beneath mound 17 was an elabora-tion of the same process found in Snape boat-grave 47. Yet the chamber con-structed within the ship interred beneath mound 1 at Sutton Hoo took the con-cept of composition to a new level. A 27m-long seaworthy clinker-built ship was interred in a 28m-long trench up to 3.5m below the contemporary ground sur-face (fig. 4.7). Within the ship, a central chamber was constructed within which a complex array of wealthy and exotic grave goods was placed and suspended from the walls. The grave goods suggest that the interment was that of an adult male, although we have no conclusive proof of this owing to the lack of preserved human remains.

Reconstructions of this complex burial assemblage have varied over the years, with differences of view expressed concerning the presence and position of the interred corpse, the presence of a coffin and the precise location of artefacts. For simplicity, this review follows the most recent reconstruction, that of Rupert Bruce-Mitford and Martin Carver, which suggests an arrangement of a body and the presence of a coffin (fig. 4.8). In terms of our discussion, the burial assemblage can provide further insights into the role of material culture and grave structures in the mnemonics of furnished burial. While in no way 'typical', and in many ways exceptional, the

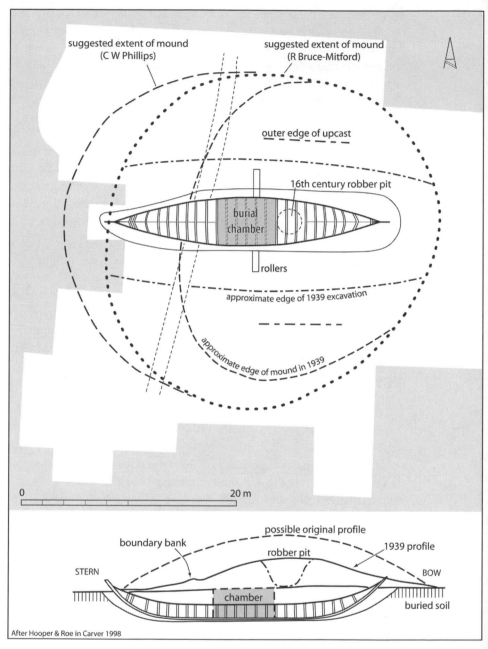

Figure 4.7   Reconstruction plan and section of the ship-burial beneath mound 1 at Sutton Hoo (redrawn by Séan Goddard after Carver 1998a).

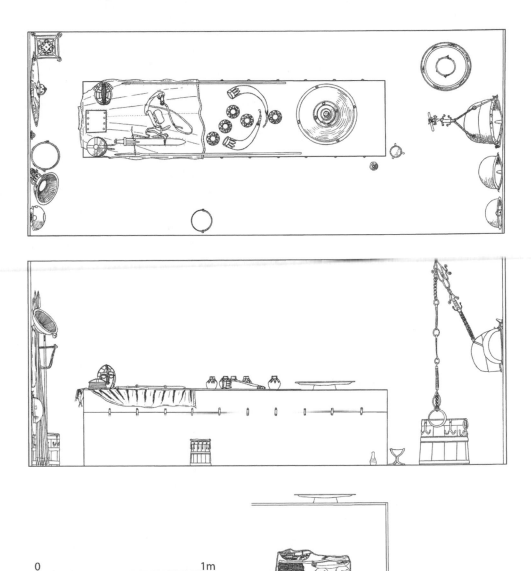

Figure 4.8 Reconstruction plan and section of the burial chamber within the ship-burial beneath mound 1 at Sutton Hoo (adapted by Séan Goddard after Carver 1998a; reproduced with the kind permission of Martin Carver & British Museum Press).

wealth of the grave allows us to pull apart the many carefully constructed mnemonic elements of the funerary process that it is difficult to pursue in the poorer graves.

It can be argued that the chamber can be divided into five main zones of activity, composed in the following simplified sequence:

1 The chamber was constructed within the ship once it had reached the site.
2 The chamber was lined with fabrics and hangings.
3 Along the eastern wall were three cauldrons.

4 The coffin was placed in the chamber.

5 Three heaps of objects were placed immediately in the coffin. The first group included a pillow, shoes, hanging bowls, a bowl and a cup. The second group included the mailcoat and flowers. Over both of these groups were placed the third group: a leather garment, a toilet bowl, a cap, a ladle, wooden bottles and combs.

6 If a coffin was in fact present, cloths were laid over it to receive sets of objects.

7 New sets of objects were placed, further 'consigning' the body, either on and obscuring the body or on the coffin lid. These included the helmet, gaming pieces, a bell, spoons, bowls, spears, a sword, bottles, horns and the silver Anastasius dish.

8 The western wall was adorned with items, including a stack of spears, a lyre, a bucket, a stag sceptre, a shield and an iron 'standard'.

9 Other items were dispersed across the floor, including a bucket, a bottle and an iron lamp.

Many of the items were wrapped in textiles, including both vessels and weapons. Regardless of the precise order in which the eastern and western wall assemblages were orchestrated, we can be reasonably confident about the sequence in which they went out of the view of the mourners. First to go would have been the objects within the coffin, followed by the range of objects within the chamber and finally the entire view of ship and chamber created in the mound. In this sense, the burial was a series of nested spaces that were displayed and concealed consecutively to construct remembrance.

The types of object involved in this display are also relevant. Warrior gear, feasting equipment, symbols of office, personal items and clothing, mariners' tools and the ship itself were all elements displayed in the grave and sequentially hidden from view (Carver 1998a; 2005). While an afterlife voyage is one metaphorical interpretation of the grave goods, Carver also emphasises how the artefacts would individually and collectively serve to create a spectacle for the living.

One aspect that could be added to Carver's account concerns the centrality of colour and brilliance within the composition and concealment of Sutton Hoo mound 1 (see also Jones 2003; 2004). The textiles, when found, are either yellow or red, mirroring the use of brilliant gold and garnet jewellery associated with the body itself. In this context it is important to remember that if the chamber was half-closed and lit by the sole iron lamp found in the grave, it would represent an animated scene, a flickering light in which gold and silver objects and the brightly coloured, painted coffin and textiles would appear to shimmer and move. Indeed, the importance of this fiery quality of objects can be found in the serpentine Style II animal art found on the goldwork; the gold buckle and helmet, for example, are more than objects that glistened and shone, they were objects that would have been animated by the zoomorphic decoration of serpents adorning them. Consequently, the display of material culture in mound 1 was a vivid spectacle indeed, but one that evoked brilliance and animation as well as wealth and splendour. One must not forget that the chamber walls, and the ship itself, may have been elaborately carved and painted with similar decorative motifs in order to mirror the textiles and metalwork of the grave. In this sense, we come close to the use of the grave as a 'technology of enchantment' as discussed by the anthropologist Alfred Gell (1992; 1998): the use of material culture to create scenes that have an impact on the senses and have an 'agency' in evoking memories. Indeed, it is possible that the distinctive experience of the mound 1 chamber was enhanced not only by visual information, but by distinctive sounds and aromas to evoke associations of energy, vitality and perhaps even the continued animation of the dead and their artefacts.

Therefore the archaeological evidence from mound 1 at Sutton Hoo can be used to emphasise the experiential and mnemonic elements of the display: a unique spectacle that was not intended to be repeated. Hence each burial at Sutton Hoo does not attempt to replicate the others, but employs the rituals of both inhumation and cremation in distinctive ways. The 'scenes' created are unique to each and memorable in their own rite, with elements of earlier funerals replaced and reconfigured, but not replicated (see chapter 5).

A cist to remember

In contrast to the furnished burials of southern and eastern England are the cist or lintel graves of western and northern Britain. This form of grave structure and cemetery date from the late Roman period through to the end of the millennium and beyond (e.g. Alcock 1992; Ludlow 2000), but their association with field cemeteries away from churchyards appears to centre upon the fifth to ninth centuries AD. Examples include Cannington in Somerset (Rahtz et al. 2000), Caer, Bayvil in Pembrokeshire (James 1987) and, from St Patrick's Isle, Peel on the Isle of Man (Freke 2002). While grave goods are rarely found in these burial rites (see chapter 2), great care and attention seem to have gone into the composition of the grave structures.

The long-cist cemeteries of southern and central Scotland have produced detailed evidence of the construction sequence of building cists and placing the body within them (e.g. Henshall 1955–6; Cowie 1978). For example, by discussing the 111 early medieval graves excavated at Thornybank, Lothian (Rees 2002), it is possible to identify ways in which such structures may have influenced the manner of commemoration. Radiocarbon dates from selected graves suggest the cemetery was in use throughout the sixth century AD, although the exact duration of cemetery use is unknown. A range of different grave structures was recognised at Thornybank, including dug graves, log-coffin graves, square-ditch/enclosed graves, pebble-lined graves and a four-posted burial, although the vast majority of burials uncovered were long-cist graves repeatedly composed in the following manner:

1 A pit was dug about 10 per cent wider than the cist to be created.
2 Upright side and end slabs were placed and chocked by numerous small rounded pebbles between grave cut and slabs.

3 The corpse was interred, probably wrapped in a shroud.
4 A lintel slab or slabs were laid across the tops of the upright slabs.
5 The cist was back-filled.

At Hallowhill in Fife (Proudfoot 1996), the excavators discussed the sequence of cist-building, and in some cases the construction is more complex. The site produced 145 burials, 122 of which were from long-cists. It was estimated that these graves represent between one-third and a half of the total original area of the long-cist cemetery. The remainder were either earth-dug graves (ten examples) or boulder-edged graves (thirteen examples). The dug and boulder graves concentrated on the south-west side of the site and included a high number of children and juveniles. This may not be the whole picture, since earth-dug graves are likely to be overlooked: they are much more difficult to recognise during excavation than the more elaborate cist-burials. Consequently, even if cist-burial was not a 'normative' rite, it was a repeated and common custom for those using the Hallowhill cemetery (fig. 4.9). The sequence of actions used in constructing the grave informs us about the effort and subsequent significance of ensuring the protection of the body in death. In the better-preserved graves, the following sequence could be identified:

1 A pit was excavated, wider than the planned cist.
2 The western-end stone and north-west side stone were first inserted. This is clear from the lack of packing stone at the western end of the grave.
3 Next, the south-west side stone was added.
4 The remaining stones were then inserted around the cist.
5 The last stone added was the eastern-end stone.
6 The body was then laid in the grave, possibly wrapped within a shroud.
7 Finally, the lintel slab or slabs were laid across the tops of the upright slabs.
8 The grave was back-filled.

These sequences are clearly practical ones; it would be difficult to construct a cist in alternative ways. Undoubtedly, there are other phases to the sequence that elude the archaeologist; we do not know the duration of each event or the intervals between them, and neither can we be sure of the possibility of there having been rituals surrounding the grave construction. The care and preparation taken to line the graves, however, is far from being a practical necessity, a fact underlined by the instances of earth-dug graves found on the same sites. The shape of cists is sometimes deliberately arranged in an attempt to evoke the shape of the body – an element of design that may not be motivated purely by functionality (Henshall 1955–6). Furthermore, the selection of materials for cists may have held significance. For instance, at the Catstane in Lothian, three different types of cist were employed: those made of shale, those of shale and sandstone, and those exclusively of sandstone (Cowie 1978: 182–3). The shale graves formed a clear group within the cemetery. Similarly, at Hallowhill in Fife, red sandstone was the most commonly employed material for cists, but in some cases white sandstone and mudstone were also employed. At Thornybank (Rees 2002), river-borne stones were employed, usually sandstone with stones of

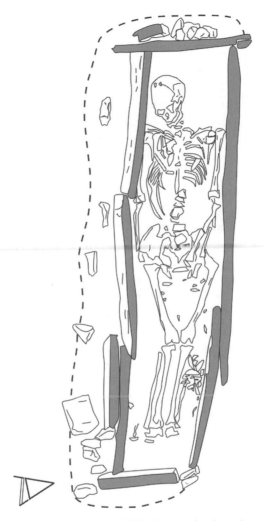

Figure 4.9   Plan of a cist-grave from Hallowhill, Fife (redrawn by the author after Proudfoot 1996).

yellow and red. The reuse of Roman material, possibly from a bathhouse, was also identified in graves 7, 10 and 64. There are instances where quern-stones are used as capstones, as found in cist 88 at Parkburn (Henshall 1955–6: 256). The utilisation of these different types of stone of different origins may have been expedient, but there remains the possibility that, with detailed research and the recording of stone-types by archaeologists, patterns might be identified suggesting the deliberate choice of certain sizes, shapes, colours and provenances of stone. In particular, the propensity for the use of white quartz is well recognised throughout northern and western Britain, both as an element of grave structure and as grave goods. For example, G. F. Bigelow's report on two kerbed cairns from Sandwick, Unst, Shetland, recognises the selection of fist-sized beach pebbles, many white quartzite, over much of the cairns (Bigelow 1984: 115).

While there has been an inevitable bias towards the discussion of furnished buri-als from southern and eastern England, these last examples serve to emphasise the symbolic and mnemonic importance of grave structures in containing and conceal-ing the dead within the grave. It is even possible that the selection of the colours, textures and shapes of the stones used to 'frame' the dead, as well as the sequence of interment, may have been an important element in the display of the dead. At the very least, the limited provision of grave goods over much of northern and western Britain does not appear to indicate a lack of concern for the grave as a context and its role in commemorating the dead.

Conclusion: the grave as mnemonic context and sequence

This chapter has addressed some of the varied grave structures found in early medieval burials. Complementing the discussion of grave goods in the last chap-ter, we have seen how the body, artefacts and the grave structure itself interacted in sequences of display and concealment. This theme has been shown to operate in different ways in different graves, from the inhumation rites of the sixth century at Snape, to the late sixth- and early seventh-century ship and chamber graves from Sutton Hoo. By way of contrast, we have considered how cist-burials operated in a different way, focusing upon the protection and enclosure of an already wrapped cadaver (see chapter 3). By considering the sequence of display and concealment in early medieval mortuary practices, we are better positioned to understand the 'scene-making' qualities of furnished and unfurnished burial rites, and the different ways in which images of the dead were manipulated to create memorable sensory engagements for the mourners. It is now necessary to move on to consider the role of monuments in early medieval mortuary commemoration.

5

Monuments and memory

Introduction – theorising monuments

Early medieval archaeologists encounter many different types of monument. Some can be described as 'mortuary' in character on account of their contextual association with the remains of the dead, others can be identifiable as commemorative of the dead on account of their form and inscriptions, even when their original loca tions and association with human remains and graves cannot be verified or were never the original intention. Further examples have mortuary and commemorative associations as only an element of their significance and function. In this chapter we shall focus upon the significance for remembering and forgetting in early medieval monumentality by looking at a series of themes rather than attempting to explore the full range of monumental forms. In particular, the discussion will focus upon the different ways in which cairns and burial mounds served to commemorate the dead. Consideration of churches, domestic architecture, and inscribed and sculpted stone monuments (including shrines, grave covers, slabs and free-standing crosses) receive limited attention here, as they will be addressed in future research by the author (see Williams, in prep.).

As with grave goods, so archaeologists have approached monuments as a means of charting early medieval migrating peoples, ideas and religious beliefs. More recently, mortuary monuments have been considered in social terms, regarded consecutively as reflections of social organisation and social differentiation (e.g. Shephard 1979), as evidence of social stress and competition in society (e.g. Arnold 1982b), and in terms of shifting ideological statements of domination and resistance (for a review, see Carver 2001; 2002). However, the precise roles of monuments in constructing social memories by creating links between the past, the present and the future and in constituting the dead have received limited attention in contrast to the consideration of these issues in prehistoric archaeology (e.g. Bradley 1998b; 2002).

Monuments can commemorate the dead in many ways, yet a common theme is that monuments are always about selective remembrance, embodying both remembering and forgetting, and that they connected retrospective pasts with prospective futures (Holtorf 1996). A single monument can commemorate a single dead person, but this is only one relationship possible, and rarely is it likely to be that simple. Even when covering a single grave, monuments can serve as nodes in complex relationships between different groups among the living, the dead person and the broader concepts of ancestors (e.g. Hope 1997). It is certainly the case that monuments can mark the end of obsequies and be raised over single graves, allowing the mourners to return to the world of the living and for the dead to be provided with a new identity as an ancestor. In other instances, monuments can be raised over collective graves, or over time attract subsequent burials and therefore commemorate the corporate or collective dead (see Bloch & Parry 1982).

Monuments can both inscribe and incorporate memories (see Connerton 1989). Images and text can be inscribed upon monuments, and their form, content and the manner of their juxtaposition can serve to promote memories of the dead and the past in particular ways (see Barrett 1993; Hope 2003). The materiality and placing of a monument can itself be commemorative, including the substances and materials used in its composition, its colour, form, decoration, size and shape. Monuments also evoke particular bodily dispositions and ritual performances, and as such can be seen as 'fields of discourse' (Barrett 1994). They can create environments for the embodiment of experiential memories, including distinctive tastes (i.e. through feasting; see Hamilakis 1998), specific acoustic effects (Watson & Keating 1999), the management of particular aromas (see Kus 1992) and even textures (Cummings 2002), all of which can mediate commemoration in mortuary and ancestral rites.

Through their multi-media and multi-sensuous character and materiality, monuments selectively inscribe memories onto place and incorporate them into the bodies of ritual participants (see Connerton 1989; see also Hope 2003; Williams 2001a). Even the biographies of monuments affect their roles in remembering and forgetting, because after their initial creation, monuments endure and can take on different meanings and commemorative roles over time (see Holtorf 1996; 1997; 1998; Moreland 1999). This can apply to monuments in ruinous states, and even when they are deliberately fragmented or destroyed (Verdery 1999). In some societies, it is the case that monuments are made for brief displays before destruction and fragmentation, and indeed their efficacy derives from the brevity of their existence (Küchler 1988; 1999; 2002).

This leads us to consider who is being remembered, and by whom. Monuments were not set up by everyone or everywhere in the early medieval period. Moreover, they are rarely set up to commemorate individuals in the early medieval world. If they are, they inevitably commemorate others, whether directly or indirectly, including craftsmen, family, social and political relationships, as well as ethnic and religious affiliations. In many cases monuments are raised over a number of burials or become the focus for sequences of mortuary rituals augmenting the monument over time. In such instances, it is a complex process to disentangle how monuments created and reproduced identities through linking past, present and future. It is also important to bear in mind that monuments can be concerned with conflict and multiple perspectives, rather than a single elite vision of authority and identity (Brück 2001).

In summary, monuments can operate in relation to social memory in many complex ways, influencing and interacting with ritual actions, embodying cosmologies and origin myths, and acting as thresholds to other worlds, the resting places of ancestors or places of repeated engagement between the living and the dead. In this sense, the mnemonic roles of monuments are closely bound up with their symbolic meanings, involvement in power relations and their experiential qualities. Yet their role in influencing the ways the past, present and future interact, their temporality and social memory, is a common theme linking monuments, including those built to last and those built to decay or be destroyed and transformed.

The variety of early medieval monuments

There is a startling variety in early medieval funerary monuments. The best-known are burial mounds or 'barrows'. These were first systematically investigated by the eighteenth-century antiquarian Bryan Faussett at a time when many survived as visible standing monuments before their destruction by agricultural and industrial improvements. Since then, few survive as earthworks, but rare instances can still be seen, notably the sixth-century cemetery at Greenwich Park (Struth & Eagles 1999), the early seventh-century barrow cemetery at Sutton Hoo, Suffolk (Carver 1998a) and the late ninth-century 'Viking' barrow cemetery at Heath Wood, Ingleby, Derbyshire (Richards et al. 1995; Richards 2004). Even in these instances, the earth-works have been severely denuded and much of the evidence lost. For example, the 'princely' burial mound at Taplow Court, Buckinghamshire (see chapter 6) has been substantially 'landscaped' in the post-medieval period as a viewing platform within the gardens of the stately home (Webster 1992; Williams 1999b). For an appre-ciation of the visual character of the largest early medieval burial mounds, we are forced to consider the reconstructed mound that now serves as the focal point of the Sutton Hoo Visitor Centre near Woodbridge in Suffolk (Carver 1998a; 2005; see fig. 5.8 below). However, even in this instance, we do not know whether structures and posts adorned the monument when originally raised, and much of the context within which the mound was raised is now lost to us.

Burial mounds were not restricted to the 'elites' of the seventh century. Cemetery excavations, particularly in Kent and adjacent regions, have often produced traces of annular and penannular ring-ditches. Classic examples were identified in the long-running cemetery of sixth- and seventh-century date from Finglesham in Kent (Hawkes 1982), and from the seventh- and early eighth-century burials at Polhill (Philp 1973) and Eastry (Philp & Keller 2002), both in Kent. Ring-ditches can vary considerably in scale and character and are often interpreted as the quarry ditches and perimeters of burial mounds. However, even this evidence is limited, because many different reconstructions are possible for these features, from quite modest to quite elaborate structures, as is reflected in discussions of the different possible reconstructions of the seventh-century ring-ditches at Orsett Cock, Essex (Hedges & Buckley 1985). There does, however, appear to be a prevalence of these fea-tures in seventh-century cemeteries, suggesting that the rise of monumental settings around graves is associated with the process of kingdom formation and conversion to Christianity (Shephard 1979).

Excavations of cemeteries reveal a range of other monuments and structures, including slots alongside graves and single posts interpreted as grave markers (Hamerow 1993a; Hogarth 1973). In contrast to the large burial mounds, such as those surviving at Sutton Hoo and Taplow, it appears that many more graves were covered by burial mounds of a much more modest size. At Appledown in Sussex, a late fifth- and sixth-century cemetery revealed circular ring-ditches but also a series of square four-post structures associated with cremated human remains and interpreted as 'mortuary houses' within which ashes were stored and displayed (Down & Welch 1990). Some cremation cemeteries have produced evidence of lines of posts, such as at Baston in Lincolnshire (Mayes & Dean 1976) and Portway Andover, Hampshire (Cook & Dacre 1985). Almost every cemetery produces some form of grave monument, but in many cases we simply are not sure whether post-holes were contemporaneous with each other. Nor can we assume that the absence of evidence is really evidence of the absence of funerary monuments. For example, burial mounds can be raised by quarrying ring-ditches, but they can equally well be constructed by cutting turfs or by scraping material from a wide area. Consequently, in the absence of a surviving earthwork some funerary monuments will have left no trace. We therefore have little direct idea of the full range of above-ground monuments that may have been present in an early medieval cemetery, but we can say that in many cemeteries a range of monument types was visible.

A further category of structure that might have held funerary and commemorative functions is that of a series of square enclosures defined by John Blair as pagan temples (Blair 1995; see also Hope-Taylor 1977). Although the dating and function of these features remain ambiguous, in many cases they form a further type of structure and could be associated with early medieval cemeteries and could have served a range of functions in ritual practices, including a focus of communal memory.

Moving beyond Anglo-Saxon England, we find a comparable variety of monuments, including posts, ledges, ring-ditches and 'mortuary houses'. To take one example: an early medieval cemetery excavated at Thornybank near Dalkeith consisted of over 100 lintel- and earth-graves. Two of the latter type were surrounded by rectangular ditched enclosures (61 and 114), while another (62) was surrounded by four post-holes, suggesting that some form of canopy adorned the grave. A similar form of structure was identified at Kenn in Devon, showing the broad geographical span of these discoveries (Weddell 2000). Possible burial mounds can also be identified from St Materiana's churchyard at Tintagel (Petts 2000: 94–5) and at Four Crosses, Llandysilio (Warrilow et al. 1986), where a series of early medieval graves focused on the south-west side of a Bronze Age cairn. In addition, David Petts (2000: 95) argues that a smaller ring-ditch close to the probable early medieval graves, itself containing a single west–east-orientated grave, may also be an early medieval burial. If so, then we may be seeing the mimicking of prehistoric graves in a way comparable to cases identified in Anglo-Saxon regions (see chapter 6).

A variation on these monumental traditions is the cairns of different shapes and sizes, as well as square-ditched burial mounds, found in northern and eastern Scotland, as at Garbeg and Whitebridge (Stevenson 1984; MacLagan Wedderburn & Grime 1984; fig. 5.1). Western and northern Britain also have traditions of inscribed stones, from early cross-inscribed stones and stones inscribed in Latin or ogham to Pictish symbol stones. While the function of these monuments may

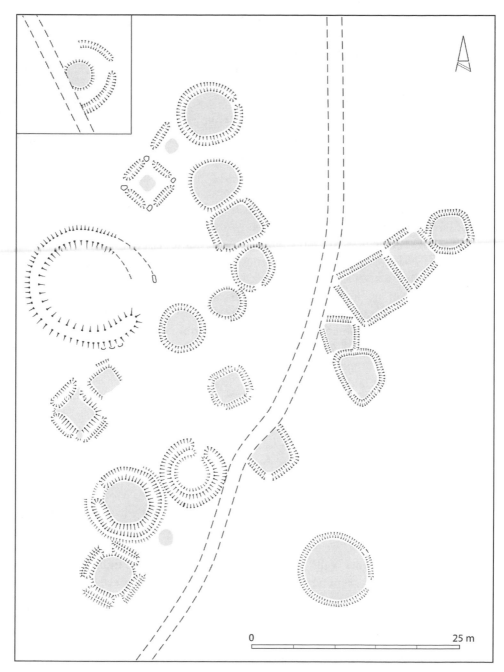

Figure 5.1 Plan of the cairn cemetery at Garbeg near Inverness (adapted by Séan Goddard after Mac-Lagan Wedderburn & Grime 1984; reproduced with the kind permission of Historic Scotland).

have been diverse, the commemoration of the dead and an association with graves can be attested in at least some examples. We shall hold back from a detailed discussion of inscribed and sculpted stones, as commemorative monuments must be left to future research, but these are also important elements of mortuary commemoration that take a variety of different forms across the British Isles, from Ireland (Edwards 1990: 161–71), Scotland (Driscoll 2000; Henderson & Henderson 2004) and Wales (Edwards 2001; Nash-Williams 1950) to Man (Cubbon 1971) and England (Bailey 1991). Yet the evidence presented so far is enough to illustrate the wide variability in monuments placed over the graves of the early medieval dead. Although the multi-period and overlapping stratigraphy of churchyards often obscures the presence of monuments, early monastic cemeteries like Whithorn (Hill 1997) and cemeteries from emporia such as Ipswich and Hamwic contain evidence of the continuation of funerary monumentality (Lucy & Reynolds 2002).

Moreover, architecture itself can serve to commemorate in a variety of ways, whether it is through the ceremonial life operating in and around large early medieval halls, such as those uncovered at Yeavering (Hope Taylor 1977), or within the complex architectural environments of churches and crypts (Gem 1983). As we have already seen, the adoption of churchyard burial did not decrease the range of possible monuments. As well as the church itself, grave slabs, grave covers and grave stones are likely to have adorned churchyards and the interiors of churches in much higher proportions than the fragmentary remains might suggest (e.g. Boddington 1996; see chapter 3).

Monuments as commemorative foci

Both in early medieval field cemeteries and in those surrounding churches, monuments could provide a focus for repeated burial activity. As such, they may have served to commemorate particular individuals, but they also served in the collective commemoration of the community of the dead. Most discussions of this evidence have focused upon Anglo-Saxon burial mounds (e.g. Carver 2001; 2002), so this section will deliberately focus upon some monuments within early medieval cemeteries from Wales (see James 1992; Knight 2003). The evidence serves to demonstrate how monuments could serve to mark and memorialise individual burials while simultaneously providing a focus and context for repeated acts of commemoration through the accumulation of subsequent burials and other ritual activity.

Capel Eithin, Anglesey

The early medieval cemetery at Capel Eithin on Anglesey is one of the most extensively excavated 'early Christian' cemeteries from western Britain. Excavations by Gwynedd Archaeological Trust revealed a cemetery of west–east graves, many in cists (fig. 5.2). Human remains were poorly preserved, but in total 102 features were identified that were of a size, shape, orientation and internal composition to suggest that they were graves (White & Smith 1999: 128). The graves focused upon

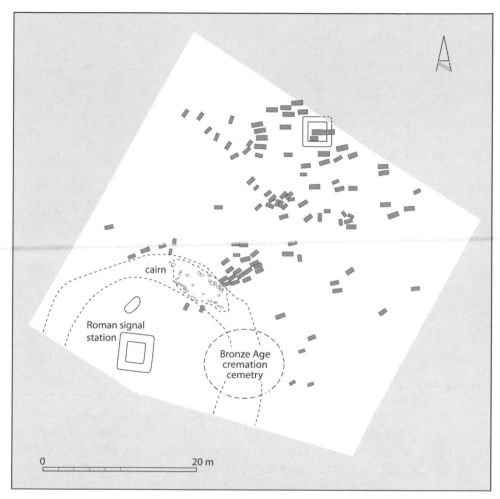

Figure 5.2 Plan of the early medieval cemetery of Capel Eithin, Anglesey (adapted by Séan Goddard after White & Smith 1999; reproduced with the kind permission of Gwynedd Archaeological Trust).

one rectangular structure that not only seems to have been an important monument marking a 'special grave', but also to have operated as a focus for subsequent burials (fig. 5.3). The structure consisted of a rectangular trench with straight sides and a flat bottom. On the northern side were traces of organic remains within the trench that may have been the remains of a wooden beam, while a scatter of stones of a type that had to be imported from 8km to the north was found within the southern trench. One possible interpretation is that a wooden structure of logs, planks or even wattle was supported by the trench, with the stone used as packing for the footings (White & Smith 1999: 136). The structure had a narrow eastern entrance the size of a doorway, 0.8m across, and a thin layer of clay provided a floor surface. It is thought to have been a roofed structure rising from the clay floor and accessed from the eastern doorway.

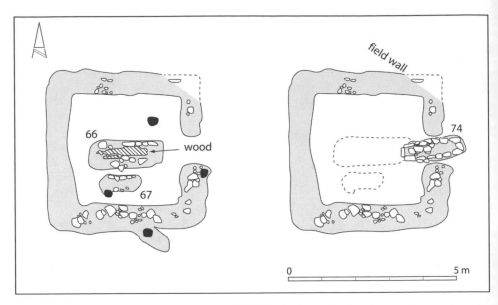

Figure 5.3 Plan of the 'special grave' at Capel Eithin, Anglesey showing the two phases of use: the construction of the mortuary 'house' and insertion of two graves (left) and the subsequent addition of a third grave (right) (adapted by Séan Goddard after White & Smith 1999; reproduced with the kind permission of Gwynedd Archaeological Trust).

The structure enclosed three graves. Grave 66 was placed centrally within the enclosure, lined with stones in a manner comparable to many other graves from the cemetery. Of the two instances with substantial traces of organic remains, one was grave 66 (White & Smith 1999: 130). The stain was shorter than the grave, suggesting that a grave structure or plank rather than a coffin covered the body.

Two further graves were associated with the Capel Eithin structure. Grave 67 was placed within the enclosure to the south of grave 66 and, to judge from its small size, may have contained the body of an infant or young child. Both graves 66 and 67 were subsequently covered by the clay floor surface, suggesting that they were integral to the earlier phases of the enclosure's use. At a later date, a cist-grave was added to the doorway area of the structure, cutting the top of grave 66 but seemingly respecting its location and that of the still-standing 'mortuary house'. Perhaps the aim was to 'seal' the doorway with the new grave and prevent further access to graves 66 and 67. In any case, the structure served as a focus for one of the three main burial clusters in the cemetery. These graves had the largest grave dimensions and contained the most frequent use of complete cist-graves from the site, hinting at the possibility that this was a preferential burial site for a higher-status group (White & Smith 1999: 140).

The interpretation of such structures as a *cella memoriae* – a memorial cell raised over the grave of a 'saint' or secular leader – was seen by the excavator to be likely, with the proviso that the lack of artefactual evidence suggested that it was not used for any length of time (White & Smith 1999: 158). However, if the structure was repeatedly cleaned and its structure repaired, the ephemeral ground-level remains may still represent an enduring structure used for years or even decades. Following the lead of Nancy Edwards (2002), we should be wary of seeing these as necessarily the graves of 'saints' or members of the religious hierarchy in early medieval Wales, because they may equally well have marked the graves of those with a special secular status. Moreover, just because in later centuries these graves may have become the focus of special attention, this need not reflect the accurate transmission of memories concerning their original occupants. Whoever their occupants were, the structure fits with other mausolea and *cellae memoriae* known from the late antique Mediterranean, western Europe and other instances identified in early medieval western and northern Britain (Petts 2004). The structure facilitated commemoration by providing continual access to the grave and subsequently attracting further graves. Although we cannot be sure whether this was the first burial at the site or one constructed later in the cemetery's history of use, it is evident that it formed part of a cluster of graves, suggesting that the location had a special importance for the community long after the initial burial.

Further evidence for the significance of the site comes from an early Christian inscribed stone. Edwards accepts that many of Nash-Williams' Class I inscribed stones were originally funerary monuments; even if not raised over graves they were certainly, in part, commemorating (mainly male) ancestors (Edwards 2002). Capel Eithin was associated with such an inscribed stone, now lost but recorded in a manuscript of c.1698. The excavators even speculate that the stone may have come from the area of the excavated cemetery, perhaps set into one of the stone-packed pits identified during excavation. The Latin inscription reads DEVORIGI, a Celtic name that Patrick Sims-Williams ascribes to the sixth or possibly the seventh century AD. An inscribed memorial stone was also found associated with the early medieval cemetery at Arfryn, Bodedern (also on Anglesey), forming the lintel of a grave. By analogy, the cemetery may have focused on a number of graves commemorating high-status individuals whose remembrance, enhanced both by inscribed stones and memorial cells, encouraged the continued use of the site for burial over a number of centuries.

Plas Gogerddan, Ceredigion

A second Welsh site provides evidence of related rectangular structures surrounding early medieval graves. At Plas Gogerddan in the Afon Clarach valley north-east of Aberystwyth, excavations focused on a Bronze Age ritual complex, including round barrows and standing stones that subsequently received burials in the late Iron Age. The excavations also revealed evidence of an early medieval cemetery of west–east alignment and arranged in rows (fig. 5.4). Nine graves produced surviving coffin soil-stains, but little human bone survived in the soil conditions. The site was broadly dated to between the third and seventh centuries AD on the basis of a single radiocarbon date (Murphy 1992: 15–17).

At Plas Gogerddan, three rectangular structures were identified, the best preserved of which (structure 373) consisted of a rectangular foundation trench with an opening at the eastern end bounded by two post-holes (fig. 5.5). Within the enclosure was a central grave, but also a stone-lined pit. The dark soil-stain, hinting at the presence

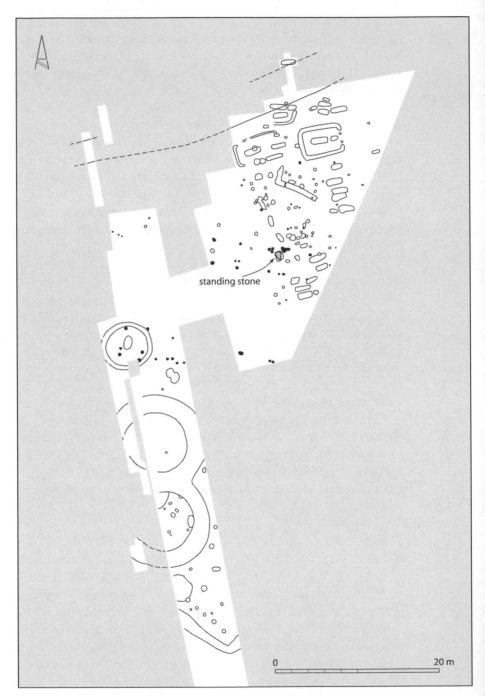

standing stone

Figure 5.4   Plan of the early medieval cemetery to the north-east of a series of Bronze Age burial mounds at Plas Gogerddan, Ceredigion (adapted by Séan Goddard after Murphy 1992; reproduced with the kind permission of Cambria Archaeology and the Royal Archaeological Institute).

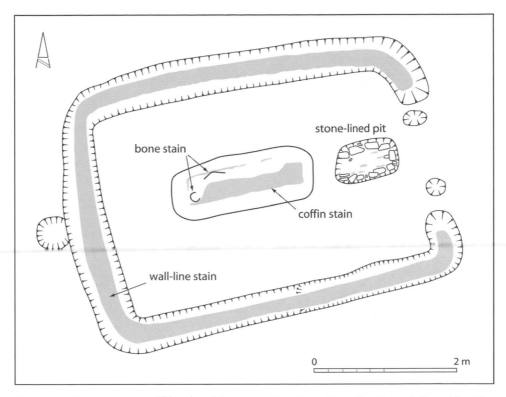

Figure 5.5 Plan of structure 373, a 'special grave' at Plas Gogerddan, Ceredigion (adapted by Séan Goddard after Murphy 1992; reproduced with the kind permission of Cambria Archaeology and the Royal Archaeological Institute).

of decayed timbers, ran throughout the trench. As at Capel Eithin, we may be seeing here evidence for a timber structure supported by the trench. At the eastern end was a gap, 1.8m wide, with two small post-holes set 1m apart, creating a narrower aperture for entering the structure. The excavators argue that the stone-lined pit, being aligned on the grave and surrounding structure, was an integral part of the funerary ritual. One suggestion arising from the excavations is that a wooden box or comparable organic container had been placed in the pit, perhaps as a grave good or offering; certainly phosphate analysis confirmed that no body was ever inhumed in it. As with Capel Eithin, it appears that the unenclosed burials cluster around the structures, hinting that they formed commemorative foci both for funerals and other ritual events.

Tandderwen, Clwyd
A different form of monument was identified during excavations at Tandderwen in the Ystrad valley of north Wales (Brassil et al. 1991). Aerial photographs revealed a series of square ditched structures that upon excavation were shown to enclose graves of early medieval date focusing upon a large ring-ditch, the surviving traces of a Bronze Age barrow (fig. 5.6). The site incorporated a mixture of monument

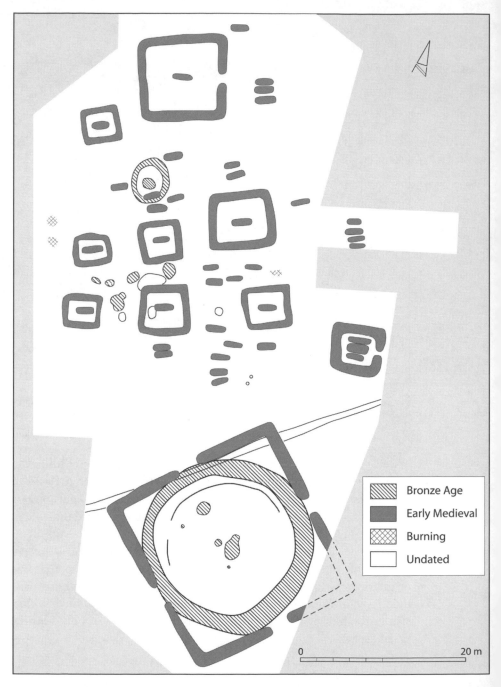

Figure 5.6   Plan of the early medieval cemetery at Tandderwen, Clwyd (adapted by Séan Goddard after Brassil et al. 1991; reproduced with the kind permission of the Royal Archaeological Institute).

reuse and monument-building as an integral part of the funerary rituals. The Bronze Age round barrow was enclosed by an enigmatic rectangular structure on the southern edge of the excavated area. The structure consisted of a four-entranced square enclosure encircling the prehistoric burial mound. The entrances were positioned half-way around each side, marked by rounded butt-ends to the ditches. This feature was excavated after a prolonged silting of the Bronze Age ditches, and an early medieval date is not unreasonable but cannot be proved (Brassil et al. 1991: 61–2). Whether this was a trench for an above-ground fence or earthen bank, or simply a way of demarcating and respecting the earlier monument, is not clear. Yet it does represent a renewed interest in the ancient monument as a focus for ceremony and ritual connected to the graves. It may even represent the deliberate choice to appropriate an old structure that may have been invested with supernatural or ancestral associations in a fashion that would not have been regarded as appropriate for a new cairn or mound. It is even possible that the barrow itself was remodelled and reused by early medieval burials that have left no trace as the burial mound was eroded by subsequent centuries of weather and farming activities. At the very least, the excavation plan clearly suggests that the ditch or mound of the original barrow was still visible in the early medieval period, and the cluster of graves to the north suggests that it provided a commemorative focus for the cemetery (see chapter 7).

The cemetery itself lay (as just stated) north of this monument, consisting of thirty-nine west–east oriented graves, some placed in rows and groups of between two and six graves. Any human remains had been completely destroyed by the soil conditions. Traces of wood from twenty-two graves suggest the former presence of coffins of some kind. Individually or collectively, many of these graves could have originally had above-ground monuments raised over them, but no evidence survived. However, interspersed between these groups were six graves surrounded by square ditches. In two further instances (28 and 574), the line of the enclosure ditches was broken half-way along its eastern side in a way comparable to the 'special graves' identified at Plas Gogerddan and Capel Eithin and discussed above. In one of these cases (28), the enclosure was of a substantial size, demarcating a sizeable space 9m by 8.5m around the grave (Brassil et al. 1991: 64). Rather than representing the footings of small buildings, it is more likely that these ditches marked the inside of an outer bank, or perhaps most probably, an internal mound. The excavator notes that the thickest ditch was associated with the only structure containing three graves (574). One scenario is that the mound was reconstituted after the second and third interments by recutting the ditch and throwing up a new mound on each occasion. The evidence hints at a succession of mortuary events, each connected to mound-building episodes, leading to augmentation of the monument (Brassil et al. 1991: 64).

Discussion
These examples suffice to illustrate the fact that the role of monuments in early medieval cemeteries could extend beyond the simplistic function of covering and

marking individual graves to commemorating groups of graves: mounds might be augmented with subsequent burials and other graves, and might consequently provide architectural settings for ancestral and commemorative rites. In the case of the inscribed stone from Capel Eithin and the enclosures for all the three sites discussed, it is possible that they provided a common focus for the cemeteries. As such, we can envisage their role as material foci for commemorative ceremonies for the communities using the sites. We have also introduced the reuse of prehistoric monuments as a way of enhancing the communal commemorative significance of cemeteries. In the case of Tandderwen, a prehistoric mound was elaborated to provide an ancient focus for the cemetery. In other cases, ancient monuments served as enclosures for cemeteries (e.g. James 1987). All these locations served to connect the past and the dead with the living communities that used the cemetery. In early medieval western Britain 'field cemeteries' were probably the norm throughout the period. Inscribed stones, grave houses and mounds appear to have been foci for commemorating high-status or 'special' individuals, but in doing so they also served as communal foci for the commemoration of kin, ancestry and group identity.

Monumental genealogies

Having explored the roles of monuments as foci for graves, let us look at how the placing of monuments in relation to each other served in the evolution of cemeteries. As a case study, we shall focus once again upon the late sixth- and early seventh-century barrow cemetery at Sutton Hoo. Since we have already considered the contents of mounds 1 and 17 (see chapter 4), our attention here turns to the cemetery as a whole as revealed through survey and excavation (Bruce-Mitford 1975; 1978; Bruce-Mitford & Care Evans 1983; Carver 1998a; 2005). A series of at least nineteen burial mounds stretched along a ridge to the east of the river Deben in south-east Suffolk. When excavated, most of the mounds were found to have been robbed, but enough can be reconstructed of the burial rites to suggest that we are dealing with a cemetery very different from the communal cemeteries of inhumations and cremations that preceded in the later fifth and sixth centuries in the region. The recent discovery of sixth-century cremation burials located within small ring-ditches during the construction of the National Trust Visitor Centre to the north of the known cemetery serves to cast new light on the development of the Sutton Hoo barrow tradition (Newman 2002). The rite clearly had local origins (*pace* Bruce-Mitford 1975; Carver 1986), but the scale of the exclusive burial plot chosen on the prominent ridge above the Deben took mound-building and the elaboration of mortuary theatre to new heights (Carver 2005; Williams 2001a). The site is in many ways exceptional: nowhere else can we demonstrate in Britain a 'dynastic' cemetery of multiple large burial mounds located in relation to each other. Whatever else can be said about the story of Sutton Hoo, memory was being manipulated here in a distinctive and exclusive way.

The variability of the burial rites performed at Sutton Hoo is its defining feature (fig. 5.7). There are wealthy cremation-burials associated with bronze vessels and (in one case) a bronze tray, richly furnished inhumation graves and two ship-burials,

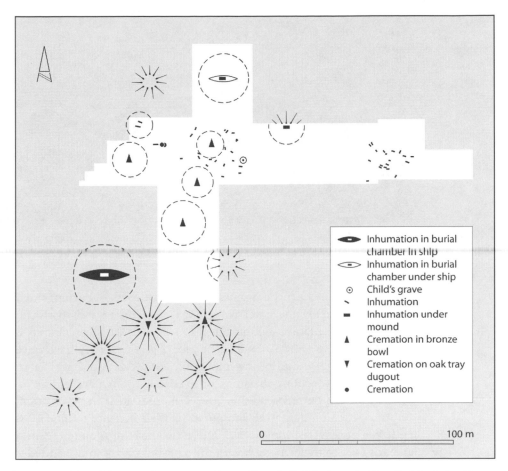

Figure 5.7   Plan of the mound-cemetery at Sutton Hoo, Suffolk (redrawn by Séan Goddard after Carver 2005).

all of which were surmounted by large burial mounds. We cannot assume the cremation burials were necessarily any poorer than the other graves, since by definition the ritual technology destroys many of the artefacts associated with earlier stages of the funeral, nor can we ascertain how unique the wealth in the mound 1 ship-burial really was, given that so many of the other graves have been looted. The chronology is also uncertain, although Martin Carver has hypothesised a possible sequence beginning with a central line of cremation burials and culminating in ship-burials 1 and 2 (Carver 1998a; Carver 2005: 311). However, the spatial organisation of the mounds, combined with the diversity of burial rites employed, has its own tale to tell about the evolving use of space and monumentality in social remembrance. It appears that in a very short period of time, mortuary practices were altering rapidly at Sutton Hoo, building upon existing traditions in distinctive ways. Yet the completion of each rich funeral with a sizeable mound was a common theme repeated throughout the use of the site.

Figure 5.8   Mound 2 at Sutton Hoo following reconstruction after excavation provides an impression of the monumental scale of the mound-building at the site (photo by the author).

The first element to be discussed is the linear spatial arrangement of the burial mounds, especially the core two groups of three mounds consisting of a central line of three cremation mound-burials (5, 6 and 7). This line may have continued to include mounds 3, 10 and 11 but for a gap that may have once contained an additional burial mound, now ploughed away. Mound 2 was later added to this line of mounds forming the spine of the cemetery. A parallel line of three mounds to the west can be recognised in the location of a further cremation mound-burial (mound 18), an inhumation and horse-sacrifice beneath mound 17 (see chapter 4), and the unexcavated mound 12. These two lines of mounds seem to have formed an early core to the cemetery, with the ship-burials mound 2 added to one line, and mound 1 to the other, as well as further mounds added to the east, such as 8, 9, 13 and 14 (Carver 1998a: 133–6).

A further observation is the surprising lack of intercutting and the broad spacing of the mounds, providing a very different sense of space from a 'normal' early medieval cemetery, in which graves may often respect each other but are located in close proximity. The mounds therefore created a distinct sense of space as well as providing individual monuments over single graves (fig. 5.8). With the exception of the satellite burials around mound 5 that appear to be later execution graves, the mounds appear to show no signs of reopening or the addition of secondary graves; these were exclusive monuments intended to commemorate individuals rather than groups.

A connected theme concerns the relative parity in the sizes of the mounds, despite the variability in the provision of the artefacts, structures and mortuary technologies they covered. It seems that each additional mound replicated the overall form of its predecessors. In other words, with each new mound mnemonic references were being constructed with earlier graves.

Moreover, individually and collectively the mounds would have stood in contrast to the scale of mound-building previously conducted in the early medieval period in the region. The only monuments of comparable size on which the mounds could have been modelled were prehistoric monuments (Carver 1998a). Consequently, while there is no categorical evidence for 'monument reuse' at Sutton Hoo, in scale, location and appearance the mounds may have been deliberately evoking associations with prehistoric barrow cemeteries in the environs.

Sutton Hoo was a restricted burial zone within which sizeable burial mounds were placed in cumulative relationship with existing graves. Each burial respected the location of earlier mounds, and each seems to represent a single funeral event: the mounds covered only single interments, by inhumation within chambers, or in association with ships, or by cremation within high-status containers such as bronze bowls. In combination, these elements seem to create a tension between the idiosyncrasy of the individual burial rites conducted and the apparent parity in the size and shape of the burial mounds raised over the graves. Admittedly, this similarity is not exact, and some mounds are considerably larger than others, but the similarity may be partly illusory because of over a millennium of denudation and the disappearance of any posts or structures raised on top of the burial mounds. However, the impression is one of each burial rite creating overt distinctions from and elaboration upon earlier ones in terms of the precise burial rite, but also adopting a symbolic emulation of earlier mounds in terms of the final form of the monuments. For those participating in the burial rite, the sequence of rituals led from the idiosyncratic and distinctive increasingly towards similarity as the corpse, objects and grave structures were covered over and incorporated into the hearts of the burial mounds, which very quickly (within a few years) would have come to resemble those that went before. In terms of social memory, we must consider the rituals as serving to create an ordered and coherent physical marker and to connect them genealogically to earlier mounds.

Interpretations of the site and the burial rites at Sutton Hoo have varied considerably over the years, focusing on the nature of the cultural influences and religious beliefs, as well as on attempts to ascribe named historical personages to individual burial mounds. Carver has suggested a broad context for the graves not only as symbols of status and claims over territory, but also as political statements of pagan independence by an incipient royal dynasty threatened by Merovingian and Kentish political hegemony (Carver 1992; 1995; 1998a). In this light, the attempt to create a monumental genealogy may have been the primary concern: a means of connecting past and present through the rapid innovation of elaborate mortuary practices, and the interment of the dead in a clear spatial relationship with earlier graves and monuments (see also Bradley 1987; Halsall 2001; Williams 1997; 1998). Whether this genealogy was a reality or no more than an aspiration, and whether (and how far) the social order and connections between past and present were a fiction or a reality, we cannot guess. But the mounds at Sutton Hoo were more than a collection of their individual parts: they were a chain of monumental episodes intended to create social memories and relations between past and present. Indeed, this may have been what made Sutton Hoo unique and perhaps successful as a monumental endeavour: not simply the elaborate furnishing of each funeral, but the way that those organising the funeral made careful references to past funerary events as the site evolved. Such an attempt at monumental genealogy at Sutton Hoo may reflect a conception of the past that is lacking at other sites, even in the other seventh-century furnished mound-burials, because they were located in relative isolation in the landscape (Webster 1992; Williams 1999b).

Having discussed the roles of monuments as foci and their relationship to each other, let us now look more precisely at the relationship symbolism of monument construction and the connection between monuments. We can combine these themes and explore more precisely the meaning of monuments with reference to early medieval cemeteries in eastern Scotland.

Monuments and symbols

The Pictish symbol stones of northern and eastern Scotland have long been a focus of fascination for archaeologists, and the symbols have over the years received many different types of interpretation (e.g. Thomas 1963; see Henderson & Henderson 2004). The classic tripartite division of the monuments into Classes I, II and III was established by Allen and Anderson (1903a and b). They defined Class I monuments as unsculpted or unworked stones with symbols along one side only, Class II monuments as sculpted stones with symbols on one side and crosses on the other, and, finally, Class III monuments as sculpted crosses with no or subsidiary Pictish symbols. Few would deny that chronology has some role in the distinction between these three types, although the relative and precise dating of these monuments remains disputed. Currently, researchers appear to concur that Class I stones are the earliest and could date from as early as the sixth and seventh centuries. Class II monuments may date from the eighth century onwards, and Class III monuments from the ninth century (Henderson & Henderson 2004). The symbols on Class I monuments are extremely varied, including animals, artefacts and abstract symbols (Allen & Anderson 1903a). These have been considered symbols of clans, lineages or rank, or records of marriage alliances (see Foster 1996). Most recently, Pictish symbols have been interpreted as a form of writing – in which pairs of symbols represent bisyllabic personal names (Forsyth 1997; Samson 1992; Carver 2004). All these interpretations can, in part, be connected to their roles in commemorating the dead in a visual and public way, forming one variant upon the widespread use of inscribed and sculpted stones found across northern Europe and Scandinavia in the later first millennium AD (e.g. Andrén 1993; Carver 1998b). Therefore, while the precise interpretation of the symbols continues to be obscure, it is evident that their possible significance as statements of identity, allegiance and authority can be suggested (Driscoll 1988; 2000; Henderson & Henderson 2004).

Class I symbol stones in particular have been interpreted as primarily funerary in function and context. This has always been difficult to demonstrate with security, because very few Class I symbol stones have been securely identified *in situ* in relation to graves (Ashmore 1980; Close-Brooks 1978–80: 335). Certainly it cannot be said that all Class 1 Pictish symbol stones had a funerary context, or that all Pictish burial sites had symbol stones associated with them. However, of the twelve sites identified by Patrick Ashmore (1980) as being of early medieval date/type with low cairns and long-cists, five were associated with symbol stones. For example, at the cemetery of Garbeg, Drumnadrochit, twenty-one low cairns were excavated, and fragments of a Class 1 symbol stone were found near the top of a circular mound (Ashmore 1980: 347; Close-Brooks 1984; MacLagan Wedderburn & Grime 1984). Similarly, a Class 1 symbol stone fragment was found at the head of a cist-burial associated with rectangular cairns and one circular cairn at Ackergill, Caithness (Ashmore 1980: 348). Five Class I stones discovered at Tillytarmont near Rothiemay were also associated with cairns (Ashmore 1980; see also Gourley 1984). Let us take one instance of this relationship that suggests a possible connection between symbol stones and the commemoration of the dead.

A cairn and symbol stone at Dunrobin
A rare example of a Class I symbol stone found in association with a burial was excavated in the Dairy Park near Dunrobin Castle near Golspie (Close-Brooks 1978–80; fig. 5.9). The area was a coastal strip of land about 6m above sea level. Two other symbol stones are known from nearby, both associated with cists and both laid over them, suggesting that they either served as horizontal grave slabs or vertical grave memorials. The first was a nineteenth-century discovery of a symbol stone used as the capstone to a cist containing two skeletons of adult men and an iron artefact. In the 1940s, a second stone was found over another cist, although it is unclear whether it served as the capstone. The evidence suggests that along the coastal plain at Dunrobin was either one dispersed burial ground or a series of discrete burial zones, in which some graves were monumentalised by having symbol stones raised over them, or by being sealed with them. Close-Brooks (1984) argued for a possible association with a fortified, high-status early medieval site that may have been located beneath Dunrobin Castle.

In 1977 the new symbol stone was found in association with a cairn containing a long-cist. The cairn was rectangular, 0.3m in height and 9.5m by 7m in extent. At the centre of the cairn was a long-cist of sandstone slabs dug into the natural subsoil and containing an extended adult female inhumation orientated with her head to the west. Radiocarbon dating of the skeleton suggested a sixth- or seventh-century AD date for the interment. The structure of the monument may have involved the clearing of turfs to expose the sand, followed by the construction of a layer of pebbles bounded by a kerb of sandstone boulders, probably obtained from the nearby beach. The original height (and hence the scale) of the monument cannot be easily reconstructed, since stone-robbing and erosion seem to have severely dilapidated it. The excavator believed that, unlike a burial mound, this cairn (as with many Pictish monuments) was never a particularly high and impressive monument. Instead it may have been a 'low cairn' of perhaps only half a metre in height (Ashmore 1980; Close-Brooks 1978–80; 1984). If this is the case, then the monuments were intended to create a zone that passers-by and those conducting ceremonies could overlook. They may have also provided a platform upon which rituals could be performed,

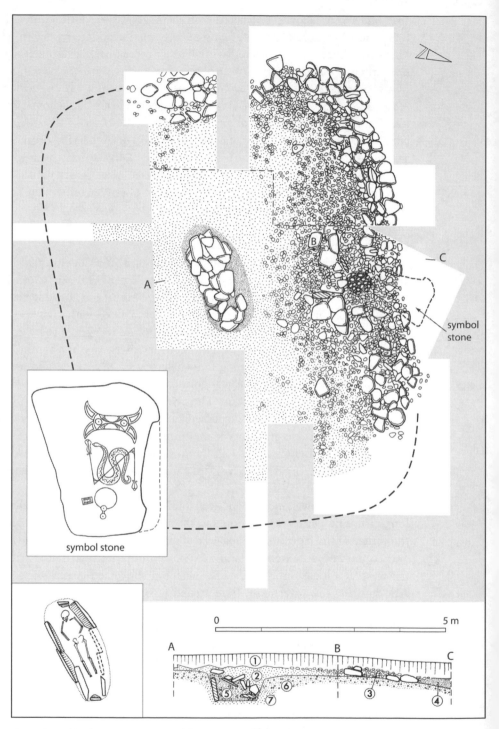

Figure 5.9   The Pictish cairn from the Dairy Park, Dunrobin associated with a symbol stone and covering an extended, supine adult female skeleton (adapted by Séan Goddard after Close-Brooks 1980; reproduced with the kind permission of J. Close-Brooks).

rather than a barrow that would seal a grave beneath a steep, upstanding monument. Although it was not possible to define the exact position of the symbol stone, which may have been moved by the plough, the excavator suggested that the stone was originally erected vertically on top of the cairn or placed vertically at its northern edge. The latter scenario is supported by the discovery of five stones placed in a west–east line that may have provided a platform upon which the stone had been placed or a support against which it rested (Close-Brooks 1978–80: 330).

While this example does not serve to demonstrate conclusively that all Class 1 Pictish symbol stones were exclusively or even primarily restricted to a mortuary context, it does sustain the argument that they were in some way connected to promoting the memory of the dead. They may have communicated the identity of individuals and their kinship and socio-political affiliations, perhaps as an exclusive symbol of elite status. They may have been raised over individual graves, as at Dunrobin, but may also have acted as a focus for further burials or communal burial sites. This provides us with an example where the stone in itself would not have been successful in commemoration, but its location and orientation in relation to a cairn covering the remains of the dead served to make a visible statement to those viewing the monument.

This discussion also draws our attention to the role of cairns in the commemoration of the dead. The cairn at Dunrobin was intended to be viewed from above and around rather than seen from a distance. It was used to demarcate a space around the grave and associated with a memorial stone. The materials from the cairn were derived, perhaps because of the convenience and availability, but possibly also because the liminal environment of the seashore brought with it specific associations with the mortuary context (see Pollard 1999). Particularly given the prominence of many possible depictions of fish and other marine animals on symbol stones (i.e. the 'Pictish beasts') and their coastal distribution (presumably close to settlement sites), a connection with water and the significance of burial location can be tentatively suggested.

A further aspect of the cairns that may have had commemorative significance was their shape. At Dunrobin, the cairn was rectangular rather than round. Indeed, in such cemeteries as Garbeg, Whitebridge and Redcastle a range of different cairns can be found, including circular, trapezoidal, square and rectangular structures (Alexander 1999). This raises the question of what the significance of monument shape was in the commemoration of the dead.

Cairns and monumental symbols at Lundin Links
Located on a south-facing slope between 5m–10m OD in an area of sand dunes on a shelf of land above the sea, the Lundin Links cemetery was placed on the edge of Largo Bay in Fife, on the north shore of the Forth estuary (Greig et al. 2000; fig. 5.10). The excavations, following storm erosion in 1965 and 1966, revealed a series of west–east-orientated long-cists that fall into three types: those without monuments, those under rectangular cairns and those under circular cairns. In addition were found two groups of long-cists associated with two unique composite cairns

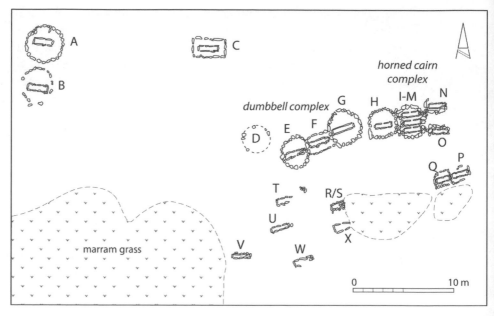

Figure 5.10 Plan of the cairns and long-cist graves excavated at Lundin Links, Fife including two composite cairns: the 'dumbbell' structure and the 'horned' structure (adapted by Séan Goddard after Greig et al. 2000; reproduced with the kind permission of Society of Antiquaries for Scotland).

constructed out of round and oblong monuments: first, a structure dubbed the 'dumbbell complex', consisting of two round cairns joined by an oval monument; and second, the 'horned-cairn complex', comprising a number of sub-circular cairns and crescentic ('horned') structures. As at Dunrobin, the cairns were low and could therefore be viewed by those standing around them. Moreover, their location on a shelf above the sea and below a steep slope meant that they could be viewed from above with ease, forming a prominent element of the local coastline. Radiocarbon dates from the skeletons centre on the fifth and sixth centuries AD (Greig et al. 2000: 611).

Unlike the Garbeg and Whitebridge cemeteries, which, although not fully published, are very much the 'classic' site-types for Pictish cemeteries (Ashmore 1980; Foster 1992), the site of Lundin Links in Fife has escaped detailed attention (see Close-Brooks 1984). Reviewed as one of the twelve sites with low cairns and long-cists by Patrick Ashmore, part of the reason for its limited discussion has been that the site has only recently been published (Ashmore 1980: 349; Greig et al. 2000).

The cemetery sits on the borders of two overlapping mortuary traditions dating from the fifth to eighth centuries AD; the symbol stones and cairns tend to be located in northern and eastern Scotland, while long-cist cemeteries are found in central and south-east Scotland (Carver 1998b; Foster 1996; see chapter 4). Both traditions (if indeed they are separate at all) share with many other areas of western and northern Britain in the middle and late first millennium AD a focus on inhumation, although some cremation burials are known (Ashmore 2003; Petts 2002). At some sites long-cist cemeteries are associated with Latin-inscribed stones with crosses. Indeed, the distribution of 'long-cist cemeteries', often seen as the first evidence for the spread of Christianity, can be charted throughout southern and central-eastern Scotland to include Fife. Classic examples of this site are the cemeteries at the Catstane and Parkburn in Lothian and Hallowhill in Fife (Alcock 1992; Henshall 1955–6; Proudfoot 1996).

The Lundin Links cemetery owes elements to both traditions. As well as the extreme variability of the monuments identified at Lundin Links, the other major observation is their referential and 'composite' character. The monuments were not raised in isolation and exclusively related to a single burial event, but located and augmented to connect burials to each other over successive mortuary rituals. Moreover, in one case convincingly (the dumbbell complex) and in a further instance possibly (the horned-cairn complex), these composite cairns resemble Pictish symbols rendered on a monumental scale.

The round and rectangular cairns at Lundin Links

Round cairns 1 and 2, respectively covering cairns A and B, begin the theme. While they are apparently similar, adjacent monuments composed of boulders and beach pebbles, they contain subtle differences that may have been intended to be recognised by visitors to the cemetery and that perhaps represent the contrasting identities of their occupants. Both covered single sandstone cist-graves, cairn 1 covering an adult male, cairn 2 an adult female. However, their structures showed distinctive variations in the arrangement of stones. Cairn 1 was the more carefully constructed monument, and over the cairn was a sandstone disc 60cm in diameter, seemingly placed to reference or mimic the overall shape of the monument. It appears that while these remained discrete monuments, their shape, materiality and location served to create a visual interaction between them.

Other monuments were physically connected. Of the three rectangular cairns around long-cists identified, each covered a single cist, but whereas C was positioned in isolation, cairns Q and P were juxtaposed end-to-end. Indeed, the arrangement of kerbed cairns around the cists suggests an overall design linking the (presumably) separate phases of monumental construction. This suggests that the monuments were augmented with successive burials, perhaps as part of a planned design. The resulting monument commemorated not an individual, but the relationships between the dead.

Composite monuments

This theme of monuments augmenting existing structures is taken to further extremes in the cases of both the dumbbell and horned-cairn complexes. The dumbbell complex consisted of two round cairns of different composition and cists. The oblong cairn linking the two monuments suggests an intended overall composite plan intended for all three graves. What is also notable is that the finished form of the monument is almost identical to common Pictish symbols, including 'pairs of circular discs' and 'double-discs' (Allen & Anderson 1903a: 59–60). Examples from close to the Lundin Links cemetery include both Class I and Class II stones (Allen & Anderson 1903b: 285, 287, 302, 346), portable artefacts, as in the Norrie's Law hoard (Allen & Anderson 1903b: 369), and cave art, like that in Doo Cave and Jonathan's Cave (Allen & Anderson 1903b: 371–2). The double-disc motif is also very similar to the handles of mirrors frequently depicted on stones (Allen & Anderson 1903a: 69). Finally, there are even examples of excavated paired circular houses from excavations at Pool on Sanday, Orkney (Hunter 1997). In combination this evidence suggests that the planned monument at Lundin Links was intended to appear as a symbol once complete. We seem in fact to be looking at a symbol found on a range of artefacts and in numerous ritual and profane contexts but rendered here on a monumental scale.

Meanwhile, the horned-cairn complex was even more elaborate. The western cairn (H) was heavily kerbed with stones and may have been an 'enclosure' rather than a 'cairn'. Structure I/M was a 'multi-storey' burial monument with two layers of graves: two lower ones and three interspersed at a higher level. Finally, two cists at the eastern end of the monumental complex were surrounded by symmetrical crescents ('horns') of stones (N and O). Therefore we have a complex of at least four discrete monuments, three overlying single graves, and a fourth associated with five cists. A parallel with Pictish symbols is less self-evident with this monument, although the crescent-stone arrangements do evoke the commonly identified 'Crescent' symbol (Allen & Anderson 1903a: 62), while the overall structure resembles the 'Notched Rectangle' motif (Allen & Anderson 1903a: 68). The monument is therefore a combination of two abstract themes of crescents/curved lines and rectangles/straight lines found on many symbol stones and contrast with the circles that form the main theme of the dumbbell complex (Forsyth 1997: 90).

Gender and genealogy
The osteological evidence from the site also shows how the monuments served to commemorate collective identities rather than discrete individuals. First, all the burials were of adults, and despite the many taphonomic biases that can exclude immature individuals from burial samples, this seems to be a significant issue, suggesting that burial monuments were intended for a select group of the living population, the rest of whom were interred elsewhere. The careful planning and selection of individuals for interment at the cemetery is not only evidenced by the absence of children, but also by the distribution of the sexes within the multiple phased monuments.

The dumbbell complex contained the juxtaposition of male and female burials. Both individuals interred beneath the circular cairns were males (40–50 years in the western cairn, 35–45 years old in the eastern cairn), whereas the oblong cairn in between overlay a younger adult female (c. 25 years). Even clearer patterns were revealed in the horned-cairn complex. All those that could be sexed (seven out of eight) were attributed as female. Moreover, non-metric traits from the crania were shared by four of the skeletons from the horned-cairn complex, which may hint at possible familial relationships between these women.

Therefore, we have a dumbbell composite cairn of a female flanked by males and on the same alignment as a horned cairn exclusively used for female burials. When we look at the overall plan of the cemetery, it appears that while males and females were mixed throughout, the exclusive use of the horned-cairn complex for adult females indicates that age and gender structured the use of monumental commemoration. Moreover, what is surprising is how these distinctive monuments must have been planned through a sequence of funerary events that may have developed over a number of generations as planned enterprises that reached some form of coherence and mnemonic project between funerary events.

Discussion

In the excavation report, the excavators were modest about the implications of the Lundin Links site, concluding that it was used by 'a fairly small Christian community with a tradition of burying men and women under different cairns . . . over three or four generations . . .' (Greig et al. 2000).

Yet Lundin Links appears to demonstrate two instances where the monuments were 'composed' as symbols. Moreover, in this light, the more simply built square, rectangular and circular monuments may equally have been regarded as 'symbolic' in a direct sense, and they were certainly positioned to reference each other and were sometimes augmented and enlarged. To understand the significance of these relationships between composite monumental symbols, we need to consider further the significance of symbols as they appear on Class I stone monuments.

There are three classes of Pictish symbols: artefacts (combs and mirrors), animals and abstract symbols, the latter being by far the most common. The extension of symbols to the cairns at Lundin Links could be regarded as simply reflecting the ubiquity of these symbols on many types of art used in contemporary Pictish society. Yet Class I symbol stones also used symbols in a composite sense, and this suggests a further significance to the use of shapes and symbols in burial monuments. Despite a reluctance on the part of recent scholars to interpret symbols directly, both Ross Samson (1992) and Kathryn Forsyth (1997) have developed the convincing argument that the symbols formed part of a writing system akin to the ogham, Latin and runic scripts found elsewhere on early medieval stones. Symbols appear in vertically arranged pairs with the occasional addition of mirrors and combs that together are thought to create the syllables of personal names. Martin Carver (2004) has recently supported this view in his discussion of the location of paired symbols on Class II symbol stones from Tarbat.

Therefore, symbols were meaningfully constituted as part of a structured writing system of personal names. Class 1 symbol stones were raised over individual graves and displayed the names of their occupants, and, as such, were an important commemorative device. Symbols were integral to remembrance, both because they composed the deceaseds' names and, perhaps on account of this fact, because they were iconic of the genealogies of these individuals. Early medieval genealogies were often alliterative: your name reflected not simply your aspired personal qualities and accumulated prestige, it also reflected your genealogy and connection to your ancestors. In this light, even personal names are a symbol of 'dividuality' – identities created from the elements of different persons, materials and substances – rather than 'individuality' in early medieval society (see Fowler 2004). This is compounded when we recognise that symbol stones – if pairs are thought to denote single names – were often raised to more than one person (Forsyth 1997: 92). When displayed on monuments, these names took on a new significance, because, like corporate logos in the modern world, they conveyed more than the identity of the individual person. They connected the named person to a wider network of relations both living and dead. Moreover, when displayed on symbol stones, the identity of the dead was projected both back into the past, as genealogies were evoked, and forward into the future, through the expectation that the monument would endure.

We are still no closer to 'decoding' the precise meanings of Pictish symbols and their monumental contexts. But that has not been the aim of this study. The suggestion that the Lundin Links monuments employ shape, space and a composite character to commemorate dividual persons does not rely on the precise meaning of individual symbols. What we can say is that at Lundin Links there is a fundamental difference between the symbols on stones and the monumental symbols created by sequences of funerary events. These contrasting uses of symbols suggest a more complex relationship between symbols and dead persons in Pictish society, one in which, at different scales, persons and symbols were enmeshed. We can take the analogy further by considering how the dumbbell and horned complexes are comparable to the pairs of symbols found on stones: perhaps the entire group was intended to create a 'name' in monumental symbols.

The importance of the lineage is supported by the fact that the clustering of graves of adult females at Lundin Links appears to mirror a comment made by the Venerable Bede, writing in the early eighth century. Bede mentions an origin myth of the Picts that they had no women when they arrived on the shores of Britain. The Irish agreed to give them wives on condition that they chose their kings from the female royal line rather than the male. Bede states that 'this custom continues among the Picts to this day' (HE I 2 in Colgrave and Mynors 1969). Whether an accurate reflection of Pictish kinship and inheritance customs or a misunderstanding of a distinctive culture by a Northumbrian monk, this does appear to find some form of resonance with the ideas behind the Lundin Links evidence in which adult females sharing close biological affinities were buried in close proximity and their graves were 'composed' into monumental symbols.

Having discussed the role of monuments in cemetery space and their meanings, let us now look at precisely how monuments interacted with the mortuary process.

Monuments and the ritual process

Two connected assumptions often made by archaeologists concerning mortuary monuments are that they are commissioned as single events and that they are associated only with the final stages of the funeral. Often this is the case, but we have already encountered monuments that acted as foci for a range of burials and were augmented through successive mortuary events. But even when a monument seems to be associated with a single mortuary sequence, the monument is not always a final act; monument-building can be an integral part of the ritual sequence, an unfolding process linked to the treatment of objects, bodies, substances, structures and spaces. In this way, monuments can serve at many successive stages to build a commemorative focus and identity for the deceased, changing in form as the identity of the deceased is transformed from deceased individual to ancestor. This section suggests that greater understanding of the relationship between the ritual process and monumentality is required to understand the mnemonic importance of mortuary monuments.

The Viking burial mounds on the Isle of Man provide one such example. At first glance they appear to be monuments that are 'familiar' and simple to understand. In common with other areas of Scandinavian colonisation in the Irish Sea during the ninth and tenth centuries, burial mounds containing furnished burial rites have been recognised (Richards 1991; 2000). In traditional terms, these are monuments of Norse settlers, bringing to a Christian island their own pagan ways of burying the dead (Bersu & Wilson 1966). Despite recent challenges to the assumption that furnished burial in this period can be simplistically linked to Scandinavian settlement (e.g. Halsall 2000), the Isle of Man is distinctive in the range of place-name and historical evidence, as well as the testimony of stone sculpture, hoards and graves, suggesting strong Scandinavian influence. While the scale and nature of the settlement remain open to debate, it is churlish to deny that direct Scandinavian influence and settlement provided the *context* for the introduction of Scandinavian-style furnished burial rites. What it is necessary to question are the assumptions regarding ethnicity and religion directly imposed upon these graves. If these are pagan and Scandinavian burial rites, why were they selected as an overt statement of difference in death from the native Christian population? Julian D. Richards notes that the rich, late ninth-century burial mounds on Man can be seen as more than evidence of the settlement of pagan Scandinavians. They may have been deliberate statements laden with symbolism aimed at asserting and legitimising claims over newly acquired territory on the island at a time of social and political stress and competition between and within settling and native communities. Whereas later Manx crosses attest to the conversion of Norse settlers and the intermarriage of individuals with Norse and Gaelic names, these elaborate funerary rituals have been seen as ways of promoting a new social order that was both aggressive and assertive in its claims, but perhaps also as holding the potential to negotiate and legitimise the positions of Norse elites through the performance of mortuary rituals. From such a perspective, the rites conducted by the Viking settlers upon Man were knowledgeable choices and public displays which, as at Sutton Hoo in early seventh-century East Anglia, were intended to serve particular purposes and communicate with certain audiences, as well as exclude others (Carver 1986; 2001; 2002).

To develop this argument further, it is necessary to make reference to Norse attitudes towards mounds as recorded in later saga literature. Admittedly, there are difficulties in directly translating the fragmentary folklore of thirteenth- and fourteenth-century Iceland onto the late first millennium in the Irish Sea region.

Yet these sources do provide insights into the meanings of mounds beyond their evident roles as landmarks and investments of materials, labour and time. The idea that burial mounds were dwellings for the dead and other supernatural beings is not exclusively Scandinavian but finds resonance in Irish and Anglo-Saxon folk traditions (Semple 1998; 2004a and b). A common trope in the Icelandic sources is the mound as a house. Barrows are regarded as containing the corporeal ghosts (*draugar*) of dead chiefs seated almost in suspended animation within their burial chambers and sometimes awaking to roam the surrounding countryside. For example, in the thirteenth-century Icelandic *Grettir's Saga*, the hero travels to Norway, where he faces the *draugr* of the dead chief Karr the Old by entering his burial mound to retrieve the chief's sword. Karr becomes animated, and Grettir wrestles and defeats the *draugr* before returning to the son of Karr, bearing the won treasure (Fox & Pálsson 1974: 35–8). The ability of the hero to enter a mound, subdue its occupant and return with treasure can be regarded as a form of other-world ordeal akin to the underwater journey of Beowulf to fight Grendel's mother (S. Bradley 1982: 451–5).

Similar concepts may have enhanced the efficacy of building large burial mounds on the newly acquired farms of Norse settlers in ninth-century Man. These were not merely retrospective monuments commemorating the life of the deceased, but places that evoked prospective memories. In other words, they were monuments intended to promote the memory of the dead ancestor onto subsequent generations to the exclusion of other memories linked to that place. This may have been seen as not just the projection of a memory of how the person once was, but also a memory of their continued active and forceful role in securing and protecting the interests of their descendants. In short, these were monuments concerned with memory-creation: the demonstration of genealogy and the linking of past, present and future. Rather than being claimed through the repeated augmentation of mound after mound as at Sutton Hoo, the ninth-century burial mounds on Man selected a single ancestor. Through the funeral and subsequent remembrance of the person buried within, claims were being made not simply on land, but on the past, present and future.

How was this form of monumentality and social memory constructed? Certainly, the display of burying grave goods with the dead and covering the grave with a substantial burial mound involved elaborate ritual performances and left behind a prominent mark on the Manx landscape. Yet the mnemonics of monumentality at these funerals could be explored further. Through a consideration of the famous excavations of Gerhard Bersu at Chapel Hill, Balladoole and Ballateare, this section will address how the interplay between the funerary process and monument-building may be the key to understand the efficacy of such monuments. This interaction was central to the creation of an 'animated' and 'prospective' memory of an ancestor dwelling within the barrow and prominent within the surrounding landscape.

Chapel Hill, Balladoole

Those who raised the burial mound covering a boat-burial at Chapel Hill, at Balladoole, selected a prominent location just within the eastern perimeter and south of the entrance of an earlier Iron Age fortification. The site had previously been reused as an early medieval cemetery and possible chapel site (Bersu & Wilson 1966: 1). The chosen site had a wide view-shed, situated at the highest point of the hill (Bersu & Wilson 1966: 3). Yet the precise position of the mound may have been equally significant. The mound commanded and 'guarded' the entrance to the hillfort and the ancestral and Christian sacred space it had contained. Moreover, cists dating to sometime between the abandonment of the hillfort and the raising of the cairn suggest that the mound was deliberately situated over an early Christian long-cist cemetery. While David Wilson suggested in the excavation report that the lack of grave markers means that this may have been accidental (the Vikings 'were not to know that they had only to move 5m to be outside the area of the Christian cemetery'), a range of monuments and structures associated with early medieval cemeteries of all periods and places makes it likely that mounds, posts and per-haps grave houses like those at Capel Eithin, Plas Gogerddan and Tandderwen were likely to have been visible when the site was selected for the burial and mound-raising (see above). Bersu provides one explanation for what he rightly saw as a deliberate connection created through the location of the burial mound over the Christian graves:

> I still feel inclined to suggest, therefore, that the pagan Viking was buried intentionally above the slightly earlier burials of the Christians who lived in the island before the advent of the Vikings. The Vikings may have wished to demonstrate that they were now masters of the island and, for that reason, deliberately slighted the Christian community with this pagan burial of a personality of high rank.
> (Bersu & Wilson 1966: 13).

Moving on to consider the sequence and contents of the burial rite, we can see how the display of the funeral may have given this location a new memorial role (fig. 5.11). Within the grave were the remains of two individuals, an adult male and an adult female, the grave goods suggesting that the male remains were the primary occupant, with a female accompanying. The female was seen either as someone who had died at the same time as the male or, just possibly, as a sacrificed slave interred with her master.

The grave goods with the male burial included a ring-headed pin, a knife, a hone and flint strike-a-light found at the belt, a belt buckle and spurs. These were pos-sibly all originally elements of the clothing in which the mourners had dressed the deceased, although post-burial disturbance made it difficult for the excavator to associate their original position in relation to the skeletal remains. A range of other artefacts was interpreted as 'gifts' placed with the dead, including a harness spread over the length of the body, an iron cauldron by the left leg and the remains of an iron bowl. Finally, a shield-boss and fragmentary remains of the grip suggest the shield was placed over the knees of the body. Also included were human bones disturbed from earlier cists and seemingly replaced within the Viking burial (Bersu & Wilson 1966: 7). This response to the earlier human remains was seen by the excavators as evidence for the disregard for earlier graves on the part of those conducting the

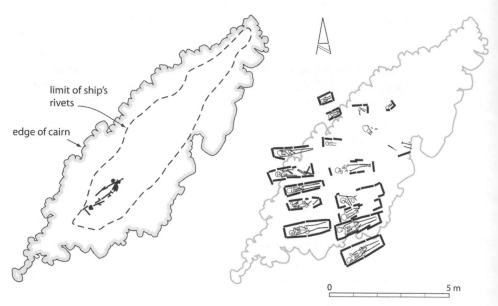

Figure 5.11   Plans of two phases of activity at Balladoole, Isle of Man. The early Christian long-cist cemetery (right) was overlain and partially disturbed by the Viking-period ship-burial (left), defined by a distribution of ship-rivets and a stone cairn (redrawn by Séan Goddard after Bersu & Wilson 1966).

funeral. There was even the suggestion that some of the bones may still have been articulated when disturbed:

> The contents of the cists thus became visible to the builders of the Viking cairn and, in some cases, the bones of the skeletons were taken out of the cists and either replaced in a disturbed state or spread out beneath the boat. In some cases the vertical walls of the cists and their paving slabs were more or less destroyed, a fact which explains the occurrence of slabs of Pooilvaish shale and isolated human bones in the body of the mound. It is clear that the Vikings had little respect for the earlier burials.
> (Bersu & Wilson 1966: 12).

Sarah Tarlow (1997) has gone further, to suggest that the deliberate and aggressive disturbance of earlier graves may have been a conscious statement of violence to the memory of the previous landowners by dispersing and desecrating their graves. A further alternative interpretation might be that this was a deliberate appropriation of earlier human remains as a form of social remembrance, perhaps creating or inventing connections with a local past while reformulating existing traditions associated with the site. Given the nature of the evidence, it is difficult to decide between these interpretations, but it does underpin the fact that engagement with the past was an inevitable consequence of the choice of location for the ship-burial.

It is in relation to this burial tableau that the monumentality of the grave was orchestrated. There are two, perhaps related, elements of monumental structure on the site, both of which *could* have remained partially visible after the raising of the cairn. The first was a large post-hole thought to be contemporary with the Viking burial and situated to the north of the south-west end of the ship. This could have served both as a mooring pole for the ship and as a memorial pole marking the location of the bow after the raising of the mound. The ship, roughly 11m in length and 3m broad amidships, was revealed through its clench nails. It appears to have been laid on the ground surface. Dry-stone walling was built up around the vessel to keep the ship in place during the raising of the cairn. Although conclusive evidence was not found, it is possible that the ship retained an erect mast – the second of the two elements – when interred that would have extended beyond the burial mound. Perhaps even a sail and ropes were erected when the ship was in place and remained visible once the cairn was raised. Both mooring pole and mast had a specific mnemonic role, serving as visible above-ground memorials in themselves but simultaneously evoking memories of the below-ground remains and the dead within the ship.

The third form of 'monument' was the cairn itself. Although difficult to reconstruct because of the decay of organic material in the mound, rabbit burrowing, erosion and stone-robbing, it seems to have been a boat-shaped mound. It was originally 12m long and perhaps 5m in height (Bersu & Wilson 1966: 9). Again, it seems that the permanent monument served as a composite marker but also evoked memories of the deposit it contained through its form.

Further ritual acts seem to have accompanied the mound-building, suggesting that the *process* of construction as well as the final result were important. The mound was capped with a heap of stone, covered by a layer of cremated bones – horse, ox, pig, sheep/goat, dog and cat – recognised from this level that '. . . apparently represent an offering of livestock to accompany the dead man to the other world' (Bersu & Wilson 1966: 10). Animal sacrifice was an integral element of mortuary practices in the early medieval period and can be regarded as a further element of conspicuous display and violence linked to the mortuary process. This theme is also reflected in the possibility that the female occupant of the boat had been a sacrificial victim linked to the mortuary ritual.

Therefore the ritual sequence involved the building of different monumental elements of the grave at different times, some of which remained visible as part of the final monumental composition. The final cairn would therefore have acted as a monument in and of itself, yet also as a reminder of the more ephemeral elements of the mortuary display that went along with its construction but that were hidden beneath the cairn.

Ballateare

Bersu's excavations at Ballateare revealed a different, but comparable, relationship between burial rites and monument-building. The relationship between the building of a circular earthen mound over a furnished male weapon burial and the funerary process began with the selection of the site, again influenced not only by topography and views, but also by the presence of a Neolithic burial ground, recognised either

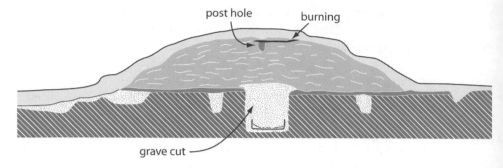

Figure 5.12   A section of the grave and mound from Ballateare, Isle of Man. The grave was covered with a turf mound with burnt animal remains, a human skeleton and a post-hole near the top of the monument (redrawn by Séan Goddard after Bersu & Wilson 1966).

because of surviving surface features or because of artefacts discovered below the surface during the excavation of the grave.

The burial sequence was itself a complex set of ritual actions (fig. 5.12). A rectangular pit was dug, into which a coffin was placed. The grave goods included a ring-headed pin (perhaps fastening a woollen cloak), a knife laid on the chest, a sword broken into at least two pieces before being replaced within its scabbard, and a spear put into the coffin, perhaps with its shaft broken. Once the lid of the coffin was in place, two further spears were placed on the coffin lid, and a shield, showing signs of damage from heavy weapon blows, was placed outside the south side of the coffin. In each case it is possible that the weapons were 'ritually broken' for the funeral. The burial pit was filled with fine sand before the raising of the monument.

The mound was constructed of turfs packed horizontally one on top of the other. The turf had not been from under the mound, since the old humus layer was intact. Nor was the turf from the immediate environs of the barrow, where the soil was fine or gravelly, quite different from that adhering to the sods. While Bersu's excavations did not have available modern scientific analysis of ancient soils to sustain the argument, it is convincingly suggested by Bersu that the very material used to build the barrows had many different places of origin, perhaps to symbolise the extent and character of the lands owned by the deceased and/or the chief mourners. Bersu's symbolic interpretation was that the sods 'may represent the fields of the dead man, so that more of his property, in addition to the grave-goods in the coffin, might be represented in his burial'. If so, then the monument itself was a crystallisation of the links between place, memory and (if a newcomer) invented claims to the past.

At Ballateare, the mound-building was accompanied by a sequence of obsequies. The mound construction ceased on at least one occasion, when a platform was created upon which a series of ritual acts took place. These included the positioning of a second human body: the skeleton was discovered of a female aged between 20 and 30, her arms raised upwards at right angles to the body, with a large hole in her skull made by the slashing of a sword or similar weapon. Bersu suggested that the body had been moved to this position from a place of death elsewhere because the posture suggested that rigor mortis had set in when it was interred. He further argued that this represents the killing of a slave girl to accompany her master, drawing upon written sources of human sacrifice such as the tenth-century account by the Arab traveller Ibn Fadlan (Warmind 1995). This act was accompanied, as at Balladoole, by the cremation of sacrificed animal remains, the cremated bones from which were scattered across the platform where the female skeleton had been positioned. This solid layer of cremated bones mixed with black earth and charcoal could either represent the mound itself being used as a platform for cremation, or the material being moved in large amounts from a nearby location. Given that the layer of charcoal and cremated animal remains created a layer in the region of around 10cm thick, it is possible that the former was the case. The pyre remains included those of a sacrificed horse, cattle, sheep/goat and dog, a sacrifice that would have reflected the wealth and status of mourners, but a rite that added to the sequence of spectacles that the funeral entailed to make the mound-building a memorable and sanctified operation. A final adornment to the mound seems to have been the erection of a post, evidenced by a central surviving post-hole. Whether this was a simple undecorated pole, a flag, a mast to create the *impression* that the mound contained a ship, or a totem inscribed with decoration and/or a runic inscription, we cannot know. Yet the earthen structure was just one among many elements used in the creation of a monument and its elaboration, serving to meld the monument-building into the mortuary sequence as an important element of commemoration.

Discussion

When thinking of Viking-period funerals of the scale and complexity of the Manx graves described above, archaeologists have tended to be influenced by the vivid account of a chief's funeral among the Viking Rus recorded by Ibn Fadlan in the tenth century (Warmind 1995). Ibn Fadlan described the cremation of a chief within a ship, accompanied with rich furnishings, sacrificed animals and the gruesome rape and sacrifice of a slave girl. Yet the account is restricted to only one stage of what was a lengthy funeral sequence. His witnesses filled in brief details of what had gone before the cremation, including the temporary burial of the body and the preparation of the funeral pyre, but little is said of the post-cremation rituals. This is possibly a bias in the sources from someone who, from the Arab world, might not expect or understand elaborate rites after the 'disposal' of the body. Archaeology has the opposite bias, rendering a clear sequence of actions attending the construction of the grave, but failing to reveal the range of rituals before and after these actions, as well as attendant rituals away from the barrow itself. However, the relationship between the spectacle of the funeral and the mound-building that followed has tended to be underplayed. At Balladoole and Ballateare, we appear to have instances of an impressive funerary display in which monumentality was integral to the proceedings. At both sites, spectacle and monumentality seem to have operated in tandem in the creation of social memory.

Conclusion: monuments in memory

This chapter has by no means exhausted the range of monument types found in early medieval Britain. What we have seen is a glimpse of the complexity of monumental form and scale and their variable roles in promoting the selective remembering and forgetting of the dead, both individually and collectively. This involves monuments acting as a focus for commemorative practices, as well as their role as enduring structures onto which memories could be portrayed or inscribed. We have also seen that monuments are tied into the sequence of the funeral itself and the sequence of burials added to the cemetery. Monuments were not always employed in mortuary practices, but when they were, it was a strategic choice to make a specific statement about the dead, the living and their evolving relationship through the mortuary process. The diversity of monumentality over time and space within early medieval Britain can be considered less a response to the changes in ethnic groups and social complexity, and more to do with the marshalling of material and symbolic resources to portray memories in increasingly diverse ways.

6

Death and landscape

Introduction – early medieval landscapes

In studies of burial in its landscape setting, there continues to be a schism. As it has developed in Britain, landscape archaeology has been closely connected to discussions of monuments, their distribution and their topographical location in prehistory. Yet for historic periods, landscape studies have tended to be affiliated with settlement archaeology, in which burial sites may provide the indirect evidence for nearby habitations. Consequently, burial sites tend to be considered a second-rate means of charting the distribution and evolution of settlements, rather than a feature of interest in themselves (e.g. Brown & Foard 1998; Hooke 1999; Rippon 2000). This chapter sets out to explore the potential for developing an understanding of the landscape locations and environs of cemeteries at a variety of scales. The particular focus will be upon the significance of landscape and burial location for constructing social memories, links both to the past in a general sense and to the ancestors in particular. In order to achieve this, it is first necessary to review previous approaches to the location of burials and cemeteries and explore recent studies of early medieval mortuary topography before considering the relationships between cemeteries and social memory. The chapter culminates in a discussion of the interaction of texts and landscape in constructing links between the early medieval past and the social histories (real or imagined) of individuals, communities and kingdoms. While studies of burial location and landscape have increased in recent years, a coherent theoretical approach has not been developed, and it is hoped that this chapter will provide pointers towards such an approach. While artefacts, bodies, graves and monuments all had contributions to make in remembering and forgetting in the early medieval period, it was in many ways the sacred and social topography of death and burial within which these ritual performances took place that informed the social and political significance of the dead in early medieval societies. To develop such an approach, we need to consider how monuments and burial sites were experienced by those moving through the landscape (Tilley 1994) and how they may have been invested with memories through their use and reuse (Ashmore & Knapp 1999).

Early medieval mortuary landscapes

The location and landscape setting of burials and cemeteries have been an intermittent focus of archaeological enquiry for a long time. The geographical distribution and location of early medieval cemeteries have always received comment since the work of the early barrow-diggers (see Marsden 1999). For example, while the illustration and description of artefacts were the principle preoccupation of Victorian antiquaries and archaeologists, many nineteenth-century cemetery reports included descriptions of the topographical and historical setting of cemeteries, including relationships with prehistoric and Roman sites (e.g. Wylie 1852). With the syntheses of Anglo-Saxon cemeteries produced in the early twentieth century, burial location continued to be considered. G. Baldwin Brown (1903–15) contrasted the topographical location of cemeteries, either on higher ground away from settlements or 'riverine' cemeteries down in valleys, while both E. T. Leeds (1913; 1936) and J. N. L. Myres (1969) discussed the distribution of cemeteries in relation to Roman towns, Roman roads and rivers, in terms of the sites where Germanic groups were established as mercenaries, followed by subsequent waves of invasion and immigration. Indeed, some scholars continue to use the geography of burials to write histories of migration and conversion in a direct and straightforward way (Blair 1994; Hawkes 1986).

Throughout the middle and later twentieth century, reports on archaeological discoveries developed a format within which the regional and local archaeological and topographical context of cemeteries was discussed (e.g. Bersu & Wilson 1966; Evison 1994; see chapter 5 here). Yet it was only with the development of the self-proclaimed 'New Archaeology' of the 1960s and 1970s that the landscape context of mortuary practices was recognised as an important window onto past social organisation (e.g. Goldstein 1980; Chapman 1980; Chapman & Randsborg 1980; Randsborg 1980). These early studies employed explicit theory-building, with new methodologies for analysing the spatial distribution and locations of cemeteries, and they have continued to inspire systematic analyses of the location of burial sites (e.g. Buikstra & Charles 1999; Goldstein 1995; Hedeager 1992b). A central argument posited was that the location of burials and monuments might be expected to define territories, and could serve to sustain and legitimise the social order through the creation of an ancestral presence so as to claim rights to land and other strategic resources (Chapman 1980).

Subsequent criticisms of these approaches have challenged the use of cross-cultural generalisations, their social evolutionary approach and the lack of contextual analysis, yet they continued to inspire studies of burial in the landscape (e.g. Bevan 1999; Parker Pearson 1993; 1999a; Thomas 1996; Tilley 1994). Most of these studies have focused upon prehistoric periods, where a range of computer-based and more impressionistic methodologies have been developed to investigate and portray the locations and settings of monuments and burial sites (e.g. Cummings et al. 2002; Field 1998; Watson 2001a and b; Woodward & Woodward 1996).

These perspectives have only had a limited impact on early medieval archaeology. Some exceptions include the influential work of Desmond Bonney on the relationship between Anglo-Saxon burials and the boundaries of later estates in Wiltshire (Bonney 1966; 1976; see also Goodier 1984). Early studies have also considered changes in burial location over time, so that it has been argued that the seventh century saw a shift in both settlement and cemeteries (the 'middle Saxon shuffle') connected to both conversion and estate formation (Arnold & Wardle 1981; Boddington 1990; Meaney & Hawkes 1970). Meanwhile, historians and archaeologists have resurrected a debate initiated by John Mitchell Kemble (1857) in the mid-nineteenth century in recognising that between conversion and the widespread adoption of church/churchyard-burial, there may have been a long period of time in which the majority of the populace in Anglo-Saxon England continued to be buried in the countryside (Blair 1994; Hadley 2002). For example, the long-running excavations at Sedgeford in Norfolk have revealed a middle Saxon cemetery away from the site of the later parish church (Davies 2000). Yet these studies share a limited engagement with the social and ideological significance of burial location and its relationship with surrounding landscape features. Despite this focus upon territories and church-burial, a specific landscape focus to early medieval burial sites was slow in its arrival, despite being advocated in repeated studies of the period (Bradley 1980; Hodder 1980). In particular, there has been little in the way of debate over the adoption of social and phenomenological approaches to landscape and their respective critiques (see Tilley 1994, see also Brück 1998; Fleming 1998). Let us first proceed by exploring how studies have investigated and interpreted burial location.

Monument reuse

Theoretically informed discussions of early medieval burial location initially focused on the phenomenon of 'monument reuse': the insertion of early medieval burials into, or close to, prehistoric and Roman-period monuments. The phenomenon had been recognised since the age of the Victorian barrow-digger, but the debate over its interpretation is more recent, dating from a seminal paper drawing upon discussions in Mediterranean and British prehistory by Richard Bradley (1987) in response to Hope-Taylor's (1977) claims for continuity at the Anglo-Saxon royal palace sites at Yeavering. Bradley (1987) argued that, rather than real continuity, we are seeing a deliberate strategy of inventing traditions at such sites, in which the dead and the living were situating themselves in connection to a timeless, mythical past. Ancient monuments may have been regarded as the residences or burial places of heroes, ancestors, ancient peoples or supernatural beings. In this sense, ritual practices, including those surrounding death, were used in the early medieval period to create senses of place and history in the landscape through monument reuse.

A number of studies have attempted to build upon Bradley's insights (Lucy 1992; Williams 1997). While Bradley focused upon the site of Yeavering, with only brief reference to other instances of monument reuse, subsequent studies have explored the frequency and character of the practice through excavations (e.g. Härke in Fulford & Rippon 1994; Scull & Harding 1990), regional surveys (Driscoll 1998; Lucy 1992; 1998; Petts 2002; Semple 2002; 2003), national assessments (Lucy 2000; Williams 1997) and comparisons with Continental and Scandinavian monument reuse (Effros 2001; Roymans 1995; Thäte 1996). Further work has emphasised the selectivity of monument reuse, not only in terms of which monuments were reused and which were avoided (Lucy 2000; Semple 1998; Williams 1999b), but also in terms of the exclusive selection of particular monuments for particular categories of the dead (Reynolds 2002; Williams 1999b). Some studies continue to ignore monument reuse in favour of more evolutionary discussions of transition from 'field-' to 'churchyard'-burial, and there remain debates over how to discern monument reuse from coincidental or expedient associations (e.g. Zadora-Rio 2003). Yet there appears to be a broad consensus that the appropriation and reuse of a range of prehistoric monuments (including earthen long mounds, megalithic tombs, round barrows, stone circles, henges, hillforts and linear earthworks) as well as Roman structures (including buildings, temples and burial sites) could attract deliberate reuse for burial and other ritual activities in early medieval Britain.

We have already come across instances of monument reuse in a number of guises in previous chapters, with prehistoric mounds acting as a common focus for the early medieval cemeteries of Mill Hill, Deal, Kent (chapter 2; see fig. 2.11 above), Harford Farm, Norfolk (chapter 3) and the Welsh sites of Plas Gogerddan, Ceredigion and Tandderwen, Clwyd (chapter 6; see figs. 5.2, 5.4 and 5.5 above). The practice seems to have indigenous roots, since many late Roman instances are known (Esmonde Clearly 2000). Indeed, the reuse of ancient monuments can be illustrated through many case studies, but for the sake of this discussion let us return to the excavations at Mill Hill, Deal. The sixth-century cemetery was excavated by the Dover Archaeological Group, directed by Keith Parfitt (Parfitt & Brugmann 1997). Previous excavations on the site had revealed Anglo-Saxon graves, suggesting two distinct cemeteries on the hill, two of four furnished burial sites known within the former parish of Mongeham, in turn suggesting a dense early medieval funerary topography of contemporary and successive burial sites (Parfitt & Brugmann 1997: 6). At the centre of the cemetery, on the highest point of the hill, was the surviving ring-ditch (20m in diameter) of a ploughed-out burial mound of prehistoric date. The size of the ditch allowed the excavators to suggest that, when built, the monument would have been a prominent local landmark, as well as being visible from seagoing vessels in the Channel (Parfitt & Brugmann 1997: 12). The local field name, from an early nineteenth-century tithe map and deeds, records the 'White Barrow' on the spot, demonstrating beyond doubt that the monument was a visible landscape feature until recent times (Parfitt & Brugmann 1997: 12; see fig. 2.12 above). The spatial organisation of the cemetery provides further evidence for a conscious reuse of a recognised feature for early medieval burial. Two separate burial plots were established on the fringes of the prehistoric mound. Further graves were probably inserted into the monument itself, but they have not survived the levelling of the mound in more recent centuries. However, the excavator suggests that the plots represent a real clustering around the monument while respecting its interior (Parfitt & Brugmann 1997: 13). A further element to the reuse can be recognised in the orientation of the graves: in the north-east group, a radial arrangement of the graves suggests an alignment upon a common focus, perhaps a centrally placed burial or a timber monument adorning the top of the prehistoric monument (see Hope-Taylor 1977). Another quality to the monument reuse seems to have been the deliberate emulation of the prehistoric monument, a practice recognised elsewhere in Kent at Saltwood (Canterbury Archaeological Trust/Wessex Archaeology 2000). Saxon burial mounds seem to be a widespread feature of early medieval cemeteries from Kent known from antiquarian sources as standing earthworks but now surviving only as annular and penannular ring-ditches (e.g. Hawkes 1982; Hogarth 1973; Struth & Eagles 1999; MOLAS 2000; see chapter 5). The Mill Hill cemetery produced no indications of ring-ditches of early medieval date, yet a group of adult male weapon-burials in the north-east sector of the cemetery was well and evenly spaced, suggesting that small mounds without ring-ditches marked their location, as discussed in chapter 2 and also as discussed above (Parfitt & Brugmann 1997: 17–22). The prehistoric mound was therefore referenced in each new burial event, with burials inserted around its edges and graves further away covered with small mounds acting as miniature copies of the ancient monument.

A different kind of monument reuse has been identified at Bromfield, Shropshire (Stanford et al. 1995: 130–41; fig. 6.1). The cemetery of thirty-one west–east-orientated inhumation burials produced few grave goods (a penannular brooch, an amber bead, a buckle and two knives) and is dated to the seventh century AD. The burial site reused the denuded rampart of an Iron Age farmstead, and while there is no evidence for the recutting of the ditch in the early medieval period or for the alignment of the enclosure being respected by the graves, the deliberate reuse of an earlier feature seems likely on the basis of the extent of the cemetery and the apparent respect shown for the entrance to the enclosure (Stanford et al. 1995: 131).

The question then needs to be asked, why was an ancient monument selected for reuse, as opposed to the building of a new monument? The usual approach to this question is to argue that prehistoric monuments provided a more convenient and easier option in terms of exploiting unused places in the landscape and in terms of energy expenditure than building a new monument. This may explain some instances, but the Mill Hill and Bromfield cemeteries show that ancient monuments were *not* being treated in a comparable manner to a newly built burial mound. The respect shown for the pre-existing monument and the use of the mound as a focus for an entire cemetery rather than simply the burial of one grave suggest that expediency cannot be the only or principle reason for reuse. It has been argued that the reuse of an ancient monument evoked particular conceptions of time and memory, and provided a communal focus for a cemetery (Bradley 1987). Such links to perceived ancestors and supernatural beings or, indeed, perhaps the deliberate appropriation and invention of new pasts through the appropriation and 'forgetting' of earlier traditions may have had a range of social and political motivations. The desire to legitimise claims over land and resources and thereby sustain inheritance claims and territory may have been a chief motivation (e.g. Lucy 2000; Shephard 1979). Yet this author has argued that the practice concerns the working and reworking of social memory at a variety of levels: links to ancestors and the sacred in a general sense, but also the creation of specific genealogies and histories for kingdoms and communities (Holtorf 1996; 1997; Williams 1997; 1998; 1999b). This was not simply a concern for the past, but also a means of staking claims over the present and the future (Holtorf 1996; Penn 2000), using the past as a means of appropriating and shaping the early medieval landscape both conceptually and physically through mortuary practices.

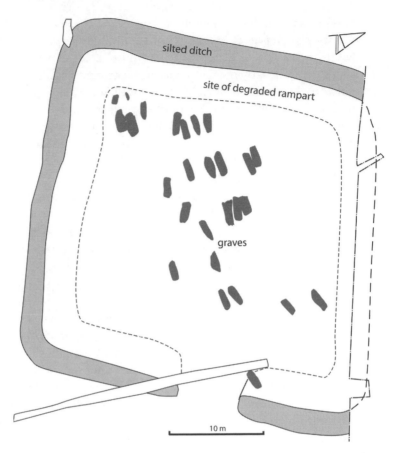

silted ditch

site of degraded rampart

graves

10 m

Figure 6.1 Plan of the seventh-century inhumation cemetery excavated at Bromfield, Shropshire (redrawn by the author after Stanford et al. 1995).

While the desire to place the dead close to pre-existing monuments can be demonstrated to be a repeated and influential factor in the location of early medieval burial sites prior to the adoption of churchyard-burial from the fifth century through to the eighth and ninth centuries, attitudes towards ancient monuments were neither static nor universal. John Blair (1994) has argued that the seventh century was a particularly important time for monument reuse because of the tensions and transformations in society, economy and religion at this time. Moreover, Sarah Semple (1998) has argued that after the seventh century the ancestral or communal associations of old earthworks were supplanted by less positive associations. Archaeological evidence demonstrates an increased use of mounds as places of execution and criminal burial from the seventh century onwards. Place-name, literary and pictorial evidence supports the view that in later Anglo-Saxon England selected earthworks (including both 'pagan-period' burial mounds and prehistoric monuments) could receive demonic and supernatural associations (Semple 1998).

Within this broad picture, there is a need for more contextual analyses of monument reuse, focusing on localities and regions. This approach has been developed by Sarah Semple, who has looked at monument reuse in the Avebury region. She recognises the preference for single, intrusive graves selectively inserted into large prehistoric round barrows, although the communal reuse of monuments is also known from the region (Semple 2003). This practice began in the sixth century but develops into the seventh and eighth centuries, and possibly into the ninth. Both genders are found buried in older monuments, but, contrary to broader trends, there is a bias towards male interments in the Avebury area (Semple 2003: 74). Over time, Semple sees topographical changes, with the West Overton burials of sixth-century date indicating reuse close to contemporary settlements in a densely populated downland landscape. Meanwhile, in the seventh century the secondary burials are placed in prominent locations, with extensive views, on the chalk escarpment, further away from the likely locations of contemporary settlements at the base of the escarpment (Semple 2003: 76; see also Lucy 1998). Semple relates this pattern to the increasing political contestation of the region in the seventh and eighth centuries between the kingdoms of Mercia and Wessex, a possible context that might also explain the building of the Wansdyke, a linear earthwork traditionally dated to the fifth century AD (Reynolds 1999).

While this author would assert that monument reuse was one of the most important factors influencing early medieval mortuary topography, it was by no means the only one. If we take the Mill Hill cemetery as an example, the choice of location may have been motivated by a variety of factors: proximity to settlement, patterns of fields and trackways, and proximity to other (archaeologically invisible) ritual and sacred sites such as temples and shrines, as well as other burial locations. Equally, the view-shed afforded from the spot may have influenced the placing of the grave as much as the presence of an ancient monument. It is likely that no single factor influenced early medieval burial location, so let us explore some other factors that may have been influential.

Routes, boundaries and topography

Landscape can be considered to be made up of not only places, but also pathways between locales (Tilley 1994). Routeways may have connected settlements and cemeteries and passed beside the graves, although it is often near-impossible to reconstruct the patterns and status of roads, tracks and paths in the early medieval landscape. Yet recently, a number of studies have attempted to tackle this issue. For example, Simon Draper has reappraised Desmond Boney's ideas concerning the location of early medieval burials in Wiltshire, arguing that Roman roads and ridge-top paths influenced the choice of both isolated graves and cemeteries (Draper 2004). Stuart Brookes has similarly argued for a close relationship between cemetery location and routes over both land and sea from a detailed GIS-analysis of eastern Kent (Brookes, in prep). This author has made the argument that the ridgeway routes along the Berkshire Downs were an important factor influencing the location of the seventh-century weapon-burial beneath a prominent barrow adjacent to a ruined Romano-Celtic temple complex upon Lowbury Hill. Of all the possible hills in the area, Lowbury is the one that provides the greatest inter-visibility with this route, making the mound a prominent landmark for travellers as well as those dwelling for miles around (Williams 1999b; see also Härke in Fulford & Rippon 1994). The potential for these approaches is their attempt to appreciate how burial mounds and cemeteries may have been encountered 'on the ground' as early medieval people inhabited and traversed their landscape, rather than consider burial location from a two-dimensional, aerial perspective provided by distribution maps (Ingold 1993; Tilley 1994). Whether an ancient monument was reused or not, the engagement with cemeteries at particular points along routes between settlements would have served to embed the ancestors both individually and collectively into the fabric of daily experience, as well as during funerals and ancestral rites (see Bevan 1999).

As already mentioned, boundaries have long been discussed in relation to burial location (Bonney 1966; 1976; Goodier 1984; Kemble 1857; Welch 1985). Similar 'territorial' approaches to the distribution of early medieval cemeteries have been applied to the long-cist cemeteries of southern and central Scotland, considering their association with hillforts, churches, roads and boundaries (Proudfoot & Aliaga-Kelly 1997). There remain many methodological difficulties with this association, not least because boundaries are often recorded only in later centuries, and their precise location and contemporaneous character cannot always be attested from topographical or archaeological evidence. Yet many studies continue to attest that the evolution of estates and territories from at least as early as the seventh century onwards could be associated with, and sustained through, the burial of certain categories of the dead on or near natural and/or socio-political boundaries (Hooke 1999; Petts 2002; Reynolds 2002). There is also growing contextual and quantitative evidence for the importance of boundaries as locations for burials, and, over time, that certain boundaries (those of hundreds and shires) became places for the execution and burial of excommunicated criminals (Reynolds 2002; Semple 1998; Pitts et al. 2002).

Boundaries were not simply physical markers, but conceptual spaces, regions of liminality that were charged with symbolic and socio-political importance for the communities and territories they defined (see Pantos 2003). Indeed, burial may have been only one of the ways in which memories were inscribed upon boundaries. Place names recorded in charter boundaries give insights into how boundaries were perceived, and while attention has tended to focus on the extremely rare instances where the names suggest supernatural associations (e.g. Semple 1998), the vast majority are descriptive, intended to have a mnemonic significance for those dwelling in and around the territory described. Moreover, the use of prominent natural and topographical features, including ancient earthworks and mounds, in charter boundaries may have been more than a practical result of utilising unambiguous and prominent features, but a way of facilitating the connection of boundaries, memory and perhaps also (for criminal burials) morality (Grinsell 1991; Reynolds 2002).

A further factor that might have influenced burial location but that has received surprisingly little attention is the actual lie of the land. Sam Lucy's study of the early medieval cemeteries of East Yorkshire provides a pioneering attempt to consider the interaction of cemetery location and local topography inspired by the work of Mike Parker Pearson and Bill Bevan (Lucy 1998; see Parker Pearson 1993; Bevan 1999). Lucy identified a range of possible associations between burial rite and burial location by studying their relationship to drift geology, their position on slopes, the direction of slope, and the distance from water. Of particular significance is her argument for a chronological change in the topographical location of burial sites over time. Comparing sixth- with seventh-century burial sites, it appears that there is a trend over time for burials to be placed higher on the Yorkshire Wolds (see also Semple 2003). She suggests that this trend might indicate an increasing marginalisation of the dead from contemporary settlements which (on partial evidence) are assumed to be situated in the valleys. As an alternative explanation she suggests that those sites visible in the seventh and eighth centuries were restricted in their use by elite groups, and that this is reflected in the selection of more inaccessible but prominent locations (Lucy 1998: 99). Lucy also considers the fact that early medieval graves may have sought out chalk areas because, once burial mounds were built, they would be visible from afar as gleaming white markers against the green of the hillsides (Lucy 1998: 99). Yet broader considerations of viewing monuments and cemeteries, and how distinctive views were afforded to those at cemeteries, are required, given the variety of potential interactions between perception and commemoration possible in different societies that might have influenced the location of funerary monuments and other sites of ritual and ceremony (Bradley 1997; Bloch 1995).

Therefore, while cemeteries could be interspersed with fields, enclosures and areas of habitation, the possibility remains that the dead were transported some distance to where they were finally interred, and that this could have involved places with specific views over the surrounding environment. A closely related issue is whether cemeteries were selected so as to be viewed by people when using particular routes or inhabiting particular zones of the landscape. Attempts to consider the view-sheds from burial sites have involved GIS analysis (Rippon & Fulford 1994) and fieldwork-based recording methods (e.g. Williams 1999b), together with more straightforward site-based interpretations of the surrounding landscape (Carver 1998a; Richards 2002; Semple 2003). In combination, they provide the potential for examining the choice of location and its visual interaction with the surrounding landscape in a more sophisticated manner.

Settlement and burial

One might expect there to be a relationship between early medieval settlements and cemeteries. Yet, as Sam Lucy has noted (1998), the proximity of settlement and cemetery is relative and connected to the way the society perceives the landscape (one group's idea of proximity is another group's idea of far apart). However, settlement and mortuary archaeology have tended to exist in isolation from each other (see for example Hamerow 2002; Lucy 2000; Welch 1992). We need to study the precise relationships of settlements and cemeteries, rather than simply their presence in the same vicinity (see also Bradley 1980; Parker Pearson 1993). With the discussion of burial location focusing on boundaries, it is often assumed that the dead were always placed away from settlement sites. However, the interconnected and changing relationships between settlements and burials have been addressed by numerous scholars over the years, with several examples being identified (e.g. Boddington 1990; Reynolds 2002). Meanwhile, examples of 'paired' and successive cemeteries, such as those at Sancton proposed by Margaret Faull (1976), have been used as evidence for the shift towards churchyard-burial. They may instead reflect a more complex early medieval mortuary topography than has previously been appreciated, with numerous settlements and farmsteads of different sizes and forms contributing to any one given burial site, and multiple burial sites serving any single community. We know nothing of whether place of birth or place of domicile, or a range of other practical, social or religious factors influenced the choice of where one was buried. For example, two burial grounds were identified in association with the late fifth- and sixth-century settlement at Mucking (Hamerow 1993b). The nineteenth-century excavations at West Stow that revealed a cemetery were later to be complemented by the excavation of the contemporary settlement (West 1985). At least two broadly contemporary cemeteries have been excavated in association with the seventh-century Northumbrian palace at Millfield (Scull & Harding 1990). In the Gwash valley in Rutland, contemporary settlements and cemeteries were identified in two instances (Cooper 1998). An extensive programme of rescue excavations combined with aerial photography in the Abingdon and Dorchester regions of the Upper Thames valley have similarly revealed a complex interpolation of settlements and cemeteries (Boyle et al. 1995; Miles 1974). Meanwhile, the large-scale excavations conducted at West Heslerton in the Vale of Pickering of North Yorkshire have identified a broadly contemporary settlement and cemetery in close proximity, the cemetery focusing upon a prehistoric barrow cemetery, the settlement seemingly coherently planned and spreading either side of the stream and spring to the south (Powlesland 2000; fig. 6.2). Building on the project, further settlements and cemeteries have been revealed close by during a programme of extensive geophysical survey on a landscape scale (Powlesland 2004; pers. comm.). This research clearly demonstrates that, in some regions of early medieval Britain at least, there was a densely occupied landscape with settlements and cemeteries interspersed hundreds of metres apart (Haughton & Powlesland 1999; Powlesland 2004; pers. comm.).

We also have instances where the distinction between settlement and cemetery appears to blur. In France (Peacquer 2003), the Netherlands (Theuws 1999) and also England, we have dispersed groups of burials among settlements and seemingly contemporaneous with their use (see Reynolds 2003: 132). For example, in the middle Saxon settlement of Yarnton, a small cemetery of at least six west–east-orientated inhumation graves was found 100m west of the settlement, but a further three graves, all sub-adults, one in a prone position and associated with portions

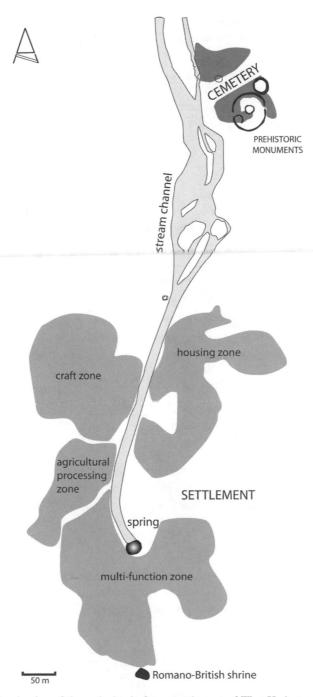

Figure 6.2 Schematic plan of the early Anglo-Saxon settlement of West Heslerton, with its adjacent cemetery focusing upon a prehistoric monument complex (redrawn by the author after Powlesland 2000).

of at least four skulls of sub-adults, were inserted into the ditch on the edge of the settlement compound itself (Hey 2004: 159–63; Boyle in Hey 2004: 321). These might be described as 'deviant' burials and form a part of a broader phenomenon (Reynolds pers. comm.), but the most famous such instance cannot be regarded in this manner. From the middle Saxon palace site of Yeavering, the west–east-orientated grave Ax contained a supine extended burial with a staff and goat's skull and was located outside the eastern entrance of one of the large halls. The grave was seemingly commemorated by the raising of a post. This monument seems to have served as a guide in the orientation of a linear arrangement of high-status buildings focusing upon a prehistoric burial mound to the east (Hope Taylor 1977). In such an instance, we may be looking at the commemoration of a dead individual connected directly to the construction sequence of the royal halls.

These patterns of proximity were enhanced with the advent of church-burial, and from the middle Saxon period sites like Flixborough in Lincolnshire (Loveluck 1998) and Staunch Meadow, Brandon, in Suffolk (Carr et al. 1988) sport a close connection of church, burial and settlement. Similarly, the proto-urban centres (wics or emporia) have produced numerous burial sites, some successively replaced as the settlements expanded, others seemingly contemporary and serving different social groups (Garner 2001; Lucy & Reynolds 2002: 13–4; Scull & Bayliss 1999).

Mortuary geography

A further area of research in recent years concerns the definition of cemeteries and their interaction with their surrounding landscape. In early studies, the discovery of numerous graves often led to the ascription of the site as a 'cemetery' based on the reasonable assumption that the graves identified were only part of a much larger whole. In many cases this assumption has been substantiated through further fieldwork. Yet this is not always the case. Archaeological research, particularly over recent years where rescue excavations sometimes involve the large-scale investigation of an extensive tract of the landscape, has increasingly identified a series of seemingly isolated early medieval burials and small groups of graves, and larger cemeteries can provide alternative locales in close proximity to each other within the settled landscape.

We have already encountered wealthy and seemingly isolated barrow-burials as a distinctive mortuary practice of the late sixth and seventh centuries (e.g. Speake 1989). In some instances, as at Tidworth, where four sixth-century weapon-burials were interred simultaneously in the same grave, the possibility of burial following conflict seems feasible (e.g. Härke 2002), but other instances suggest a more dispersed mortuary geography than is usually appreciated. For example, at Tattershall Thorpe in Lincolnshire, large-scale excavations ahead of gravel extraction revealed a single, isolated seventh-century early medieval burial interred with a range of metal-working tools, leading to the ascription of the grave to a smith (Hinton 2000). Similarly, the wealthy female burial of sixth-century date from Winthorpe Road, Newark, appears to be situated in complete isolation, and extensive excavations around the grave produced no further burials (Samuels & Russell 1999). The increasing discovery of isolated burials in the early medieval landscape situated in earlier monuments, along routes and on boundaries is likely to become more frequent and may not simply be restricted to deviant burials, as for instance the adult male supine extended skeleton uncovered at the site of a later cross-road at Broad Town, Wiltshire (Clarke 2004). These instances encourage us to accept the possibility that 'cemeteries' are a modern term that bring with them a set of assumptions about defined burial zones that may not always be appropriate when applied to the early medieval period. Rather than thinking of defined cemeteries, we need to consider mortuary geography, both when dealing with field cemeteries and churchyards and when considering church complexes.

Pre-Christian sacred and political geography linking high-status settlements to temples and burial sites has been increasingly studied for first millennium AD Scandinavia (e.g. Brink 2004; Hedeager 2001; 2002). An element of these 'central places' is the ancient monument operating as a focus for rituals, assembly, settlement and, sometimes, burial. A commemorative element to assembly places has also been recognised in the association with burial mounds, boat-graves and rune-stones (Brink 2004: 209). Comparable ritual complexes of ceremony and assembly of pre-Christian and early Christian date are known from Britain and Ireland. Timothy Darvill has reviewed the archaeological evidence for the development of Tynwald Hill, the assembly place of the Isle of Man, whose origins as a place of assembly can be charted back to the late first millennium AD at least. Geophysical, geochemical and topographical surveys were combined to ascertain the nature of the site, and, while it was not tested by excavation, Darvill is able to suggest that the four-tiered circular mound may have had prehistoric origins, and evidence of other prehistoric mounds is known from close by. Moreover, the mound itself was enclosed with a rectangular enclosure (Darvill 2004: 220–1). The second phase of activity on the site represents a possible reuse of the mound and enclosure in the mid-late first millennium AD with the establishment of a keeil (chapel), cemetery and a possible associated burial mound (Darvill 2004: 221). Other high-status settlements within a double-ditched enclosure, a further keeil and cemeteries are known from the immediate environment, suggesting an evolving ritual landscape from the sixth to the ninth centuries AD focusing upon the site of assembly. The third phase is suggested for the Viking period and is indicated by a rectangular enclosure around the mound and chapel. Burial was clearly an integral part of the practices focusing upon the ritual and assembly site at Tynwald, perhaps serving as a high-status burial place for Man's elite.

The same picture can be gleaned from the wide-ranging archaeological and literary evidence for assembly and central places in early medieval Ireland and Scotland. In Ireland, Richard Warner has argued for Iron Age origins for royal inauguration sites situated upon mounds that were perceived as places of intercession with the other world. This architecture of power seems to have endured, in part at least, through the early medieval period at sites like Clogher (Warner 2004: 35–9). For Scotland, the connections between royal centres and monasteries as central places in which death and the dead were an integral part have been discussed by

Stephen Driscoll for Scone and Forteviot (Driscoll 1998; 2000; 2004). For Anglo-Saxon England, the picture is less clear, although the barrow cemetery at Sutton Hoo has been argued to be but one element of a high-status central place (Carver 1998a; Semple 2004a). Similarly, the royal palace of Yeavering evolved focusing upon two prehistoric monuments, and it incorporated an open-air assembly site, a series of halls and two successive burial sites (Hope-Taylor 1977). Other assembly sites may have had pre-Christian origins: the focal points of social, political and religious life, as well as being connected to the reuse of ancient monuments (Meaney 1995; Semple 2004a). Despite the lack of surviving literary traditions associating mounds with the dead, ancestors and supernatural peoples, the role of barrows as not only a focus for burial, but also for other ceremonies connecting to ancestors and the past seems likely. Sarah Semple has developed the idea of the burial mound as a focus for socio-political and religious activity in Anglo-Saxon England, drawing upon the Irish and Scandinavian traditions as an analogy for the role of the mound as burial place but also as a conduit to the supernatural and a place of inauguration and administration (Brink 2004; Warner 2004). She proceeds to identify a series of early Anglo-Saxon cemeteries with multiple foci upon prehistoric monuments, such as Winklebury Hill (Wiltshire), Garton Station (East Yorkshire), Harford Farm (Norfolk) and Dorchester-on-Thames (Oxfordshire) (Semple 2004a: 140–2). As well as burials, some of these sites show evidence for square timber structures, interpreted by John Blair as pagan shrines, as at Harford Farm (Blair 1995; Penn 2000), and timber posts, as at Roche Court Down (Semple 2004a: 145). This idea of sacred and political geographies encapsulating more than one monument emphasises the possibility that burial was one among many types of ritual practice taking place at early medieval cemeteries.

If, as Semple argues, sites like Sutton Hoo (see Carver 1998a) and Yeavering (see Hope-Taylor 1977) were experimentations in the creation of sacred spaces and central places during the process of kingdom formation and conversion (Semple 2004a), then their commemorative and mortuary roles were replaced in the later seventh century by monasteries and minster churches (Blair 1989; 1992). Excavations and surveys around minster churches are revealing their dispersed topography, an element of which was a complex series of churches, chapels, oratories and crypts, many of which could have had a mortuary association in commemorating different saints, abbots and abbesses, the burial sites of the religious community and the secular communities of the monastery or minster's estates (Hadley 2001). For example, at Ripon, North Yorkshire, Hall and Whyman have compiled a range of topographical and archaeological evidence to suggest a dispersed series of burial sites associated with the early medieval monastery. As well as from the minster church itself, burials have been produced from at least two sites to the north and a natural knoll called Ailcy Hill situated immediately to the east, and serving as an extension of an alignment of churches and chapels (Hall & Whyman 1996, fig. 6.3). Similar topographies of remembrance can be suggested for other early medieval monasteries, such as Lindisfarne (O'Sullivan 2001), Glastonbury (Rahtz & Watts 2003), Whithorn (Hill 1997), Crowland (Meaney 2001; Stocker 1993; see below), St David's (James 1993) and

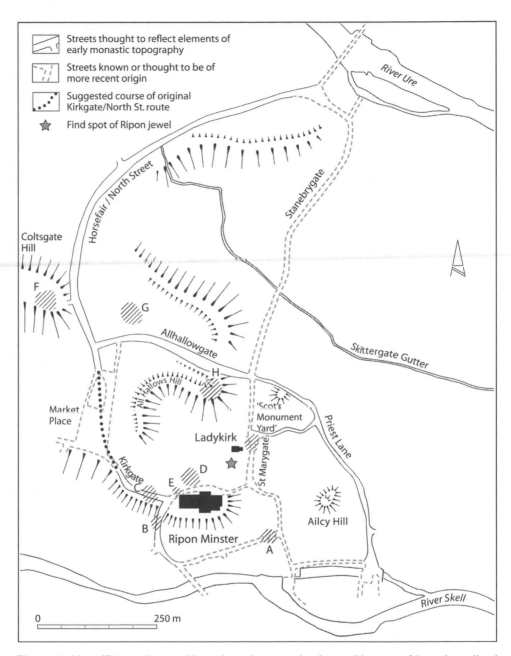

Figure 6.3 Map of Ripon minster and its environs demonstrating the possible extent of the early medieval religious complex and its multiple burial grounds (adapted by Séan Goddard after Hall & Whyman 1996; reproduced with the kind permission of York Archaeological Trust).

St Andrews (Foster 1998), to name a selection. It is possible that this Christian sacred geography, focusing in part upon the cult of saints and kings, was directly copied from Mediterranean and Frankish exemplars, in which multiple church groups formed the commemorative core of monastic and ecclesiastical centres where the power of the sacred and the secular was combined (Thacker 1985; Theuws 2001; Wood 2001).

Natural places

A further theme in recent landscape archaeology that could have relevance for the study of early medieval mortuary topography is the role of natural places (Barnett & Edmonds 2002; Bradley 2000; Pollard 1999) and the interaction of landscape with monumental and grave constructions (Cummings et al. 2002). For example, as well as reusing a series of prehistoric monuments, early medieval burials often reuse prominent natural features, either for their own qualities or because they were mistaken for ancient mounds. For example, at Ailcy Hill, Ripon, a large natural knoll became the focus for a multi-phase inhumation cemetery from the sixth and seventh centuries AD (Hall & Whyman 1996; Williams 1997; Härke 2001). There are other types of natural place that may have attracted burial. Richard Neville (1852) noted the close proximity of the Little Wilbraham sixth-century burial site to a spring, and yet such relationships have received scant consideration since. Certainly, the West Heslerton cemetery was located adjacent to, and over, a series of prehistoric burial mounds, but the site selected was also adjacent to a stream channel fed from a spring (Powlesland 2000).

Could such associations have more than a coincidental or practical significance? Bill Bevan (1999) has argued for a symbolic significance to seasonal water courses for the Yorkshire Wolds, influencing the situation of Iron Age square-barrow cemeteries (Bevan 1999), while Fowler and Cummings (2003) have explored the integration of allusions to water within Neolithic monuments. Meanwhile, recent research by David Stocker and Paul Everson (2003) has argued for a ritual significance of certain water courses surviving from prehistory through the early Middle Ages, such as the River Witham in Lincolnshire. The Witham pins (Webster & Backhouse 1991) and Witham bowl (Graham Campbell 2004) are but some of the treasures found associated with causeways across the river to a series of sites that were to become important early medieval monasteries (see below). Given the deposition of early medieval weaponry in water contexts that, some have argued, could have a votive or funerary significance (Hines 1997b; Härke 2001), it is hoped that future studies will investigate the patterns.

Certainly, watery locations could be regarded as 'liminal' boundary-locations (see Reynolds 2002) and hence appropriate places for the disposal of 'deviants'. Such an individual might be represented by the burial found near the Wiltshire Avon and dated to the fifth or sixth century AD, and bearing all the hall-marks of pre-Iron Age 'bog bodies'. The body was that of a young adult female interred in an extended posture but prone and covered with fourteen oak timbers (McKinley 2003; see chapter 3). Other instances of such burials, often but not exclusively adult females, have been found along the Thames foreshore, in one case surmounted by a mound and wooden post. These seemingly deviant burials have been dated to between the seventh and ninth centuries AD and suggest that watery places could be among the locations singled out for the disposal of bad deaths (Cohen 2003: 17–18).

Of course, there are many other forms of 'natural' feature that do not survive. The nature of vegetation can affect the visibility of cemeteries and graves as well as affect the views achievable when at the sites, and this is often difficult for archaeologists to reconstruct (see Cummings & Whittle 2003). Vegetation can also serve as an important element of the mortuary environment, as in Roman 'garden' cemeteries (Evans & Maynard 1997; Toynbee 1971: 94–100). For instance, the ubiquity of trees as the focus of early medieval assembly places as revealed in place-name evidence does not produce an archaeological correlate (Pantos 2004a and b). In other periods, trees have been regarded as places attracting ritual activity (Evans, Pollard & Knight 1999) and as enduring 'time-marks' in the rural landscape, socialised through their use as resting and meeting places (see Ingold 1993). Similarly, if trees formed foci for cemeteries, we would often be none the wiser in terms of the surviving evidence. The possibility that stones might equally have served to connect the living with the dead and with ancestors, either their burial places or acts connected to their life-histories, is a theme fully discussed in prehistoric archaeology (e.g. Bradley 1998a; Gillings & Pollard 1999; Tilley 1996b; see also Tilley 2004) but also finds resonance in Icelandic literature (Overing & Osbern 1994: 79–80). Yet, at the very least, this discussion hints at the potential for considering a broader range of factors influencing the location and organisation of early medieval burial sites.

Theorising mortuary landscapes
So far we have discussed a range of factors that may have influenced early medieval burial location. Inevitably, the introduction of new techniques and methods in land-scape fieldwork, as well as new means of data management and analysis, is likely to have a valuable role in our understanding of early medieval mortuary topography. In particular, the combination of increasing volumes of cemetery data brought about by excavations, landscape surveys and metal-detector finds, together with more rig-orous techniques with which to handle spatial data including GIS (Geographical Information Systems), will increasingly provide a detailed and more nuanced appre-ciation of death in the early medieval landscape (Chester-Kadwell 2004; Powlesland 2004; see also Williams 2002b). However, although the studies addressed above have alluded to the potential role of landscape in mortuary commemoration, a coherent theory of memory and landscape has yet to be applied to early medieval mortuary archaeology.

In order to theorise early medieval mortuary geography, we need to consider two related factors linking landscape and mortuary practices. The first element deals with how mortuary practices are inherently concerned with spatial and temporal movement and directionality (Parkin 1992), and so the mortuary process is inher-ently implicated in creating memories through places and pathways (Tilley 1994). The second aspect concerns how cemeteries operate as places where the ancestors can be contacted and reside, places that accrue memories through their use as the end-point of repeated mortuary events. Let us look at some of the aspects of each in turn.

Mortuary geographies of remembrance

Cemeteries are merely the end-points of complex mortuary sequences that might incorporate many locations in the landscape including settlements, temples/churches, pyre-sites (for cremation) and other locations of assembly and congregation (see above; Williams 2004c). The landscape is significant not only for the locales associated with different stages of mortuary practices, but the routes between them. Much of this sequence is lost, but as we have already discussed archaeologists have already recognised relationships between burial sites and a range of other locations and routes in the early medieval landscape. My argument is that memories of the dead were manipulated, promoted and suppressed through the use of the geographical and temporal sequence of events during the funeral, not just the burial site itself.

Movement across the landscape is not only a physical aspect of mortuary practices, it is also a metaphorical and symbolic aspect. Movement took place in mortuary practices to symbolise journeys made in life, perhaps the funeral procession itself, and hence was concerned with retrospective remembrance. Alternatively, it concerned otherworld journeys to a new supernatural realm or ancestral state, and in this sense was concerned with prospective remembrance. Archaeology reveals a surprising variety of evidence for these metaphorical journeys. Obvious and explicit examples include horses buried or cremated with the dead, as well as the ships placed in mounds, as at Sutton Hoo and Snape (Carver 1998a; Filmer-Sankey & Pestell 2001). Further evidence of metaphors for retrospective remembrance might include the inclusion with the dead of exotic artefacts from other places. These might evoke other times, but also other places and the journeys made both by the deceased during life and the artefacts associated with his or her biography.

A further type of movement concerns the metaphysics of bodily transformation in death. The dead body undergoes movements of its own. In cremation rites, the body moves downwards in the pyre as it collapses, but upwards and around the pyre in the form of heat, light, ash and smoke (Williams 2004b). Continued communication with the living and the expectation of resurrection are also integral elements of movement in mortuary practices in a cosmological sense, if not a physical sense (if this distinction was recognised in early medieval societies). In this sense, the geographical movement of the dead both physically and symbolically serves in the construction of identities and social remembrance involving landscapes both real and imagined. In this sense, the cemetery can be considered less a permanent end-point of funerals, and more a conduit in the ongoing transformation of memory.

Places of remembrance

This leads us to consider the role of the cemetery as a place. A paper by Heinrich Härke (2001) has come closer than any other in creating a general theory for the significance of the cemetery in early medieval Europe. The strength of Härke's argument is that he considers the various ways in which cemeteries operate in social relations and reflect, participate in, and promote sacred and social power. He notes nine different ways in which cemeteries operate as social places rather than simply as collections of graves. He discusses cemeteries as places for the disposal of corpses, which he notes was a deliberate and conscious decision, since (as he reminds us) in many periods and places formal burial grounds are not known. In this sense, cemeteries are not a 'natural' consequence of death in human society: they are in themselves the result of human agency and social decisions concerning how to dispose of the dead in ways relating to particular social and historical contexts. Härke then considers cemeteries as places of remembrance, where the past and the present are connected and the dead are remembered. He also considers cemeteries as places where rites of passage occur, in which the living and the dead undergo transformations. Cemeteries are also regarded by Härke as places laden with emotion, as places where mortality is encountered and therefore an awareness of being-in-the-world is manifest. He also suggests that cemeteries enhanced claims over property and resources, and notes how they can serve to connect people to the land. Next, Härke suggests that cemeteries can operate as locales, points in the landscape linked by pathways that both constrained and influenced ritual processions and social routines within the landscape. Härke considers cemeteries as places linked to mental topographies and sacred geographies, places connected to particular ways of viewing the world. Finally, Härke considers the temporality of cemeteries, that they are places with distinct essences of time separate from the routines and cycles of activities operating in other spheres of social life. These points coalesce in three interrelated ways in which cemeteries are related to power. First, there is the power *of* cemeteries through their association with ancestors and the sacred. Second, there is the power *in* cemeteries: the use of cemeteries as places of social and political display in which identities and memories are negotiated and reproduced. Third, we must appreciate the importance of power *over* cemeteries: how the control of the mortuary practices and the meaning of place can serve as a means of negotiating identities and memories.

Although Härke's discussion does not focus specifically on social memory, all of the themes he identifies have a mnemonic significance, influencing how the dead are remembered and forgotten by the living. In terms of the power of cemeteries, the graves of the dead can act as visual reminders of the deceased, both individually and collectively. Memories were constructed through the repeated use of the burial sites and the journeys, real and metaphorical, that were performed through mortuary practices and inscribed on the landscape. The construction of genealogical and mythical relationships between burial and place is a key theme in this regard. Cemeteries can serve in commemoration through the rituals conducted at them, both during burial rites and in ancestor rites that celebrated the memories of the dead (fig. 6.4). Finally, power over cemeteries influenced remembrance in the sense that those controlling the mortuary practices and access to, and use of, the cemetery could manipulate which memories were promoted and which were suppressed and

Figure 6.4   An artistic interpretation of the rituals surrounding the reuse of a prehistoric barrow-cemetery for burial in the later seventh century on the downland of southern England (artwork by Aaron Watson).

dispersed. In this sense, cemeteries as places of remembrance are concerned with ancestors and performance, as well as domination and resistance.

Texts and monuments – inherited, invented, imagined and inhabited landscapes

To allow us to appreciate further the relationship between death, memory and landscape, we need to consider medieval literature. There are many pitfalls in using later medieval sources to understand the ideologies and experiences of landscape of early medieval societies, but they can provide a set of insights into how death and landscape were related to an ideology that had its manifestations in both literature and ritual practices. For example, Sarah Semple has discussed the demonic and supernatural associations of selected burial mounds in the landscape of later Anglo-Saxon England, as revealed in place names, written sources and in the placing of execution graves at prehistoric monuments (Semple 1998). More recently, she has argued that portrayals of hell-mouths in manuscripts are a further representation of a subterranean hell entered through mounds (Semple 2004b). Therefore, text, image, place names and ritual practices form elements of an evolving ideology of landscape.

How was social memory implicated in this interaction of word and the mortuary landscape location? The symbolic and narrative role of landscape in the Icelandic sagas provides us with one instance. Landscape features, including burial mounds, are widely used in the Icelandic sagas not as accurate representations of the tenth-century landscapes in which the narratives were set, but as ways of inscribing narratives onto the thirteenth- and fourteenth-century landscapes of the saga-writers and their audience of wealthy Icelandic farmers wishing to affirm and invent identities with reference to the heroic past and the days of settlement. Landscape and genealogy are enmeshed in the sagas and, most importantly, are sustained through reference to prominent natural features, farmsteads and, occasionally, the mounds of the dead (see for example Fentress & Wickham 1992: 162–72; Wyatt 2004).

Similar ideas can be developed in relation to the Anglo-Saxon landscape. Nicholas Howe has discussed the various ways in which later Anglo-Saxon written sources construct ideologies of space and place (Howe 2000; 2002). In particular, Howe suggests that the literary portrayal of landscape focuses upon three interleaving themes: inherited, invented and imagined landscapes. The inherited landscape of the Anglo-Saxons constituted an origin myth built upon a model derived from the Old Testament of a chosen people migrating to reach a promised land. Through the writings of the Venerable Bede, this perception of the Anglo-Saxons, their rightful inheritance of Britain and their Continental origins, was widely circulated and perpetuated through religious and secular texts (Howe 1989). The presence of ancient monuments in the landscapes of later Anglo-Saxon England was reflected in such poems as *The Ruin*, in which an abandoned Roman town, the 'work of giants', is depicted. The landscape is perceived as the material accumulation of the past (Howe 2002: 95). Ancient monuments embodied an awareness in the literary sources that the landscape was inherited from former occupants. These abandoned structures became attached to stories, names and memories through their enduring presence in the landscape, and provided a conception of time and place. Yet Howe does not engage with the possibility that these ideas may have been materialised through social and ritual practices in burial rituals by, for instance, monument reuse (see above).

This leads us to Howe's second aspect of later Anglo-Saxon landscape perception: invented landscapes. In a sense this focuses upon the creation of new landscapes. One example of such a landscape discussed by Howe is the creation of territory manifest in the proliferation of land charters. These were written documents, but the use of Old English for the description of charter boundaries suggests they were intended to be read aloud as part of ritual performance and the exchange of land from kings to lords, bishops and abbots. Their intention was to consolidate and commemorate the social relations of giver and receiver. Moreover, through their recording and utterance, charters served to inscribe memories of these social relationships onto the landscape, so that both the charters themselves and the boundaries they define become commemorative of the gift-giving that they record. Land charters also invented memories, in so far as they were intended to be mnemonics during routes of procession around the boundaries. The embodied and ritualised aspect of land charters is emphasised by the fact that 'landscape is not a vista to be enjoyed but a sequence of signs to be walked' (Howe 2002: 102). The inscribed aspect of land charters comes from their incorporation of prominent features, both natural and human-made, including burial mounds and earthworks, into the boundaries. In doing so, land surveyors were using recognised and permanent features of the landscape not only to render the boundaries beyond dispute, but also to inscribe memories of land ownership and identities onto a place. Indeed, the frequent use of ancient and natural features represents an aspiration to render permanent and enduring social relations and ownership within what was by definition a fleeting relationship between people and land.

The third element of landscape is the imagined landscapes, usually the wilderness of *The Seafarer*, *The Wanderer* or *The Wife's Lament*, in which seascapes and land-scapes are places of abandonment and confinement. In *Beowulf*, the juxtaposition and opposition of home and wild – the hall Heorot and Grendel's mere – serve to emphasise the use of landscape as a focus of crisis in heroic culture.

No single coherent vision of landscape is presented in Anglo-Saxon texts, but Howe's literary perspective prevents him from engaging with a fourth type of land-scape found in the texts: one of inhabitation. Certainly, the landscape of settlements, farms, fields and tracks is lost in these literary sources. Yet the theme of inhabiting takes other forms. Landscapes and seascapes in *Beowulf* are thickly inhabited by spirits and dragons, inhabited by people focusing on the hall and inhabited by the dead in their burial mounds. The landscape was not a surface but an interface, in these texts, just as they are represented in the Harley Psalter depictions of entrances to hell discussed by Semple (2004b).

Beowulf's mound

Archaeologists have long used and abused the poem *Beowulf*, and great caution needs to be taken in regarding the poem as an historical document illustrating early medieval material culture and funerary rites (Cramp 1957; Hills 1997). Yet in terms of landscape and memory, the poem provides a vision of the burial mound as a focus of commemoration at a number of levels, but also as a mnemonic structural element within the oral performance of the poem, and perhaps also as a material anchor for aristocratic memories of pagan and heroic pasts. The mound of the hero Beowulf in particular incorporates all three of the literary perceptions of landscape discussed by Howe and the theme of inhabited landscapes. The mound materialises the inherited, invented and imagined landscapes, and also alludes to the importance of mounds in inhabited landscapes.

Rather than discussing the poem as a whole, this discussion will focus upon the grave of the hero as portrayed in the final section of the work. After Beowulf has killed the dragon in the ancient burial mound, he himself dies and is carried to a nearby funeral pyre, where he is cremated together with the dragon's treasure. A mound is raised over his tomb on a prominent headland, where it is visible to seafarers:

Command men famous as fighters to build a burial mound, a conspicuous one, on the ocean bluff, following the cremation. It must tower high on Hronesnæs as a reminder to my people, so that seafarers who from afar come navigating their tall ships over the gloom of the waters may thereafter call it Beowulf's Barrow.
(Bradley 1982: 485).

Then the Geatish people erected for him a funeral fire on the ground, one not mean, but hung about with helmets, with battle-shields, with bright mail-coats, as he had asked . . . And so the warriors proceeded to kindle upon the hill-top a most mighty funeral pyre.
(Bradley 1982: 493).

Then the Weder Geatish people built a resting place on the headland, which was high and broad and widely visible to those journeying the ocean; and over ten days they constructed the monument of a man renowned for his striving.
(Bradley 1982: 494).

The funeral interacted with its landscape in all three of the ways discussed by Howe. The mound was raised in the *imaginary* landscape in the mythical homeland of the Geats, by the ocean, on a hill-top, close to the conceptual and physical edges of the kingdom, a location comparable to the liminal landscapes depicted in *The Seafarer*, *The Wanderer* and *The Wife's Lament*. The mound incorporates *inherited* aspects, for it is itself situated close to the ancient dragon's mound wrought by an ancient race. For the Geats, the dragon's mound embodied the ancient past; for the Anglo-Saxon audience, Beowulf's mound also served this purpose, juxtaposed close to the dragon's mound that embodied the past in the past. Beowulf's mound even incorporated this ancient monument into its structure through the placing of the dragon's treasure on Beowulf's funeral pyre. The *invented* landscape can be found in the monumentality of the barrow itself, as a statement of the endeavours of the hero and king Beowulf, promoting his fame into the future for all who passed by to see. The *inhabited* landscape is implicit, the threatened landscape that Beowulf saves by slaying the dragon. The inhabitation is, however, explicit earlier in the poem, depicted clearly in Hrothgar's hall Heorot, the axis mundi for the inhabited world of kingship and hospitality (Bradley 1982: 413).

In all these senses, the funeral of Beowulf was a ritual performance embedded within a poetic performance, serving as a mnemonic nexus for a range of associations linking the Anglo-Saxon audience to the heroic past. For the Geats in the poem, Beowulf's mound is portrayed as linked to the world before their rise to power and promoted the memory of their dead ruler into the future, but also forewarned them of their eventual demise. In this way, the landscape of Beowulf's mound connected, but maintained a distance between, the Anglo-Saxon audience and the Scandinavian past of the poem. Rather than attempting to consider its accuracy and the precise choice of names employed for the landscape (see Gelling 2002), we can instead consider the landscape as literary fantasy. Yet it was a fantasy that incorporates elements that were meaningful and given a material focus through the description of Beowulf's funeral and burial mound. The mound creates a mnemonic focus for the inherited, invented, imagined and inhabited landscapes of the poem and in turn provides a set of ideas and associations that may have interacted with the early medieval perception of the British landscape.

Materialising the landscape of Beowulf's mound

With these ideas in mind, we can return to the archaeology of high-status barrow-burials with an invigorated understanding of the relationships between death, memory and landscape that were embodied in the funerary rites. Let us take, for the sake of argument, two sites in the Thames Valley: Taplow Court and Asthall.

The burial mound at Taplow Court was excavated in the late nineteenth century and found to be a primary mound raised over a large timber burial chamber containing an extremely wealthy, even 'princely', early seventh-century adult male-gendered weapon-burial with feasting gear (Webster 1992; fig. 6.5). The location 'inherited' the ancient past: recent excavations by the Oxford Archaeological Unit have revealed that the burial mound had been situated within an Iron Age hillfort that encompassed the hill-top but that had long been obscured by the destruction caused by the post-medieval landscaped gardens (Allen & Lamdin-Whymark 2001). The choice of location may have served to emphasise the view that the dead experienced, since the mound was placed on the only hill in the area with long-distance views in most directions, rather than views in only one direction. Through this prominent location, it can be argued that the spectacular mortuary display of Taplow Court served to assert claims over land and territory, and express a new identity for the deceased and his kin. The imaginary and inhabited landscape is embodied within the burial chamber itself: the range of aristocratic practices embodied in the drinking-horns, lyre and weaponry allude to an idealised lifestyle in this world and the next. As such, the idealised hall-life is embodied in the grave: the connection between two dwellings, one for the living, one for the dead. As such, the 'presence' of the Taplow mound may have been more than a 'marker' for the dead, but something evoked that status, and aspired pasts and futures, and perhaps also the presence of the dead active within the mound (see chapter 5).

Broadly contemporary with the Taplow mound is the early seventh-century cremation burial found beneath a large earthen mound at Asthall in north Oxfordshire (fig. 6.6). The spectacle of the funerary rites, the prominent location with wide views over the surrounding landscape, and the association with routes and ancient monuments can all be attested (Dickinson & Speake 1992). The cremation was extremely high-status, and while only some of the objects survived and were recognised by the early twentieth-century excavators, a kin-group of comparable status to those performing the cremation ceremonies at Sutton Hoo can be suggested. The mound overlooked the Roman road Akeman Street and was immediately above the abandoned site of the Roman settlement that straddled the road where it crossed the River Windrush (Williams 1999b). There is no direct evidence that the mound itself reused an earlier

Figure 6.5 The early seventh-century barrow-burial at Taplow, Buckinghamshire. The mound is now situated in the grounds of Taplow Court amidst the eighteenth- and nineteenth-century graves and tombs of the abandoned churchyard. The mound is situated on a south-facing spur enjoying extensive views over the Thames Valley (Photo by the author).

Figure 6.6   The early seventh-century barrow-burial at Asthall, Oxfordshire, dominates a ridge overlooking the valley of the River Windrush, with long-distance views in all directions (photo by the author).

site, although it is possible, given the large number of prominently sited prehistoric mounds in the Wychwood district immediately to the north. As such, the mound may have emphasised, or created, a sense of territory, connections to the past and domination of the contemporary landscape, and may even have been regarded as the dwelling place of the dead person. Such 'sentinel' burials of the seventh century (see Everson 1993; O'Brien 1999; Williams 1999b; Williams 2001a) served to inscribe and perform new pasts and assert new futures upon the early medieval landscape. Evoking the mnemonic presence of the dead within their graves, and hence dominating their environs, mound-burials allowed the dead to inhabit the landscape.

Beowulf does not portray the early medieval landscape or mortuary practices in a direct and objective way, and archaeologists cannot 'dig up' the reality of *Beowulf*, because it probably never existed. However, by thinking about the mnemonics of the burial mound in the poem, it helps us to conceptualise the mnemonic role of seventh-century burial mounds through their interaction with the surrounding landscape.

Guthlac's mound

One of the tropes of early medieval hagiography is the monk leaving the monastery for a solitary life as a hermit in a wilderness inhabited by devils. This is manifest clearly in the second famous early medieval depiction of a burial mound: that in the eighth-century *Life of St Guthlac* by Felix. The *Life* was written only a couple of decades after the saint's death and can be regarded as a primary source. While part of a developing literary genre and written to a hagiographic template inspired directly by the lives of the early desert fathers and indirectly via Bede's *Life of Cuthbert* written about Lindisfarne, as well as a range of other borrowings, Felix's *Life* was a selection of motifs and themes that seems to have been a response to the ideals of Anglo-Saxon secular and religious life and the topography of the Cambridge fenland (Meaney 2001: 30).

The commemorative aspects of the *Life* can be summarised to illustrate the central commemorative role of the burial mound and its landscape. The *Life* was itself commemorative through its dedication to the East Anglian King Aelfwald, who ruled c. 713 to 749. From birth, Guthlac was marked as a holy man through the bright light that illuminated the house where the saint was born (Meaney 2001: 31). As a young man, Guthlac pursued a secular life as a soldier for nine years before turning to the religious life, going first to the double monastery at Repton. Two years later he sought the anchoretic life in the fens:

> There is in the midland district of Britain a most dismal fen of immense size, which begins at the banks of the river Granta not far from the camp which is called Cambridge, and stretches from the south as far north as the sea. It is a very long tract, now consisting of marshes, now of bogs, sometimes of black waters overhung by fog, sometimes studded with wooded islands and traversed by the windings of tortuous streams. So when this same man of blessed memory, Guthlac, had learned about the wild places of this vast desert, he made his way thither with divine assistance by the most direct route.
> (Colgrave 1956: 87).

The place was therefore secretive, 'untilled and known to a very few' (Colgrave 1956: 89). It was a liminal place, haunted by 'phantoms of demons', yet it was only revealed by divine will, and Guthlac 'loved the remoteness of the spot seeing that God had given it him . . .' (Colgrave 1956: 89). On the island was a 'mound built of clods of earth which greedy comers to the waste had dug open, in the hope of finding treasure there; in the side of this there seemed to be a sort of cistern, and in this Guthlac the man of blessed memory began to dwell, after building a hut over it' (Colgrave 1956: 95).

Over this mound an oratory was later built. The mound is taken to be a prehistoric or Saxon barrow, perhaps one of a series of prehistoric burial mounds, and may have been a prominent element of the island's topography (Meaney 2001: 34–5; Stocker 1993). The portrayal of a burial mound as a place for a hermitage evokes the tombs used as retreats by the desert fathers, a theme that has resonances in the British landscape in Welsh hagiography (Corner 1985).

The significance of the mound extends to Guthlac's death. The manipulation of time and space was a key element in the perfect saintly death in Anglo-Saxon England, and Guthlac was able to predict his own death and prophesied his successor (Colgrave 1956: 147–9, 155–7). A linen cloth for a shroud and a lead coffin were sent by Abbess Ecgburh, and, when close to death, Guthlac instructs his sister Pega to perform the simple burial rites (Colgrave 1956: 147). Guthlac was already in a heavenly state prior to burial, for he had conversations with angels in his cell every morning and evening. His death was accompanied by a sweet odour of nectar issuing from his last breath, and a bright light filled his cell all night (Colgrave 1956: 157–9). The ascension of his soul was demonstrated by a bright light leading to heaven and the sound of angelic singing. Pega arrived the day after Guthlac's death to find the whole island and dwellings filled with an 'ambrosial odour'. She then spent three days praying for his soul before burying him in his oratory over the burial mound (Colgrave 1956: 161).

A year later, 'God put it into the heart of his sister to place her brother's body in another sepulchre' (Colgrave 1956: 161). The body was found incorrupt: 'the limbs flexible and much more like those of a sleeping man', and his garments 'shone' (Colgrave 1956: 161). Subsequently, the body was translated to an above-ground shrine in a church nearby. These acts linked the burial mound, presumably still visible in Felix's day, to a topography of commemoration propagated through the saint's *Life* but also through the landscape of Crowland. This was sustained through post-mortem miracles and an appearance to the Mercian over-king Aethelbald in a vision (Colgrave 1956: 165–71).

Archaeologists have focused upon debating the accuracy of this description and the precise form of the monument, but the literary significance of the monument's description lies in the role of the burial mound as part of inherited, invented, imaginary and inhabited landscapes. There are three elements to its significance. First, the monument must have had a supernatural origin if the island had never before been inhabited. Therefore, the monument was *inherited*, serving to mark the distinction between pagan past and Christian present through its present reuse as a hermit's cell. Second, it is a monument of futility, a vain monument to the 'wretched deaths and the shameful ends of the ancient kings of his race in the course of the past ages' (Colgrave 1956: 83). Third, the location in the wilderness away from human habitation is doubled by emphasising the failure of treasure-hunters to find 'the fleeting riches of this world' (Colgrave 1956: 83). The liminal setting fits the criteria of an *imagined* location, while Guthlac *invented* the monument anew through dwelling upon it. Indeed, in this instance, the mound was *inhabited*, and inhabitation is the key theme linking the associations of the mound and the focus of conflict between Guthlac and the demons.

The monument is therefore inherited, invented, imagined and inhabited by the saint in life and subsequently in death. On Crowland, Guthlac became a 'soldier of the true God' (Colgrave 1956: 91) in combating the temptations of demons and the Devil and in performing miracles (Shook 1960). Archaeological evidence shows that the fenland was still an occupied environment of dispersed early Anglo-Saxon settlement followed by middle Saxon nucleation, even if less densely inhabited than in the Romano-British period (Lane & Hayes 1993). Consequently, Felix's description is an exaggeration to suit the desired metaphor of fenland as desert and the mound as a focus of conflict between the demons and the saint (Meaney 2001; Shook 1960).

Alfred K. Siewers (2003) has recently argued for a broader, Mercian political context to the portrayal of landscape in the *Life of St Guthlac* connected to the demonising of the native and the assertion of an Anglo-Saxon nation, but the primary focus of the hagiographic writing was upon the promotion of Crowland as a holy place through its connection to the cult of the saint as a focus of local and regional identities and memories connected to the monastery. The barrow was more than a literary metaphor: it had a physical presence, surmounted by the oratory, associated with the memory of the saint's life, miracles and death, as well as his translation and subsequent miraculous occurrences. The mound was a mnemonic focus of the inherited, invented, imagined and inhabited landscape of the early medieval fenland connecting the saint to his spiritual kin among the living.

This perspective provides the theoretical connection between death, memory and landscape with which we can re-approach the archaeological evidence for the pro-liferation of monasteries on islands in the Lincolnshire and Cambridgeshire fenland (Stocker 1993; fig. 6.7). The stations of crosses that defined the monastic bound-aries, as well as the dispersed topography of early medieval monasteries with mul-tiple churches and burial grounds, together with the physical boundaries provided by the islands themselves, all served as settings for, but also integral components in, the topographies of memory promoted by these monasteries throughout the Middle Ages. The promulgation of the cult of saints required not just hagiographies but also landscape, and in the case of St Guthlac a burial mound provided a mnemonic focus for the life, death and later enshrinement of the saint (see Harvey 2002).

The curse of Cwichelm's mound
We have so far discussed plenty of burial mounds, both early medieval and reused prehistoric and Roman monuments. Yet the only shire-moot – the meeting place of the shirt court – known as a field monument is that for Berkshire at Scutchamer Knob on Cuckhamsley Hill (fig. 6.8). The site as it is preserved is a huge mound situated on the Berkshire Ridgeway overlooking the Vale of the White Horse to the north and with views over the Downs towards the distant hills of Hampshire to the south. The site is recorded in the Anglo-Saxon Chronicle's entry for 1006 recording how a raiding Danish force camped at *Cwichelmes hlaewe* in defiance of the curse of the site that any invading army reaching the mound would be doomed (Pantos 2003; Semple 2004a):

> [the raiding army] . . . sought out Cwichelm's Barrow, and there awaited
> the boasted threats, because it had often been said that if they sought
> out Cwichelm's Barrow they would never get to the sea. Then they
> turned homewards by another route.
> (Swanton 2000: 137).

The site was, clearly, associated with a certain Cwichelm and is one of a number of ancient burial mounds attributed to mythological, heroic and (in some instances) infamous personages and recorded in land charters (Grinsell 1991; see Reynolds 2002). Cwichelm's mound was a place of fame and of infamy: a place where disputes

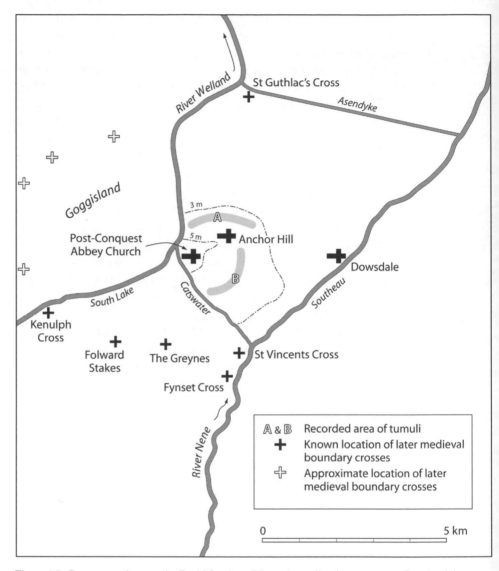

Figure 6.7 Reconstruction map by David Stocker of the early medieval monastery at Crowland, incorporating the known and postulated locations of later medieval boundary crosses (redrawn by Séan Goddard after Stocker 1993).

were settled, the fate of criminals was decided and where armies might meet their fate in battle.

There are two Cwichelms recorded in Anglo-Saxon sources, both notable figures in the early history of the West Saxon kingdom. The first we know little about other than that he met his death in battle fighting alongside the powerful West Saxon king Ceawlin against his rivals in the late sixth century. This Cwichelm might have been remembered in oral tradition for good or ill, but, given the detail that the

Figure 6.8 Scutchamer Knob, Cuckhamsley Hill, Oxfordshire (in Berkshire until 1974). This vast mound, now hidden in woodland, is the site of *Cwichelmes Hlaewe* recorded in late tenth- and early eleventh-century sources as the assembly site for the shire-court for Berkshire (photo by the author).

Venerable Bede and the Anglo-Saxon Chronicle employ in recording the acts of the second Cwichelm, it seems more likely that Cwichelm's mound was connected to the memory of this West Saxon leader. As a king (at least according to Bede), Cwichelm fought alongside his brother King Cynegils 'on Bea's mount' and allegedly killed 2,065 Welsh (Swanton 2000: 22). Later he fought again alongside Cynegils against the Mercians. Although he was defeated and perhaps lost land in an agreement, it is notable that this battle may have also been remembered in a positive light in West Saxon folk memory. This is because father and son did not lose their lives or kingdoms, for they had fought against the powerful pagan Mercian King Penda, who was much maligned by the Venerable Bede as the slayer of the Northumbrian Christian Kings Edwin and Oswald. It is also notable that the Anglo-Saxon Chronicle records his place of baptism as Dorchester, the first episcopal see of the West Saxons, not far to the north of *Cwichelmes hlaewe* (Blair 1994; Swanton 2000: 25–6). Yet Cwichelm was not recorded simply as a hero-king by the Anglo-Saxon Chronicle. He was also remembered for ill as the king who sent an assassin to try to kill the godly King Edwin of Northumbria, the first Christian king of that kingdom (Swanton 2000: 25). Consequently, it may have been the mixture of good and bad associations, the juxtaposition of sin and repentance, that made Cwichelm so memorable a figure in the folk history of the Upper Thames valley.

Whether Cwichelm was actually interred beneath *Cwichelmes hlaewe* cannot be demonstrated. The site was excavated in the early twentieth century, but no conclusive evidence for burials or a date for the monument could be ascertained (Meaney 1964: 45–6), although nearby there are prominently sited burial sites containing richly furnished seventh-century burials. This again returns us to sites that may materialise the 'heroic' ideals of *Beowulf* discussed above, namely Taplow Court and Asthall, but also Cuddesdon and Lowbury Hill (e.g. Dickinson 1974; Williams 1999b). A likely, if completely hypothetical, scenario is that Scutchamer Knob began life as a Bronze Age burial mound, was reused in the seventh century as a burial site and was enlarged in the later Saxon period as an assembly mound. This possibility must, however, remain speculation, until extensive excavations on the much-denuded monument are pursued. The accuracy of the association is, however, not the issue, but the association with the memory and fame of Cwichelm combined with its use as an assembly place. By the later Anglo-Saxon period, it may have been regarded as Cwichelm's burial mound or it may equally have been thought to be the site of 'Bea's mount', where the second Cwichelm and his father defeated the Welsh. This latter association may have been the source of the myth that invading armies reaching the mound would never again leave the kingdom. It may even be the case that the mound was selected for Cwichelm's interment because it had been the site of his famous victory. What we can argue is that, to an early eleventh-century aristocracy and clergy (and perhaps to those in earlier centuries) who were familiar with heroic tales like *Beowulf* in which war-heroes are interred in prominently sited burial mounds, it is likely that Scutchamer Knob would have been perceived as an appropriate burial place and battle site associated with one of the founding fathers of the West Saxon kingdom. This theme of conflict may have had a spiritual element to it, found in both Beowulf's conflict with the dragon and Guthlac's struggle with demons. For Cwichelm, the struggle was for faith, and the remembrance of a pagan king who converted to Christianity before death may have made Cwichelm's mound a monument commemorating morality as well as heroic kingship.

These associations may have been particularly important to add gravitas and legitimacy to the complex legal functions of assembly sites, but the association of the mound with Cwichelm may have had a particular poignancy, since while the Upper Thames region in the early seventh century had been at the heart of the West Saxon kingdom, throughout the seventh, eighth and ninth centuries it became a contested landscape between the West Saxons and the Mercians (Blair 1994). The 'fame' of the site may have been intended to stand as a warning against enemies of the West Saxons long after the Welsh and Mercians had ceased to be a threat, when the Danes had appeared on the scene. Sadly for the kingdom of Aethelred II (the ill-counselled), the curse of Cwichelm proved ineffective against the powerful Danish army that ravaged the kingdom in the winter of 1006/7, but it does suggest that mythologies were embedded within the early medieval landscape beyond the cult centres of the saints and were employed to create heroic histories in times of crisis.

It is against the mnemonic significance of the naming of the large assembly mound on Cuckhamsley Hill that many other named mounds and topographical features found in documentary sources and charter bounds can be understood (see Grinsell 1991; Hines 1997a). Rather than references to memories, or folklore concerning the occupant of the mound, or 'pagan mythology', named monuments may instead be regarded as forming a central part of a later Anglo-Saxon landscape of fear, fate and morality. Combining aristocratic heroic and Christian moral traditions, Cwichelm's mound embodies one version of themes that might find expression in other named mounds. For instance, the prehistoric monuments attributed to Germanic gods and heroes, such as Neolithic monuments renamed in the early medieval period 'Wayland's Smithy' and 'Woden's mound', as well as purpose-built meeting mounds named after bishops, such as 'Oswald's mound' in Worcestershire (Adkins & Petchy 1984), seem like poor interpretive bed-fellows. Yet all served to commemorate the past and inscribe onto the landscape heroic and powerful famed personalities.

Accumulating memories: Cannington

The discussion has so far engaged with the significance of single burial mounds and the 'fame' of individuals in death, whether installed within new mounds or reusing ancient monuments. However, the very evidence of communal burial sites from the early medieval landscape helps us to consider the power of place and of accumulated memory beyond isolated acts of commemoration. For example, long-running furnished burial sites such as the Buckland cemetery in Dover can be shown from the construction of a chronological sequence to evolve as a poly-focal mortuary space for over 200 years (Evison 1987).

In the Christian context of early medieval western Britain, the promotion of the significance of place in cemeteries was connected to the powerful presence of 'special graves', whether they represented local saints or secular elites (see chapter 5). One of the largest excavated cemeteries of relevance to this phenomenon is the Somerset cemetery of Cannington (Rahtz, Hirst & Wright 2000; fig. 6.9), an example of the numerous sub-Roman cemeteries dominated by west–east-orientated, poorly furnished inhumation graves in south-west England (see Rahtz 1977).

The site can be regarded as situated within a region defined by dispersed settlement that has continued from prehistory to the present day (Rahtz, Hirst & Wright 2000: 22–3). The cemetery was located on a prominent hill, the smaller and easterly of a pair rising to the west of the lower stretches of the valley of the River Parrett. The immediate surroundings of the cemetery are worthy of note. The Roman settlements of Combwich and Crandon Bridge close by provide the suggestion that Cannington was part of a local central place or 'central zone' in the early medieval period. Moreover, the most prominent site in the immediate area is the adjacent Iron Age hillfort 'Cannington Camp', located on the larger hill to the west. The hillfort has produced evidence of use in the Roman period (or at least the deposition of Roman-period material) and may have been reoccupied and refortified as an elite site in the fifth and sixth centuries AD equivalent to those known from elsewhere in Somerset at South Cadbury and Cadbury Congresbury (Rahtz, Hirst & Wright 2000: 12–13, 396). In this location, it follows a pattern recognised at other early medieval cemeteries of the region, including the burials at Hicknoll Slait overlooking the hillfort with sub-Roman reuse at South Cadbury (Davey 2004: 50–2), the reuse of a Romano-Celtic temple at Henley Wood by a sub-Roman inhumation

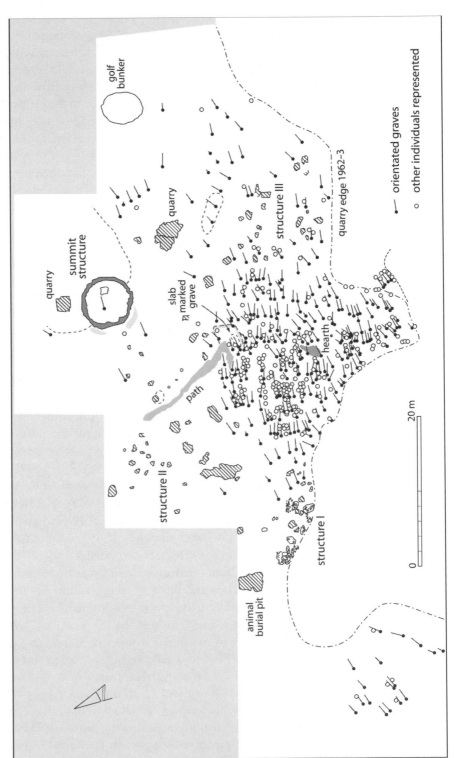

Figure 6.9 The large sub-Roman cemetery at Cannington, Somerset (redrawn by Séan Goddard after Rahtz et al. 2000).

cemetery (Watts & Leach 1996) and the graves adjoining the Romano-Celtic temple at Lamyatt Beacon (Leech 1986).

The excavated cemetery consisted of up to 542 burials dating to between the fourth and eighth centuries AD, excavated between 1962 and 1963 (Rahtz, Hirst & Wright 2000: 391–2). The graves are thought to have formed part of a much larger burial site destroyed by quarrying that has been estimated to have possibly consisted of over 1,500 burials. Despite the long duration of the cemetery, this is still an impressive size, suggesting that the burial site may have served many communities in the surrounding landscape (Rahtz, Hirst & Wright 2000: 420–2).

It may be unsurprising at this stage that there is some evidence, if not conclusive, that the location of the cemetery may have overlain, and perhaps deliberately reused, a site of early Bronze Age burial (Rahtz, Hirst & Wright 2000: 395). The development of the cemetery was examined in detail by the excavators, who noted that there were nuclei or foci of burials in at least four places, one of which was the Summit Structure (FT 43), a feature that has attracted a number of interpretations, from Roman barrow to pagan temple. The Summit Structure was a low mound prior to excavation, consisting of Devonian red sandstone blocks not native to the hill (and therefore brought for the construction) forming a polygonal kerb that surrounded a circular trench and mound (Rahtz, Hirst & Wright 2000: 45–51). The precise sequence seems hazy, but the associated burials appear to be secondary additions, including a centrally placed grave 424 (Rahtz, Hirst & Wright 2000: 47). In its final form, the structure may have been a trench holding posts which went up through the mound, surmounted by a central platform, and surrounded by a raised polygonal kerb that at some point became adapted to receive burials, possibly in the fourth or fifth century AD (Rahtz, Hirst & Wright 2000: 49–51). Despite the prominent location on the summit of the hill and the secondary graves, most burials respected its location and are located at some distance to the south.

The second monumental focus for the cemetery attracted a dense concentration of later graves. This focus was a mound on the northern side of the cemetery, found upon excavation to cover a west–east arrangement of large horizontal and vertical slabs of Lias brought to the site from over a kilometre away over which a mound had been raised (FT 26: Rahtz, Hirst & Wright 2000: 51–7). To its east was a possible post-hole with a packing of Lias stones and one stone of red sandstone decorated with incised lines and a circular motif, interpreted as a possible grave marker (Rahtz, Hirst & Wright 2000: 51). This structure was associated with numerous pieces of red sandstone, Lias, bone, stone, Roman metal-finds and pottery, and upon further excavation was found to overlie grave 409, which contained the partially disarticulated bones of a young person c. 13 years of age. The mound seems to have formed a focal point for a dense concentration of subsequent graves, particularly to the south, as well as the west and east. By contrast, to the north of the mound few graves were inserted, and instead a well-worn path approached the mound, suggesting that burial 409 attracted repeated visits (Rahtz, Hirst & Wright 2000: 54). Indeed, the excavators interpret the distribution of Roman and post-Roman finds on the site as an indication of religious or mortuary activity contemporaneous with the use of the site as a cemetery (Rahtz, Hirst & Wright 2000: 398).

Further structures (I and II), while difficult to interpret, support the excavators' interpretation of the cemetery as a focus for more than burials. A chapel and settlement may have also been adjacent to and overlapped with the cemetery. For example, structures I and II are tentatively associated with the cemetery. Meanwhile, structure III was associated with ferrous and non-ferrous metal-working and antler-working that may very well have been contemporaneous with the cemetery (Rahtz, Hirst & Wright 2000: 400). The possibility that artefact production and burial were associated may have more than a passing significance that cannot be enlarged upon here, but it is nonetheless relevant in this regard because of the implicitly public and ritualised nature of communal activity on the site.

The burials on the hilltop at Cannington indicate the role of the cemetery as the accumulation of memories focusing upon special graves: social memories constituted through procession from settlement to burial site through the landscape, and through inscription onto the place in relation to earlier burials. Despite the major socio-political changes of the fifth century (with the collapse of Roman control) and of the seventh century (associated with West Saxon expansion in the region), the burial site continues to have been used as a focal point for social and ritual gatherings by local communities.

Conclusions – landscapes of memory

Landscape studies focusing upon early medieval mortuary practices are very much in their infancy, and the potential remains for considerable new research through developing new fieldwork projects, employing a range of archaeological techniques and compiling the data in a more rigorous manner. However, a theory is required to link death, memory and the early medieval landscape. This chapter has attempted to address this issue by focusing upon the interplay of texts and monumentality in social remembrance. While texts can reveal attitudes towards monuments, the archaeology can allow us to appreciate the mnemonic significance of mortuary monuments and cemeteries in terms of location and landscape settings.

7

Remembering, forgetting and the mortuary context

Introduction

From the discussion of previous chapters, we have seen how different elements of the materiality of early medieval death were employed in remembering and forgetting the dead, and we have seen instances of how these formed a part of strategies of commemoration in different times and places. This book has introduced a new theoretical argument concerning how we investigate the relationships between death, memory and material culture in early medieval Britain. Artefacts, the body, graves, monuments and landscape have been explored in terms of their roles in remembering and forgetting.

In many ways, this book does not break any moulds, focusing within accepted period boundaries of the fifth and eleventh centuries, without charting the many themes linking the societies and mortuary practices on either side of these chronological parameters. Equally traditional is the focus on Britain, without consideration of Ireland, Scandinavia or Continental Europe. A further emphasis has been upon the evidence from cemeteries and an avoidance of detailed discussions of settlements and other archaeological contexts, again a consequence of the space available and the questions asked. However, taking the argument further in time, space and context would require more research and space than is possible here. Within this traditional period and geographical division, the book has attempted to explore thematically a range of different archaeological sites, many of which have not been discussed in archaeological syntheses. In so doing, a coherent chronological and geographical narrative has been deliberately avoided; such a story is for another study, but it is also a narrative that would in any case not have been familiar or meaningful to early medieval people. Focusing on social practices and strategies rather than the evolution of these practices and strategies, we are able to get closer to how early medieval people would have employed material culture and used it to mediate with the dead and various, different conceptions of past, present and future. Finally, I might be required by some to justify my focus on material evidence as opposed to textual sources of evidence. By definition, the argument pursued in this book is that while historical approaches to early medieval memory have failed to fully grasp the rich potential of material culture as a medium of remembrance and archaeological evidence to act as a window onto these strategies and material culture use, so archaeologists have failed to grasp the potential of this evidence and these ideas for engaging with interdisciplinary debates on the construction and reproduction of memories and identities in early medieval Britain. To this end, the book has attempted to deliberately focus on the contexts and uses of material culture in mortuary practices as a means of complementing and developing an archaeological contribution to the study of early medieval social memory.

Beyond Swallowcliffe Down: strategies and variability in mortuary commemoration

This book has drawn upon a range of examples from many different areas of early medieval Britain to address the relationship between mortuary practices and social memory. We began with a discussion of the high-status female bed-burial inserted into a prehistoric burial mound on Swallowcliffe Down in Wiltshire. This burial mound encapsulates many of the themes discussed in subsequent chapters, showing how the deposition of grave goods, body, structures, monumentality and location combine to make the funeral a memorable event and communicate specific aspects of the deceased's identities and those of the mourners. However, focusing upon a single time and a single grave does not allow us to fully engage with the changing variability in mortuary commemoration available from the early medieval period. This introduction takes us only so far, so the core of the book takes specific themes further, moving on from Swallowcliffe to explore how, in many different places and different centuries, memories were mediated by funerals.

The mainstay of early medieval archaeology has traditionally been the study of artefacts from graves, particularly those from the late fifth to the early eighth centuries AD. This study has attempted to consider grave goods in a new way (in chapter 2). It has been argued that, for sixth-century inhumation cemeteries, artefacts were employed to create memorable images that were responded to in subsequent burial rites conducted on the same site. While this approach does not fully reject the value of social and symbolic approaches towards early medieval grave goods, it does suggest the possibility that a focus on the creation of memorable scenes helps us to understand the relationships between graves in the evolution of any individual cemetery. Admittedly, the commemorative significance of grave goods may not be the only quality they possess, or be the only motivation for their presence in early medieval graves, yet a mnemonic perspective provides a means of considering the contextual associations, biographies and materiality of objects beyond their function and style. The focus on a select number of cemeteries, chiefly the cemetery of Berinsfield in Oxfordshire, but also Mill Hill, Deal, in Kent, far from exhausts the possibilities of future study developing and consolidating these perspectives using larger samples of data and more rigorous analyses. Yet the diverse and complex relationship between portable artefacts and social memory is one that requires careful and more detailed consideration by archaeologists, who have been tempted to divide grave goods into unhelpful categories of 'possessions' and 'gifts'.

This argument was developed through a consideration of the changing roles of grave goods in the seventh and early eighth centuries, focusing again on a select cemetery at Harford Farm, Norfolk. We were able to suggest that grave goods were used to do more than create memorable images: they were both displayed and hidden within graves as part of complex gift exchanges between the living and the dead. This in turn led to a consideration that a view of grave goods as citations (see Fowler 2001) used to create memorable images can be extended to objects in 'final-phase' graves: they also created relational concepts of the social person in death linked through exchange relations with the living.

In chapter 3 we moved on to consider the mnemonics of the cadaver in early medieval mortuary practices. The discussion began by exploring the transformation of the body in cremation rituals of the fifth and sixth centuries, including evidence from eastern England at sites like Sancton in East Yorkshire, Spong Hill in Norfolk and Newark in Nottinghamshire, and from mixed-rite cemeteries from southern England such as Kingsworthy in Hampshire. Cremation can be considered a 'technology of remembrance' in which the body suffers dissolution, fragmentation and reconstitution. Cremation involved many artefacts, materials and substances, but it was the cadaver and its transformation that were the central focus of the ritual process. In these rites, the hair and nails of the deceased were used in post-cremation rites to evoke the metaphorical rebuilding of the body following its destruction on the pyre. Such 'regenerative' and 'embodying' acts of remembrance are common in many societies and may have served to articulate the construction of a new ancestral identity for the dead. The contrasting relationship between the body position and artefact provision in the sixth and seventh centuries was discussed by focusing upon 'deviant' burials from Sewerby, East Yorkshire and Edix Hill, Cambridgeshire. Rather than an objective 'deviant' status being assigned to individuals of a particular social status and personal identity, it was argued that memorable images were afforded or denied to different individuals through the posture and clothing of the body, depending on the circumstances of their death and fears over death pollution.

Moving into the Christian era and burial rites associated with churches, the body was treated in relation to social tradition and religious expectations but also remained a vehicle for social remembrance. The orchestration of the body in later Saxon churchyard burials from Raunds Furnells was addressed, showing how the body was the focus of commemoration through its posture, orientation and location, and even through cases of exhuming and translating human remains after burial.

Artefacts and bodies were composed in graves, and in chapter 4 we moved on to consider the complex sequential mnemonic images created through display and concealment in the furnished burial rites of Snape and Sutton Hoo, both in Suffolk, and in early medieval cist-graves from eastern Scotland. At Snape, the excellent preservation of organic remains allows us to reconstruct the complex sequence of display and concealment that accompanied a furnished burial rite often over-simplistically considered as a form of tableau. The use of burial chambers beneath mound 1 at Sutton Hoo, together with the sequence of ritual actions identified beneath mound 17, serves to illustrate how colour, light and the concealment of spectacle was as important as display in these mortuary practices. Finally, the sequence of constructing cist-graves at Thornybank and Hallowhill served to show how this theme is not exclusive to the study of early medieval furnished burial rites. There is a tendency to regard grave contexts as backdrops to the bodies and grave goods they contain, but it was argued that the structures, linings and layers that are often invisible but that can be identified at certain sites were what *made* the memorable spectacles of early medieval mortuary practices. This study also challenged the interpretative primacy of metal artefacts over organic materials and textiles employed in graves.

Only once we had reviewed the mnemonic roles of objects, bodies and graves did the discussion move on to address the commemorative roles of monuments in chapter 5. In many ways, monuments are a mainstay in the study of commemoration in past societies, and archaeologists from many periods have developed new ways of studying the diversity of monumentality found associated with the graves of the dead. Monuments found in association with mortuary remains need not be exclusively or primarily 'mortuary' in character but might serve instead as foci for a range of other ritual practices, many of which may be commemorative in nature. No attempt was made to explore the full range of early medieval monuments known to be associated with the dead or to engage in the full range of ways that we can consider their mnemonic significance. Instead, the chapter focused on four different case studies that serve to illustrate how we can consider four themes in how mortuary monuments operated in remembering and forgetting. The monuments and monument reuse identified in recent excavations of early medieval cemeteries from central and north Wales were used to illustrate how monuments served as commemorative foci, influencing the engagement of early medieval ritual participants and observers with the topography of cemeteries. The Sutton Hoo barrow cemetery in Suffolk illustrated a different theme, for while individual monuments provided monumental foci, collectively they cross-referenced each other as a means of creating monumental *genealogies*, sequences of monuments that were meaningful only in relation to each other and the materialising of the history of a social group through the burial mounds of selected individuals. The symbol stone and cairn from Dunrobin and the composite cairns from Lundin Links were used to illustrate the construction of social memories by incorporating the graves of the dead into monumental *symbols*. At Lundin Links these symbols were not commemorating the graves of discrete individuals but were built up through successive mortuary events, subsuming individual graves into larger monumental projects that commemorated gendered groups of dead persons. Finally, two Viking burials from the Isle of Man, Balladoole and Ballateare, were selected to illustrate not how monuments were raised after early medieval funerals, but how monumentality was integral to the *ritual process*. In combination, these case studies demonstrated the complex relationships between monuments, mortuary practices and social memory that challenge the simplistic modern expectation of single monuments raised over single graves that retrospectively commemorate the dead *individual*. Instead, these examples show how monumental projects were enmeshed in manifold ways with the commemoration of specific dead individuals, social groups, genealogies and mythologies.

The final theme for discussion addressed in chapter 6 is the landscape context of early medieval mortuary practices and how it affected the commemoration of the dead. The study of the location of burial in the early medieval landscape has tended to focus on specific themes. For many 'field cemeteries', their distribution and location has been used as an indirect way of recognising settlements and therefore the presence or influence of immigrant groups. Meanwhile, cemetery location has been considered in religious terms and used in the debate over the timing and extent of conversion and the adoption of churchyard-burial. More recently, burial location has been considered in terms of territoriality, socio-politics and ideology in early medieval societies. It was here argued that these approaches can be developed by considering the way burial location served in strategies of remembering and forgetting the dead. Rather than a linear evolution from 'field cemetery' to 'churchyard-burial', we can instead perceive many factors influencing the location of early medieval burial sites before, during and after conversion to Christianity. The influence of ancient monuments, relationships with settlements, routes and boundaries, the location of a burial ground within a wider sacred geography and associations with natural places were all considered important factors guiding early medieval communities and groups when selecting repositories for the dead and the memories that enshrouded them. The chapter moved on to consider the relationship between texts and landscape in the construction of early medieval mortuary memories. Employing case studies taken from the poem *Beowulf*, the *Life of Saint Guthlac* and the Anglo-Saxon Chronicle, it was possible to show the interaction of text, place and space in the creation of social memories through the portrayal of mortuary monuments. Each example, in contrasting ways, illustrated how monuments and tombs were central to the perception and construction of the past in early medieval societies. The discussion finished by moving away from single, isolated burial mounds to consider the accumulation of memories through repeated burial in the large, late Roman and early medieval cemetery excavated at Cannington in Somerset. Situated away from a church on a hill-top, the excavations provided evidence for how the cemetery was the focus of repeated burial events over many centuries but perhaps also became a focus for the veneration of 'special' graves in a location prominent within the surrounding landscape. Together, these elements provide a more sophisticated understanding of the role of the dead in social remembrance, illustrating how we can consider the many different and shifting forms of commemorative topography and mortuary places that would have been encountered as one traversed the countryside and towns of the early medieval landscape.

Return to Swallowcliffe Down: mortuary commemoration and early medieval identities

In many ways, these chapters can be considered in isolation, but together they are intended to provide strands towards a broader argument concerning how we approach, study and interpret the material culture of early medieval mortuary practices. With this in mind, we can return to the rich, seventh-century bed-burial inserted into a prehistoric burial mound on Swallowcliffe Down in Wiltshire discussed in the introduction to this volume.

Early medieval mortuary practices were performances, sequences of actions that transformed substances, bodies, ideas and emotions. Mortuary practices serve to mediate remembrance, and material culture is implicated in this process by means of many strategies. This theme transcends many of the traditional divisions that have broken up the study of early medieval death and burial and the sources used to study them. These include ethnic, religious, spatial and chronological false dichotomies, such as 'Germanic and British', 'native and Viking', 'pagan and Christian', 'field- and church-burial', 'country and town' and so on.

The ubiquity of the application of the themes discussed in this volume is both a strength and a weakness of the mnemonic approach. In side-lining or down-grading the centrality of ethnic, religious, cultural, social and ideological approaches, and instead foregrounding the theme of memory, we risk reducing all mortuary rites to being universally explained in terms of 'memory' without explaining precisely how and why specific commemorative strategies were employed. Yet by using memory as a starting-point, we are not rejecting the importance of the cultural, religious, social or ideological elements of mortuary practices, but conversely see them all as elements for understanding the commemorative significance of mortuary practices. Rather than seeing mortuary practices as a direct window onto any of these more abstract phenomena, we can first and foremost regard them as strategies for negotiating between the living and the dead to create memories and identities.

This approach serves to link together the practices of what people actually did with the ideas that drove these practices and developed from them. It also takes the focus away from particular categories of material to consider how different sources of evidence and different contexts provided complementary and distinctive strategies of commemoration.

In this light, the mnemonic qualities of material culture and their use in mortuary contexts can be seen as a way in which funerals were rendered memorable, and how traditions of mortuary practices were generated and perpetuated. It is an approach that allows us to consider both how traditions of ritual behaviour are transmitted over time and space and how they can show considerable consistency even in pre-literate or semi-literate societies. Yet it is an approach that also encapsulates how innovation can develop in order to make distinctive memorable performances and ritual processes. It helps archaeologists understand how overtly contrasting traditions of mortuary practice can sometimes develop in close proximity to make distinctive mnemonic experiences for those participating in and observing them.

Of course, an issue central to this entire discussion is exactly what is being remembered. The discussion has deliberately kept this vague. Memories are rarely exclusive or focused; rather, multi-layered and complex aspects of identity and the past are evoked and interact during funerals, some highlighted, others repressed and dispersed. Memories can take many forms, from mythologies and social histories to personal recollections, that can interact and coalesce in mortuary events, motivating at different scales the conduct of individuals and groups in the disposal and commemoration of the dead. It may seem ironic in a discussion that focuses on memory to admit that our ability as archaeologists to recognise specific forms and types of memory in the form of personal recollection may not ever be possible, given the nature of the material evidence we have at our disposal. Yet the reconstruction of precise mnemonic information recalled and transmitted has not been the aim of this study. Instead, by examining the strategies, practices and performances involving material culture at funerals, we can engage with the archaeological evidence to identify how memories were produced and reproduced over time and space using artefacts, bodies, technologies, structures, monuments and landscape. If our task is ever to get inside the heads of past people or to simply describe what they did, archaeologists are simply wasting their time. However, by exploring the structuring themes and the variability of mortuary practices in mnemonic terms, we might be getting closer to understanding the centrality of rituals surrounding death for the lives of early medieval people, their understanding of their world, perceptions of their pasts, and aspirations regarding both physical and metaphysical futures. If, as archaeologists, we can begin to engage with such questions, we might find ourselves in a better position to address the big questions about the shifting nature of death and commemoration from the ancient into the medieval world than we have previously thought possible.

REFERENCES

Adams, M. 1996. 'Excavation of a Pre-Conquest Cemetery at Addingham, West Yorkshire', *Medieval Archaeology* 40: 62–150.

Adkins, R. A. & Petchy, M. R. 1984. 'Secklow Hundred Mound and Other Meeting-Place Mounds in England', *Archaeological Journal* 141: 243–51.

Alcock, E. 1992. 'Burials and Cemeteries in Scotland', in N. Edwards & A. Lane (eds.) *The Early Church in Wales and the West*, Oxford: Oxbow Monograph 16, pp. 125–9.

Alcock, L. 1981. 'Quantity or Quality: The Anglian Graves of Bernicia', in V. Evison (ed.) *Angles, Saxons and Jutes*, Oxford: Clarendon, pp. 168–86.

Alexander, D. 1999. 'Redcastle Barrow Cemetery', *Current Archaeology* 166(10): 395–7.

Allen, J. R. & Anderson, J. 1993a (1903). *The Early Christian Monuments of Scotland*, volume I (Parts 1 & 2), Angus: Pinkfoot Press.

1993b (1903). *The Early Christian Monuments of Scotland*, volume II (Part 3), Angus: Pinkfoot Press.

Allen, T. & Lamdin-Whymark, H. 2001. 'The Taplow Hillfort', *Current Archaeology* 15(175): 186–9.

Anderson, G. 2005. 'With Thor on Our Side: The Symbolism of the Thor Hammer-Ring in Viking Age Burial Ritual', in T. Artelius & F. Svanberg (eds.) *Dealing with the Dead: Archaeological Perspectives on Prehistoric Scandinavian Burial Ritual*, Stockholm: National Heritage Board, pp. 45–62.

Andrén, A. 1993. 'Doors to Other Worlds: Scandinavian Death Rituals in Gotlandic Perspectives', *Journal of European Archaeology* 1: 33–56.

Arnold, C. J. 1980. 'Wealth and Social Structure: A Matter of Life and Death', in P. Rahtz, T. Dickinson & L. Watts (eds.) *Anglo-Saxon Cemeteries 1979*, Oxford: BAR British Series, pp. 81–142.

1982a. *The Anglo-Saxon Cemeteries of the Isle of Wight*, London: British Museum.

1982b. 'Stress as a Factor in Social and Economic Change', in C. Renfrew & S. Shennan (eds.) *Ranking, Resource and Exchange*, Cambridge: Cambridge University Press, pp. 124–31.

1997. *An Archaeology of the Early Anglo-Saxon Kingdoms*. 2nd edn. London: Routledge.

Arnold, C. & Wardle, P. 1981. 'Early Medieval Settlement Patterns in England', *Medieval Archaeology* 25: 145–8.

Arrhenius, B. 2002. 'Kinship and Social Organisation in the Early Medieval Period in Svealand Elucidated by DNA', in J. Jesch (ed.) *The Scandinavians from the Vendel Period to the Tenth Century*, Woodbridge: Suffolk, pp. 45–51.

Ashmore, P. 1980. 'Low Cairns, Long Cists and Symbol Stones', *Proceedings of the Society of Antiquaries of Scotland* 110: 346–55.

2003. 'Orkney Burials in the First Millennium AD', in J. Downes & A. Ritchie (eds.) *Sea Change: Orkney and Northern Europe in the Later Iron Age AD 300–800*, Balgavies: Pinkfoot Press, pp. 35–50.

Austin, D. 1990. 'The "Proper Study" of Medieval Archaeology', in D. Austin & L. Alcock (eds.) *From the Baltic to the Black Sea*, London: Routledge, pp. 9–42.

Avent, R. & Evison, V. 1982. 'Anglo-Saxon Button Brooches', *Archaeologia* 107: 77–124.

Axboe, M. 1981. 'The Scandinavian Gold Bracteates', *Acta Archaeologica* 52: 1–57.

Bailey, R. 1980. *Viking Age Sculpture in Northern England*, London: Collins.

 1991. *England's Earliest Sculptors*, Toronto: Pontifical Institute of Medieval Studies.

Baldwin Brown, G. 1903–15. *The Arts of Early England: Saxon Art and Industry in the Pagan Period*, vols. 1–4, London: John Murray.

Barber, P. 1988. *Vampires, Burial and Death – Folklore and Reality*, Yale: Yale University Press.

Barnett, J. & Edmonds, M. 2002. 'Places Apart? Caves and Monuments in Neolithic and Earlier Bronze Age Britain', *Cambridge Archaeological Journal* 12(1): 113–29.

Barrett, J. C. 1990. 'The Monumentality of Death: The Character of Early Bronze Age Mortuary Mounds in Southern Britain', *World Archaeology* 22(2): 179–89.

 1993. 'Chronologies of Remembrance: The Interpretation of Some Roman Inscriptions', *World Archaeology* 25(2): 236–47.

 1994. *Fragments from Antiquity*, Oxford: Blackwell.

Bartel, B. 1982. 'A Historical Review of Ethnological and Archaeological Analyses of Mortuary Practice', *Journal of Anthropological Archaeology* 1: 32–58.

Battaglia, D. 1990. *On the Bones of the Serpent: Person, Memory, and Mortality in Sabarl Island Society*, Chicago: University of Chicago Press.

 1992. 'The Body in the Gift: Memory and Forgetting in Sabarl Mortuary Exchange', *American Ethnologist* 19: 3–18.

Bazelmans, J. 2000. 'Beyond Power: Ceremonial Exchanges in *Beowulf*', F. Theuws & J. L. Nelson (eds.) *Rituals of Power from Late Antiquity to the Early Middle Ages*, Leiden: Brill, pp. 311–75.

 2002. 'Moralities of Dress and the Dress of the Dead in Early Medieval Europe', in Y. Hamilakis, M. Pluciennik & S. Tarlow (eds.) *Thinking through the Body: Archaeologies of Corporeality*, New York: Kluwer/Plenum, pp. 71–84.

Bentley, R. A., Krause, R., Price, T. D. & Kaufmann, B. 2003. 'Human Mobility at the Early Neolithic Settlement of Vaihingen, Germany: Evidence from Strontium Isotope Analysis', *Archaeometry* 45(3): 471–86.

Bethell, P. H. & Carver, M. 1987. 'Detection and Enhancement of Decayed Inhumations at Sutton Hoo', in A. Boddington, A. N. Garland & R. C. Janaway (eds.) *Death, Decay and Reconstruction*, Manchester: Manchester University Press, pp. 10–21.

Bersu, G. & Wilson, D. M. 1966. *Three Viking Graves in the Isle of Man*, London: Society for Medieval Archaeology.

Bevan, W. 1999. 'The Landscape Context of the Iron-Age Square-Barrow Burials', in J. Downes & T. Pollard (eds.) *The Loved Body's Corruption: Archaeological Contributions to the Study of Human Mortality*, Glasgow: Cruithne, pp. 69–93.

Biddle, M. 1986. 'Archaeology, Architecture, and the Cult of Saints in Anglo-Saxon England', in L. A. S. Butler & R. K. Morris (eds.) *The Anglo-Saxon Church*, London: CBA Research Report 60, pp. 1–31.

Biddle, M. & Kjlbye-Biddle, B. 1992. 'Repton and the Vikings', *Antiquity* 66: 36–51.

 2001. 'Repton and the "Great Heathen Army", 873–4', in J. Graham-Campbell, R. Hall, J. Jesch & D. N. Parsons (eds.) *Vikings and the Danelaw*, Oxford: Oxbow, pp. 45–96.

Bigelow, G. F. 1984. 'Two Kerbed Cairns from Sandwick, Unst, Shetland', in J. G. P. Friell & W. G. Watson (eds.) *Pictish Studies: Settlement, Burial and Art in Dark Age Northern Britain*, Oxford: BAR British Series 125, pp. 115–29.

Binford, L. R. 1971. 'Mortuary Practices: Their Study and Their Potential', in J. Brown (ed.) *Approaches to the Social Dimensions of Mortuary Practices*, Washington: Memoir of the Society of American Archaeology 25: 6–29.

Binski, P. 1996. *Medieval Death: Ritual and Representation*, London: British Museum.

Birkbeck, V. 2005. *The Origins of Mid-Saxon Southampton: Excavations at the Friends Provident St Mary's Stadium 1998–2000*, Old Sarum: Wessex Archaeology.

Blair, J. 1989. 'Minster Churches in the Landscape', in D. Hooke (ed.) *Anglo-Saxon Settlements*, Oxford: Oxford University Press, pp. 35–58.

    1992. 'Anglo-Saxon Minsters: A Topographical Review', *Pastoral Care before the Parish*, Leicester: Leicester University Press, pp. 226–66.

    1994. *Anglo-Saxon Oxfordshire*, Stroud: Sutton.

    1995. 'Anglo-Saxon Pagan Shrines and their Prototypes', in D. Griffiths (ed.) *Anglo-Saxon Studies in Archaeology and History 8*, Oxford: Oxford Committee for Archaeology, pp. 1–28.

Bloch, M. 1971. *Placing the Dead: Tombs, Ancestral Villages, and Kinship Organisation in Madagascar*, Prospect Heights, Illinois: Waveland.

    1998. *How We Think They Think: Anthropological Approaches to Cognition, Memory and Literacy*, Boulder, Colorado: Westerview.

    1995. 'People into Places: Zafimaniry Concepts of Clarity', in E. Hirsch & M. O'Hanlon (eds.) *The Anthropology of Landscape*, Oxford: Oxford University Press, pp. 63–77.

Bloch, M. & Parry, J. 1982. 'Introduction: Death and the Regeneration of Life', in M. Bloch & J. Parry (eds.) *Death and the Regeneration of Life*, Cambridge: Cambridge University Press, pp. 1–44.

Boddington, A. 1987a. 'Raunds, Northamptonshire: Analysis of a Country Churchyard', *World Archaeology* 18(3): 411–25.

    1987b. 'From Bones to Population: The Problem of Numbers', in A. Boddington, A. N. Garland & R. C. Janaway (eds.) *Death, Decay and Reconstruction: Approaches to Archaeology and Forensic Science*, Manchester: Manchester University Press, pp. 180–97.

    1990. 'Models of Burial, Settlement and Worship: The Final Phase Reviewed', in E. Southworth (ed.) *Anglo-Saxon Cemeteries: A Reappraisal*, Sutton: Stroud, pp. 177–99.

    1996. *Raunds Furnells: The Anglo-Saxon Church and Churchyard*, London: English Heritage, Archaeological Report 7.

Bond, J. 1996. 'Burnt Offerings: Animal Bone in Anglo-Saxon Cremations', *World Archaeology* 28(1): 76–88.

Bondeson, J. 2001. *Buried Alive: The Terrifying History of Our Most Primal Fear*, London: Norton.

Bonney, D. 1966. 'Pagan Saxon Burials and Boundaries in Wiltshire', *Wiltshire Archaeological Magazine* 61: 25–30.

    1976. 'Early Boundaries and Estates in Southern England', in P. Sawyer (ed.) *Medieval Settlement: Continuity and Change*, London: Macmillan, pp. 72–82.

Boyle, A., Dodd, A., Miles, D. & Mudd, A. 1995. *Two Oxfordshire Anglo-Saxon Cemeteries: Berinsfield and Didcot*. Oxford: Oxford Archaeological Unit, Thames Valley Landscapes Monograph No. 8.

Boyle, A., Jennings, D., Miles, D. & Palmer, S. 1998. *The Anglo-Saxon Cemetery at Butler's Field, Lechlade, Gloucestershire*, Oxford: Oxford Archaeological Unit, Thames Valley Landscapes Monograph No. 10.

Bradley, R. 1980. 'Anglo-Saxon Cemeteries: Some Suggestions for Research', in P. Rahtz, T. Dickinson & L. Watts (eds.). *Anglo-Saxon Cemeteries 1979*, Oxford: BAR British Series 82, pp. 171–8.

    1987. 'Time Regained: The Creation of Continuity', *Journal of the British Archaeology Association* 140: 1–17.

    1997. 'Death by Water: Boats and Footprints in the Rock Art of Western Sweden', *Oxford Journal of Archaeology* 16(3): 315–24.

1998a. 'Ruined Buildings, Ruined Stones: Enclosures, Tombs and Natural Places in the Neolithic of South-West England', *World Archaeology* 30(1): 13–22.

1998b. *The Significance of Monuments*, London: Routledge.

2000. *An Archaeology of Natural Places*, London: Routledge.

2002. *The Past in Prehistoric Societies*, London: Routledge.

Bradley, S. A. J. (ed. & trans.) 1982. *Anglo-Saxon Poetry*, London: Dent.

Brassil, K. S., Owen, W. G. & Britnell, W. J. 1991. 'Prehistoric and Early Medieval Cemeteries at Tandderwen, near Denbigh, Clwyd', *Archaeological Journal* 148: 46–97.

Brink, S. 2004. 'Legal Assembly Sites in Early Scandinavia', in A. Pantos & S. Semple (eds.) *Assembly Places and Practices in Medieval Europe*, Dublin: Four Courts, pp. 205–16.

Britnell, W. J. 1990. 'Capel Maelog, Llandrindod Wells, Powys: Excavations 1984–87', *Medieval Archaeology* 34: 27–96.

Brookes, S. (in prep.) 'Walking with Anglo-Saxons: Landscapes of the Living and Landscapes of the Dead in Early Anglo-Saxon Kent', in S. Semple & H. Williams (eds.) *Anglo-Saxon Studies in Archaeology and History* 14, Oxford: Oxford University Committee for Archaeology.

Brothwell, D. 1987. 'Decay and Disorder in the York Jewbury Skeletons', in A. Boddington, A. N. Garland & R. C. Janaway (eds.) *Death, Decay and Reconstruction: Approaches to Archaeology and Forensic Science*, Manchester: Manchester University Press, pp. 22–42.

Brown, J. 1980. 'The Search for Rank in Prehistoric Burials', in R. Chapman, I. Kinnes & K. Randsborg (eds.) *The Archaeology of Death*, Cambridge: Cambridge University Press, pp. 25–37.

Brown, P. 1981. *The Cult of the Saints: Its Rise and Function in Latin Christianity*, Chicago: University of Chicago Press.

Brown, T. & Foard, G. 1998. 'The Saxon Landscape: A Regional Perspective', in P. Everson & T. Williamson (eds.) *The Archaeology of Landscape: Studies presented to Christopher Taylor*, Manchester: Manchester University Press, pp. 67–94.

Browne, T. 1658. *Hydriotaphia, Urne-Burial, or, a discourse of the Supulchrall Urnes lately found in Norfolk . . .* London: Brome.

Bruce-Mitford, R. 1975. *The Sutton Hoo Ship-Burial I: Excavations, Background, the Ship, Dating and Inventory*, London: British Museum.

1978. *The Sutton Hoo Ship-Burial II: Arms, Armour and Regalia*, London: British Museum.

Bruce-Mitford, R. & Evans, A. C. 1983. *The Sutton Hoo Ship-Burial III Late Roman and Byzantine Silver, Hanging-Bowls, Drinking Vessels, Cauldrons and Other Containers, Textiles, the Lyre, Pottery Bottle and Other Items*, London: British Museum.

Brück, J. 1998. 'In the Footsteps of the Ancestors: A Review of Christopher Tilley's *A Phenomenology of Landscape: Places, Paths and Monuments*', *Archaeological Review from Cambridge* 15(1): 23–36.

2001. 'Monuments, Power and Personhood in the British Neolithic', *Journal of the Royal Anthropological Institute* 7: 649–67.

2004. 'Material Metaphors: The Relational Construction of Identity in Early Bronze Age Burials in Ireland and Britain', *Journal of Social Archaeology* 4(3): 307–33.

Budd, P., Millard, A., Chenery, C., Lucy, S. and Roberts, C. 2004. 'Investigating Population Movement by Stable Isotopes: A Report From Britain', *Antiquity* 78: 127–41.

Buckberry, J. (in prep.) 'On Sacred Ground: Social Identity and Churchyard Burial in Lincolnshire and Yorkshire, c. 700–1100 AD', in S. Semple & H. Williams (eds.) *Anglo-Saxon Studies in Archaeology and History* 14, Oxford: Oxbow.

Buikstra, J. E. 1981. 'Mortuary Practices, Palaeodemography and Palaeopathology: A Case Study from the Koster Site (Illinois)', in R. Chapman, I. Kinnes & K. Randsborg (eds.) *The Archaeology of Death*, Cambridge: Cambridge University Press, pp. 123–32.

Buikstra, J. E. & Charles, D. K. 1999. 'Centering the Ancestors: Cemeteries, Mounds, and Sacred Landscapes of the Ancient North American Midcontinent', in W. Ashmore & A. B. Knapp (eds.) *Archaeologies of Landscape – Contemporary Perspectives*, Oxford: Blackwell, pp. 201–28.

Bullough, D. A. 1983. 'Burial, Community and Belief in the Early Medieval West', in P. Wormald (ed.) *Ideal and Reality in Frankish and Anglo-Saxon Society*, Oxford: Clarendon, pp. 175–201.

Bush, H. & Zvelebil, M. 1991. 'Pathology and Health in Past Societies: An Introduction', in H. Bush & M. Zvelebil (eds.) *Health in Past Societies*, Oxford: BAR International Series 567, pp. 3–9.

Butterworth, C. A. & Lobb, S. 1992. *Excavations in the Burghfield Area, Berkshire: Developments of the Bronze Age and Saxon Landscapes*, Salisbury: Trust for Wessex Archaeology, Wessex Archaeology Reports 1.

Caciola, N. 1996. 'Wraiths, Revenants and Ritual in Medieval Culture', *Past and Present*, 152: 1–45.

Callmer, J. 1994. 'The Clay Paw Burial Rite of the Åland Islands and Central Russia', *Current Swedish Archaeology* 2: 13–46.

Campbell, J. 1982. 'The Tomb of St Cuthbert', in J. Campbell (ed.) *The Anglo-Saxons*, London: Penguin, pp. 80–1.

Cannon, A. 1989. 'The Historical Dimension in Mortuary Expressions of Status and Sentiment', *Current Anthropology* 30(4): 4–58.

Canterbury Archaeological Trust/Wessex Archaeology. 2000. 'Saltwood', *Current Archaeology* 14(168): 462–3.

Carnegie, S. & Filmer-Sankey, W. 1993. 'A Saxon "Cremation Pyre" from the Snape Anglo-Saxon Cemetery, Suffolk', in W. Filmer-Sankey & D. Griffiths (eds.) *Anglo-Saxon Studies in Archaeology and History* 6, Oxford: Oxbow, pp. 107–11.

Carr, C. 1995. 'Mortuary Practices: Their Social, Philosophical-Religious, Circumstantial, and Physical Determinants', *Journal of Archaeological Method and Theory* 2: 105–200.

Carr, R. D., Tester, A. & Murphy, P. 1988. 'The Middle Saxon Settlement at Staunch Meadow, Brandon', *Antiquity* 62: 371–7.

Carver, M. 1986. 'Sutton Hoo in Context', *Settimane di Studio del Centro Italiano di Studi sull'Alto Medioevo* 32: 77–117.

  1992. 'Ideology and Allegiance in East Anglia', in R. Farrell & C. Newman de Vegvar (eds.) *Sutton Hoo: Fifty Years After*, Oxford: Oxbow, pp. 173–82.

  1995. 'Boat-Burial in Britain: Ancient Custom or Political Signal?', in O. Crumlin-Pedersen & B. Munch Thye (eds.) *The Ship as Symbol in Prehistoric and Medieval Scandinavia*, Publications of the National Museum Studies in Archaeology & History vol. I, Copenhagen, pp. 111–24.

  1998a. *Sutton Hoo: Burial Ground of Kings?* London: British Museum.

  1998b. 'Conversion and Politics on the Eastern Seaboard of Britain: Some Archaeological Indicators', in B. E. Crawford (ed.) *Conversion and Christianity in the North Sea World*, St Andrews: St John's House Papers No. 8, pp. 11–40.

  1999. 'Exploring, Explaining, Imagining: Anglo-Saxon Archaeology 1998', in C. Karkov (ed.) *The Archaeology of Anglo-Saxon England: Basic Readings*, London: Garland, pp. 25–52.

  2000. 'Burial as Poetry: The Context of Treasure in Anglo-Saxon Graves', in E. Tyler (ed.) *Treasure in the Medieval West*, York: York Medieval Press, pp. 25–48.

  2001. 'Why That? Why There? Why Then? The Politics of Early Medieval Monumentality', in H. Hamerow & A. MacGregor (eds.) *Image and Power in the Archaeology of Early Medieval Britain*, Oxford: Oxbow, pp. 1–23.

2002. 'Reflections on the Meanings of Anglo-Saxon Barrows', in S. Lucy & A. Reynolds (eds.) *Burial in Early Medieval England and Wales*, Leeds: Maney, pp. 132–43.

2004. 'An Iona of the East: The Early-Medieval Monastery at Portmahomack, Tarbat Ness', *Medieval Archaeology* 48: 1–30.

2005. *Sutton Hoo: A Seventh-Century Princely Burial Ground and its Context*, London: British Museum.

Chamberlain, A. 1994. *Human Remains*, London: British Museum.

Chamberlain, A. & Parker Pearson, M. 2001. *Earthly Remains: The History and Science of Preserved Human Bodies*, London: British Museum.

Chapman, J. 2000. 'Tensions at Funerals: Social Practices and the Subversion of Community Structure in Later Hungarian Prehistory', in M.-A. Dobres & J. E. Robb (eds.) *Agency in Archaeology*, London: Routledge, pp. 21–33.

Chapman, R. 1980. 'The Emergence of Formal Disposal Areas and the "Problem" of Megalithic Tombs in Prehistoric Europe', in R. Chapman, I. Kinnes & K. Randsborg (eds.) *The Archaeology of Death*, Cambridge: Cambridge University Press, pp. 71–81.

Chapman, R. & Randsborg, K. 1980. 'Approaches to the Archaeology of Death', in R. Chapman, I. Kinnes & K. Randsborg (eds.) *The Archaeology of Death*, Cambridge: Cambridge University Press, pp. 1–24.

Cherryson, A. (in prep.) 'Disturbing the Dead: Urbanisation, the Church and the Post-Burial Treatment of Human Remains in Early Medieval Wessex, c. 600–1100 AD', in S. Semple & H. Williams (eds.) *Anglo-Saxon Studies in Archaeology and History* 14, Oxford: Oxford University Committee for Archaeology.

Chesson, M. S. 2001. 'Social Memory, Identity, and Death: An Introduction', in M. S. Chesson (ed.) *Social Memory, Identity and Death: Anthropological Perspectives on Mortuary Rituals*, Arlington VA: Archaeological Papers of the American Anthropological Association No. 10, pp. 1–11.

Chester-Kadwell, M. 2004. 'Early Anglo-Saxon Cemeteries in the Landscape of Norfolk: Metal-Detector Finds in Context', conference paper presented at the 55th Sachsymposium, Cambridge, University of Cambridge, 11th–15th September 2004.

Childe, V. E. 1945. 'Directional Changes in Funerary Practices during 50,000 Years', *Man* 4: 13–18.

Clarke, B. 2004. 'An Early Anglo-Saxon Cross-Roads Burial from Broad Town, North Wiltshire', *Wiltshire Archaeological and Natural History Magazine* 97: 89–94.

Cleary, S. 1989. *The Ending of Roman Britain*, London: Batsford.

Close-Brooks, J. 1978–80. 'Excavations in the Dairy Park, Dunrobin, Sutherland, 1977', *Proceedings of the Society of Antiquaries of Scotland* 110: 328–45.

1984. 'Pictish and Other Burials', in J. G. P. Friell & W. G. Watson (eds.) *Pictish Studies: Settlement, Burial and Art in Dark Age Northern Britain*, Oxford: BAR British Series 125, pp. 87–115.

Collis, J. 1983. *Wigber Low*, Sheffield: University of Sheffield Press.

Coatsworth, E. 1989. 'The Pectoral Cross and Portable Altar from the Tomb of St Cuthbert', in G. Bonner, D. Rollason & C. Stancliffe (eds.) *St Cuthbert, His Cult and His Community to AD 1200*, Woodbridge: Boydell, pp. 287–302.

2001. 'The Embroideries from the Tomb of St Cuthbert', in N. J. Higham & D. H. Hill (eds.) *Edward the Elder 899–924*, London: Routledge, pp. 280–91.

Cohen, N. 2003. 'Boundaries and Settlement: The Role of the River Thames', in D. Griffiths, A. Reynolds & S. Semple (eds.) *Boundaries in Early Medieval Britain. Anglo-Saxon Studies in Archaeology and History* 12, pp. 9–20.

Colgrave, B. (ed. & trans.) 1940. *Two Lives of Saint Cuthbert*, Cambridge: Cambridge University Press.

(ed.) 1956. *Felix's Life of Guthlac*, Cambridge: Cambridge University Press.

Colgrave, B. & Mynors, R. A. B. (trans.) *Bede's Ecclesiastical History of the English People*, Oxford: Clarendon.

Cook, A. & Dacre, M. 1985. *Excavations at Portway, Andover 1973–5*, Oxford: Oxford University Committee for Archaeology Monograph No. 4.

Cooper, N. J. 1998. 'Anglo-Saxon Settlement in the Gwash Valley, Rutland', in J. Bourne (ed.) *Anglo-Saxon Landscapes in the East Midlands*, Leicester: Leicester Museums, pp. 165–79.

Corner, D. J. 1985. 'The *Vita Cadoci* and a Cotswold-Severn Chambered Cairn', *The Bulletin of the Board of Celtic Studies* 32: 50–67.

Connerton, P. 1989. *How Societies Remember*, Cambridge: Cambridge University Press.

Connor, L. 1995. 'The Action of the Body on Society: Washing a Corpse in Bali', *Journal of the Royal Anthropological Institute* 1: 537–59.

Cowie, T. G. 1978. 'Excavations at the Catstane, Midlothian 1977', *Proceedings of the Society of Antiquaries of Scotland* 109: 166–201.

Cramp, R. 1957. 'Beowulf and Archaeology', *Medieval Archaeology* 1: 57–77.

Crawford, S. 1993. 'Children, Death and the Afterlife in Anglo-Saxon England', in W. Filmer-Sankey (ed.) *Anglo-Saxon Studies in Archaeology and History* 6, Oxford: Oxbow, pp. 83–91.

2000. 'Children, Grave Goods and Social Status in Early Anglo-Saxon England', in J. Sofaer Derevenski (ed.) *Children and Material Culture*, London: Routledge, pp. 169–79.

2004. 'Votive Deposition, Religion and the Anglo-Saxon Furnished Burial Ritual', *World Archaeology* 36(1): 83–102.

Crick, J. 2000. 'Posthumous Obligation and Family Identity', in W. O. Frazer & A. Tyrell (eds.) *Social Identity in Early Medieval Britain*, Leicester: Leicester University Press, pp. 193–208.

Cubbon, A. M. 1971. *The Art of the Manx Crosses*, Douglas: Manx Museum.

Cubitt, C. 1998. 'Memory and Narrative in the Cult of Early Anglo-Saxon Saints', in Y. Hen & M. Innes (eds.) *The Uses of the Past in the Early Middle Ages*, Cambridge: Cambridge University Press, pp. 29–66.

2000. 'Monastic Memory and Identity in Early Anglo-Saxon England', in W. O. Frazer & A. Tyrell (eds.) *Social Identity in Early Medieval Britain*, Leicester: Leicester University Press, pp. 253–76.

Cummings, V. 2002. 'Experiencing Texture and Transformation in the British Neolithic', *Oxford Journal of Archaeology* 21(3): 249–61.

Cummings, V., Jones, A. & Watson, A. 2002. 'Divided Places: Phenomenology and Asymmetry in the Monuments of the Black Mountains, Southeast Wales', *Cambridge Archaeological Journal* 12(1): 57–70.

Cummings, V. & Whittle, A. 2003. 'Tombs with a View: Landscape, Monuments and Trees', *Antiquity* 77 (296): 255–66.

Danforth, L. M. & Tsiaras, A. 1982. *The Death Rituals of Rural Greece*, Princeton: University of Princeton Press.

Daniell, C. 1997. *Death and Burial in Medieval England*, London: Routledge.

2002. 'Conquest, Crime and Theology in the Burial Record: 1066–1200', in S. Lucy & A. Reynolds (eds.) *Burial in Early Medieval England and Wales*, London: Society for Medieval Archaeology Monograph 17, pp. 241–54.

Daniels, R. 1999. 'The Anglo-Saxon Monastery at Hartlepool, England', in J. Hawkes & S. Mills (eds.) *Northumbria's Golden Age*, Stroud: Sutton, pp. 105–12.

Dark, K. R. 1994. *Civitas to Kingdom: British Political Continuity 300–800*, Leicester: Leicester University Press.

2000. *Britain and the End of the Roman Empire*, London: Tempus.

Davey, J. 2004. 'The Environs of South Cadbury in the Late Antique and Early Medieval periods', in R. Collins & J. Gerrard (eds.) *Debating Late Antiquity in Britain AD300–700*, Oxford: BAR British Series 365, pp. 43–54.

Davies, G. J. 2000. 'Boneyard and Reeddam', in R. Hoggett (ed.) *Sedgeford Historical and Archaeological Research Project Interim Report 2000*, Sedgeford.

Darvill, T. 2004. 'Tynwald Hill and the "Things" of Power', in A. Pantos & S. Semple (eds.) *Assembly Places and Practices in Medieval Europe*, Dublin: Four Courts, pp. 217–32.

David, N. & Kramer, C. 2001. *Ethnoarchaeology in Action*. Cambridge, Cambridge University Press.

Davies, D. J. 1997. *Death, Ritual & Belief: The Rhetoric of Funerary Rites*, London: Cassell.

Davidson, S. 1863. '. . . account of the discovery . . . of Antiquities on Snape Common, Suffolk', *Proceeding of the Society of Antiquaries London*, 2nd Series, 2: 177–82.

Dickinson, T. 1974. *Cuddesdon and Dorchester-upon-Thames*, Oxford: BAR British Series 1.

1979. 'On the Origin and Chronology of the Early Anglo-Saxon Disc Brooch', in S. Chadwick Hawkes, D. Brown & J. Campbell (eds.) *Anglo-Saxon Studies in Archaeology and History 1*, Oxford: BAR British Series 72, pp. 39–80.

1980. 'The Present State of Anglo Saxon Cemetery Studies', in P. Rahtz, T. Dickinson & L. Watts (eds.) *Anglo-Saxon Cemeteries 1979*, Oxford: BAR British Series 82, pp. 11–34.

1991. 'Material Culture as Social Expression: The Case of Saxon Saucer Brooches with Running Spiral Decoration', in H.-J. Häßler (ed.) *Studien zur Sachsenforschung 7*, Hildesheim: August, pp. 39–70.

1993. 'An Anglo-Saxon "Cunning Woman" from Bidford-upon-Avon', in M. Carver (ed.) *In Search of Cult: Archaeological Investigations in Honour of Philip Rahtz*, Woodbridge: Boydell, pp. 45–54.

2002a. 'Review article: What's New in Early Medieval Burial Archaeology?', *Early Medieval Europe* 11(1): 71–87.

2002b. 'Translating Animal Art: Salin's Style I and Anglo-Saxon Cast Saucer Brooches', *Hikuin* 29: 163–86.

Dickinson, T. & Härke, H. 1992. *Early Anglo-Saxon Shields*, London: Society of Antiquaries of London, Archaeologia 110.

Dickinson, T. & Speake, G. 1992. 'The Seventh-Century Cremation Burial in Asthall Barrow, Oxfordshire: A Reassessment', in M. Carver (ed.) *The Age of Sutton Hoo*, Woodbridge: Boydell, pp. 95–30.

Dommasnes, L. 1982. 'Late Iron Age in Western Norway: Female Roles and Ranks as Deduced from an Analysis of Burial Customs', *Norwegian Archaeological Review* 15: 70–84.

Douglas, J. 1793. *Nenia Britannica*, London: Nichols.

Down, A. & Welch, M. 1990. *Chichester Excavations VII*, Chichester: Chichester District Council.

Downes, J. 1999. 'Cremation: A Spectacle and a Journey', in J. Downes & T. Pollard (eds.) *The Loved Body's Corruption: Archaeological Contributions to the Study of Human Mortality*, Glasgow: Cruithne, pp. 19–29.

Downes, J. with Morris, C. 1997. 'Hermisgarth, Sanday: The Investigation of Pyre Settings and Pictish Cist Burials in Orkney', *Proceedings of the Society of Antiquaries in Scotland* 127: 609–26.

Draper, S. 2004. 'Roman Estates to English Parishes? The Legacy of Desmond Bonney Reconsidered', in R. Collins & J. Gerrard (eds.) *Debating Late Antiquity in Britain AD300–700*, Oxford: BAR British Series 365, pp. 55–64.

Driscoll, S. 1984. 'The New Medieval Archaeology: Theory vs. History', *Scottish Archaeological Review* 3(2): 104–12.

1988. 'The Relationship between History and Archaeology: Artefacts, Documents and Power', in S. Driscoll & M. Nieke (eds.) *Power and Politics in Early Medieval Britain and Ireland*, Edinburgh: Edinburgh University Press, pp. 162–87.

1998. 'Picts and Prehistory: Cultural Resource Management in Early Medieval Scotland', *World Archaeology* 30(1): 142–58.

2000. 'Christian Monumental Sculpture and Ethnic Expression in Early Scotland', in W. O. Frazer & A. Tyrell (eds.) *Social Identity in Early Medieval Britain*, Leicester: Leicester University Press, pp. 233–52.

2004. 'The Archaeological Context of Assembly in Early Medieval Scotland – Scone and its Comparanda', in A. Pantos & S. Semple (eds.) *Assembly Places and Practices in Medieval Europe*, Dublin: Four Courts, pp. 73–94.

Dumville, D. 1985. 'The West Saxon Genealogical Regnal List and the Chronology of early Wessex', *Peritia* 4: 21–66.

Eaton, T. 2000. *Plundering the Past: Roman Stonework in Medieval Britain*, Stroud: Tempus.

Eckardt, H. & Williams, H. 2003. 'Objects without a Past? The Use of Roman Objects in early Anglo-Saxon Graves', in H. Williams (ed.) *Archaeologies of Remembrance: Death and Memory in Past Societies*, New York: Kluwer/Plenum, pp. 141–70.

Edmonds, M. 1999. *Ancestral Geographies of the Neolithic: Landscapes, Monuments and Memory*, London: Routledge.

Edwards, N. 1990. *The Archaeology of Early Medieval Ireland*, London: Routledge.

2001. 'Monuments in the Landscape: The Early Medieval Sculpture of St. David's', in H. Hamerow & A. MacGregor (eds.) *Images and Power in the Archaeology of Early Medieval Britain: Essays in Honour of Rosemary Cramp*, Oxford: Oxbow, pp. 55–79.

2002. 'Celtic Saints and Early Medieval Archaeology', in A. Thacker & R. Sharpe (eds.) *Local Saints and Local Churches in the Early Medieval West*, Oxford: Oxford University Press, pp. 225–65.

Effros, B. 1996. 'Symbolic Expressions of Sanctity: Gertrude of Nivelles in the Context of Merovingian Mortuary Custom', *Viator* 27: 1–10.

1997. 'Beyond Cemetery Walls: Early Medieval Funerary Topography and Christian Salvation', *Early Medieval Europe* 6(1): 1–23.

2001. 'Monuments and Memory: Repossessing Ancient Remains in Early Medieval Gaul', in M. de Jong & F. Theuws (eds.) *Topographies of Power in the Early Middle Ages*, Leiden: Brill, pp. 93–118.

2002a. *Creating Community with Food and Drink in Merovingian Gaul*, London: Macmillan.

2002b. *Caring for Body and Soul*, Pennsylvania: Pennsylvania State University Press.

2003. *Merovingian Mortuary Archaeology and the Making of the Early Middle Ages*, Berkeley: University of California Press.

2004. 'Dressing Conservatively: Women's Brooches as Markers of Ethnic Identity?', in L. Brubaker & J. M. H. Smith (eds.) *Gender in the Early Medieval World*, Cambridge: Cambridge University Press, pp. 165–84.

Eliade, M. 1954. *Shamanism: Archaic Techniques of Ecstasy*, Harmondsworth: Penguin.

Ellis Davidson, H. 1962. *The Sword in Anglo-Saxon England*, Woodbridge: Boydell.

Esmonde Cleary, S. 2000. 'Putting the Dead in their Place: Burial Location in Roman Britain', in J. Pearce, M. Millett & M. Struck (eds.) *Burial, Society and Context in the Roman World*, Oxford: Oxbow, pp. 127–42.

Evans, C., Pollard, J. & Knight, M. 1999. 'Life in Woods: Tree-Throws, "Settlement" and Forest Cognition', *Oxford Journal of Archaeology* 18(3): 241–54.

Evans, E. & Maynard, D. J. 1997. 'Caerleon Lodge Hill Cemetery: The Abbeyfield Site 1992', *Britannia* 28: 169–244.

Everson, P. 1993. 'Pre-Viking Settlement in Lindsey', in A. Vince (ed.) *Pre-Viking Lindsey*, Lincoln: City of Lincoln Archaeology Unit, pp. 91–100.

Eves, R. 1996. 'Remembrance of Things Passed: Memory, Body and the Politics of Feasting in New Ireland, Papua New Guinea', *Oceania* 66: 266–77.

Evison, V. 1987. *Dover: Buckland Anglo-Saxon Cemetery*, London: Historic Buildings and Monuments Commission for England Archaeological Report No. 3.

1994. *An Anglo-Saxon Cemetery at Great Chesterford, Essex*, London: CBA Research Report 91.

Faull, M. L. 1976. 'The Location and Relationship of the Sancton Anglo-Saxon Cemeteries', *Antiquaries Journal* 56: 227–33.

Fentress, J. & Wickham, C. 1992. *Social Memory*, Oxford: Blackwell.

Field, D. 1998. 'Round Barrows and the Harmonious Landscape: Placing Early Bronze Age Burial Monuments in South-East England', *Oxford Journal of Archaeology* 17(3): 309–26.

Filmer-Sankey, W. & Pestell, T. 1995. 'The Snape Logboats: Excavation, Construction and Performance', in O. Olsen, J. Skamby Madsen & F. Rieck (eds.) *Shipshape, Essays for Ole Crumlin-Pedersen*, Vikingeskibshallen i Roskilde, pp. 81–8.

2001. *Snape Anglo-Saxon Cemetery: Excavations and Surveys 1824–1992*, Ipswich: East Anglian Archaeology Report No. 95.

Finch, J. 2000. *Church Monuments in Norfolk before 1850: An Archaeology of Commemoration*, Oxford: BAR British Series 317.

Fisher, G. 1988. 'Style and Sociopolitical Organisation: A Preliminary Study from Early Anglo-Saxon England', in S. Driscoll & M. Nieke (eds.) *Power and Politics in Early Medieval Britain and Ireland*, Edinburgh: Edinburgh University Press, pp. 6–21.

1995. 'Kingdom and Community in Early Anglo-Saxon Eastern England', in L. Beck (ed.) *Regional Approaches to Mortuary Analysis*, New York: Plenum, pp. 147–66.

Fitzpatrick, E. 2004. 'Royal Inauguration Mounds in Medieval Ireland: Antique Landscape and Tradition', in A. Pantos & S. Semple (eds.) *Assembly Places and Practices in Medieval Europe*, Dublin: Four Courts, pp. 44–72.

Fleming, A. 1998. 'Phenomenology and the Megaliths of Wales: A Dreaming too Far?' *Oxford Journal of Archaeology* 18(2): 119–25.

Foot, S. 1999. 'Remembering, Forgetting and Inventing: Attitudes to the Past in England at the End of the First Viking Age', *Transactions of the Royal Historical Society* 6th series, 9: 185–200.

Forsyth, K. 1997. 'Some Thoughts on Pictish Symbols as a Formal Writing System', in D. Henry (ed.) *Pictish and Related Studies Presented to Isabel Henderson*, Balgavies, Angus: Pinkfoot, pp. 85–98.

Foster, R. J. 1990. 'Nurture and Force-Feeding: Mortuary Feasting and the Construction of Collective Individuals in a New Ireland Society', *American Ethnologist* 17: 431–48.

Foster, S. M. 1992. 'The State of Pictland in the Age of Sutton Hoo', in M. Carver (ed.) *The Age of Sutton Hoo*, Woodbridge: Boydell, pp. 217–34.

1996. *Picts, Gaels and Scots*, London: Batsford.

1998. 'Discovery, Recovery, Context and Display', in S. M. Foster (ed.) *The St Andrews Sarcophagus: A Pictish Masterpiece and its International Connections*, Dublin: Four Courts Press, pp. 36–62.

Fowler, C. 2001. 'Personhood and Social Relations in the British Neolithic with a Study from the Isle of Man', *Journal of Material Culture* 6: 137–63.

2002. 'Body Parts: Personhood and Materiality in the Earlier Manx Neolithic', in Y. Hamilakis, M. Pluciennik & S. Tarlow (eds.) *Thinking through the Body: Archaeologies of Corporeality*, New York: Kluwer/Plenum, pp. 47–69.

2003. 'Rates of (Ex)change: Decay and Growth, Memory and the Transformation of the Dead in Early Neolithic Southern Britain', in H. Williams (ed.) *Archaeologies of Remembrance: Death and Memory in Past Societies*, New York: Kluwer/Plenum, pp. 45–63.

2004. *The Archaeology of Personhood*, London: Routledge.

Fowler, C. & Cummings, V. 2003. 'Places of Transformation: Building Monuments from Water and Stone in the Neolithic of the Irish Sea', *Journal of the Royal Anthropological Institute* 9(1): 1–20.

Fox, D. & Pálsson, H. (trans.) 1974. *Grettir's Saga*, Toronto: University of Toronto Press.

Fulford, M. & Rippon, S. 1994. 'Lowbury Hill, Oxon: A Re-assessment of the Probable Romano-Celtic Temple and the Anglo-Saxon Barrow', *Archaeological Journal* 151: 158–211.

Freke, D. 2002. *Excavations on St Patrick's Isle Peel, Isle of Man, 1982–88: Prehistoric, Viking, Medieval and Later*, Liverpool: Liverpool University Press, Centre for Manx Studies Monographs 2.

Fyfe, R. & Rippon, S. 2004. 'A Landscape in Transition? Palaeoenvironmental Evidence for the End of the "Romano-British" Period in Southwest England', in R. Collins & J. Gerrard (eds.) *Debating Late Antiquity in Britain AD300–700*, Oxford: BAR British Series 365, pp. 33–42.

Gage, J., Jones, A., Bradley, R., Spence, K., Barber, E. J. W. & Taçon, P. S. C. 1999. 'What Meaning had Colour in Early Societies?' *Cambridge Archaeological Journal* 9(1): 109–26.

Gaimster, M. 1992. 'Scandinavian Gold Bracteates in Britain: Money and Media in the Dark Ages', *Medieval Archaeology* 36: 1–28.

1998. *Vendel Period Bracteates on Gotland: On the Significance of Germanic Art*, Lund, Acta Archaeologica Lundensia 27.

Garland, A. N. & Janaway, R. C. 1989. 'The Taphonomy of Inhumation Burials', in C. A. Roberts, F. Lee & J. Bintliff (eds.) *Burial Archaeology: Current Research, Methods and Developments*, Oxford: BAR British Series 211, pp. 15–37.

Garner, M. F. 2001. 'A Middle Saxon Cemetery at Cook Street, Southampton', *Hampshire Studies 2001: Proceedings of the Hampshire Field Club and Archaeological Society* 56: 170–91.

Geake, H. 1992. 'Burial Practice in Seventh- and Eighth-Century England', in M. Carver (ed.) *The Age of Sutton Hoo*, Woodbridge: Boydell, pp. 83–94.

1997. *The Use of Grave-Goods in Conversion-Period England*, Oxford: BAR British Series 261.

1999a. 'Invisible Kingdoms: The Use of Grave Goods in Seventh-Century England', in T. Dickinson & D. Griffiths (eds.) *The Making of Kingdoms: Anglo-Saxon Studies in Archaeology and History* 10, Oxford: Oxford University Committee for Archaeology, pp. 203–15.

1999b. 'When Were Hanging Bowls Deposited in Anglo-Saxon Graves?' *Medieval Archaeology* 43: 1–18.

2002. 'Persistent Problems in the Study of Conversion-Period Burials in England', in S. Lucy & A. Reynolds (eds.) *Burial in Early Medieval England and Wales*, Leeds: Maney, Society for Medieval Archaeology Monograph 17, pp. 144–55.

2003. 'The Control of Burial Practice in Middle Anglo-Saxon England', in M. Carver (ed.) *The Cross Goes North: Processes of Conversion in Northern Europe, AD 300–1300*, Woodbridge: Boydell, pp. 259–70.

Geary, P. 1986. 'Sacred Commodities: The Circulation of Medieval Relics', in A. Appadurai (ed.) *The Social Life of Things: Commodities in Cultural Perspective*, Cambridge: Cambridge University Press, pp. 169–94.

1991. 'Ethnic Identity as a Situational Construct in the Early Middle Ages', in E. Peters (ed.) *Folk Life in the Middle Ages*, Richmond, Kentucky: Southeastern Medieval Association, pp. 1–17.

1994a. *Living with the Dead in the Middle Ages*, Ithaca: Cornell University Press.

1994b. *Phantoms of Remembrance: Memory and Oblivion at the End of the First Millennium*, Princeton: Princeton University Press.

1999. 'Land, Language and Memory in Europe 700–1100', *Transactions of the Royal Historical Society* 6th series 9: 169–84.

Gell, A. 1992. 'The Technology of Enachantment and the Enchantment of Technology' in J. Coote & A. Shelton (eds.) *Anthropology: Art and Aesthetics*, Oxford: Clarendon, pp. 40–67.

1998. *Art and Agency: An Anthropological Theory*, Oxford: Oxford University Press.

Gelling, M. 2002. 'The Landscape of *Beowulf*', *Anglo-Saxon England* 31: 7–11.

Gem, R. 1983. 'Towards an Iconography of Anglo-Saxon Architecture', *Journal of the Warburg and Courtauld Institutes* 46: 1–18.

Gillespie, S. D. 2001. 'Personhood, Agency and Mortuary Ritual', *Journal of Anthropological Archaeology* 20(1): 73–112.

Gillings, M. & Pollard, J. 1999. 'Non-Portable Stone Artifacts and Contexts of Meaning: The Tale of Grey Wether', *World Archaeology* 31(2): 179–93.

Gittos, H. 2002. 'Creating the Sacred: Anglo-Saxon Rites for Consecrating Cemeteries', in S. Lucy & A. Reynolds (eds.) *Burial in Early Medieval England and Wales*, Leeds: Maney, pp. 195–208.

Goldstein, L. 1980. 'One-Dimensional Archaeology and Multidimensional People: Spatial Organization and Mortuary Analysis', in R. Chapman, I. Kinnes & K. Randsborg (eds.) *The Archaeology of Death*, Cambridge: Cambridge University Press, pp. 53–69.

Goldstein, L. 1995. 'Landscapes and Mortuary Practices: A Case for Regional Perspectives', in L. A. Beck (ed.) *Regional Approaches to Mortuary Analysis*, New York: Plenum, pp. 101–21.

Goodier, A. 1984. 'The Formation of Boundaries in Anglo-Saxon England: A Statistical Study', *Medieval Archaeology* 28: 1–21.

Gourley, R. 1984. 'A Symbol Stone and Cairn at Watenan, Caithness', in J. G. P. Friell & W. G. Watson (eds.) *Pictish Studies: Settlement, Burial and Art in Dark Age Northern Britain*, Oxford, BAR British Series 125, pp. 131–3.

Gowland, R. 2001. 'Playing Dead: Implications of Mortuary Evidence for the Social Construction of Childhood in Roman Britain', in G. Davies, A. Gardner & K. Lockyear (eds.) *TRAC 2000: Proceedings of the Tenth Annual Theoretical Roman Archaeology Conference, London 2000*: Oxford: Oxbow, pp. 152–68.

2002. *Examining Age as an Aspect of Social Identity in Fourth- to Sixth-Century England through the Analysis of Mortuary Evidence*, Durham: Unpublished Ph.D. thesis, University of Durham.

2004. 'The Social Identity of Health in Late Roman Britain', in B. Croxford, H. Eckardt, J. Meade & J. Weekes (eds.) *TRAC 2003: Proceedings of the Thirteenth Annual Theoretical Roman Archaeology Conference*, Oxford: Oxbow, pp. 135–46.

(in prep). 'Beyond Ethnicity: Symbols of Social Identity from the Fourth to the Sixth Centuries in England', in S. Semple & H. Williams (eds.) *Anglo-Saxon Studies in Archaeology and History* 14, Oxford: Oxford University Committee for Archaeology.

Graham-Campbell, J. 2004. 'On the Witham Bowl', *Antiquaries Journal* 84: 358–70.

Graham-Campbell, J. & Batey, C. E. 1998. *Vikings in Scotland*, Edinburgh: Edinburgh University Press.

Gransden, A. 1994. 'The Alleged Incorruption of the Body of St. Edmund, King and Martyr', *Antiquaries Journal* 74: 135–68.

Gräslund, B. 1994. 'Prehistoric Soul Beliefs in Northern Europe', *Proceedings of the Prehistoric Society* 60: 15–26.

Greig, C., Greig, M. & Ashmore, P. 2000. 'Excavations of a Cairn Cemetery at Lundin Links, Fife, in 1965–6', *Proceedings of the Society of Antiquaries of Scotland* 130: 585–636.

Grinsell, L. V. 1991. 'Barrows in the Anglo-Saxon Land Charters', *Antiquaries Journal* 71: 46–63.

Hadley, D. M. 2000. 'Burial Practice in the Northern Danelaw, c. 650–1100', *Northern History* 36: 199–216.

2001. *Death in Medieval England*, Stroud: Tempus.

2002. 'Burial Practices in Northern England in the Later Anglo-Saxon Period', in S. Lucy & A. Reynolds (eds.) *Burial in Early Medieval England and Wales*, Leeds: Maney, Society for Medieval Archaeology Monograph 17, pp. 209–28.

Halbwachs, M. 1992. *On Collective Memory*, Chicago: University of Chicago Press.

Hall, R. A. & Whyman, M. 1996. 'Settlement and Monasticism at Ripon, North Yorkshire, from the 7th to 11th Centuries AD', *Medieval Archaeology* 40: 62–150.

Hallam, E., Hockey, J. & Howarth, G. 1999. *Beyond the Body*, London: Routledge.

Hallam, E. & Hockey, J. 2001. *Death, Memory and Material Culture*, Oxford: Berg.

Halsall, G. 1992. 'The Origins of the *Reihengräberzivilisation*: Forty Years on', in J. Drinkwater & H. Elton (eds.) *Fifth-Century Gaul: A Crisis of Identity?* Cambridge: Cambridge University Press, pp. 196–207.

1998. 'Burial, Ritual and Merovingian Society', in J. Hill & M. Swan (eds.) *The Community, the Family and the Saint: Patterns of Power in Early Medieval Europe*, Turnhout: Brepols, pp. 325–38.

2000. 'The Viking Presence in England? The Burial Evidence Reconsidered', in D. M. Hadley & J. D. Richards (eds.) *Cultures in Contact: Scandinavian Settlement in England in the Ninth and Tenth Centuries*, Turnhout: Brepols, pp. 261–76.

2001. 'Childeric's Grave, Clovis' Succession, and the Origins of the Merovingian Kingdom', in R. W. Mathisen & D. Shanzer (eds.) *Society and Culture in Late Antique Gaul*, Aldershot: Ashgate, pp. 116–33.

2003. 'Burial Writes: Graves, Texts and Time in Early Merovingian Northern Gaul', in J. Jarnut & M. Wemhoff (eds.) *Erinnerungskultur im Bestattungsritual*, Munich: Wilhelm Fink, pp. 61–74.

Hamerow, H. 1993a. 'An Anglo-Saxon Cemetery near West Hendred, Oxon', in W. Filmer-Sankey (ed.) *Anglo-Saxon Studies in Archaeology and History*, Oxford: Oxford University Committee for Archaeology, pp. 113–24.

1993b. *Excavations at Mucking Volume 2: The Anglo-Saxon Settlement*, London: English Heritage.

2002. *Early Medieval Settlements: The Archaeology of Rural Communities in North-West Europe 400–900*, Oxford: Oxford University Press.

Hamilakis, Y. 1998. 'Eating the Dead: Mortuary Feasting and the Politics of Memory in the Aegean Bronze Age Societies', in K. Branigan (ed.) *Cemetery and Society in the Aegean Bronze Age*, Sheffield: Sheffield University Press, pp. 115–32.

Härke, H. 1989a. 'Early Saxon Weapon Burials: Frequencies, Distributions and Weapon Combinations', in S. C. Hawkes (ed.) *Weapons and Warfare in Anglo-Saxon England*, Oxford: Oxford University Committee for Archaeology Monograph No. 21, pp. 49–61.

1989b. 'Knives in Early Saxon Burials: Blade Length and Age at Death', *Medieval Archaeology* 33: 144–8.

1990. '"Warrior Graves"? The Background of The Anglo-Saxon Weapon Burial Rite', *Past and Present* 126: 22–43.

1992. 'Changing Symbols in a Changing Society: The Anglo-Saxon Weapon Burial Rite in the Seventh Century', in M. Carver (ed.) *The Age of Sutton Hoo*, Woodbridge: Boydell, pp. 149–66.

1997a. 'The Nature of Burial Data', in C. Kjeld Jensen & K. Høilund Nielsen (eds.) *Burial and Society*, Aarhus: Aarhus University Press, pp. 19–27.

1997b. 'Final Comments: Ritual, Symbolism and Social Inference', in C. K. Jensen & K. Høilund Nielsen (eds.) *Burial and Society*, Aarhus: University of Aarhus, pp. 191–5.

1997c. 'Material Culture as Myth: Weapons in Anglo-Saxon Graves', in C. K. Jensen & K. Høilund Nielsen (eds.) *Burial and Society*, Aarhus: Aarhus University Press, pp. 119–27.

1997d. 'Early Anglo-Saxon Social Structure', in J. Hines (ed.) *The Anglo-Saxons from the Migration Period to the Eighth Century: An Ethnographic Perspective*, Woodbridge: Boydell, pp. 125–59.

2000a. 'The Circulation of Weapons in Anglo-Saxon Society', in F. Theuws & J. L. Nelson (eds.) *Rituals of Power from Late Antiquity to the Early Middle Ages*, Leiden: Brill, pp. 377–99.

2000b. 'Social Analysis of Mortuary Evidence in German Protohistoric Archaeology', *Journal of Anthropological Archaeology* 19: 369–84.

2001. 'Cemeteries as Places of Power', in M. de Jong & F. Theuws (eds.) *Topographies of Power in the Early Middle Ages*, Leiden: Brill, pp. 9–30.

2002. 'An Anglo-Saxon Quadruple Weapon Burial at Tidworth: A Battle-Site Burial on Salisbury Plain?', *Proceedings of the Hampshire Field Club and Archaeological Society* 57: 38–52.

Harman, M., Molleson, T. I. & Price, J. L. 1981. 'Burials, Bodies and Beheadings in Romano-British and Anglo-Saxon Cemeteries', *Bulletin of the British Museum of Natural History* 35(3): 145–88.

Harrington, S. (in prep.) 'Soft Furnished Burial: An Assessment of the Role of Textiles in Early Anglo-Saxon Inhumations, with Particular Reference to East Kent', in S. Semple & H. Williams (eds.) *Anglo-Saxon Studies in Archaeology and History* 14, Oxford: Oxford University Press.

Harvey, D. C. 2002. 'Constructed Landscapes and Social Memory: Tales of St Samson in Early Medieval Cornwall', *Environment and Planning D: Society and Space* 20: 231–48.

Hawkes, S. C. 1977. 'Orientation at Finglesham: Sunrise Dating of Death and Burial in an Anglo-Saxon Cemetery in East Kent', *Archaeologia Cantiana* 92: 33–51.

1982. 'Finglesham: A Cemetery in East Kent', in J. Campbell (ed.) *The Anglo-Saxons*, London: Penguin, pp. 24–5.

1986. 'The Early Saxon Period', in G. Briggs, J. Cook & T. Rowley (eds.) *The Archaeology of the Oxford Region*, Oxford: Oxford University Committee for Archaeology, pp. 64–108.

Hawkes, S. C. & Grainger, G. 2003. *The Anglo-Saxon Cemetery at Worthy Park, Kingsworthy, near Winchester, Hampshire*, Oxford: Oxford University School of Archaeology Monograph No. 59.

Hawkes, S. C. & Wells, C. 1975. 'Crime and Punishment in an Anglo-Saxon Cemetery?', *Antiquity* 49: 118–22.

Haughton, C. & Powlesland, D. 1999. *West Heslerton: The Anglian Cemetery volume I: The Excavation and Discussion of the Evidence*. London: English Heritage. 2 vols.

Hedeager, L. 1992a. *Iron Age Societies*, Oxford: Blackwell.

1992b. 'Kingdoms, Ethnicity and Material Culture: Denmark in a European Perspective', in M. Carver (ed.) *The Age of Sutton Hoo*, Woodbridge: Boydell, pp. 279–300.

1998. 'Cosmological Endurance: Pagan Identities in Early Christian Europe', *European Journal of Archaeology* 1(3): 382–96.

1999. 'Myth and Art: A Passport to Political Authority in Scandinavia during the Migration Period', in T. Dickinson & D. Griffiths (eds.) *The Making of Kingdoms: Anglo-Saxon Studies in Archaeology and History* 10, Oxford: Oxford University Committee for Archaeology, pp. 151–6.

2000. 'Migration Period Europe: The Formation of a Political Mentality', in F. Theuws & J. L. Nelson (eds.) *Rituals of Power from Late Antiquity to the Early Middle Ages*, Leiden: Brill, pp. 15–57.

2001. '*Asgard* Reconstructed? Gudme – A "Central Place" in the North', in M. de Jong & F. Theuws (eds.) *Topographies of Power in the Early Middle Ages*, Leiden: Brill, pp. 467–508.

2002. 'Scandinavian "Central Places" in a Cosmological Setting', in B. Hardh & L. Larsson (eds.) *Central Places in the Migration and Merovingian Periods*, Lund: Uppåkrastudier 6, pp. 3–18.

Hedges, J. D. & Buckley, D. G. 1985. 'Anglo-Saxon Burials and Later Features Excavated at Orsett, Essex, 1975', *Medieval Archaeology* 29: 1–24.

Heighway, C. & Bryant, R. 1999. *The Golden Minster: The Anglo-Saxon Minster and Later Medieval Priory of St Oswald at Gloucester*, London: CBA Research Report 117.

Henderson, G. & Henderson, I. 2004. *The Art of the Picts: Sculpture and Metalwork in Early Medieval Scotland*, London: Thames & Hudson.

Henshall, A. S. 1955–6. 'A Long Cist Cemetery at Parkburn Sand Pit, Lasswade, Midlothian', *Proceedings of the Society of Antiquaries of Scotland* 89: 252–83.

Hertz, R. 1960. 'A Contribution to the Study of the Collective Representation of Death', in R. Needham & C. Needham (trans.) *Death and the Right Hand*, New York: Free Press.

Hey, G. 2004. *Yarnton: Saxon and Medieval Settlement and Landscape*, Oxford: Oxford Archaeological Unit.

Higham, N. 1992. *Rome, Britain and the Anglo-Saxons*, London: Seaby.

Hill, P. 1997. *Whithorn and St Ninian: The Excavation of a Monastic Town, 1984–91*, Stroud: Sutton.

Hills, C. 1977. *The Anglo-Saxon Cemetery at Spong Hill, North Elmham, part I: Catalogue of Cremations*, Dereham: East Anglian Archaeology 6.

    1980. 'Anglo-Saxon Cremation Cemeteries, with Particular Reference to Spong Hill, Norfolk', in P. Rahtz, T. Dickinson & L. Watts (eds.) *Anglo-Saxon Cemeteries 1979*, Oxford: BAR British Series 82, pp. 197–208.

    1997. '*Beowulf* and Archaeology', in R. E. Bjork & J. D. Niles (eds.) *A Beowulf Handbook*, Exeter: University of Exeter Press, pp. 291–11.

    2003. *Origins of the English*, London: Duckworth.

Hills, C. & Penn, K. 1981. *The Anglo-Saxon Cemetery at Spong Hill, North Elmham, part II: Catalogue of Cremations*, Dereham: East Anglian Archaeology 11.

Hills, C., Penn, K. & Rickett, R. 1984. *The Anglo-Saxon Cemetery at Spong Hill, North Elmham, part III: Catalogue of Inhumations*, Dereham: East Anglian Archaeology 21.

    1987. *The Anglo-Saxon Cemetery at Spong Hill, North Elmham, part IV: Catalogue of Cremations*, Dereham: East Anglian Archaeology 34.

    1994. *The Anglo-Saxon Cemetery at Spong Hill, North Elmham, part V: Catalogue of Cremations*, Dereham: East Anglian Archaeology 67.

Hines, J. 1984. *The Scandinavian Character of Anglian England in the pre-Viking Period*, Oxford: BAR British Series 124.

    1997a. 'Religion: The Limits of Knowledge', in J. Hines (ed.) *The Anglo-Saxons from the Migration Period to the Eighth Century*, Woodbridge: Boydell, pp. 375–400.

    1997b. *A New Corpus of Anglo-Saxon Great Square-Headed Brooches*, Woodbridge: Boydell.

    1999. 'The Sixth-Century Transition in Anglian England: An Analysis of Female Graves from Cambridgeshire', in J. Hines, K. Høilund Nielsen & F. Siegmund (eds.) *The Pace of Change: Studies in Early-Medieval Chronology*, Oxford: Oxbow, pp. 65–79.

    2002. 'Lies, Damned Lies, and the Curriculum Vitae: Reflections on Statistics and the Populations of Early Anglo-Saxon Inhumation Cemeteries', in S. Lucy & A. Reynolds (eds.) *Burial in Early Medieval England and Wales*, London: Society for Medieval Archaeology, pp. 88–102.

Hinton, D. 1990. *Archaeology, Economy & Society*, London: Seaby.

    2000. *A Smith in Lindsey: The Anglo-Saxon Grave at Tattershall Thorpe, Lincolnshire*, London: Society for Medieval Archaeology Monograph Series No. 16.

Hirst, S. 1985. *An Anglo-Saxon Inhumation Cemetery at Sewerby, East Yorkshire*, York: York University Archaeological Publications 4.

Hodder, I. 1980. 'Social Structure and Cemeteries: A Critical Appraisal', in P. Rahtz, T. Dickinson & L. Watts (eds.) *Anglo-Saxon Cemeteries 1979*, Oxford: BAR British Series 82, pp. 161–70.

Hogarth, A. C. 1973. 'Structural Features in Anglo-Saxon Graves', *Archaeological Journal* 130: 104–19.

Høilund Nielsen, K. 1997a. 'From Society to Burial and from Burial to Society? Some Modern Analogies', in C. K. Jensen & K. H. Nielsen (eds.) *Burial and Society: The Chronological and Social Analysis of Archaeological Burial Data*, Aarhus: Aarhus University Press, pp. 103–10.

1997b. 'Animal Art and the Weapon Burial Rite – A Political Badge?', in C. Kjeld Jensen & K. Høilund Nielsen (eds.) *Burial and Society*, Aarhus: Aarhus University Press, pp. 129–48.

1998. 'Animal Style – A Symbol of Might and Myth: Salin's Style II in a European Context', *Acta Archaeologia* 69: 1–52.

Holtorf, C. 1996. 'Towards a Chronology of Megaliths: Understanding Monumental Time and Cultural Memory', *Journal of European Archaeology* 4: 119–52.

1997. 'Megaliths, Monumentality and Memory', *Archaeological Review from Cambridge* 14(2): 45–66.

1998. 'The Life-Histories of Megaliths in Mecklenburg-Vorpommern (Germany)', *World Archaeology* 30(1): 23–38.

Hooke, D. 1999. *The Landscape of Anglo-Saxon England*, Leicester: Leicester University Press.

Hope, V. 1997. 'Words and Pictures: The Interpretation of Romano-British Tombstones', *Britannia* 38: 245–58.

2003. 'Remembering Rome: Memory, Funerary Monuments and the Roman Soldier', in H. Williams (ed.) *Archaeologies of Remembrance*, New York: Kluwer/Plenum, pp. 113–40.

Hope-Taylor, B. 1977. *Yeavering: An Anglo-British Centre of Early Northumbria*, London: HMSO.

Hoskins, J. 1998. *Biographical Objects*, London: Routledge

Hosler, D. 1995. 'Sound, Color and Meaning in the Metallurgy of Ancient West Mexico', *World Archaeology* 27(1): 100–15.

Howe, N. 1989. *Migration and Mythmaking in Anglo-Saxon England*, New Haven: Yale University Press.

2000. 'An Angle on this Earth: Sense of Place in Anglo-Saxon England', *Bulletin of the John Rylands University Library of Manchester* 82(1): 1–25.

2002. 'The Landscape of Anglo-Saxon England, Inherited, Invented, Imagined', in J. Howe & M. Wolfe (eds.) *Inventing Medieval Landscapes – Senses of Place in Western Europe*, Gainesville: University of Florida Press, pp. 91–112.

Hunter, J. 1997. *A Personal for the Northern Picts*, Rosemarkie: Groam House Museum.

Hyslop, M. 1963. 'Two Anglo-Saxon Cemeteries at Chamberlains Barn, Leighton Buzzard, Bedfordshire', *Archaeological Journal* 120: 161–200.

Ingold, T. 1993. 'The Temporality of Landscape', *World Archaeology* 25(2): 152–74.

Innes, M. 1998. 'Memory, Orality and Literacy in an Early Medieval Society', *Past and Present* 158: 3–36.

2001. 'Keeping it in the Family: Women and Aristocratic Memory, 700–1200', in E. van Houts (ed.) *Medieval Memories: Men, Women and the Past, 700–1300*, London. Longman, pp. 17–35.

James, E. 1980. 'Merovingian Cemetery Studies, and Some Implications for Anglo-Saxon England', in P. Rahtz, T. Dickinson & L. Watts (eds.) *Anglo-Saxon Cemeteries 1979*, Oxford: BAR British Series 82, pp. 35–58.

1988. *The Franks*, Oxford: Blackwell.

James, H. 1987. 'Excavations at Caer, Bayvil, 1979', *Archaeologia Cambrensis* 136: 51–76.

1992. 'Early Medieval Cemeteries in Wales', in N. Edwards & A. Lane (eds.) *The Early Church in Wales and the West*, Oxford: Oxbow Monograph 16, pp. 90–103.

1993. 'The Cult of St. David in the Middle Ages', in M. Carver (ed.) *In Search of Cult: Archaeological Investigations in Honour of Philip Rahtz*, Woodbridge: Boydell, pp. 105–12.

Janes, D. 2000. 'Treasure, Death and Display from Rome to the Middle Ages', in E. Tyler (ed.) *Treasure in the Medieval West*, York: York Medieval Press, pp. 1–11.

Jennbert, K. 2000. 'Archaeology and Pre-Christian Religion in Scandinavia', *Current Swedish Archaeology* 8: 127–41.

Joyce, R. A. 2001. 'Burying the Dead at Tlatilco: Social Memory and Social Identities', in M. S. Chesson (ed.) *Social Memory, Identity and Death: Anthropological Perspectives on Mortuary Rituals*, Arlington VA: Archaeological Papers of the American Anthropological Association No. 10, pp. 12–26.

2003. 'Concrete Memories: Fragments of the Past in the Classic Maya Present (500–1000AD)', in R. M. van Dyke & S. E. Alcock (eds.) *Archaeologies of Memory*, Oxford: Blackwell, pp. 104–25.

Jones, A. 2001a. 'Drawn from Memory: The Archaeology of Aesthetics and the Aesthetics of Archaeology in Earlier Bronze Age Britain and the Present', *World Archaeology* 33(2): 334–56.

2001b. 'Enduring Images? Image Production and Memory in Earlier Bronze Age Scotland', in J. Brück (ed.) *Bronze Age Landscapes*, Oxford: Oxbow, pp. 217–28.

2002. 'A Biography of Colour: Colour, Material Histories and Personhood in the Early Bronze Age of Britain and Ireland', in A. Jones & G. MacGregor (eds.) *Colouring the Past: The Significance of Colour in Archaeological Research*, Oxford: Berg, pp. 159–74.

2003. 'Technologies of Remembrance', in H. Williams (ed.) *Archaeologies of Remembrance: Death and Memory in Past Societies*, New York: Kluwer/Plenum, pp. 65–88.

2004. 'Matter and Memory: Colour, Remembrance and the Neolithic/Bronze Age Transition', in E. DeMarrais, C. Gosden & C. Renfrew (eds.), *Rethinking Materiality: The Engagement of Mind with the Material World*, Cambridge: McDonald Institute, pp. 167–78.

Jørgensen, L. 1987. 'Family Burial Practices and Inheritance Systems: The Development of an Iron Age Society from 500BC to AD1000 on Bornholm, Denmark', *Acta Archaeologia* 58: 17–53.

2003. 'Manor and Market at Lake Tissø in the Sixth to Eleventh Centuries: The Danish "Productive" Sites', in T. Pestell & K. Ulmschneider (eds.) *Markets in Early Medieval Europe: Trading and Productive Sites, 650–850*, Macclesfield: Windgather, pp. 175–207.

Kaliff, A. 2005. 'The Grave as Concept and Phenomenon: Reflections on the Relation between Archaeological Terminology and Interpretation', in T. Artelius & F. Svanberg (eds.) *Dealing with the Dead: Archaeological Perspectives on Prehistoric Scandinavian Burial Ritual*, Stockholm: National Heritage Board, pp. 125–42.

Karkov, C. E. 1999. 'Whitby, Jarrow and the Commemoration of Death in Northumbria', in J. Hawkes & S. Mills (eds.) *Northumbria's Golden Age*, Stroud: Sutton, pp. 126–35.

2003. 'The Body of St Æthelthryth: Desire, Conversion and Reform in Anglo-Saxon England', in M. Carver (ed.) *The Cross Goes North: Processes of Conversion in Northern Europe, AD 300–1300*, York: York Medieval Press, pp. 397–411.

Kemble, J. M. 1857. 'Notices of Heathen Interment in the Codex Diplomaticus', *Archaeological Journal* 14: 119–43.

King, J. 2004. 'Grave-Goods as Gifts in Early Saxon Burials', *Journal of Social Archaeology* 4(2): 214–38.

Kinsley, A. 1989. *The Anglo-Saxon Cemetery at Millgate, Newark-on-Trent, Nottinghamshire*, Nottingham: University of Nottingham.

Knapp, A. B. & Ashmore, W. 1999. 'Archaeological Landscapes: Constructed, Conceptualized, Ideational', in W. Ashmore & A. B. Knapp (eds.) *Archaeologies of Landscape – Contemporary Perspectives*, Oxford: Blackwell, pp. 1–32.

Knight, J. 2003. 'Basilicas and Barrows: Christian Origins in Wales and Western Britain', in M. Carver (ed.) *The Cross Goes North: Processes of Conversion in Northern Europe, AD 300–1300*, York: York Medieval Press, pp. 119–26.

Knüsel, C. J., Janaway, R. C. & King, S. E. 1996. 'Death, Decay and Ritual Reconstruction: Archaeological Evidence for Cadaveric Spasm', *Oxford Journal of Archaeology* 15(2): 121–8.

Kornbluth, G. A. 1989. 'The Alfred Jewel: Reuse of Roman', *Spolia, Medieval Archaeology* 33: 32–7.

Küchler, S. 1988. 'Malanggan: Objects, Sacrifice and the Production of Memory', *American Ethnologist* 15(4): 625–37.

1999. 'The Place of Memory', in A. Forty & S. Küchler (eds.) *The Art of Forgetting*, Oxford: Berg, pp. 53–72.

2002. *Malanggan. Art, Memory and Sacrifice*, Oxford: Berg.

Kuijt, I. 2001. 'Place, Death, and the Transmission of Social Memory in Early Agricultural Communities of the Near Eastern Pre-pottery Neolithic', in M. S. Chesson (ed.) *Social Memory, Identity and Death: Anthropological Perspectives on Mortuary Rituals*, Arlington VA: Archaeological Papers of the American Anthropological Association No. 10, pp. 80–99.

Kus, S. 1992. 'Toward an Archaeology of Body and Soul', in J.-C. Gardin & C. S. Peebles (eds.) *Representations in Archaeology*, Bloomington & Indianapolis: Indiana University Press, pp. 168–77.

Kus, S. & Raharijaona, V. 2001. 'To Dare to Wear the Cloak of Another before Their Very Eyes: State Co-optation and Location Re-appropriation in Mortuary Rituals of Central Madagascar', in M. S. Chesson (ed.) *Social Memory, Identity and Death: Anthropological Perspectives on Mortuary Rituals*, Arlington VA: Archaeological Papers of the American Anthropological Association No. 10, pp. 114–31.

Lahiri, N. 2003. 'Commemorating and Remembering 1857: The Revolt in Delhi and its Afterlife', *World Archaeology* 35(1): 35–60.

Lane, T. W. with Hayes, P. 1993. *The Fenland Project No. 8: Lincolnshire Survey: The Northern Fen-Edge*, Dereham: East Anglian Archaeology No. 66.

Lang, J. 1984. 'The Hogback: A Viking Colonial Monument', in S. C. Hawkes, J. Campbell & D. Brown (eds.) *Anglo-Saxon Studies in Archaeology and History* 3, pp. 85–176.

Last, J. 1998. 'Books of Life: Biography and Memory in a Bronze Age Barrow', *Oxford Journal of Archaeology* 17(1): 43–53.

Leech, R. 1986. 'The Excavation of a Romano-Celtic Temple and a Later Cemetery on Lamyatt Beacon, Somerset', *Britannia* 17: 259–328.

Lee, F. & Magilton, J. 1989. 'The Cemetery of the Hospital of St James and St Mary Magdalene Chichester – A Case Study', *World Archaeology* 21(2): 273–82.

Leeds, E. T. 1913. *The Archaeology of the Anglo-Saxon Settlements*, Oxford: Clarendon.

1936. *Early Anglo-Saxon Art and Archaeology*, Oxford: Clarendon.

1945. 'The Distribution of the Angles and Saxons Archaeologically Considered', *Archaeologia* 91: 1–106.

Leeds, E. T. & Harden, D. 1936. *The Anglo-Saxon Cemetery at Abingdon, Berkshire*, Oxford: Ashmolean.

Lillios, K. T. 1999. 'Objects of Memory: The Ethnography and Archaeology of Heirlooms', *Journal of Archaeological Method and Theory*, 6(3): 235–62.

Longley, D. 2002. 'Orientation within Early Medieval Cemeteries: Some Data from North-West Wales', *Antiquaries Journal*: 309–21.

Loveluck, C. 1998. 'A High-Status Anglo-Saxon Settlement at Flixborough, Lincolnshire', *Antiquity* 72: 146–61.

Lucy, S. 1992. 'The Significance of Mortuary Ritual in the Political Manipulation of the Landscape', *Archaeological Review from Cambridge*: 93–103.

'Housewives, Warriors and Slaves? Sex and Gender in Anglo-Saxon Burials', in J. Moore and E. Scott (eds.) *Invisible People and Processes*, Leicester: Leicester University Press, pp. 150–68.

1998. *The Early Anglo-Saxon Cemeteries of East Yorkshire*, Oxford: BAR British Series 272.

2000. *The Anglo-Saxon Way of Death*, Stroud: Sutton.

2002. 'Burial Practice in Early Medieval Eastern England: Constructing Local Identities, Deconstructing Ethnicity', in S. Lucy & A. Reynolds (eds.) *Burial in Early Medieval England and Wales*, Leeds: Maney, pp. 72–87.

Lucy, S. & Reynolds, A. 2002. 'Burial in Early Medieval England and Wales: Past, Present and Future', in S. Lucy & A. Reynolds (eds.) *Burial in Early Medieval England and Wales*, Leeds: Maney, pp. 1–23.

Ludlow, N. 2000. 'St Cristiolus' Churchyard, Eglwyswrw, Pembrokeshire: A Post-Conquest Cist Cemetery', *Archaeologia Cambrensis* 149: 21–48.

MacLagan Wedderburn, L. M. & Grime, D. M. 1984. 'The Cairn Cemetery at Garbeg, Drumnadrochit', in J. G. P. Friell & W. G. Watson (eds.) *Pictish Studies: Settlement, Burial and Art in Dark Age Northern Britain*, Oxford: BAR British Series 125, pp. 151–68.

Magilton, J. & Lee, F. 1989. 'The Leper Hospital of St James and St Mary Magdalene, Chichester', in C. Roberts, F. Lee & J. Bintliff (eds.) *Burial Archaeology: Current Research, Methods and Developments*, Oxford: BAR British Series, pp. 249–65.

Malim, T. & Hines, J. 1998. *The Anglo-Saxon Cemetery at Edix Hill (Barrington A), Cambridgeshire*, London: Council for British Archaeology 112.

Manchester, K. 1987. 'Medieval Leprosy: The Disease and its Management', in M. Deegan & D. G. Scragg (eds.) *Medicine in Early Medieval England*, Manchester: Manchester Centre for Anglo-Saxon Studies, pp. 27–32.

Marsden, B. 1999. *The Early Barrow Diggers*, Stroud: Tempus.

Marzinzik, S. 2000. 'Grave Goods in Conversion Period and Later Burials – A Case of Early Medieval Religious Double Standards?', in K. Pollmann (ed.) *Double Standards in the Ancient and Medieval World*, Göttingen: Göttinger Forum für Altertumswissenschaften, Beiheft 1, pp. 149–66.

2003. *Early Anglo-Saxon Belt Buckles (Late 5th to Early 8th Centuries AD): Their Classification and Context*, Oxford: BAR British Series 357.

Mayes, P. & Dean, M. J. 1976. *An Anglo-Saxon Cemetery at Baston, Lincolnshire*, Sleaford: Society for Lincolnshire History and Archaeology.

Mays, S. 1998. *The Archaeology of Human Bones*, London: Routledge.

McKinley, J. 1994. *The Anglo-Saxon Cemetery at Spong Hill, North Elmham, part VII: The Cremations*, Dereham: East Anglian Archaeology 69.

McKinley, J. 2003. 'A Wiltshire "Bog Body"?: Discussion of a Fifth/Sixth-Century AD Burial in the Woodford Valley', *Wiltshire Archaeological and Natural History Magazine* 96: 7–18.

Meaney, A. 1964. *A Gazetteer of Early Anglo-Saxon Burial Sites*, London: Allen & Unwin.

1981. *Anglo-Saxon Amulets and Curing Stones*, Oxford: BAR British Series 96.

1995. 'Pagan English Sanctuaries, Place-Names and Hundred Meeting Places' in D. Griffiths (ed.) *Anglo-Saxon Studies in Archaeology and History* 8, Oxford: Oxbow. pp. 29–42.

2001. 'Felix's Life of St Guthlac: Hagiography and/or Truth', *Proceedings of the Cambridge Antiquarian Society* 90: 29–48.

Meaney, A. L. & Hawkes, S. C. 1970. *Two Anglo-Saxon Cemeteries at Winnall*, London: Society for Medieval Archaeology Monograph Series No. 4.

Meskell, L. 1996. 'The Somatization of Archaeology: Institutions, Discourses and Corporeality', *Norwegian Archaeological Review* 29: 1–17.

2003. 'Memory's Materiality: Ancestral Presence, Commemorative Practice and Disjunctive Locales', in R. M. van Dyke & S. E. Alcock (eds.) *Archaeologies of Memory*, Oxford: Blackwell, pp. 34–55.

Metcalf, D. & Huntingdon, R. 1991. *Celebrations of Death: The Anthropology of Mortuary Ritual*, 2nd edn. Cambridge: Cambridge University Press.

Miles, D. 1974. 'Abingdon and Region: Early Anglo-Saxon Settlement Evidence', in T. Rowley (ed.) *Anglo-Saxon Settlement and Landscape*, Oxford: BAR British Series 6, pp. 36–41.

Mitford, J. 1963. *The American Way of Death*, London: Quartet.

Mizoguchi, K. 1993. 'Time in the Reproduction of Mortuary Practices', *World Archaeology* 25(2): 223–35.

MOLAS. 2000. 'Cuxton Anglo-Saxon Cemetery', *Current Archaeology* 14 (168): 460–1.

MOLAS. 2004. 'Prittlewell: Treasures of a King of Essex', *Current Archaeology* 16(190): 430–6.

Montgomery, J., Budd, P. & Evans, J. 2000. 'Reconstructing the Lifetime Movements of Ancient People', *European Journal of Archaeology* 3(3): 370–86.

Montgomery, J., Evans, J. A., Powlesland, D. & Roberts, C. A. 2005. 'Continuity or Colonization in Anglo-Saxon England? Isotope Evidence for Mobility, Subsistence Practice, and Status at West Heslerton', *American Journal of Physical Anthropology* 126: 123–38.

Moreland, J. 1997. 'The Middle Ages, Theory and Post-Modernism', *Acta Archaeologia* 68: 163–82.

1999. 'The World(s) of the Cross', *World Archaeology* 31(2): 194–213.

2001. *Archaeology and Text*, London: Duckworth.

Morris, I. 1992. *Death-Ritual and Social Structure in Classical Antiquity*, Cambridge: Cambridge University Press.

Mulville, J., Parker Pearson, M., Sharples, N., Smith, H. & Chamberlain, A. 2003. 'Quarters, Arcs and Squares: Human and Animal Remains in the Hebridean Late Iron Age', in J. Downes & A. Ritchie (eds.) *Sea Change: Orkney and Northern Europe in the Later Iron Age AD 300–800*, Balgavies: Pinkfoot Press, pp. 20–34.

Murphy, K. 1992. 'Plas Gogerddan, Dyfed: A Multi-Period Burial and Ritual Site', *Archaeological Journal* 149: 1–39.

Myres, J. N. L. 1969. *Anglo-Saxon Pottery and the Settlement of England*, Oxford: Clarendon.

1977. *A Corpus of Anglo-Saxon Pottery of the Pagan Period*, Cambridge: Cambridge University Press.

Myres, J. N. L. & Green, B. 1973. *The Anglo-Saxon Cemeteries of Caistor-by-Norwich and Markshall*, London: Society of Antiquaries.

Nash-Williams, V. E. 1950. *The Early Christian Monuments of Wales*, Cardiff: University of Wales Press.

Newman, J. 2002. 'Sutton Hoo before Raedwald', *Current Archaeology* 15(180): 498–505.

Neville, R. C. 1852. *Saxon Obsequies*, London: Murray.

Nilsson Stutz, L. 2003. *Embodied Rituals and Ritualized Bodies*, Lund: Acta Archaeologica Lundensia No. 46.

Oestigaard, T. 2000. 'Sacrifices of Raw, Cooked and Burnt Humans', *Norwegian Archaeological Review* 33(1): 41–58.

O' Brien, E. 1999. *Post-Roman Britain to Anglo-Saxon England: Burial Practices Reviewed*, Oxford: BAR British Series 289.

2003. 'Burial Practices in Ireland: First to Seventh Centuries AD', in J. Downes & A. Ritchie (eds.) *Sea Change: Orkney and Northern Europe in the Later Iron Age AD 300–800*, Balgavies: Pinkfoot Press, pp. 62–74.

O'Sullivan, D. 2001. 'Space, Silence and Shortages on Lindisfarne', in H. Hamerow & A. MacGregor (eds.) *Image and Power in the Archaeology of Early Medieval Britain*, Oxford: Oxbow, pp. 33–52.

Overing, G. R. & Osborn, M. 1994. *Landscape of Desire: Partial Stories of the Medieval Scandinavian World*, Minneapolis: University of Minnesota Press.

Owen-Crocker, G. R. 2004. *Dress in Anglo-Saxon England*, Woodbridge: Boydell.

Ozanne, A. 1962–3. 'The Peak Dwellers', *Medieval Archaeology* 6–7: 15–52.

Pader, E. J. 1980. 'Material Symbolism and Social Relations in Mortuary Studies', in P. Rahtz, T. Dickinson & L. Watts (eds.) *Anglo-Saxon Cemeteries 1979*, Oxford: BAR British Series 82, pp. 143–60.

1982. *Symbolism, Social Relations and the Interpretation of Mortuary Remains*, Oxford: BAR International Series 130.

Pantos, A. 2003. '"On the Edge of Things": The Boundary Location of Anglo-Saxon Assembly Sites', in D. Griffiths, A. Reynolds & S. Semple (eds.) *Boundaries in Early Medieval Britain: Anglo-Saxon Studies in Archaeology and History* 12, Oxford: Oxbow, pp. 38–49.

2004a. 'The Location and Form of Anglo-Saxon Assembly-Places', in A. Pantos & S. Semple (eds.) *Assembly Places and Practices in Medieval Europe*, Dublin: Four Courts Press, pp. 155–80.

2004b. '"*in medle oððe an þinge*": The Old English Vocabulary of Assembly', in A. Pantos & S. Semple (eds.) *Assembly Places and Practices in Medieval Europe*, Dublin: Four Courts Press, pp. 181–204.

Parfitt, K. & Brugmann, B. 1997. *The Anglo-Saxon Cemetery on Mill Hill, Deal, Kent*, Leeds: The Society for Medieval Archaeology Monograph Series No. 14.

Parker, S. J. 1989. 'Skulls, Symbols and Surgery: A Review of the Evidence for Trepanation in Anglo-Saxon England and a Consideration of the Motives behind the Practice', in D. G. Scragg (ed.) *Superstition and Popular Medicine in Anglo-Saxon England*, Manchester: Manchester Centre for Anglo-Saxon Studies, pp. 73–84.

Parker Pearson, M. 1982. 'Mortuary Practices, Society and Ideology: An Ethnoarchaeological Study', in I. Hodder (ed.) *Symbolic and Structural Archaeology*, Cambridge: Cambridge University Press, pp. 99–113.

1993. 'The Powerful Dead: Archaeological Relationships between the Living and the Dead', *Cambridge Archaeological Journal* 3(2): 203–29.

1999a. 'Food, Sex and Death: Cosmologies in the British Iron Age with Particular Reference to East Yorkshire', *Cambridge Archaeological Journal* 9: 43–69.

1999b. 'Fearing and Celebrating the Dead in Southern Madagascar', in J. Downes & T. Pollard (eds.) *The Loved Body's Corruption: Archaeological Contributions to the Study of Human Mortality*, Glasgow: Cruithne, pp. 19–29.

1999c. *The Archaeology of Death and Burial*, Stroud: Sutton.

Parker Pearson, M., van de Noort, R. & Woolf, A. 1993. 'Three Men and a Boat: Sutton Hoo and the East Anglian Kingdom', *Anglo-Saxon England* 22: 27–50.

Parker Pearson, M. & Ramilisonina, 1998. 'Stonehenge for the Ancestors: The Stones Pass on the Message', *Antiquity* 72: 308–26.

Parker Pearson, M., Ramilisonina and Resihisatse. 1999. 'Ancestors, Forests and Ancient Settlements: Tandroy Readings of the Archaeological Past', in P. J. Ucko & R. Layton (eds.) *The Archaeology and Anthropology of Landscape: Shaping your Landscape*, London: Routledge, pp. 397–410.

Parkin, D. 1992. 'Ritual as Spatial Direction and Bodily Division', in D. de Coppett (ed.) *Understanding Rituals*, London: Routledge, pp. 11–25.

Peacquer, L. 2003. 'Des Morts chez les vivants. Les Inhumations dan les habitats ruraux du haut Moyen Âge en Île-de-France', *Archéologie Médiévale*, 33: 1–31.

Penn, K. 2000. *Excavations on the Norwich Southern Bypass, 1989–91, part II: The Anglo-Saxon Cemetery at Harford Farm, Caistor St Edmund, Norfolk*, Gressenhall: East Anglian Archaeology Report No. 92.

Petts, D. 1998. 'Burial and Gender in Late- and Sub-Roman Britain', in C. Forcey, J. Hawthorne & R. Witcher (eds.) *TRAC97 – Proceedings of the Seventh Annual Theoretical Roman Archaeology Conference*, Oxford: Oxbow, pp. 112–24.

2000. *Burial and Religion in Sub-Roman and Early Medieval Britain: AD 400–800*, Unpublished Ph.D. thesis, University of Reading.

2002. 'Cemeteries and Boundaries in Western Britain', in S. Lucy & A. Reynolds (eds.) *Burial in Early Medieval England and Wales*, Leeds: Maney, Society for Medieval Archaeology Monograph 17, pp. 24–46.

2004. 'Burial in Western Britain, AD 400–800: Late Antique or Early Medieval', in R. Collins & J. Gerrard (eds.) *Debating Late Antiquity in Britain AD 300–700*, Oxford: BAR British Series 365, pp. 77–88.

Phillips, D. & Heywood, B. 1995. *Excavations at York Minster vol. I, From Roman Fortress to Norman cathedral*, London: HMSO.

Philp, B. 1973. 'The Anglo-Saxon Cemetery at Polhill, Dunton Green, Kent', in B. Philp (ed.) *Excavations in West Kent 1960–1970*, West Wickham: Kent Archaeological Rescue Unit, pp. 164–214.

Philp, B. & Keller, P. 2002. *The Anglo-Saxon Cemetery at Eastry, near Dover*, West Wickham: Kent Archaeological Rescue Unit.

Philpott, R. 1991. *Burial Practices in Roman Britain: A Survey of Grave Treatment and Furnishing, AD* 43–410, Oxford: BAR British Series 219.

Pitts, M., Bayliss, A., McKinley, J., Boylston, A., Budd, A., Evans, J., Chenery, C., Reynolds, A. & Semple, S. 2002. 'An Anglo-Saxon Decapitation and Burial at Stonehenge', *Wiltshire Archaeological and Natural History Magazine* 95: 131–46.

Pohl, W. 1997. 'Ethnic Names and Identities in the Britsh Isles: A Comparative Perspective', in J. Hines (ed.) *The Anglo-Saxons from the Migration Period to the Eighth Century*, Woodbridge: Boydell, pp. 1–40.

Pointon, M. 2002. 'Materializing Mourning: Hair, Jewellery and the Body', in M. Kwint, C. Breward & J. Aynsley (eds.) *Material Memories: Design and Evocation*, Oxford: Berg, pp. 39–58.

Pollard, T. 1999. 'The Drowned and the Saved: Archaeological Perspectives on the Sea as Grave', in J. Downes & T. Pollard (eds.) *The Loved Body's Corruption: Archaeological Contributions to the Study of Human Mortality*, Glasgow: Cruithne, pp. 30–51.

Powlesland, D. 2000. 'West Heslerton Settlement Mobility: A Case of Static Development', in H. Geake & J. Kenny (eds.) *Early Deira: Archaeological Studies of the East Riding in the Fourth to Ninth Centuries AD*, Oxford: Oxbow, pp. 19–26.

2004. 'Early Anglo-Saxon Settlement and Landscape in the Vale of Pickering', conference paper presented at 55th Sachsensymposium, Cambridge, University of Cambridge, 11–15 September 2004.

Price, N. 2002. *The Viking Way: Religion and War in Late Iron Age Scandinavia*. Uppsala: University of Uppsala.

Proudfoot, E. 1996. 'Excavations at the Long Cist Cemetery on the Hallow Hill, St Andrews, Fife', *Proceedings of the Society of Antiquaries of Scotland* 126: 387–454.

Proudfoot, E. & Aliaga-Kelly, C. 1997. 'Aspects of Settlement and Territorial Arrangements in South-East Scotland in the Late Prehistoric and Early Medieval Period', *Medieval Archaeology* 41: 33–50.

Raharijaona, V. & Kus, S. 2001. 'Matters of Life and Death: Mortuary Rituals as Part of a Larger Whole among the Betsileo of Madagascar', in M. S. Chesson (ed.) *Social Memory, Identity and Death: Anthropological Perspectives on Mortuary Rituals*, Arlington VA: Archaeological Papers of the American Anthropological Association No. 10, pp. 56–68.

Rahtz, P. 1977. 'Later Roman Cemeteries and beyond' in R. Reece (ed.) *Burial in the Roman World*, London: Council for British Archaeology Research Report 22, pp. 1–22.

Rahtz, P., Hirst, S. & Wright, S. 2000. *Cannington Cemetery*. London: Britannia Monograph Series, 17.

Rahtz, P. & Watts, L. 2003. *Glastonbury: Myth and Archaeology*, Stroud: Tempus.

Randsborg, K. 1980. 'Burial, Succession and Early State Formation in Denmark', in R. Chapman, I. Kinnes & K. Randsborg (eds.) *The Archaeology of Death*, Cambridge: Cambridge University Press, pp. 105–21.

Ravn, M. 1999. 'Theoretical and Methodological Approaches to Migration Period Burials', in M. Rundkvist (ed.) *Grave Matters: Eight Studies of First Millennium AD Burials in Crimea, England and Southern Scandinavia*, Oxford: BAR International Series 781, pp. 41–56.

2003. *Death Ritual and Germanic Social Structure*, Oxford: BAR International Series 1164.

Rees, A. R. 2002. 'A First Millennium AD Cemetery, Rectangular Bronze Age Structure and Late Prehistoric Settlement at Thornybank, Midlothian', *Proceedings of the Society of Antiquaries of Scotland* 132: 313–57.

Reynolds, A. 1997. 'The Identification and Ideology of Anglo-Saxon Execution Sites and Cemeteries', conference presentation at *Bruges Medieval Europe Conference*.

1999. *Later Anglo-Saxon England: Life and Landscape*, Stroud: Tempus.

2002. 'Burials, Boundaries and Charters in Anglo-Saxon England: A Reassessment', in S. Lucy & A. Reynolds (eds.) *Burial in Early Medieval England and Wales*, Leeds: Maney, Society for Medieval Archaeology Monograph 17, pp. 171–94.

2003. 'Boundaries and Settlements in Later Sixth to Eleventh-Century England', in D. Griffiths, A. Reynolds & S. Semple (eds.) *Boundaries in Early Medieval Britain: Anglo-Saxon Studies in Archaeology & History* 12, Oxford: Oxbow, pp. 98–136.

Reynolds, N. 1976. 'The Structure of Anglo-Saxon Graves', *Antiquity* 50: 140–4.

1988. 'The Rape of the Anglo-Saxon Women', *Antiquity* 62: 715–18.

Richards, J. D. 1987. *The Significance of Form and Decoration of Anglo-Saxon Cremation Urns*, Oxford: BAR British Series 166.

1991. *Viking Age England*, London: Batsford.

1992. 'Anglo-Saxon Symbolism', in M. Carver (ed.) *The Age of Sutton Hoo*, Woodbridge: Boydell, pp. 131–49.

1995. 'An Archaeology of Anglo-Saxon England', in G. Ausenda (ed.) *After Empire: Towards an Ethnology of Europe's Barbarians*, Woodbridge: Boydell, pp. 51–66.

1999. 'Cottam: An Anglo-Scandinavian Settlement on the Yorkshire Wolds', *Archaeological Journal* 156: 1–111.

2000. *Viking Age England*, 2nd edn, Stroud: Tempus.

2001. 'Boundaries and Cult Centres: Viking Burial in Derbyshire', in J. Graham-Campbell, R. Hall, J. Jesch & D. N. Parsons (eds.) *Vikings and the Danelaw*, Oxford: Oxbow, pp. 97–104.

2002. 'The Case of the Missing Vikings: Scandinavian Burial in the Danelaw', in S. Lucy & A. Reynolds (eds.) *Burial in Early Medieval England and Wales*, Leeds: Maney, Society for Medieval Archaeology Monograph 17, pp. 156–70.

2003. 'Pagans and Christians at the Frontier: Viking Burial in the Danelaw,' in M. Carver (ed.) *The Cross Goes North: Processes of Conversion in Northern Europe, AD 300–1300*, York: York Medieval Press, pp. 383–96.

2004. 'Excavations at the Viking Barrow Cemetery at Heath Wood, Ingleby, Derbyshire', *Antiquaries Journal* 84: 117–84.

Richards, J. D., Jecock, M., Richmond, L. & Tuck, C. 1995. 'The Viking Barrow Cemetery at Heath Wood, Ingleby, Derbyshire', *Medieval Archaeology* 39: 51–70.

Richards, P. 1977. *The Medieval Leper*, Cambridge: Brewer.

Rippon, S. 2000. 'Landscapes in Transition: The Later Roman and Early Medieval Periods', in D. Hooke (ed.) *Landscape: The Richest Historical Record*, Amesbury: Society for Landscape Studies, pp. 47–62.

Robb, J. 2002. 'Time and Biography: Osteobiography of the Italian Neolithic Lifespan', in Y. Hamilakis, M. Pluciennik & S. Tarlow (eds.) *Thinking through the Body*, New York: Kluwer/Plenum, pp. 153–72.

Roberts, C. & Manchester, K. 1995. *The Archaeology of Disease*, Stroud: Sutton.

Rodwell, W. & Rodwell, K. 1983. 'St Peter's Church, Barton-upon-Humber: Excavation and Structural Study, 1978–81', *Antiquaries Journal* 62(2): 283–315.

Rowlands, M. 1993. 'The Role of Memory in the Transmission of Culture', *World Archaeology* 25(2): 141–51.

Roymans, N. 1995. 'The Cultural Biography of Urnfields and the Long-Term History of a Mythical Landscape', *Archaeological Dialogues* 2(1): 2–38.

Samson, R. 1987. 'Social Structures from Reihengräber: Mirror or Mirage?' *Scottish Archaeological Review* 4: 116–26.

1992. 'The Reinterpretation of the Pictish Symbol Stones', *Journal of the British Archaeological Association* 145: 29–65.

Samuels, J. & Russell, A. 1999. 'An Anglo-Saxon Burial near Winthorpe Road, Newark, Nottinghamshire', *Transactions of the Thoroton Society of Nottinghamshire*, 103: 57–83.

Saunders, N. J. 1999. 'Biographies of Brilliance: Pearls, Transformations of Matter and Being, c. AD 1492', *World Archaeology* 31(2): 243–57.

2002. 'The Colours of Light. Materiality and Chromatic Cultures of the Americas', in A. Jones & G. MacGregor (eds.) *Colouring the Past: The Significance of Colour in Archaeological Research*, Oxford: Berg, pp. 209–27.

2003. 'Crucifix, Calvary, and Cross: Materiality and Spirituality in Great War Landscapes', *World Archaeology* 35(1): 7–21.

Scull, C. 1992. 'Excavation and Survey at Watchfield, Oxfordshire, 1983–92', *Archaeological Journal* 149: 124–281.

Scull, C. & Harding, A. 1990. 'Two Early Medieval Cemeteries at Millfield, Northumberland', *Durham Archaeological Journal* 6: 1–29.

Scull, C. & Bayliss, A. 1999. 'Dating Burials of the Seventh and Eighth Centuries: A Case Study from Ipswich, Suffolk', in J. Hines, K. Høilund Nielsen & F. Siegmund (eds.) *The Pace of Change: Studies in Early Medieval Chronology*, Oxford. Oxbow, pp. 80–92.

Semple, S. 1998. 'A Fear of the Past: The Place of the Prehistoric Burial Mound in the Ideology of Middle and Later Anglo-Saxon England', *World Archaeology* 30(1): 109–26.

2002. *Anglo-Saxon Attitudes to the Past: A Landscape Perspective*, Unpublished Ph.D. thesis, University of Oxford.

2003. 'Burials and Political Boundaries in the Avebury Region, North Wiltshire', in D. Griffiths, A. Reynolds & S. Semple (eds.) *Anglo-Saxon Studies in Archaeology & History* 12, Oxford: Oxbow, pp. 72–91.

2004a. 'Locations of Assembly in Early Anglo-Saxon England', in A. Pantos & S. Semple (eds.) *Assembly Places and Practices in Medieval Europe*, Dublin: Four Courts Press, pp. 135–54.

2004b. 'Illustrations of Damnation in Late Anglo-Saxon Manuscripts', *Anglo-Saxon England* 32: 231–45.

Serematakis, N. 1991. *The Last Word: Women, Death and Divination in Inner Mani*, Chicago: University of Chicago Press.

Shanks, M. & Tilley, C. 1982. 'Ideology, Symbolic Power and Ritual Communication: A Reinterpretation of Neolithic Mortuary Practices', in I. Hodder (ed.) *Symbolic and Structural Archaeology*, Cambridge: Cambridge University Press, pp. 129–54.

Shennan, S. 1975. 'The Social Organization at Branc', *Antiquity* 49: 279–88.

Shephard, J. 1979. 'The Social Identity of the Individual in Isolated Barrows and Barrow Cemeteries in Anglo-Saxon England', in B. C. Burnham & J. Kingsbury (eds.) *Space, Hierarchy and Society: Interdisciplinary Studies in Social Area Analysis*, Oxford: BAR International Series 59, pp. 47–79.

Shook, L. 1960. 'The Burial Mound in *Guthlac A*', *Modern Philology* 58: 1–10.

Siewers, A. K. 2003. 'Landscapes of Conversion: Guthlac's Mound and Grendel's Mere as Expressions of Anglo-Saxon Nation-Building', *Viator* 34: 1–39.

Sims-Williams, P. 1983. 'The Settlement of England in Bede and the *Chronicle*', *Anglo-Saxon England* 12: 1–41.

Smith. C. R. 1848. 'Warwickshire Antiquities', *Collectanea Antiqua* 1: 33–48.

(ed.) 1856. *Inventorium Sepulchre: An Account of Some Antiquities Dug up at Gilton, Kingston, Sibertswold, Barfriston, Beakesbourne, Chartham, and Crundale . . . Kent, from AD 1757 to AD 1773, by Rev. Bryan Faussett*. London: privately printed.

1868. 'Anglo-Saxon Remains Recently Discovered in Kent, in Cambridgeshire, and in Some Other Counties', *Collectanea Antiqua* 6 (II): 136–72.

Sofaer Derevenski, J. 2000. 'Rings of Life: The Role of Early Metalwork in Mediating the Gendered Life Course', *World Archaeology* 31(3): 389–406.

Solberg, B. 1985. 'Social Status in the Merovingian and Viking Periods in Norway from Archaeological and Historical Sources', *Norwegian Archaeological Review* 18: 61–76.

Speake, G. 1989. *A Saxon Bed Burial on Swallowcliffe Down*, London: Historic Buildings and Monuments Commission for England Archaeological Report No. 10.

Speed, G. & Walton Rogers, P. 2004. 'A Burial of a Viking Woman at Adwick-le-Street, South Yorkshire', *Medieval Archaeology* 48: 51–90.

Stanford, S. C. with Bayliss, A., Moffet, L., Morris, E. L. & Walker, A. J. 1995. 'A Cornovian Farm and Saxon Cemetery at Bromfield, Shopshire', *Transactions of the Shropshire Archaeological and History Society* 70: 95–142.

Stevenson, J. B. 1984. 'Garbeg and Whitebridge: Two Square-Barrow Cemeteries in Inverness-shire', in J. G. P. Friell & W. G. Watson (eds.) *Pictish Studies: Settlement, Burial and Art in Dark Age Northern Britain*, Oxford: BAR British Series 125, pp. 145–50.

Stocker, D. 1993. 'The Early Church in Lincolnshire', in A. Vince (ed.) *Pre-Viking Lindsey*, Lincoln: City of Lincoln Archaeology Unit, pp. 101–22.

Stocker, D. & Everson, P. 2003. 'The Straight and Narrow Way: Fenland Causeways and the Conversion of the Landscape in the Witham Valley, Lincolnshire', in M. Carver (ed.) *The Cross Goes North: Processes of Conversion in Northern Europe, AD 300–1300*, York: York Medieval Press, pp. 271–88.

Stoodley, N. 1999a. *The Spindle and the Spear*, Oxford: BAR British Series 288.

1999b. 'Burial Rites, Gender and The Creation of Kingdoms: The Evidence from Seventh-Century Wessex', in T. Dickinson & D. Griffiths (eds.) *The Making of Kingdoms: Anglo-Saxon Studies in Archaeology and History* 10, Oxford: Oxford University Committee for Archaeology, pp. 99–108.

2000. 'From the Cradle to the Grave: Age Organization and the Early Anglo-Saxon Burial Rite', *World Archaeology* 31(3): 456–72.

2002. 'Multiple Burials, Multiple Meanings? Interpreting the Early Anglo-Saxon Multiple Interment', in S. Lucy & A. Reynolds (eds.) *Burial in Early Medieval England and Wales*, London: Society for Medieval Archaeology Monograph 17, pp. 103–21.

(in prep.) 'Strontium and Oxygen Isotope Assessment of the Immigrant Population from Lankhills, Winchester'.

Stoodley, N. & Stedman, M. 2001. 'Excavations at Shavards Farm, Meonstoke: The Anglo-Saxon cemetery', *Hampshire Studies 2001: Proceedings of the Hampshire Field Club and Archaeological Society* 56: 129–69.

Struth, P. & Eagles, B. 1999. 'An Anglo-Saxon Barrow Cemetery in Greenwich Park', in P. Pattison, D. Field & S. Ainsworth (eds.) *Patterns of the Past: Essays in Landscape Archaeology for Christopher Taylor*, Oxford: Oxbow, pp. 37–52.

Swanton, M. 1973. *The Spearheads of the Anglo-Saxon Settlements*, London: Royal Archaeological Institute.

(trans.) 2000. *The Anglo-Saxon Chronicles*, London: Phoenix.

Tarlow, S. 1997. 'The Dread of Something after Death: Violation and Desecration on the Isle of Man in the Tenth Century', in J. Carmen (ed.) *Material Harm: Archaeological Studies of War and Violence*, Glasgow: Cruithne, pp. 133–42.

1999. *Bereavement and Commemoration*, Oxford: Blackwell.

2002. 'The Aesthetic Corpse in Nineteenth-Century Britain', in Y. Hamilakis, M. Pluciennik & S. Tarlow (eds.) *Thinking through the Body: Archaeologies of Corporeality*, New York: Kluwer/Plenum, pp. 85–97.

Taylor, A. 2001. *Burial Practice in Early England*, Stroud: Tempus.

Taylor, T. 2002. *The Buried Soul: How Humans Invented Death*, London: Fourth Estate.

Thacker, A. 1985. 'Kings, Saints, and Monasteries in Pre-Viking Mercia', *Midland History* 10: 1–25.

Thäte, E. 1996. 'Alte Denkmäler und frühgeschichtliche Bestattungen: Ein sächsisch-angelsächsischer Totenbrauch und seine Kontinuität', *Archäologische Informationen* 19/1&2: 105–16.

Theuws, F. 1999. 'Changing Settlement Patterns, Burial Grounds and the Symbolic Construction of Ancestors and Communities in the Late Merovingian Southern Netherlands', in C. Fabech & J. Ringtved (eds.) *Settlement and Landscape*, Moesgrd: Jutland Archaeological Society, pp. 337–49.

2001. 'Maastricht as a Centre of Power in the Early Middle Ages', in M. de Jong & F. Theuws (eds.) *Topographies of Power in the Early Middle Ages*, Leiden: Brill, pp. 155–216.

Theuws, F. & Alkemade, M. 2000. 'A Kind of Mirror for Men: Sword Depositions in Late Antique Northern Gaul', in F. Theuws & J. L. Nelson (eds.) *Rituals of Power from Late Antiquity to the Early Middle Ages*, Leiden: Brill, pp. 401–76.

Thomas, C. 1963. 'The Interpretation of the Pictish Symbols', *Archaeological Journal* 120: 31–97.

Thomas, J. 1996. *Time, Culture and Identity: An Interpretive Archaeology*, London: Routledge.

1999. *Understanding the Neolithic*, London: Routledge.

2000. 'Death, Identity and the Body in Neolithic Britain', *Journal of the Royal Anthropological Institute* 6: 603–17.

2002. 'Archaeology's Humanism and the Materiality of the Body', in Y. Hamilakis, M. Pluciennik & S. Tarlow (eds.) *Thinking through the Body: Archaeologies of Corporeality*, New York: Kluwer/Plenum, pp. 29–46.

Thompson, V. 2002. 'Constructing Salvation: A Homiletic and Penitential Context for Late Anglo-Saxon Burial Practice', in S. Lucy & A. Reynolds (eds.) *Burial in Early Medieval England and Wales*, Leeds: Maney, pp. 229–40.

2003a. 'Memory, Salvation and Ambiguity', in H. Williams (ed.) *Archaeologies of Remembrance: Death and Memory in Past Societies*, New York: Kluwer/Plenum, pp. 215–26.

2003b. 'The View from the Edge: Dying, Power and Vision in Late Saxon England', in D. Griffiths, A. Reynolds & S. Semple (eds.) *Boundaries in Early Medieval Britain: Anglo-Saxon Studies in Archaeology and History* 12, Oxford: Oxbow, pp. 92–7.

2004. *Dying and Death in Later Anglo-Saxon England*, Woodbridge: Boydell.

Tilley, C. 1994. *A Phenomenology of the Landscape*, Oxford: Berg.

1996a. *An Ethnography of the Neolithic*, Cambridge: Cambridge University Press.

1996b. 'The Power of Rocks: Topography and Monument Construction on Bodmin Moor', *World Archaeology* 28(2): 161–76.

1999. *Metaphor and Material Culture*, Oxford: Blackwell.

2004. *The Materiality of Stone*, Oxford: Berg.

Timby, J. 1993. 'Sancton I Anglo-Saxon Cemetery: Excavations Carried out between 1976 and 1980', *Archaeological Journal* 150: 243–365.

1996. *The Anglo-Saxon Cemetery at Empingham II, Rutland*, Oxford: Oxbow Monograph 70.

Todd, M. 1992. *The Early Germans*, Oxford: Blackwell.

Trigger, B. 1989. *A History of Archaeological Thought*, Cambridge: Cambridge University Press.

Toynbee, J. M. C. 1971. *Death and Burial in the Roman World*, London: Johns Hopkins University Press.

Tyrell, A. 2000. '*Corpus Saxonum*: Early Medieval Bodies and Corporeal Identity', in W. O. Frazer & A. Tyrrell (eds.) *Social Identity in Early Medieval Britain*, Leicester: Leicester University Press, pp. 137–56.

Ucko, P. 1969. 'Ethnography and Archaeological Interpretation of Funerary Remains', *World Archaeology* 1(2): 262–80.

van Gennep, A. 1960. *Rites of Passage*, London: Routledge.

van Houts, E. 1999. *Memory and Gender in Medieval Europe 900–1200*, London: Macmillan.

Verdery, K. 1999. *The Political Lives of Dead Bodies: Reburial and Postsocialist Change*, New York: Columbia University Press.

Vitebsky, P. 1993. *Dialogues with the Dead: The Discussion of Mortality among the Sora of Eastern India*, Cambridge: Cambridge University Press.

Warmind, M. L. 1995. 'Ibn Fadlan in the Context of his Age', in O. Crumlin-Pedersen & B. Munch Thye, *The Ship as Symbol*, Copenhagen: National Museum, pp. 131–7.

Warner, R. 2004. 'Notes in the Inception and Early Development of the Royal Mound in Ireland', in A. Pantos & S. Semple (eds.) *Assembly Places and Practices in Medieval Europe*, Dublin: Four Courts Press, pp. 27–40.

Warrilow, W., Owen, G. & Britnell, O. 1986. 'Eight Ring-Ditches at Four Crosses, Llandysilio, Powys', *Proceedings of the Prehistoric Society* 52: 53–87.

Watson, A. 2001a. 'Composing Avebury', *World Archaeology* 33(2): 296–314.

   2001b. 'Round Barrows in a Circular World: Monumentalising Landscapes in Early Bronze Age Wessex', in J. Brück (ed.) *Bronze Age Landscapes: Tradition and Transformation*, Oxford: Oxbow, pp. 207–16.

Watson, A. & Keating, D. 1999. 'Architecture and Sound: An Acoustic Analysis of Megalithic Monuments in Prehistoric Britain', *Antiquity* 73: 325–36.

Watt, M. 1999. 'Kings or Gods? Iconographic Evidence from Scandinavian Gold Foil Figures', in T. Dickinson & D. Griffiths (eds.) *The Making of Kingdoms: Anglo-Saxon Studies in Archaeology and History* 10, Oxford: Oxford University Committee for Archaeology, pp. 173–84.

Watts, L. & Leach, P. 1996. *Henley Wood Temples and Cemetery – Excavations 1962–9*, London: CBA Research Report 99.

Watts, D. 1991. *Christians and Pagans in Roman Britain*, London: Routledge.

Webb, J. F. (trans.) 1965. 'Bede: Lives of the Abbots of Wearmouth and Jarrow', in J. F. Webb (trans.) & D. H. Farmer (ed.) *The Age of Bede*, London: Penguin, pp. 183–208.

Webster, L. 1992. 'Death's Diplomacy: Sutton Hoo in the Light of Other Male Princely Burials', in R. Farrell & C. Newman de Vegvar (eds.) *Sutton Hoo: Fifty Years After*, Oxford: Oxbow, pp. 75–82.

Webster, L. & Backhouse, J. (eds.) 1991. *The Making of England: Anglo-Saxon Art and Culture AD 600–900*, Toronto: University of Toronto Press.

Weddell, P. J. 2000. 'The Excavation of a Post-Roman Cemetery near Kenn, South Devon', *Proceedings of the Devon Archaeological Society* 58: 93–126.

Welch, M. 1985. 'Rural Settlement Patterns in the Early and Middle Anglo-Saxon Periods', *Landscape History* 7: 13–25.

   1992. *Anglo-Saxon England*, London: Batsford.

Wells, C. & Green, C. 1973. 'Sunrise Dating of Death and Burial', *Norfolk and Norwich Archaeological Society* 35(4): 435–42.

Wenham, S. J. 1989. 'Anatomical Interpretations of Anglo-Saxon Weapon Injuries', in S. C. Hawkes (ed.) *Weapons and Warfare in Anglo-Saxon England*, Oxford: Oxford University Press, pp. 123–39.

West, S. 1985. *West Stow: The Anglo-Saxon Village*, Ipswich: East Anglian Archaeology 24.

White, R. 1988. *Roman and Celtic Objects from Anglo-Saxon Graves*, Oxford: BAR British Series 191.

White, S. I. & Smith, G. 1999. 'A Funerary and Ceremonial Centre at Capel Eithin, Gaerwen, Anglesey', *Transactions of the Anglesey Antiquarian Society* 1999.

Whitley, J. 2002. 'Too Many Ancestors', *Antiquity* 76: 119–26.

Whyte, N. 2003. 'The Deviant Dead in the Norfolk Landscape', *Landscapes* I: 24–39.

Williams, H. 1997. 'Ancient Landscapes and the Dead: The Reuse of Prehistoric and Roman Monuments as Early Anglo-Saxon burial sites', *Medieval Archaeology* 41: 1–31.

1998. 'Monuments and the Past in Early Anglo-Saxon England', *World Archaeology* 30(1): 90–108.

1999a. 'Identities and Cemeteries in Roman and Early Medieval Archaeology', in P. Baker, C. Forcey, S. Jundi & R. Witcher (eds.) *TRAC 98 Proceedings of the Eighth Annual Theoretical Roman Archaeology Conference*, Oxford: Oxbow Books, pp. 96–108.

1999b. 'Placing the Dead: Investigating the Location of Wealthy Barrow Burials in Seventh-Century England', in M. Rundkvist (ed.) *Grave Matters: Eight Studies of Burial Data from the First Millennium AD from Crimea, Scandinavia and England*, Oxford: BAR International Series 781, pp. 57–86.

2001a. 'Death, Memory and Time: A Consideration of Mortuary Practices at Sutton Hoo', in C. Humphrey & W. Ormrod (eds.) *Time in the Middle Ages*, Woodbridge: Boydell & Brewer, pp. 35–71.

2001b. 'An Ideology of Transformation: Cremation Rites and Animal Sacrifice in Early Anglo-Saxon England', in N. Price (ed.) *The Archaeology of Shamanism*, London: Routledge, pp. 193–212.

2002a. '"The Remains of Pagan Saxondom"? Studying Anglo-Saxon Cremation Practices', in S. Lucy & A. Reynolds (eds.) *Burial in Early Medieval England and Wales*, Leeds: Maney, Society of Medieval Archaeology Monograph Series 17, pp. 47–71.

2002b. 'Cemeteries as Central Places: Landscape and Identity in Early Anglo-Saxon England', in B. Hardh & L. Larsson (eds.) *Central Places in the Migration and Merovingian Periods: Papers from the 52nd Sachsensymposium*, Lund: Almqvist, pp. 341–62.

2003. 'Material Culture as Memory: Combs and Cremation in Early Medieval Britain', *Early Medieval Europe* 12(2): 89–128.

2004a. 'Artefacts in Early Medieval Graves – A New Perspective', in R. Collins & J. Gerrard (eds.) *Proceedings of 'Debating Late Antiquity' Conference*, Oxford: BAR British Series 365, pp. 89–102.

2004b. 'Death Warmed Up: The Agency of Bodies and Bones in Early Anglo-Saxon Cremation Rites', *Journal of Material Culture* 9(3): 263–91.

2004c. 'Assembling the Dead', in A. Pantos & S. Semple (eds.) *Assembly Places and Practices in Medieval Europe*, Dublin: Four Courts Press, pp. 109–34.

2005a. 'Keeping the Dead at Arm's Length: Memory, Weaponry and Early Medieval Mortuary Technologies', *Journal of Social Archaeology* 5(2): 253–75.

2005b. 'Animals, Ashes and Ancestors', in A. Plusowski (ed.) *Beyond Skin and Bones? New Perspectives on Human–Animal Relations in the Historical Past*, Oxford: BAR International Series 1410, pp. 19–40.

(in prep.) *Memory and Monumentality in Early Medieval Britain*.

Williams, M. 2003. 'Tales from the Dead: Remembering the Bog Bodies in the Iron Age of North-Western Europe', in H. Williams (ed.) *Archaeologies of Remembrance: Death and Memory in Past Societies*, New York: Kluwer/Plenum, pp. 89–112.

Wilson, D. 1992. *Anglo-Saxon Paganism*, London: Routledge.
Wilson, D. M. 1964. *Anglo-Saxon Ornamental Metalwork 700–1100*, London: British Museum.
   (ed.) 1976. *The Archaeology of Anglo-Saxon England*, Cambridge: Cambridge University
   Press.
Wood, I. 2001. 'Topographies of Holy Power in Sixth-Century Gaul', in M. de Jong & F.
   Theuws (eds.) *Topographies of Power in the Early Middle Ages*, Leiden: Brill, pp. 137–54.
Wood, J. W., Milner, G. R., Harpending, H. C. & Weiss, K. M. 1992. 'The Osteological
   Paradox', *Current Anthropology* 33: 343–70.
Woodward, A. & Woodward, P. 1996. 'The Topography of Some Barrow Cemeteries in Bronze
   Age Wessex', *Proceedings of the Prehistoric Society* 62: 275–91.
Wyatt, I. 2004. 'Narrative Functions of Landscape in the Old Icelandic Family Sagas', in J.
   Hines, A. Lane & M. Redknap (eds.) *Land, Sea and Home*, Leeds: Maney, pp. 273–82.
Wylie, W. M. 1852. *Fairford Graves*, Oxford: Parker.
   1857. 'The Burning and Burial of the Dead', *Archaeologia* 37: 455–78.
Wymer, J. J. 1996. *Barrow Excavations in Norfolk, 1984–88*, Dereham: East Anglian Archae-
   ology 77.
Zadora-Rio, E. 2003. 'The Making of Churchyards and Parish Territories in the Early
   Medieval Landscape of France and England in the 7th–12th Centuries: A Reconsid-
   eration', *Medieval Archaeology* 47: 1–20.

CAMBRIDGE STUDIES IN ARCHAEOLOGY